DICTIONARY
THEME–BASED

British English Collection

ENGLISH-
GERMAN

The most useful words
To expand your lexicon and sharpen
your language skills

9000 words

Theme-based dictionary British English-German - 9000 words

By Andrey Taranov

T&P Books vocabularies are intended for helping you learn, memorize and review foreign words. The dictionary is divided into themes, covering all major spheres of everyday activities, business, science, culture, etc.

The process of learning words using T&P Books' theme-based dictionaries gives you the following advantages:

- Correctly grouped source information predetermines success at subsequent stages of word memorization
- Availability of words derived from the same root allowing memorization of word units (rather than separate words)
- Small units of words facilitate the process of establishing associative links needed for consolidation of vocabulary
- Level of language knowledge can be estimated by the number of learned words

T&P Books Publishing
www.tpbooks.com

This book is also available in E-book formats.
Please visit www.tpbooks.com or the major online bookstores.

GERMAN THEME-BASED DICTIONARY
British English collection

T&P Books vocabularies are intended to help you learn, memorize, and review foreign words. The vocabulary contains over 9000 commonly used words arranged thematically.

- Vocabulary contains the most commonly used words
- Recommended as an addition to any language course
- Meets the needs of beginners and advanced learners of foreign languages
- Convenient for daily use, revision sessions, and self-testing activities
- Allows you to assess your vocabulary

Special features of the vocabulary

- Words are organized according to their meaning, not alphabetically
- Words are presented in three columns to facilitate the reviewing and self-testing processes
- Words in groups are divided into small blocks to facilitate the learning process
- The vocabulary offers a convenient and simple transcription of each foreign word

The vocabulary has 256 topics including:

Basic Concepts, Numbers, Colors, Months, Seasons, Units of Measurement, Clothing & Accessories, Food & Nutrition, Restaurant, Family Members, Relatives, Character, Feelings, Emotions, Diseases, City, Town, Sightseeing, Shopping, Money, House, Home, Office, Working in the Office, Import & Export, Marketing, Job Search, Sports, Education, Computer, Internet, Tools, Nature, Countries, Nationalities and more ...

TABLE OF CONTENTS

PRONUNCIATION GUIDE

T&P phonetic alphabet	German example	English example

Vowels

[a]	Blatt	shorter than in 'ask'
[ɐ]	Meister	nut
[e]	Melodie	elm, medal
[ɛ]	Herbst	man, bad
[ə]	Leuchte	driver, teacher
[ɔ]	Knopf	bottle, doctor
[o]	Operette	pod, John
[œ]	Förster	German Hölle
[ø]	nötig	eternal, church
[æ]	Los Angeles	candle, lamp
[i]	Spiel	shorter than in 'feet'
[ɪ]	Absicht	big, America
[ʊ]	Skulptur	good, booklet
[u]	Student	book
[y]	Pyramide	fuel, tuna
[Y]	Eukalyptus	fuel, tuna

Consonants

[b]	Bibel	baby, book
[d]	Dorf	day, doctor
[f]	Elefant	face, food
[ʒ]	Ingenieur	forge, pleasure
[dʒ]	Jeans	joke, general
[j]	Interview	yes, New York
[g]	August	game, gold
[h]	Haare	home, have
[ç]	glücklich	humor
[χ]	Kochtopf	as in Scots 'loch'
[k]	Kaiser	clock, kiss
[l]	Verlag	lace, people
[m]	Messer	magic, milk
[n]	Norden	name, normal
[ŋ]	Onkel	English, ring
[p]	Gespräch	pencil, private

T&P phonetic alphabet	German example	English example
[r]	Force majeure	rice, radio
[ʁ]	Kirche	French (guttural) R
[ʀ]	fragen	uvular vibrant [r]
[s]	Fenster	city, boss
[t]	Foto	tourist, trip
[ts]	Gesetz	cats, tsetse fly
[ʃ]	Anschlag	machine, shark
[tʃ]	Deutsche	church, French
[w]	Sweater	vase, winter
[v]	Antwort	very, river
[z]	langsam	zebra, please

Diphthongs

[aɪ]	Speicher	tie, driver
[ɪa]	Miniatur	Kenya, piano
[ɪo]	Radio	New York
[jo]	Illustration	New York
[ɔɪ]	feucht	oil, boy, point
[ɪe]	Karriere	yesterday, yen

Other symbols used in transcription

[']	['aːbe]	primary stress
[ˌ]	['dɛŋkˌmaːl]	secondary stress
[ʔ]	[o'liːvənˌʔøːl]	glottal stop
[ː]	['myːle]	long-vowel mark
[·]	['ʀaɪzə·byˌʀoː]	interpunct

ABBREVIATIONS
used in the dictionary

English abbreviations

ab.	-	about
adj	-	adjective
adv	-	adverb
anim.	-	animate
as adj	-	attributive noun used as adjective
e.g.	-	for example
etc.	-	et cetera
fam.	-	familiar
fem.	-	feminine
form.	-	formal
inanim.	-	inanimate
masc.	-	masculine
math	-	mathematics
mil.	-	military
n	-	noun
pl	-	plural
pron.	-	pronoun
sb	-	somebody
sing.	-	singular
sth	-	something
v aux	-	auxiliary verb
vi	-	intransitive verb
vi, vt	-	intransitive, transitive verb
vt	-	transitive verb

German abbreviations

f	-	feminine noun
f pl	-	feminine plural
f, n	-	feminine, neuter
m	-	masculine noun
m pl	-	masculine plural
m, f	-	masculine, feminine
m, n	-	masculine, neuter
n	-	neuter
n pl	-	neuter plural
pl	-	plural
v mod	-	modal verb

vi	-	intransitive verb
vi, vt	-	intransitive, transitive verb
vt	-	transitive verb

BASIC CONCEPTS

Basic concepts. Part 1

1. Pronouns

I, me	ich	[ɪç]
you	du	[duː]
he	er	[eːɐ]
she	sie	[ziː]
it	es	[ɛs]
we	wir	[viːɐ]
you (to a group)	ihr	[iːɐ]
you (polite, sing.)	Sie	[ziː]
you (polite, pl)	Sie	[ziː]
they	sie	[ziː]

2. Greetings. Salutations. Farewells

Hello! (fam.)	Hallo!	[haˈloː]
Hello! (form.)	Hallo!	[haˈloː]
Good morning!	Guten Morgen!	[ˈguːtən ˈmɔʁgən]
Good afternoon!	Guten Tag!	[ˈguːtən ˈtaːk]
Good evening!	Guten Abend!	[ˈguːtən ˈaːbənt]
to say hello	grüßen (vi, vt)	[ˈgʁyːsən]
Hi! (hello)	Hallo!	[haˈloː]
greeting (n)	Gruß (m)	[gʁuːs]
to greet (vt)	begrüßen (vt)	[bəˈgʁyːsən]
How are you?	Wie geht's?	[ˌviː ˈgeːts]
What's new?	Was gibt es Neues?	[vas giːpt ɛs ˈnɔɪəs]
Bye-Bye! Goodbye!	Auf Wiedersehen!	[aʊf ˈviːdɐˌzeːən]
See you soon!	Bis bald!	[bɪs balt]
Farewell! (to a friend)	Lebe wohl!	[ˈleːbə voːl]
Farewell! (form.)	Leben Sie wohl!	[ˈleːbən ziː voːl]
to say goodbye	sich verabschieden	[zɪç fɛɐˈapʃiːdən]
Cheers!	Tschüs!	[tʃyːs]
Thank you! Cheers!	Danke!	[ˈdaŋkə]
Thank you very much!	Dankeschön!	[ˈdaŋkəʃøːn]
My pleasure!	Bitte!	[ˈbɪtə]
Don't mention it!	Keine Ursache!	[ˈkaɪnə ˈuːɐˌzaxə]
It was nothing	Nichts zu danken!	[nɪçts tsu ˈdaŋkən]
Excuse me! (fam.)	Entschuldige!	[ɛntˈʃʊldɪgə]

15

| Excuse me! (form.) | Entschuldigung! | [ɛnt'ʃʊldɪgʊŋ] |
| to excuse (forgive) | entschuldigen (vt) | [ɛnt'ʃʊldɪgən] |

to apologize (vi)	sich entschuldigen	[zɪç ɛnt'ʃʊldɪgən]
My apologies	Verzeihung!	[fɛɐ'tsaɪʊŋ]
I'm sorry!	Entschuldigung!	[ɛnt'ʃʊldɪgʊŋ]
to forgive (vt)	verzeihen (vt)	[fɛɐ'tsaɪən]
It's okay! (that's all right)	Das macht nichts!	[das maχt nɪçts]
please (adv)	bitte	['bɪtə]

Don't forget!	Nicht vergessen!	[nɪçt fɛɐ'gɛsən]
Certainly!	Natürlich!	[na'ty:ɐlɪç]
Of course not!	Natürlich nicht!	[na'ty:ɐlɪç 'nɪçt]
Okay! (I agree)	Gut! Okay!	[gu:t], [o'ke:]
That's enough!	Es ist genug!	[ɛs ist gə'nu:k]

3. How to address

mister, sir	Herr	[hɛʁ]
madam	Frau	[fʀaʊ]
miss	Frau	[fʀaʊ]
young man	Junger Mann	['jʏŋɐ man]
young man (little boy)	Junge	['jʊŋə]
miss (little girl)	Mädchen	['mɛ:tçən]

4. Cardinal numbers. Part 1

0 zero	null	[nʊl]
1 one	eins	[aɪns]
2 two	zwei	[tsvaɪ]
3 three	drei	[dʀaɪ]
4 four	vier	[fi:ɐ]

5 five	fünf	[fʏnf]
6 six	sechs	[zɛks]
7 seven	sieben	['zi:bən]
8 eight	acht	[aχt]
9 nine	neun	[nɔɪn]

10 ten	zehn	[tse:n]
11 eleven	elf	[ɛlf]
12 twelve	zwölf	[tsvœlf]
13 thirteen	dreizehn	['dʀaɪtse:n]
14 fourteen	vierzehn	['fiʁtse:n]

15 fifteen	fünfzehn	['fʏnftse:n]
16 sixteen	sechzehn	['zɛçtse:n]
17 seventeen	siebzehn	['zi:ptse:n]
18 eighteen	achtzehn	['aχtse:n]
19 nineteen	neunzehn	['nɔɪntse:n]
20 twenty	zwanzig	['tsvantsɪç]
21 twenty-one	einundzwanzig	['aɪn·ʊnt·'tsvantsɪç]

22 twenty-two	zweiundzwanzig	['tsvaɪ·ʊnt·'tsvantsɪç]
23 twenty-three	dreiundzwanzig	['dʀaɪ·ʊnt·'tsvantsɪç]

30 thirty	dreißig	['dʀaɪsɪç]
31 thirty-one	einunddreißig	['aɪn·ʊnt·'dʀaɪsɪç]
32 thirty-two	zweiunddreißig	['tsvaɪ·ʊnt·'dʀaɪsɪç]
33 thirty-three	dreiunddreißig	['dʀaɪ·ʊnt·'dʀaɪsɪç]

40 forty	vierzig	['fɪʁtsɪç]
41 forty-one	einundvierzig	['aɪn·ʊnt·'fɪʁtsɪç]
42 forty-two	zweiundvierzig	['tsvaɪ·ʊnt·'fɪʁtsɪç]
43 forty-three	dreiundvierzig	['dʀaɪ·ʊnt·'fɪʁtsɪç]

50 fifty	fünfzig	['fʏnftsɪç]
51 fifty-one	einundfünfzig	['aɪn·ʊnt·'fʏnftsɪç]
52 fifty-two	zweiundfünfzig	['tsvaɪ·ʊnt·'fʏnftsɪç]
53 fifty-three	dreiundfünfzig	['dʀaɪ·ʊnt·'fʏnftsɪç]

60 sixty	sechzig	['zɛçtsɪç]
61 sixty-one	einundsechzig	['aɪn·ʊnt·'zɛçtsɪç]
62 sixty-two	zweiundsechzig	['tsvaɪ·ʊnt·'zɛçtsɪç]
63 sixty-three	dreiundsechzig	['dʀaɪ·ʊnt·'zɛçtsɪç]

70 seventy	siebzig	['ziːptsɪç]
71 seventy-one	einundsiebzig	['aɪn·ʊnt·'ziːptsɪç]
72 seventy-two	zweiundsiebzig	['tsvaɪ·ʊnt·'ziːptsɪç]
73 seventy-three	dreiundsiebzig	['dʀaɪ·ʊnt·'ziːptsɪç]

80 eighty	achtzig	['aχtsɪç]
81 eighty-one	einundachtzig	['aɪn·ʊnt·'aχtsɪç]
82 eighty-two	zweiundachtzig	['tsvaɪ·ʊnt·'aχtsɪç]
83 eighty-three	dreiundachtzig	['dʀaɪ·ʊnt·'aχtsɪç]

90 ninety	neunzig	['nɔɪntsɪç]
91 ninety-one	einundneunzig	['aɪn·ʊnt·'nɔɪntsɪç]
92 ninety-two	zweiundneunzig	['tsvaɪ·ʊnt·'nɔɪntsɪç]
93 ninety-three	dreiundneunzig	['dʀaɪ·ʊnt·'nɔɪntsɪç]

5. Cardinal numbers. Part 2

100 one hundred	einhundert	['aɪn‚hʊndɐt]
200 two hundred	zweihundert	['tsvaɪ‚hʊndɐt]
300 three hundred	dreihundert	['dʀaɪ‚hʊndɐt]
400 four hundred	vierhundert	['fiːɐ‚hʊndɐt]
500 five hundred	fünfhundert	['fʏnf‚hʊndɐt]

600 six hundred	sechshundert	[zɛks‚hʊndɐt]
700 seven hundred	siebenhundert	['ziːbən‚hʊndɐt]
800 eight hundred	achthundert	['aχt‚hʊndɐt]
900 nine hundred	neunhundert	['nɔɪn‚hʊndɐt]

1000 one thousand	eintausend	['aɪn‚taʊzənt]
2000 two thousand	zweitausend	['tsvaɪ‚taʊzənt]
3000 three thousand	dreitausend	['dʀaɪ‚taʊzənt]

10000 ten thousand	**zehntausend**	['tsen͵tauzənt]
one hundred thousand	**hunderttausend**	['hundət͵tauzənt]
million	**Million** (f)	[mɪ'ljoːn]
billion	**Milliarde** (f)	[mɪ'lɪaʁdə]

6. Ordinal numbers

first (adj)	**der erste**	[deːɐ 'ɛʁstə]
second (adj)	**der zweite**	[deːɐ 'tsvaɪtə]
third (adj)	**der dritte**	[deːɐ 'dʁɪtə]
fourth (adj)	**der vierte**	[deːɐ 'fiːɐtə]
fifth (adj)	**der fünfte**	[deːɐ 'fʏnftə]
sixth (adj)	**der sechste**	[deːɐ 'zɛkstə]
seventh (adj)	**der siebte**	[deːɐ 'ziːptə]
eighth (adj)	**der achte**	[deːɐ 'aχtə]
ninth (adj)	**der neunte**	[deːɐ 'nɔɪntə]
tenth (adj)	**der zehnte**	[deːɐ tseːntə]

7. Numbers. Fractions

fraction	**Bruch** (m)	[bʁuχ]
one half	**Hälfte** (f)	['hɛlftə]
one third	**Drittel** (n)	['dʁɪtəl]
one quarter	**Viertel** (n)	['fɪʁtəl]
one eighth	**Achtel** (m, n)	['aχtəl]
one tenth	**Zehntel** (m, n)	['tseːntəl]
two thirds	**zwei Drittel**	[tsvaɪ 'dʁɪtəl]
three quarters	**drei Viertel**	[dʁaɪ 'fɪʁtəl]

8. Numbers. Basic operations

subtraction	**Subtraktion** (f)	[zuptʁak'tsjoːn]
to subtract (vi, vt)	**subtrahieren** (vt)	[zuptʁa'hiːʁən]
division	**Division** (f)	[divi'zjoːn]
to divide (vt)	**dividieren** (vt)	[divi'diːʁən]
addition	**Addition** (f)	[adi'tsjoːn]
to add up (vt)	**addieren** (vt)	[a'diːʁən]
to add (vi)	**hinzufügen** (vt)	[hɪn'tsuː͵fyːgən]
multiplication	**Multiplikation** (f)	[multiplika'tsjoːn]
to multiply (vt)	**multiplizieren** (vt)	[multipli'tsiːʁən]

9. Numbers. Miscellaneous

digit, figure	**Ziffer** (f)	['tsɪfɐ]
number	**Zahl** (f)	[tsaːl]

numeral	**Zahlwort** (n)	['tsaːlˌvɔʁt]
minus sign	**Minus** (n)	['miːnʊs]
plus sign	**Plus** (n)	[plʊs]
formula	**Formel** (f)	['fɔʁməl]

calculation	**Berechnung** (f)	[bə'ʁɛçnʊŋ]
to count (vi, vt)	**zählen** (vt)	['tsɛːlən]
to count up	**berechnen** (vt)	[bə'ʁɛçnən]
to compare (vt)	**vergleichen** (vt)	[fɛʁ'glaɪçən]

How much?	**Wie viel?**	['viː fiːl]
How many?	**Wie viele?**	[viː 'fiːlə]

sum, total	**Summe** (f)	['zʊmə]
result	**Ergebnis** (n)	[ɛʁ'geːpnɪs]
remainder	**Rest** (m)	[ʁɛst]

a few (e.g., ~ years ago)	**einige**	['aɪnɪgə]
little (I had ~ time)	**wenig ...**	['veːnɪç]
the rest	**Übrige** (n)	['yːbʁɪgə]
one and a half	**anderthalb**	['andɐt'halp]
dozen	**Dutzend** (n)	['dʊtsənt]

in half (adv)	**entzwei**	[ɛn'tsvaɪ]
equally (evenly)	**zu gleichen Teilen**	[tsu 'glaɪçən 'taɪlən]
half	**Hälfte** (f)	['hɛlftə]
time (three ~s)	**Mal** (n)	[maːl]

10. The most important verbs. Part 1

to advise (vt)	**raten** (vt)	['ʁaːtən]
to agree (say yes)	**zustimmen** (vi)	['tsuːˌʃtɪmən]
to answer (vi, vt)	**antworten** (vi)	['antˌvɔʁtən]
to apologize (vi)	**sich entschuldigen**	[zɪç ɛnt'ʃʊldɪgən]
to arrive (vi)	**ankommen** (vi)	['anˌkɔmən]

to ask (~ oneself)	**fragen** (vt)	['fʁaːgən]
to ask (~ sb to do sth)	**bitten** (vt)	['bɪtən]
to be (vi)	**sein** (vi)	[zaɪn]

to be afraid	**Angst haben**	['aŋst 'haːbən]
to be hungry	**hungrig sein**	['hʊŋʁɪç zaɪn]
to be interested in ...	**sich interessieren**	[zɪç ɪntəʁɛ'siːʁən]
to be needed	**nötig sein**	['nøːtɪç zaɪn]
to be surprised	**staunen** (vi)	['ʃtaunən]

to be thirsty	**Durst haben**	['dʊʁst 'haːbən]
to begin (vt)	**beginnen** (vt)	[bə'gɪnən]
to belong to ...	**gehören** (vi)	[gə'høːʁən]
to boast (vi)	**prahlen** (vi)	['pʁaːlən]
to break (split into pieces)	**brechen** (vt)	['bʁɛçən]
to call (~ for help)	**rufen** (vi)	['ʁuːfən]
can (v aux)	**können** (v mod)	['kœnən]
to catch (vt)	**fangen** (vt)	['faŋən]

to change (vt)	ändern (vt)	['ɛndɐn]
to choose (select)	wählen (vt)	['vɛːlən]
to come down (the stairs)	herabsteigen (vi)	[hɛˈʀapˌʃtaɪɡən]

to compare (vt)	vergleichen (vt)	[fɛɐ̯ˈɡlaɪçən]
to complain (vi, vt)	klagen (vi)	['klaːɡən]
to confuse (mix up)	verwechseln (vt)	[fɛɐ̯ˈvɛksəln]
to continue (vt)	fortsetzen (vt)	['fɔʁtˌzɛtsən]
to control (vt)	kontrollieren (vt)	[kɔntʀɔˈliːʀən]
to cook (dinner)	zubereiten (vt)	['tsuːbəˌʀaɪtən]

to cost (vt)	kosten (vt)	['kɔstən]
to count (add up)	rechnen (vt)	['ʀɛçnən]
to count on ...	auf ... zählen	[aʊf ... 'tsɛːlən]
to create (vt)	schaffen (vt)	['ʃafən]
to cry (weep)	weinen (vi)	['vaɪnən]

11. The most important verbs. Part 2

to deceive (vi, vt)	täuschen (vt)	['tɔɪʃən]
to decorate (tree, street)	schmücken (vt)	['ʃmʏkən]
to defend (a country, etc.)	verteidigen (vt)	[fɛɐ̯ˈtaɪdɪɡən]
to demand (request firmly)	verlangen (vt)	[fɛɐ̯ˈlaŋən]
to dig (vt)	graben (vt)	['ɡʀaːbən]

to discuss (vt)	besprechen (vt)	[bəˈʃpʀɛçən]
to do (vt)	machen (vt)	['maxən]
to doubt (have doubts)	zweifeln (vi)	['tsvaɪfəln]
to drop (let fall)	fallen lassen	['falən 'lasən]
to enter (room, house, etc.)	hereinkommen (vi)	[hɛˈʀaɪnˌkɔmən]

to exist (vi)	existieren (vi)	[ˌɛksɪsˈtiːʀən]
to expect (foresee)	voraussehen (vt)	[foˈʀaʊsˌzeːən]
to explain (vt)	erklären (vt)	[ɛɐ̯ˈklɛːʀən]
to fall (vi)	fallen (vi)	['falən]

to fancy (vt)	gefallen (vi)	[ɡəˈfalən]
to find (vt)	finden (vt)	['fɪndən]
to finish (vt)	beenden (vt)	[bəˈʔɛndən]
to fly (vi)	fliegen (vi)	['fliːɡən]
to follow ... (come after)	folgen (vi)	['fɔlɡən]

to forget (vi, vt)	vergessen (vt)	[fɛɐ̯ˈɡɛsən]
to forgive (vt)	verzeihen (vt)	[fɛɐ̯ˈtsaɪən]
to give (vt)	geben (vt)	['ɡeːbən]
to give a hint	andeuten (vt)	['anˌdɔɪtən]
to go (on foot)	gehen (vi)	['ɡeːən]

to go for a swim	schwimmen gehen	['ʃvɪmən 'ɡeːən]
to go out (for dinner, etc.)	ausgehen (vi)	['aʊsˌɡeːən]
to guess (the answer)	richtig raten (vt)	['ʀɪçtɪç 'ʀaːtən]

| to have (vt) | haben (vt) | [haːbən] |
| to have breakfast | frühstücken (vi) | ['fʀyːˌʃtʏkən] |

to have dinner	zu Abend essen	[tsu 'a:bənt 'ɛsən]
to have lunch	zu Mittag essen	[tsu 'mɪta:k 'ɛsən]
to hear (vt)	hören (vt)	['hø:ʀən]

to help (vt)	helfen (vi)	['hɛlfən]
to hide (vt)	verstecken (vt)	[fɛɐ'ʃtɛkən]
to hope (vi, vt)	hoffen (vi)	['hɔfən]
to hunt (vi, vt)	jagen (vi)	['jagən]
to hurry (vi)	sich beeilen	[zɪç bə'ʔaɪlən]

12. The most important verbs. Part 3

to inform (vt)	informieren (vt)	[ɪnfɔʀ'mi:ʀən]
to insist (vi, vt)	bestehen auf	[bə'ʃte:ən aʊf]
to insult (vt)	kränken (vt)	['kʀɛŋkən]
to invite (vt)	einladen (vt)	['aɪn͵la:dən]
to joke (vi)	Witz machen	[vɪts 'maχən]

to keep (vt)	aufbewahren (vt)	['aʊfbə͵va:ʀən]
to keep silent, to hush	schweigen (vi)	['ʃvaɪɡən]
to kill (vt)	ermorden (vt)	[ɛɐ'mɔʀdən]
to know (sb)	kennen (vt)	['kɛnən]
to know (sth)	wissen (vt)	['vɪsən]
to laugh (vi)	lachen (vi)	['laχən]

to liberate (city, etc.)	befreien (vt)	[bə'fʀaɪən]
to look for ... (search)	suchen (vt)	['zu:χən]
to love (sb)	lieben (vt)	['li:bən]
to make a mistake	sich irren	[zɪç 'ɪʀən]
to manage, to run	leiten (vt)	['laɪtən]
to mean (signify)	bedeuten (vt)	[bə'dɔɪtən]
to mention (talk about)	erwähnen (vt)	[ɛɐ'vɛ:nən]
to miss (school, etc.)	versäumen (vt)	[fɛɐ'zɔɪmən]
to notice (see)	bemerken (vt)	[bə'mɛʀkən]
to object (vi, vt)	einwenden (vt)	['aɪn͵vɛndən]

to observe (see)	beobachten (vt)	[bə'ʔo:baχtən]
to open (vt)	öffnen (vt)	['œfnən]
to order (meal, etc.)	bestellen (vt)	[bə'ʃtɛlən]
to order (mil.)	befehlen (vt)	[͵bə'fe:lən]
to own (possess)	besitzen (vt)	[bə'zɪtsən]

to participate (vi)	teilnehmen (vi)	['taɪl͵ne:mən]
to pay (vi, vt)	zahlen (vt)	['tsa:lən]
to permit (vt)	erlauben (vt)	[ɛɐ'laʊbən]
to plan (vt)	planen (vt)	['pla:nən]
to play (children)	spielen (vi, vt)	['ʃpi:lən]

to pray (vi, vt)	beten (vi)	['be:tən]
to prefer (vt)	vorziehen (vt)	['foɐ͵tsi:ən]
to promise (vt)	versprechen (vt)	[fɛɐ'ʃpʀɛçən]
to pronounce (vt)	aussprechen (vt)	['aʊsʃpʀɛçən]
to propose (vt)	vorschlagen (vt)	['fo:ɐ͵ʃla:gən]
to punish (vt)	bestrafen (vt)	[bə'ʃtʀa:fən]

13. The most important verbs. Part 4

to read (vi, vt)	lesen (vi, vt)	['le:zən]
to recommend (vt)	empfehlen (vt)	[ɛm'pfe:lən]
to refuse (vi, vt)	sich weigern	[zɪç 'vaɪgɐn]
to regret (be sorry)	bedauern (vt)	[bə'daʊɐn]
to rent (sth from sb)	mieten (vt)	['mi:tən]
to repeat (say again)	noch einmal sagen	[nɔχ 'aɪnma:l 'za:gən]
to reserve, to book	reservieren (vt)	[ʁezɛʁ'vi:ʁən]
to run (vi)	laufen (vi)	['laʊfən]
to save (rescue)	retten (vt)	['ʁɛtən]
to say (~ thank you)	sagen (vt)	['za:gən]
to scold (vt)	schelten (vt)	['ʃɛltən]
to see (vt)	sehen (vi, vt)	['ze:ən]
to sell (vt)	verkaufen (vt)	[fɛɐ'kaʊfən]
to send (vt)	abschicken (vt)	['apʃɪkən]
to shoot (vi)	schießen (vi)	['ʃi:sən]
to shout (vi)	schreien (vi)	['ʃʁaɪən]
to show (vt)	zeigen (vt)	['tsaɪgən]
to sign (document)	unterschreiben (vt)	[ˌʊntɐ'ʃʁaɪbən]
to sit down (vi)	sich setzen	[zɪç 'zɛtsən]
to smile (vi)	lächeln (vi)	['lɛçəln]
to speak (vi, vt)	sprechen (vi)	['ʃpʁɛçən]
to steal (money, etc.)	stehlen (vt)	['ʃte:lən]
to stop (for pause, etc.)	stoppen (vt)	['ʃtɔpən]
to stop (please ~ calling me)	einstellen (vt)	['aɪnʃtɛlən]
to study (vt)	lernen (vt)	['lɛʁnən]
to swim (vi)	schwimmen (vi)	['ʃvɪmən]
to take (vt)	nehmen (vt)	['ne:mən]
to think (vi, vt)	denken (vi, vt)	['dɛŋkən]
to threaten (vt)	drohen (vi)	['dʁo:ən]
to touch (with hands)	berühren (vt)	[bə'ʁy:ʁən]
to translate (vt)	übersetzen (vt)	[ˌy:bə'zɛtsən]
to trust (vt)	vertrauen (vi)	[fɛɐ'tʁaʊən]
to try (attempt)	versuchen (vt)	[fɛɐ'zu:χən]
to turn (e.g., ~ left)	abbiegen (vi)	['apˌbi:gən]
to underestimate (vt)	unterschätzen (vt)	[ˌʊntɐ'ʃɛtsən]
to understand (vt)	verstehen (vt)	[fɛɐ'ʃte:ən]
to unite (vt)	vereinigen (vt)	[fɛɐ'ʔaɪnɪgən]
to wait (vt)	warten (vi)	['vaʁtən]
to want (wish, desire)	wollen (vt)	['vɔlən]
to warn (vt)	warnen (vt)	['vaʁnən]
to work (vi)	arbeiten (vi)	['aʁbaɪtən]
to write (vt)	schreiben (vi, vt)	['ʃʁaɪbən]
to write down	aufschreiben (vt)	['aʊfʃʁaɪbən]

14. Colours

colour	Farbe (f)	['faʁbə]
shade (tint)	Schattierung (f)	[ʃa'tiːʁʊŋ]
hue	Farbton (m)	['faʁpˌtoːn]
rainbow	Regenbogen (m)	['ʀeːɡənˌboːɡən]

white (adj)	weiß	[vaɪs]
black (adj)	schwarz	[ʃvaʁts]
grey (adj)	grau	[ɡʀaʊ]

green (adj)	grün	[ɡʀyːn]
yellow (adj)	gelb	[ɡɛlp]
red (adj)	rot	[ʀoːt]

blue (adj)	blau	[blaʊ]
light blue (adj)	hellblau	['hɛlˌblaʊ]
pink (adj)	rosa	['ʀoːza]
orange (adj)	orange	[o'ʀaŋʃ]
violet (adj)	violett	[vɪo'lɛt]
brown (adj)	braun	[bʀaʊn]

| golden (adj) | golden | ['ɡɔldən] |
| silvery (adj) | silbrig | ['zɪlbʀɪç] |

beige (adj)	beige	[beːʃ]
cream (adj)	cremefarben	['kʀɛːmˌfaʁbən]
turquoise (adj)	türkis	[tʏʁ'kiːs]
cherry red (adj)	kirschrot	['kɪʁʃʀoːt]
lilac (adj)	lila	['liːla]
crimson (adj)	himbeerrot	['hɪmbeːɐ̯ˌʀoːt]

light (adj)	hell	[hɛl]
dark (adj)	dunkel	['dʊŋkəl]
bright, vivid (adj)	grell	[ɡʀɛl]

coloured (pencils)	Farb-	['faʁp]
colour (e.g. ~ film)	Farb-	['faʁp]
black-and-white (adj)	schwarz-weiß	['ʃvaʁtsˌvaɪs]
plain (one-coloured)	einfarbig	['aɪnˌfaʁbɪç]
multicoloured (adj)	bunt	[bʊnt]

15. Questions

Who?	Wer?	[veːɐ̯]
What?	Was?	[vas]
Where? (at, in)	Wo?	[voː]
Where (to)?	Wohin?	[vo'hɪn]
From where?	Woher?	[vo'heːɐ̯]
When?	Wann?	[van]
Why? (What for?)	Wozu?	[vo'tsuː]
Why? (~ are you crying?)	Warum?	[va'ʀʊm]
What for?	Wofür?	[vo'fyːɐ̯]

How? (in what way)	Wie?	[viː]
What? (What kind of ...?)	Welcher?	['vɛlçɐ]
Which?	Welcher?	['vɛlçɐ]

To whom?	Wem?	[veːm]
About whom?	Über wen?	['yːbɐ veːn]
About what?	Wovon?	[voːˈfɔn]
With whom?	Mit wem?	[mɪt veːm]

How many?	Wie viele?	[viː ˈfiːlə]
How much?	Wie viel?	['viː fiːl]
Whose?	Wessen?	['vɛsən]

16. Prepositions

with (accompanied by)	mit	[mɪt]
without	ohne	['oːnə]
to (indicating direction)	nach	[naːχ]
about (talking ~ ...)	über	['yːbɐ]
before (in time)	vor	[foːɐ]
in front of ...	vor	[foːɐ]

under (beneath, below)	unter	['ʊntɐ]
above (over)	über	['yːbɐ]
on (atop)	auf	[aʊf]
from (off, out of)	aus	['aʊs]
of (made from)	aus, von	['aʊs], [fɔn]

| in (e.g. ~ ten minutes) | in | [ɪn] |
| over (across the top of) | über | ['yːbɐ] |

17. Function words. Adverbs. Part 1

Where? (at, in)	Wo?	[voː]
here (adv)	hier	[hiːɐ]
there (adv)	dort	[dɔʁt]

| somewhere (to be) | irgendwo | ['ɪʁɡənt'voː] |
| nowhere (not in any place) | nirgends | ['nɪʁɡənts] |

| by (near, beside) | an | [an] |
| by the window | am Fenster | [am 'fɛnstɐ] |

Where (to)?	Wohin?	[voˈhɪn]
here (e.g. come ~!)	hierher	['hiːɐ'heːɐ]
there (e.g. to go ~)	dahin	[daˈhɪn]
from here (adv)	von hier	[fɔn hiːɐ]
from there (adv)	von da	[fɔn daː]

close (adv)	nah	[naː]
far (adv)	weit	[vaɪt]
near (e.g. ~ Paris)	in der Nähe von ...	[ɪn deːɐ 'nɛːə fɔn]

| nearby (adv) | in der Nähe | [ɪn deːɐ 'nɛːə] |
| not far (adv) | unweit | ['ʊnvaɪt] |

left (adj)	link	[lɪŋk]
on the left	links	[lɪŋks]
to the left	nach links	[naːx lɪŋks]

right (adj)	recht	[ʀɛçt]
on the right	rechts	[ʀɛçts]
to the right	nach rechts	[naːx ʀɛçts]

in front (adv)	vorne	['foʀnə]
front (as adj)	Vorder-	['foʀdɐ]
ahead (the kids ran ~)	vorwärts	['foːevɛʀts]

behind (adv)	hinten	['hɪntən]
from behind	von hinten	[fɔn 'hɪntən]
back (towards the rear)	rückwärts	['ʀʏk͜vɛʀts]

| middle | Mitte (f) | ['mɪtə] |
| in the middle | in der Mitte | [ɪn deːɐ 'mɪtə] |

at the side	seitlich	['zaɪtlɪç]
everywhere (adv)	überall	[yːbɐ'ʔal]
around (in all directions)	ringsherum	[ˌʀɪŋshɛ'ʀʊm]

from inside	von innen	[fɔn 'ɪnən]
somewhere (to go)	irgendwohin	['ɪʀɡənt·vo'hɪn]
straight (directly)	geradeaus	[ɡəʀaːdə'ʔaʊs]
back (e.g. come ~)	zurück	[tsu'ʀʏk]

| from anywhere | irgendwoher | ['ɪʀɡənt·vo'heːɐ] |
| from somewhere | von irgendwo | [fɔn ˌɪʀɡənt'voː] |

firstly (adv)	erstens	['eːestəns]
secondly (adv)	zweitens	['tsvaɪtəns]
thirdly (adv)	drittens	['dʀɪtəns]

suddenly (adv)	plötzlich	['plœtslɪç]
at first (in the beginning)	zuerst	[tsu'ʔeːest]
for the first time	zum ersten Mal	[tsʊm 'eːestən 'maːl]
long before ...	lange vor ...	['laŋə foːɐ]
anew (over again)	von Anfang an	[fɔn 'anˌfaŋ an]
for good (adv)	für immer	[fyːɐ 'ɪmɐ]

never (adv)	nie	[niː]
again (adv)	wieder	['viːdɐ]
now (at present)	jetzt	[jɛtst]
often (adv)	oft	[ɔft]
then (adv)	damals	['daːmaːls]
urgently (quickly)	dringend	['dʀɪŋənt]
usually (adv)	gewöhnlich	[ɡə'vøːnlɪç]

by the way, ...	übrigens, ...	['yːbʀɪɡəns]
possibly	möglicherweise	['møːklɪçe'vaɪzə]
probably (adv)	wahrscheinlich	[vaːɐ'ʃaɪnlɪç]

maybe (adv)	vielleicht	[fi'laɪçt]
besides ...	außerdem ...	['auseːde:m]
that's why ...	deshalb ...	['dɛs'halp]
in spite of ...	trotz ...	[tʀɔts]
thanks to ...	dank ...	[daŋk]

what (pron.)	was	[vas]
that (conj.)	das	[das]
something	etwas	['ɛtvas]
anything (something)	irgendwas	['ɪʁgənt'vas]
nothing	nichts	[nɪçts]

who (pron.)	wer	[ve:ɐ]
someone	jemand	['je:mant]
somebody	irgendwer	['ɪʁgənt've:ɐ]

nobody	niemand	['ni:mant]
nowhere (a voyage to ~)	nirgends	['nɪʁgənts]
nobody's	niemandes	['ni:mandəs]
somebody's	jemandes	['je:mandəs]

so (I'm ~ glad)	so	[zo:]
also (as well)	auch	['auχ]
too (as well)	ebenfalls	['e:bən‚fals]

18. Function words. Adverbs. Part 2

Why?	Warum?	[va'ʀʊm]
for some reason	aus irgendeinem Grund	['aus 'ɪʁgənt'ʔaɪnəm gʀʊnt]
because ...	weil ...	[vaɪl]
for some purpose	zu irgendeinem Zweck	[tsu 'ɪʁgənt'ʔaɪnəm tsvɛk]

and	und	[ʊnt]
or	oder	['o:dɐ]
but	aber	['a:bɐ]
for (e.g. ~ me)	für	[fy:ɐ]

too (excessively)	zu	[tsu:]
only (exclusively)	nur	[nu:ɐ]
exactly (adv)	genau	[gə'nau]
about (more or less)	etwa	['ɛtva]

approximately (adv)	ungefähr	['ʊngəfɛ:ɐ]
approximate (adj)	ungefähr	['ʊngəfɛ:ɐ]
almost (adv)	fast	[fast]
the rest	Übrige (n)	['y:bʀɪgə]

the other (second)	der andere	[de:ɐ 'andəʀə]
other (different)	andere	['andəʀə]
each (adj)	jeder (m)	['je:dɐ]
any (no matter which)	beliebig	[bɛ'li:bɪç]
many, much (a lot of)	viel	[fi:l]
many people	viele Menschen	['fi:lə 'mɛnʃən]

all (everyone)	alle	['alə]
in return for ...	im Austausch gegen ...	[ɪm 'aʊsˌtaʊʃ 'geːgən]
in exchange (adv)	dafür	[da'fyːɐ]
by hand (made)	mit der Hand	[mɪt deːɐ hant]
hardly (negative opinion)	schwerlich	['ʃveːɐlɪç]
probably (adv)	wahrscheinlich	[vaːɐ'ʃaɪnlɪç]
on purpose (intentionally)	absichtlich	['apˌzɪçtlɪç]
by accident (adv)	zufällig	['tsuːfɛlɪç]
very (adv)	sehr	[zeːɐ]
for example (adv)	zum Beispiel	[tsʊm 'baɪʃpiːl]
between	zwischen	['tsvɪʃən]
among	unter	['ʊntɐ]
so much (such a lot)	so viel	[zoː 'fiːl]
especially (adv)	besonders	[bə'zɔndɐs]

Basic concepts. Part 2

19. Opposites

rich (adj)	reich	[ʀaɪç]
poor (adj)	arm	[aʁm]
ill, sick (adj)	krank	[kʀaŋk]
well (not sick)	gesund	[gə'zʊnt]
big (adj)	groß	[gʀoːs]
small (adj)	klein	[klaɪn]
quickly (adv)	schnell	[ʃnɛl]
slowly (adv)	langsam	['laŋzaːm]
fast (adj)	schnell	[ʃnɛl]
slow (adj)	langsam	['laŋzaːm]
glad (adj)	froh	[fʀoː]
sad (adj)	traurig	['tʀaʊʀɪç]
together (adv)	zusammen	[tsu'zamən]
separately (adv)	getrennt	[gə'tʀɛnt]
aloud (to read)	laut	[laʊt]
silently (to oneself)	still	[ʃtɪl]
tall (adj)	hoch	[hoːχ]
low (adj)	niedrig	['niːdʀɪç]
deep (adj)	tief	[tiːf]
shallow (adj)	flach	[flaχ]
yes	ja	[jaː]
no	nein	[naɪn]
distant (in space)	fern	[fɛʁn]
nearby (adj)	nah	[naː]
far (adv)	weit	[vaɪt]
nearby (adv)	nebenan	[ne:bən'ʔan]
long (adj)	lang	[laŋ]
short (adj)	kurz	[kʊʁts]
good (kindhearted)	gut	[guːt]
evil (adj)	böse	['bøːzə]

married (adj)	verheiratet	[fɛɐ'haɪʀaːtət]
single (adj)	ledig	['leːdɪç]
to forbid (vt)	verbieten (vt)	[fɛɐ'biːtən]
to permit (vt)	erlauben (vt)	[ɛɐ'laʊbən]
end	Ende (n)	['ɛndə]
beginning	Anfang (m)	['anfaŋ]
left (adj)	link	[lɪŋk]
right (adj)	recht	[ʀɛçt]
first (adj)	der erste	[deːɐ 'ɛʁstə]
last (adj)	der letzte	[deːɐ 'lɛtstə]
crime	Verbrechen (n)	[fɛɐ'bʀɛçən]
punishment	Bestrafung (f)	[bə'ʃtʀaːfʊŋ]
to order (vt)	befehlen (vt)	[ˌbə'feːlən]
to obey (vi, vt)	gehorchen (vi)	[gə'hɔʁçən]
straight (adj)	gerade	[gə'ʀaːdə]
curved (adj)	krumm	[kʀʊm]
paradise	Paradies (n)	[paʀa'diːs]
hell	Hölle (f)	['hœlə]
to be born	geboren sein	[gə'boːʀən zaɪn]
to die (vi)	sterben (vi)	['ʃtɛʁbən]
strong (adj)	stark	[ʃtaʁk]
weak (adj)	schwach	['ʃvax]
old (adj)	alt	[alt]
young (adj)	jung	[jʊŋ]
old (adj)	alt	[alt]
new (adj)	neu	[nɔɪ]
hard (adj)	hart	[haʁt]
soft (adj)	weich	[vaɪç]
warm (tepid)	warm	[vaʁm]
cold (adj)	kalt	[kalt]
fat (adj)	dick	[dɪk]
thin (adj)	mager	['maːgɐ]
narrow (adj)	eng	[ɛŋ]
wide (adj)	breit	[bʀaɪt]
good (adj)	gut	[guːt]
bad (adj)	schlecht	[ʃlɛçt]
brave (adj)	tapfer	['tapfɐ]
cowardly (adj)	feige	['faɪgə]

20. Weekdays

Monday	Montag (m)	['moːntaːk]
Tuesday	Dienstag (m)	['diːnstaːk]
Wednesday	Mittwoch (m)	['mɪtvɔχ]
Thursday	Donnerstag (m)	['dɔnɛstaːk]
Friday	Freitag (m)	['fʀaɪtaːk]
Saturday	Samstag (m)	['zamstaːk]
Sunday	Sonntag (m)	['zɔntaːk]

today (adv)	heute	['hɔɪtə]
tomorrow (adv)	morgen	['mɔʁɡən]
the day after tomorrow	übermorgen	['yːbɐˌmɔʁɡən]
yesterday (adv)	gestern	['gɛstɐn]
the day before yesterday	vorgestern	['foːɐgɛstɐn]

day	Tag (m)	[taːk]
working day	Arbeitstag (m)	['aʁbaɪtsˌtaːk]
public holiday	Feiertag (m)	['faɪɐˌtaːk]
day off	freier Tag (m)	['fʀaɪɐ taːk]
weekend	Wochenende (n)	['vɔχənˌʔɛndə]

all day long	den ganzen Tag	[den 'gantsən 'taːk]
the next day (adv)	am nächsten Tag	[am 'nɛːçstən taːk]
two days ago	zwei Tage vorher	[tsvaɪ 'taːgə 'foːɐheːɐ]
the day before	am Vortag	[am 'foːɐˌtaːk]
daily (adj)	täglich	['tɛːklɪç]
every day (adv)	täglich	['tɛːklɪç]

week	Woche (f)	['vɔχə]
last week (adv)	letzte Woche	['lɛtstə 'vɔχə]
next week (adv)	nächste Woche	['nɛːçstə 'vɔχə]
weekly (adj)	wöchentlich	['vœçəntlɪç]
every week (adv)	wöchentlich	['vœçəntlɪç]
twice a week	zweimal pro Woche	['tsvaɪmaːl pʀɔ 'vɔχə]
every Tuesday	jeden Dienstag	['jeːdən 'diːnstaːk]

21. Hours. Day and night

morning	Morgen (m)	['mɔʁɡən]
in the morning	morgens	['mɔʁɡəns]
noon, midday	Mittag (m)	['mɪtaːk]
in the afternoon	nachmittags	['naːχmɪˌtaːks]

evening	Abend (m)	['aːbənt]
in the evening	abends	['aːbənts]
night	Nacht (f)	[naχt]
at night	nachts	[naχts]
midnight	Mitternacht (f)	['mɪtɐˌnaχt]

second	Sekunde (f)	[zeˈkʊndə]
minute	Minute (f)	[miˈnuːtə]
hour	Stunde (f)	['ʃtʊndə]

half an hour	eine halbe Stunde	['aɪnə 'halbə 'ʃtʊndə]
a quarter-hour	Viertelstunde (f)	['fɪʁtəlˌʃtʊndə]
fifteen minutes	fünfzehn Minuten	['fʏnftseːn mi'nuːtən]
24 hours	Tag und Nacht	['taːk ʊnt 'naχt]

sunrise	Sonnenaufgang (m)	['zɔnənˌʔaʊfɡaŋ]
dawn	Morgendämmerung (f)	['mɔʁɡənˌdɛmərʊŋ]
early morning	früher Morgen (m)	['fʁyːɐ 'mɔʁɡən]
sunset	Sonnenuntergang (m)	['zɔnənˌʔʊntɐɡaŋ]

early in the morning	früh am Morgen	[fʁyː am 'mɔʁɡən]
this morning	heute morgen	['hɔɪtə 'mɔʁɡən]
tomorrow morning	morgen früh	['mɔʁɡən fʁyː]

this afternoon	heute Mittag	['hɔɪtə 'mɪtaːk]
in the afternoon	nachmittags	['naːχmɪˌtaːks]
tomorrow afternoon	morgen Nachmittag	['mɔʁɡən 'naːχmɪˌtaːk]

| tonight (this evening) | heute Abend | ['hɔɪtə 'aːbənt] |
| tomorrow night | morgen Abend | ['mɔʁɡən 'aːbənt] |

at 3 o'clock sharp	Punkt drei Uhr	[pʊŋkt dʁaɪ uːɐ]
about 4 o'clock	gegen vier Uhr	['ɡeːɡn fiːɐ uːɐ]
by 12 o'clock	um zwölf Uhr	[ʊm tsvœlf uːɐ]

in 20 minutes	in zwanzig Minuten	[ɪn 'tsvantsɪç mi'nuːtən]
in an hour	in einer Stunde	[ɪn 'aɪnɐ 'ʃtʊndə]
on time (adv)	rechtzeitig	['ʁɛçtˌtsaɪtɪç]

a quarter to ...	Viertel vor ...	['fɪʁtəl foːɐ]
within an hour	innerhalb einer Stunde	['ɪnɐhalp 'aɪnɐ 'ʃtʊndə]
every 15 minutes	alle fünfzehn Minuten	['alə 'fʏnftseːn mi'nuːtən]
round the clock	Tag und Nacht	['taːk ʊnt 'naχt]

22. Months. Seasons

January	Januar (m)	['januaːɐ]
February	Februar (m)	['feːbʁuaːɐ]
March	März (m)	[mɛʁts]
April	April (m)	[a'pʁɪl]
May	Mai (m)	[maɪ]
June	Juni (m)	['juːni]

July	Juli (m)	['juːli]
August	August (m)	[aʊ'ɡʊst]
September	September (m)	[zɛp'tɛmbɐ]
October	Oktober (m)	[ɔk'toːbɐ]
November	November (m)	[no'vɛmbɐ]
December	Dezember (m)	[de'tsɛmbɐ]

spring	Frühling (m)	['fʁyːlɪŋ]
in spring	im Frühling	[ɪm 'fʁyːlɪŋ]
spring (as adj)	Frühlings-	['fʁyːlɪŋs]
summer	Sommer (m)	['zɔmɐ]

| in summer | im Sommer | [ɪm 'zɔmɐ] |
| summer (as adj) | Sommer- | ['zɔmɐ] |

autumn	Herbst (m)	[hɛʁpst]
in autumn	im Herbst	[ɪm hɛʁpst]
autumn (as adj)	Herbst-	[hɛʁpst]

winter	Winter (m)	['vɪntɐ]
in winter	im Winter	[ɪm 'vɪntɐ]
winter (as adj)	Winter-	['vɪntɐ]
month	Monat (m)	['moːnat]
this month	in diesem Monat	[ɪn 'diːzəm 'moːnat]
next month	nächsten Monat	['nɛːçstən 'moːnat]
last month	letzten Monat	['lɛtstən 'moːnat]

a month ago	vor einem Monat	[foːɐ 'aɪnəm 'moːnat]
in a month (a month later)	über eine Monat	['yːbɐ 'aɪnə 'moːnat]
in 2 months (2 months later)	in zwei Monaten	[ɪn tsvaɪ 'moːnatən]
the whole month	einen ganzen Monat	['aɪnən 'gantsən 'moːnat]
all month long	den ganzen Monat	[deːn 'gantsən 'moːnat]

monthly (~ magazine)	monatlich	['moːnatlɪç]
monthly (adv)	monatlich	['moːnatlɪç]
every month	jeden Monat	['jeːdən 'moːnat]
twice a month	zweimal pro Monat	['tsvaɪmaːl pʁo 'moːnat]

year	Jahr (n)	[jaːɐ]
this year	dieses Jahr	['diːzəs jaːɐ]
next year	nächstes Jahr	['nɛːçstəs jaːɐ]
last year	voriges Jahr	['foːʁɪgəs jaːɐ]
a year ago	vor einem Jahr	[foːɐ 'aɪnəm jaːɐ]
in a year	in einem Jahr	[ɪn 'aɪnəm jaːɐ]
in two years	in zwei Jahren	[ɪn tsvaɪ 'jaːʁən]
the whole year	ein ganzes Jahr	[aɪn 'gantsəs jaːɐ]
all year long	das ganze Jahr	[das 'gantsə jaːɐ]

every year	jedes Jahr	['jeːdəs jaːɐ]
annual (adj)	jährlich	['jɛːɐlɪç]
annually (adv)	jährlich	['jɛːɐlɪç]
4 times a year	viermal pro Jahr	['fiːɐmaːl pʁo jaːɐ]

date (e.g. today's ~)	Datum (n)	['daːtʊm]
date (e.g. ~ of birth)	Datum (n)	['daːtʊm]
calendar	Kalender (m)	[ka'lɛndɐ]

half a year	ein halbes Jahr	[aɪn 'halbəs jaːɐ]
six months	Halbjahr (n)	['halpjaːɐ]
season (summer, etc.)	Saison (f)	[zɛ'zɔn]
century	Jahrhundert (n)	[jaːɐ'hʊndɐt]

23. Time. Miscellaneous

| time | Zeit (f) | [tsaɪt] |
| moment | Augenblick (m) | [ˌaʊgən'blɪk] |

instant (n)	Moment (m)	[mo'mɛnt]
instant (adj)	augenblicklich	[ˌaʊɡən'blɪklɪç]
lapse (of time)	Zeitspanne (f)	['tsaɪtˌʃpanə]
life	Leben (n)	['leːbən]
eternity	Ewigkeit (f)	['eːvɪçkaɪt]

epoch	Epoche (f)	[e'pɔχə]
era	Ära (f)	['ɛːʀa]
cycle	Zyklus (m)	['tsyːklʊs]
period	Periode (f)	[pe'ʀɪoːdə]
term (short-~)	Frist (f)	[fʀɪst]

the future	Zukunft (f)	['tsuːˌkʊnft]
future (as adj)	zukünftig	['tsuːˌkʏnftɪç]
next time	nächstes Mal	['nɛːçstəs mal]
the past	Vergangenheit (f)	[ˌfɛɐ'ɡaɲənhaɪt]
past (recent)	vorig	['foːʀɪç]
last time	letztes Mal	['lɛtstəs maːl]

later (adv)	später	['ʃpɛːtɐ]
after (prep.)	danach	[da'naːχ]
nowadays (adv)	zur Zeit	[tsuːɐ 'tsaɪt]
now (at this moment)	jetzt	[jɛtst]
immediately (adv)	sofort	[zo'foɐt]
soon (adv)	bald	[balt]
in advance (beforehand)	im Voraus	[ɪm fo'ʀaʊs]

a long time ago	lange her	['laŋə heːɐ]
recently (adv)	vor kurzem	[foːɐ 'kʊɐtsəm]
destiny	Schicksal (n)	['ʃɪkˌzaːl]
recollections	Erinnerungen (pl)	[ɛɐ'ʔɪnəʀʊŋən]
archives	Archiv (n)	[aɐ'çiːf]
during …	während …	['vɛːʀənt]
long, a long time (adv)	lange	['laŋə]
not long (adv)	nicht lange	[nɪçt 'laŋə]
early (in the morning)	früh	[fʀyː]
late (not early)	spät	[ʃpɛːt]

forever (for good)	für immer	[fyːɐ 'ɪmɐ]
to start (begin)	beginnen (vt)	[bə'ɡɪnən]
to postpone (vt)	verschieben (vt)	[fɛɐ'ʃiːbən]

at the same time	gleichzeitig	['glaɪçˌtsaɪtɪç]
permanently (adv)	ständig	['ʃtɛndɪç]
constant (noise, pain)	konstant	[kɔn'stant]
temporary (adj)	zeitweilig	['tsaɪtvaɪlɪç]
sometimes (adv)	manchmal	['mançmaːl]
rarely (adv)	selten	['zɛltən]
often (adv)	oft	[ɔft]

24. Lines and shapes

| square | Quadrat (n) | [kva'dʀaːt] |
| square (as adj) | quadratisch | [kva'dʀaːtɪʃ] |

circle	Kreis (m)	[kʀaɪs]
round (adj)	rund	[ʀʊnt]
triangle	Dreieck (n)	['dʀaɪʔɛk]
triangular (adj)	dreieckig	['dʀaɪʔɛkɪç]

oval	Oval (n)	[o'vaːl]
oval (as adj)	oval	[o'vaːl]
rectangle	Rechteck (n)	['ʀɛçtʔɛk]
rectangular (adj)	rechteckig	['ʀɛçtʔɛkɪç]

pyramid	Pyramide (f)	[pyʀa'miːdə]
rhombus	Rhombus (m)	['ʀɔmbʊs]
trapezium	Trapez (n)	[tʀa'peːts]
cube	Würfel (m)	['vʏʀfəl]
prism	Prisma (n)	['pʀɪsma]

circumference	Kreis (m)	[kʀaɪs]
sphere	Sphäre (f)	['sfɛːʀə]
ball (solid sphere)	Kugel (f)	['kuːgəl]
diameter	Durchmesser (m)	['dʊʀç.mɛsɐ]
radius	Radius (m)	['ʀaːdɪʊs]
perimeter (circle's ~)	Umfang (m)	['ʊmfaŋ]
centre	Zentrum (n)	['tsɛntʀʊm]

horizontal (adj)	waagerecht	['vaːgəʀɛçt]
vertical (adj)	senkrecht	['zɛŋkʀɛçt]
parallel (n)	Parallele (f)	[paʀa'leːlə]
parallel (as adj)	parallel	[paʀa'leːl]

line	Linie (f)	['liːniə]
stroke	Strich (m)	[ʃtʀɪç]
straight line	Gerade (f)	[gə'ʀaːdə]
curve (curved line)	Kurve (f)	['kʊʀvə]
thin (line, etc.)	dünn	[dʏn]
contour (outline)	Kontur (m, f)	[kɔn'tuːɐ]

intersection	Schnittpunkt (m)	['ʃnɪt.pʊŋkt]
right angle	rechter Winkel (m)	['ʀɛçtɐ 'vɪŋkəl]
segment	Segment (n)	[zɛ'gmɛnt]
sector (circular ~)	Sektor (m)	['zɛktoːɐ]
side (of a triangle)	Seite (f)	['zaɪtə]
angle	Winkel (m)	['vɪŋkəl]

25. Units of measurement

weight	Gewicht (n)	[gə'vɪçt]
length	Länge (f)	['lɛŋə]
width	Breite (f)	['bʀaɪtə]
height	Höhe (f)	['høːə]
depth	Tiefe (f)	['tiːfə]
volume	Volumen (n)	[vo'luːmən]
area	Fläche (f)	['flɛçə]
gram	Gramm (n)	[gʀam]
milligram	Milligramm (n)	['mɪli.gʀam]

kilogram	Kilo (n)	['ki:lo]
ton	Tonne (f)	['tɔnə]
pound	Pfund (n)	[pfʊnt]
ounce	Unze (f)	['ʊntsə]

metre	Meter (m, n)	['me:tɐ]
millimetre	Millimeter (m)	['mɪli‚me:tɐ]
centimetre	Zentimeter (m, n)	[‚tsɛnti'me:tɐ]
kilometre	Kilometer (m)	[‚kilo'me:tɐ]
mile	Meile (f)	['maɪlə]

inch	Zoll (m)	[tsɔl]
foot	Fuß (m)	[fu:s]
yard	Yard (n)	[ja:ɐt]

| square metre | Quadratmeter (m) | [kva'dʀa:t‚me:tɐ] |
| hectare | Hektar (n) | ['hɛkta:ɐ] |

litre	Liter (m, n)	['li:tɐ]
degree	Grad (m)	[gʀa:t]
volt	Volt (n)	[vɔlt]
ampere	Ampere (n)	[am'pe:ɐ]
horsepower	Pferdestärke (f)	['pfe:ɐdəˌʃtɛʀkə]

quantity	Anzahl (f)	['antsa:l]
a little bit of ...	etwas ...	['ɛtvas]
half	Hälfte (f)	['hɛlftə]
dozen	Dutzend (n)	['dʊtsənt]
piece (item)	Stück (n)	[ʃtʏk]

| size | Größe (f) | ['gʀø:sə] |
| scale (map ~) | Maßstab (m) | ['ma:sˌʃta:p] |

minimal (adj)	minimal	[mini'ma:l]
the smallest (adj)	der kleinste	[de:ɐ 'klaɪnstə]
medium (adj)	mittler, mittel-	['mɪtlɐ], ['mɪtəl]
maximal (adj)	maximal	[maksi'ma:l]
the largest (adj)	der größte	[de:ɐ 'gʀø:stə]

26. Containers

canning jar (glass ~)	Glas (n)	[gla:s]
tin, can	Dose (f)	['do:zə]
bucket	Eimer (m)	['aɪmɐ]
barrel	Fass (n), Tonne (f)	[fas], ['tɔnə]

wash basin (e.g., plastic ~)	Waschschüssel (n)	['vaʃʃʏsəl]
tank (100L water ~)	Tank (m)	[taŋk]
hip flask	Flachmann (m)	['flaχman]
jerrycan	Kanister (m)	[ka'nɪstɐ]
tank (e.g., tank car)	Zisterne (f)	[tsɪs'tɛʀnə]

| mug | Kaffeebecher (m) | ['kafeˌbɛçɐ] |
| cup (of coffee, etc.) | Tasse (f) | ['tasə] |

saucer	Untertasse (f)	['ʊntɐˌtasə]
glass (tumbler)	Wasserglas (n)	['vasɐˌglaːs]
wine glass	Weinglas (n)	['vaɪnˌglaːs]
stock pot (soup pot)	Kochtopf (m)	['kɔχˌtɔpf]

bottle (~ of wine)	Flasche (f)	['flaʃə]
neck (of the bottle, etc.)	Flaschenhals (m)	['flaʃənˌhals]

carafe (decanter)	Karaffe (f)	[ka'ʀafə]
pitcher	Tonkrug (m)	['toːnˌkʀuːk]
vessel (container)	Gefäß (n)	[gə'fɛːs]
pot (crock, stoneware ~)	Tontopf (m)	['toːnˌtɔpf]
vase	Vase (f)	['vaːzə]

flacon, bottle (perfume ~)	Flakon (n)	[fla'kɔŋ]
vial, small bottle	Fläschchen (n)	['flɛʃçən]
tube (of toothpaste)	Tube (f)	['tuːbə]

sack (bag)	Sack (m)	[zak]
bag (paper ~, plastic ~)	Tüte (f)	['tyːtə]
packet (of cigarettes, etc.)	Schachtel (f)	['ʃaχtəl]

box (e.g. shoebox)	Karton (m)	[kaʁ'tɔŋ]
crate	Kiste (f)	['kɪstə]
basket	Korb (m)	[kɔʁp]

27. Materials

material	Stoff (n)	[ʃtɔf]
wood (n)	Holz (n)	[hɔlts]
wood-, wooden (adj)	hölzern	['hœltsɐn]

glass (n)	Glas (n)	[glaːs]
glass (as adj)	gläsern, Glas-	['glɛːzɐn], [glaːs]

stone (n)	Stein (m)	[ʃtaɪn]
stone (as adj)	steinern	['ʃtaɪnɐn]

plastic (n)	Kunststoff (m)	['kʊnstˌʃtɔf]
plastic (as adj)	Kunststoff-	['kʊnstˌʃtɔf]

rubber (n)	Gummi (m, n)	['gʊmi]
rubber (as adj)	Gummi-	['gʊmi]

cloth, fabric (n)	Stoff (m)	[ʃtɔf]
fabric (as adj)	aus Stoff	['aʊs ʃtɔf]

paper (n)	Papier (n)	[pa'piːɐ]
paper (as adj)	Papier-	[pa'piːɐ]

cardboard (n)	Pappe (f)	['papə]
cardboard (as adj)	Pappen-	['papən]
polyethylene	Polyäthylen (n)	[polyʔɛty'leːn]
cellophane	Zellophan (n)	[tsɛlo'faːn]

linoleum	**Linoleum** (n)	[liˈnoːleʊm]
plywood	**Furnier** (n)	[fʊɐˈniːɐ]

porcelain (n)	**Porzellan** (n)	[pɔɐtsɛˈlaːn]
porcelain (as adj)	**aus Porzellan**	[ˈaʊs pɔɐtsɛˈlaːn]
clay (n)	**Ton** (m)	[toːn]
clay (as adj)	**Ton-**	[toːn]
ceramic (n)	**Keramik** (f)	[keˈʀaːmɪk]
ceramic (as adj)	**keramisch**	[keˈʀaːmɪʃ]

28. Metals

metal (n)	**Metall** (n)	[meˈtal]
metal (as adj)	**metallisch, Metall-**	[meˈtalɪʃ], [meˈtal]
alloy (n)	**Legierung** (f)	[leˈgiːʀʊŋ]

gold (n)	**Gold** (n)	[gɔlt]
gold, golden (adj)	**golden**	[ˈgɔldən]
silver (n)	**Silber** (n)	[ˈzɪlbə]
silver (as adj)	**silbern, Silber-**	[ˈzɪlbɐn], [ˈzɪlbə]

iron (n)	**Eisen** (n)	[ˈaɪzən]
iron-, made of iron (adj)	**eisern, Eisen-**	[ˈaɪzɐn], [ˈaɪzən]
steel (n)	**Stahl** (m)	[ʃtaːl]
steel (as adj)	**stählern**	[ˈʃtɛːlɐn]
copper (n)	**Kupfer** (n)	[ˈkʊpfə]
copper (as adj)	**kupfern, Kupfer-**	[ˈkʊpfɐn], [ˈkʊpfə]

aluminium (n)	**Aluminium** (n)	[aluˈmiːnjʊm]
aluminium (as adj)	**Aluminium-**	[aluˈmiːnjʊm]
bronze (n)	**Bronze** (f)	[ˈbʀɔŋsə]
bronze (as adj)	**bronzen**	[ˈbʀɔŋsən]

brass	**Messing** (n)	[ˈmɛsɪŋ]
nickel	**Nickel** (n)	[ˈnɪkəl]
platinum	**Platin** (n)	[ˈplaːtiːn]
mercury	**Quecksilber** (n)	[ˈkvɛkˌzɪlbə]
tin	**Zinn** (n)	[tsɪn]
lead	**Blei** (n)	[blaɪ]
zinc	**Zink** (n)	[tsɪŋk]

HUMAN BEING

Human being. The body

29. Humans. Basic concepts

human being	**Mensch** (m)	[mɛnʃ]
man (adult male)	**Mann** (m)	[man]
woman	**Frau** (f)	[fʀaʊ]
child	**Kind** (n)	[kɪnt]
girl	**Mädchen** (n)	['mɛːtçən]
boy	**Junge** (m)	['jʊŋə]
teenager	**Teenager** (m)	['tiːneːdʒɐ]
old man	**Greis** (m)	[gʀaɪs]
old woman	**alte Frau** (f)	['altə 'fʀaʊ]

30. Human anatomy

organism (body)	**Organismus** (m)	[ˌɔʀga'nɪsmʊs]
heart	**Herz** (n)	[hɛʀts]
blood	**Blut** (n)	[bluːt]
artery	**Arterie** (f)	[aʀ'teːʀiə]
vein	**Vene** (f)	['veːnə]
brain	**Gehirn** (n)	[gə'hɪʀn]
nerve	**Nerv** (m)	[nɛʀf]
nerves	**Nerven** (pl)	['nɛʀfən]
vertebra	**Wirbel** (m)	['vɪʀbəl]
spine (backbone)	**Wirbelsäule** (f)	['vɪʀbəlˌzɔɪlə]
stomach (organ)	**Magen** (m)	['maːgən]
intestines, bowels	**Gedärm** (n)	[gə'dɛʀm]
intestine (e.g. large ~)	**Darm** (m)	[daʀm]
liver	**Leber** (f)	['leːbɐ]
kidney	**Niere** (f)	['niːʀə]
bone	**Knochen** (m)	['knɔxən]
skeleton	**Skelett** (n)	[ske'lɛt]
rib	**Rippe** (f)	['ʀɪpə]
skull	**Schädel** (m)	['ʃɛːdəl]
muscle	**Muskel** (m)	['mʊskəl]
biceps	**Bizeps** (m)	['biːtsɛps]
triceps	**Trizeps** (m)	['tʀiːtsɛps]
tendon	**Sehne** (f)	['zeːnə]
joint	**Gelenk** (n)	[gə'lɛŋk]

lungs	Lungen (pl)	['lʊŋən]
genitals	Geschlechtsorgane (pl)	[gə'ʃlɛçts?ɔʁˌga:nə]
skin	Haut (f)	[haʊt]

31. Head

head	Kopf (m)	[kɔpf]
face	Gesicht (n)	[gə'zɪçt]
nose	Nase (f)	['na:zə]
mouth	Mund (m)	[mʊnt]

eye	Auge (n)	['aʊgə]
eyes	Augen (pl)	['aʊgən]
pupil	Pupille (f)	[pu'pɪlə]
eyebrow	Augenbraue (f)	['aʊgənˌbʁaʊə]
eyelash	Wimper (f)	['vɪmpɐ]
eyelid	Augenlid (n)	['aʊgənˌli:t]

tongue	Zunge (f)	['tsʊŋə]
tooth	Zahn (m)	[tsa:n]
lips	Lippen (pl)	['lɪpən]
cheekbones	Backenknochen (pl)	['bakənˌknɔxən]
gum	Zahnfleisch (n)	['tsa:nˌflaɪʃ]
palate	Gaumen (m)	['gaʊmən]

nostrils	Nasenlöcher (pl)	['na:zənˌlœçɐ]
chin	Kinn (n)	[kɪn]
jaw	Kiefer (m)	['ki:fɐ]
cheek	Wange (f)	['vaŋə]

forehead	Stirn (f)	[ʃtɪʁn]
temple	Schläfe (f)	['ʃlɛ:fə]
ear	Ohr (n)	[o:ɐ]
back of the head	Nacken (m)	['nakən]
neck	Hals (m)	[hals]
throat	Kehle (f)	['ke:lə]

hair	Haare (pl)	['ha:ʁə]
hairstyle	Frisur (f)	[ˌfʁi'zu:ɐ]
haircut	Haarschnitt (m)	['ha:ɐˌʃnɪt]
wig	Perücke (f)	[pe'ʁʏkə]

moustache	Schnurrbart (m)	['ʃnʊʁˌba:ɐt]
beard	Bart (m)	[ba:ɐt]
to have (a beard, etc.)	haben (vt)	[ha:bən]
plait	Zopf (m)	[tsɔpf]
sideboards	Backenbart (m)	['bakənˌba:ɐt]

red-haired (adj)	rothaarig	['ʁo:tˌha:ʁɪç]
grey (hair)	grau	[gʁaʊ]
bald (adj)	kahl	[ka:l]
bald patch	Glatze (f)	['glatsə]
ponytail	Pferdeschwanz (m)	['pfe:ɐdəˌʃvants]
fringe	Pony (m)	['pɔni]

39

32. Human body

hand	**Hand** (f)	[hant]
arm	**Arm** (m)	[aʁm]
finger	**Finger** (m)	['fɪŋɐ]
toe	**Zehe** (f)	['tse:ə]
thumb	**Daumen** (m)	['daʊmən]
little finger	**kleiner Finger** (m)	['klaɪnɐ 'fɪŋɐ]
nail	**Nagel** (m)	['na:gəl]
fist	**Faust** (f)	[faʊst]
palm	**Handfläche** (f)	['hant·ˌflɛçə]
wrist	**Handgelenk** (n)	['hant·gəˌlɛŋk]
forearm	**Unterarm** (m)	['ʊntɐˌʔaʁm]
elbow	**Ellbogen** (m)	['ɛlˌbo:gən]
shoulder	**Schulter** (f)	['ʃʊltɐ]
leg	**Bein** (n)	[baɪn]
foot	**Fuß** (m)	[fu:s]
knee	**Knie** (n)	[kni:]
calf	**Wade** (f)	['va:də]
hip	**Hüfte** (f)	['hʏftə]
heel	**Ferse** (f)	['fɛʁzə]
body	**Körper** (m)	['kœʁpɐ]
stomach	**Bauch** (m)	['baʊχ]
chest	**Brust** (f)	[bʁʊst]
breast	**Busen** (m)	['bu:zən]
flank	**Seite** (f), **Flanke** (f)	['zaɪtə], ['flaŋkə]
back	**Rücken** (m)	['ʁʏkən]
lower back	**Kreuz** (n)	[kʁɔɪts]
waist	**Taille** (f)	['taljə]
navel (belly button)	**Nabel** (m)	['na:bəl]
buttocks	**Gesäßbacken** (pl)	[gə'zɛ:sˈbakən]
bottom	**Hinterteil** (n)	['hɪntɐˌtaɪl]
beauty spot	**Leberfleck** (m)	['le:bɐˌflɛk]
birthmark (café au lait spot)	**Muttermal** (n)	['mu:tɐˌma:l]
tattoo	**Tätowierung** (f)	[tɛto'vi:ʁʊŋ]
scar	**Narbe** (f)	['naʁbə]

Clothing & Accessories

33. Outerwear. Coats

clothes	Kleidung (f)	['klaɪdʊŋ]
outerwear	Oberkleidung (f)	['oːbɐ̯klaɪdʊŋ]
winter clothing	Winterkleidung (f)	['vɪntɐ̯klaɪdʊŋ]
coat (overcoat)	Mantel (m)	['mantəl]
fur coat	Pelzmantel (m)	['pɛlts̩mantəl]
fur jacket	Pelzjacke (f)	['pɛltsˌjakə]
down coat	Daunenjacke (f)	['daʊnənˌjakə]
jacket (e.g. leather ~)	Jacke (f)	['jakə]
raincoat (trenchcoat, etc.)	Regenmantel (m)	['ʀeːgənˌmantəl]
waterproof (adj)	wasserdicht	['vasɐ̯dɪçt]

34. Men's & women's clothing

shirt (button shirt)	Hemd (n)	[hɛmt]
trousers	Hose (f)	['hoːzə]
jeans	Jeans (f)	[dʒiːns]
suit jacket	Jackett (n)	[ʒa'kɛt]
suit	Anzug (m)	['anˌtsuːk]
dress (frock)	Kleid (n)	[klaɪt]
skirt	Rock (m)	[ʀɔk]
blouse	Bluse (f)	['bluːzə]
knitted jacket (cardigan, etc.)	Strickjacke (f)	['ʃtʀɪkˌjakə]
jacket (of a woman's suit)	Jacke (f)	['jakə]
T-shirt	T-Shirt (n)	['tiːˌʃøːɐt]
shorts (short trousers)	Shorts (pl)	[ʃɔɐts]
tracksuit	Sportanzug (m)	['ʃpɔɐtˌantsuːk]
bathrobe	Bademantel (m)	['baːdəˌmantəl]
pyjamas	Schlafanzug (m)	['ʃlaːfʔanˌtsuːk]
jumper (sweater)	Sweater (m)	['swɛtɐ]
pullover	Pullover (m)	[pʊ'loːvɐ]
waistcoat	Weste (f)	['vɛstə]
tailcoat	Frack (m)	[fʀak]
dinner suit	Smoking (m)	['smoːkɪŋ]
uniform	Uniform (f)	['ʊniˌfɔɐm]
workwear	Arbeitskleidung (f)	['aɐbaɪtsˌklaɪdʊŋ]
boiler suit	Overall (m)	['oːvəʀal]
coat (e.g. doctor's smock)	Kittel (m)	['kɪtəl]

35. Clothing. Underwear

underwear	**Unterwäsche** (f)	['ʊntɐˌvɛʃə]
pants	**Herrenslip** (m)	['hɛʀənˌslɪp]
panties	**Damenslip** (m)	['da:mənˌslɪp]
vest (singlet)	**Unterhemd** (n)	['ʊntɐˌhɛmt]
socks	**Socken** (pl)	['zɔkən]

nightdress	**Nachthemd** (n)	['naχtˌhɛmt]
bra	**Büstenhalter** (m)	['bystənˌhaltɐ]
knee highs (knee-high socks)	**Kniestrümpfe** (pl)	['kni:ˌʃtʀʏmpfə]
tights	**Strumpfhose** (f)	['ʃtʀʊmpfˌho:zə]
stockings (hold ups)	**Strümpfe** (pl)	['ʃtʀʏmpfə]
swimsuit, bikini	**Badeanzug** (m)	['ba:dəˌʔantsu:k]

36. Headwear

hat	**Mütze** (f)	['mʏtsə]
trilby hat	**Filzhut** (m)	['fɪltsˌhu:t]
baseball cap	**Baseballkappe** (f)	['bɛɪsbɔ:lˌkapə]
flatcap	**Schiebermütze** (f)	['ʃi:bɐˌmʏtsə]

beret	**Baskenmütze** (f)	['baskənˌmʏtsə]
hood	**Kapuze** (f)	[ka'pu:tsə]
panama hat	**Panamahut** (m)	['panama:ˌhu:t]
knit cap (knitted hat)	**Strickmütze** (f)	['ʃtʀɪkˌmʏtsə]

headscarf	**Kopftuch** (n)	['kɔpfˌtu:χ]
women's hat	**Damenhut** (m)	['da:mənˌhu:t]

hard hat	**Schutzhelm** (m)	['ʃʊtsˌhɛlm]
forage cap	**Feldmütze** (f)	['fɛltˌmʏtsə]
helmet	**Helm** (m)	[hɛlm]

bowler	**Melone** (f)	[me'lo:nə]
top hat	**Zylinder** (m)	[tsy'lɪndɐ]

37. Footwear

footwear	**Schuhe** (pl)	['ʃu:ə]
shoes (men's shoes)	**Stiefeletten** (pl)	[ʃti:fə'lɛtən]
shoes (women's shoes)	**Halbschuhe** (pl)	['halpˌʃu:ə]
boots (e.g., cowboy ~)	**Stiefel** (pl)	['ʃti:fəl]
carpet slippers	**Hausschuhe** (pl)	['haʊsˌʃu:ə]

trainers	**Tennisschuhe** (pl)	['tɛnɪsˌʃu:ə]
trainers	**Leinenschuhe** (pl)	['laɪnənˌʃu:ə]
sandals	**Sandalen** (pl)	[zan'da:lən]

cobbler (shoe repairer)	**Schuster** (m)	['ʃu:stɐ]
heel	**Absatz** (m)	['apˌzats]

pair (of shoes)	**Paar** (n)	[pa:ɐ]
lace (shoelace)	**Schnürsenkel** (m)	[ˈʃnyːɐˌsɛŋkəl]
to lace up (vt)	**schnüren** (vt)	[ˈʃnyːʁən]
shoehorn	**Schuhlöffel** (m)	[ˈʃuːˌlœfəl]
shoe polish	**Schuhcreme** (f)	[ˈʃuːˌkʁɛːm]

38. Textile. Fabrics

cotton (n)	**Baumwolle** (f)	[ˈbaʊmˌvɔlə]
cotton (as adj)	**Baumwolle-**	[ˈbaʊmˌvɔlə]
flax (n)	**Leinen** (m)	[ˈlaɪnən]
flax (as adj)	**Leinen-**	[ˈlaɪnən]

silk (n)	**Seide** (f)	[ˈzaɪdə]
silk (as adj)	**Seiden-**	[ˈzaɪdən]
wool (n)	**Wolle** (f)	[ˈvɔlə]
wool (as adj)	**Woll-**	[ˈvɔl]

velvet	**Samt** (m)	[zamt]
suede	**Wildleder** (n)	[ˈvɪltˌleːdɐ]
corduroy	**Cord** (m)	[kɔʁt]

nylon (n)	**Nylon** (n)	[ˈnaɪlɔn]
nylon (as adj)	**Nylon-**	[ˈnaɪlɔn]
polyester (n)	**Polyester** (m)	[polɪˈɛstɐ]
polyester (as adj)	**Polyester-**	[polɪˈɛstɐ]

leather (n)	**Leder** (n)	[ˈleːdɐ]
leather (as adj)	**Leder**	[ˈleːdɐ]
fur (n)	**Pelz** (m)	[pɛlts]
fur (e.g. ~ coat)	**Pelz-**	[pɛlts]

39. Personal accessories

gloves	**Handschuhe** (pl)	[ˈhantʃuːə]
mittens	**Fausthandschuhe** (pl)	[ˈfaʊst·hantʃuːə]
scarf (muffler)	**Schal** (m)	[ʃaːl]

glasses	**Brille** (f)	[ˈbʁɪlə]
frame (eyeglass ~)	**Brillengestell** (n)	[ˈbʁɪlən·gəˈʃtɛl]
umbrella	**Regenschirm** (m)	[ˈʁeːgənʃɪʁm]
walking stick	**Spazierstock** (m)	[ʃpaˈtsiːɐʃtɔk]
hairbrush	**Haarbürste** (f)	[ˈhaːɐˌbʏʁstə]
fan	**Fächer** (m)	[ˈfɛçɐ]

tie (necktie)	**Krawatte** (f)	[kʁaˈvatə]
bow tie	**Fliege** (f)	[ˈfliːgə]
braces	**Hosenträger** (pl)	[ˈhoːzənˌtʁɛːgɐ]
handkerchief	**Taschentuch** (n)	[ˈtaʃənˌtuːx]

| comb | **Kamm** (m) | [kam] |
| hair slide | **Haarspange** (f) | [ˈhaːɐʃpaŋə] |

hairpin	Haarnadel (f)	[ˈhaːɐˌnaːdəl]
buckle	Schnalle (f)	[ˈʃnalə]

belt	Gürtel (m)	[ˈɡʏʁtəl]
shoulder strap	Umhängegurt (m)	[ˈʊmhɛŋəˌɡʊʁt]

bag (handbag)	Tasche (f)	[ˈtaʃə]
handbag	Handtasche (f)	[ˈhantˌtaʃə]
rucksack	Rucksack (m)	[ˈʁʊkˌzak]

40. Clothing. Miscellaneous

fashion	Mode (f)	[ˈmoːdə]
in vogue (adj)	modisch	[ˈmoːdɪʃ]
fashion designer	Modedesigner (m)	[ˈmoːdəˈdiˈzaɪnɐ]

collar	Kragen (m)	[ˈkʁaːɡən]
pocket	Tasche (f)	[ˈtaʃə]
pocket (as adj)	Taschen-	[ˈtaʃən]
sleeve	Ärmel (m)	[ˈɛʁməl]
hanging loop	Aufhänger (m)	[ˈaʊfˌhɛŋɐ]
flies (on trousers)	Hosenschlitz (m)	[ˈhoːzənˌʃlɪts]

zip (fastener)	Reißverschluss (m)	[ˈʁaɪsˌfɛɐʃlʊs]
fastener	Verschluss (m)	[fɛɐˈʃlʊs]
button	Knopf (m)	[knɔpf]
buttonhole	Knopfloch (n)	[ˈknɔpfˌlɔx]
to come off (ab. button)	abgehen (vi)	[ˈapˌɡeːən]

to sew (vi, vt)	nähen (vi, vt)	[ˈnɛːən]
to embroider (vi, vt)	sticken (vt)	[ˈʃtɪkən]
embroidery	Stickerei (f)	[ʃtɪkəˈʁaɪ]
sewing needle	Nadel (f)	[ˈnaːdəl]
thread	Faden (m)	[ˈfaːdən]
seam	Naht (f)	[naːt]

to get dirty (vi)	sich beschmutzen	[zɪç bəˈʃmʊtsən]
stain (mark, spot)	Fleck (m)	[flɛk]
to crease, to crumple	sich knittern	[zɪç ˈknɪtən]
to tear, to rip (vt)	zerreißen (vt)	[tsɛɐˈʁaɪsən]
clothes moth	Motte (f)	[ˈmɔtə]

41. Personal care. Cosmetics

toothpaste	Zahnpasta (f)	[ˈtsaːnˌpasta]
toothbrush	Zahnbürste (f)	[ˈtsaːnˌbʏʁstə]
to clean one's teeth	Zähne putzen	[ˈtsɛːnə ˈpʊtsən]

razor	Rasierer (m)	[ʁaˈziːʁɐ]
shaving cream	Rasiercreme (f)	[ʁaˈziːɐˌkʁɛːm]
to shave (vi)	sich rasieren	[zɪç ʁaˈziːʁən]
soap	Seife (f)	[ˈzaɪfə]

shampoo	Shampoo (n)	['ʃampu]
scissors	Schere (f)	['ʃeːʀə]
nail file	Nagelfeile (f)	['naːgəlˌfaɪlə]
nail clippers	Nagelzange (f)	['naːgəlˌtsaŋə]
tweezers	Pinzette (f)	[pɪn'tsɛtə]

cosmetics	Kosmetik (f)	[kɔs'meːtɪk]
face mask	Gesichtsmaske (f)	[gə'zɪçtsˌmaskə]
manicure	Maniküre (f)	[mani'kyːʀə]
to have a manicure	Maniküre machen	[mani'kyːʀə 'maχən]
pedicure	Pediküre (f)	[pedi'kyːʀə]

make-up bag	Kosmetiktasche (f)	[kɔs'meːtɪkˌtaʃə]
face powder	Puder (m)	['puːdɐ]
powder compact	Puderdose (f)	['puːdɐˌdoːzə]
blusher	Rouge (n)	[ʀuːʒ]

perfume (bottled)	Parfüm (n)	[paʁ'fyːm]
toilet water (lotion)	Duftwasser (n)	['dʊftˌvasə]
lotion	Lotion (f)	[lo'tsjoːn]
cologne	Kölnischwasser (n)	['kœlnɪʃˌvasə]

eyeshadow	Lidschatten (m)	['liːtʃatən]
eyeliner	Kajalstift (m)	[ka'jaːlˌʃtɪft]
mascara	Wimperntusche (f)	['vɪmpɐnˌtʊʃə]

lipstick	Lippenstift (m)	['lɪpənˌʃtɪft]
nail polish	Nagellack (m)	['naːgəlˌlak]
hair spray	Haarlack (m)	['haːɐˌlak]
deodorant	Deodorant (n)	[deodo'ʀant]

cream	Creme (f)	[kʀɛːm]
face cream	Gesichtscreme (f)	[gə'zɪçtsˌkʀɛːm]
hand cream	Handcreme (f)	['hantˌkʀɛːm]
anti-wrinkle cream	Anti-Falten-Creme (f)	[ˌanti'faltən·kʀɛːm]
day cream	Tagescreme (f)	['taːgəsˌkʀɛːm]
night cream	Nachtcreme (f)	['naχtˌkʀɛːm]
day (as adj)	Tages-	['taːgəs]
night (as adj)	Nacht-	[naχt]

tampon	Tampon (m)	['tampoːn]
toilet paper (toilet roll)	Toilettenpapier (n)	[toa'lɛtən·paˌpiːɐ]
hair dryer	Föhn (m)	['føːn]

42. Jewellery

jewellery, jewels	Schmuck (m)	[ʃmʊk]
precious (e.g. ~ stone)	Edel-	['eːdəl]
hallmark stamp	Repunze (f)	[ʀe'pʊntsə]

ring	Ring (m)	[ʀɪŋ]
wedding ring	Ehering (m)	['eːəˌʀɪŋ]
bracelet	Armband (n)	['aʁmˌbant]
earrings	Ohrringe (pl)	['oːɐˌʀɪŋə]

necklace (~ of pearls)	Kette (f)	['kɛtə]
crown	Krone (f)	['kʀoːnə]
bead necklace	Halskette (f)	['hals͵kɛtə]

diamond	Brillant (m)	[bʀɪl'jant]
emerald	Smaragd (m)	[sma'ʀakt]
ruby	Rubin (m)	[ʀu'biːn]
sapphire	Saphir (m)	['zaːfiɐ]
pearl	Perle (f)	['pɛʀlə]
amber	Bernstein (m)	['bɛʀnʃtaɪn]

43. Watches. Clocks

watch (wristwatch)	Armbanduhr (f)	['aʀmbant͵ʔuːɐ]
dial	Zifferblatt (n)	['tsɪfɐ͵blat]
hand (clock, watch)	Zeiger (m)	['tsaɪgɐ]
metal bracelet	Metallarmband (n)	[me'tal͵ʔaʀmbant]
watch strap	Uhrenarmband (n)	['uːʀən͵ʔaʀmbant]

battery	Batterie (f)	[batə'ʀiː]
to be flat (battery)	verbraucht sein	[fɛ'bʀaʊχt zaɪn]
to change a battery	die Batterie wechseln	[di batə'ʀi: 'vɛksəln]
to run fast	vorgehen (vi)	['foːɐ͵geːən]
to run slow	nachgehen (vi)	['naːχ͵geːən]

wall clock	Wanduhr (f)	['vant͵ʔuːɐ]
hourglass	Sanduhr (f)	['zant͵ʔuːɐ]
sundial	Sonnenuhr (f)	['zɔnən͵ʔuːɐ]
alarm clock	Wecker (m)	['vɛkɐ]
watchmaker	Uhrmacher (m)	['uːɐ͵maχɐ]
to repair (vt)	reparieren (vt)	[ʀepa'ʀiːʀən]

Food. Nutricion

meat	Fleisch (n)	[flaɪʃ]
chicken	Hühnerfleisch (n)	['hy:nəˌflaɪʃ]
poussin	Küken (n)	['ky:kən]
duck	Ente (f)	['ɛntə]
goose	Gans (f)	[gans]
game	Wild (n)	[vɪlt]
turkey	Pute (f)	['pu:tə]
pork	Schweinefleisch (n)	['ʃvaɪnəˌflaɪʃ]
veal	Kalbfleisch (n)	['kalpˌflaɪʃ]
lamb	Hammelfleisch (n)	['haməlˌflaɪʃ]
beef	Rindfleisch (n)	['ʀɪntˌflaɪʃ]
rabbit	Kaninchenfleisch (n)	[ka'ni:nçənˌflaɪʃ]
sausage (bologna, etc.)	Wurst (f)	[vuʀst]
vienna sausage (frankfurter)	Würstchen (n)	['vʀstçən]
bacon	Schinkenspeck (m)	['ʃɪŋkənˌʃpɛk]
ham	Schinken (m)	['ʃɪŋkən]
gammon	Räucherschinken (m)	['ʀɔɪçəˌʃɪŋkən]
pâté	Pastete (f)	[pas'te:tə]
liver	Leber (f)	['le:bɐ]
mince (minced meat)	Hackfleisch (n)	['hakˌflaɪʃ]
tongue	Zunge (f)	['tsʊŋə]
egg	Ei (n)	[aɪ]
eggs	Eier (pl)	['aɪɐ]
egg white	Eiweiß (n)	['aɪvaɪs]
egg yolk	Eigelb (n)	['aɪgɛlp]
fish	Fisch (m)	[fɪʃ]
seafood	Meeresfrüchte (pl)	['me:ʀəsˌfʀʏçtə]
crustaceans	Krebstiere (pl)	['kʀe:psˌti:ʀə]
caviar	Kaviar (m)	['ka:vɪaʀ]
crab	Krabbe (f)	['kʀabə]
prawn	Garnele (f)	[gaʀ'ne:lə]
oyster	Auster (f)	['aʊstɐ]
spiny lobster	Languste (f)	[laŋ'gʊstə]
octopus	Krake (m)	['kʀa:kə]
squid	Kalmar (m)	['kalmaʀ]
sturgeon	Störfleisch (n)	['ʃtø:ɐˌflaɪʃ]
salmon	Lachs (m)	[laks]
halibut	Heilbutt (m)	['haɪlbʊt]
cod	Dorsch (m)	[dɔʀʃ]

mackerel	Makrele (f)	[ma'kʀeːlə]
tuna	Tunfisch (m)	['tuːnfɪʃ]
eel	Aal (m)	[aːl]

trout	Forelle (f)	[ˌfo'ʀɛlə]
sardine	Sardine (f)	[zaʁ'diːnə]
pike	Hecht (m)	[hɛçt]
herring	Hering (m)	['heːʀɪŋ]

bread	Brot (n)	[bʀoːt]
cheese	Käse (m)	['kɛːzə]
sugar	Zucker (m)	['tsʊkɐ]
salt	Salz (n)	[zalts]

rice	Reis (m)	[ʀaɪs]
pasta (macaroni)	Teigwaren (pl)	['taɪkˌvaːʀən]
noodles	Nudeln (pl)	['nuːdəln]

butter	Butter (f)	['bʊtɐ]
vegetable oil	Pflanzenöl (n)	['pflantsənˌʔøːl]
sunflower oil	Sonnenblumenöl (n)	['zɔnənbluːmənˌʔøːl]
margarine	Margarine (f)	[maʁga'ʀiːnə]

| olives | Oliven (pl) | [o'liːvən] |
| olive oil | Olivenöl (n) | [o'liːvənˌʔøːl] |

milk	Milch (f)	[mɪlç]
condensed milk	Kondensmilch (f)	[kɔn'dɛnsˌmɪlç]
yogurt	Joghurt (m, f)	['joːgʊʁt]
soured cream	saure Sahne (f)	['zaʊʀə 'zaːnə]
cream (of milk)	Sahne (f)	['zaːnə]

| mayonnaise | Mayonnaise (f) | [majo'nɛːzə] |
| buttercream | Buttercreme (f) | ['bʊtɐˌkʀeːm] |

groats (barley ~, etc.)	Grütze (f)	['gʀʏtsə]
flour	Mehl (n)	[meːl]
tinned food	Konserven (pl)	[kɔn'zɛʁvən]

cornflakes	Maisflocken (pl)	[maɪs'flɔkən]
honey	Honig (m)	['hoːnɪç]
jam	Marmelade (f)	[ˌmaʁmə'laːdə]
chewing gum	Kaugummi (m, n)	['kaʊˌgʊmi]

45. Drinks

water	Wasser (n)	['vasɐ]
drinking water	Trinkwasser (n)	['tʀɪŋkˌvasɐ]
mineral water	Mineralwasser (n)	[mine'ʀaːlˌvasɐ]

still (adj)	still	[ʃtɪl]
carbonated (adj)	mit Kohlensäure	[mɪt 'koːlənˌzɔɪʀə]
sparkling (adj)	mit Gas	[mɪt gaːs]
ice	Eis (n)	[aɪs]

with ice	mit Eis	[mɪt aɪs]
non-alcoholic (adj)	alkoholfrei	['alkoho:l·fʀaɪ]
soft drink	alkoholfreies Getränk (n)	['alkoho:l·fʀaɪəs gə'tʀɛŋk]
refreshing drink	Erfrischungsgetränk (n)	[ɛɐ'fʀɪʃʊŋs·gə͵tʀɛŋk]
lemonade	Limonade (f)	[limo'na:də]
spirits	Spirituosen (pl)	[ʃpiʀi'tʊo:zən]
wine	Wein (m)	[vaɪn]
white wine	Weißwein (m)	['vaɪs͵vaɪn]
red wine	Rotwein (m)	['ʀo:t͵vaɪn]
liqueur	Likör (m)	[li'kø:ɐ]
champagne	Champagner (m)	[ʃam'panjɐ]
vermouth	Wermut (m)	['ve:ɐmu:t]
whisky	Whisky (m)	['vɪski]
vodka	Wodka (m)	['vɔtka]
gin	Gin (m)	[dʒɪn]
cognac	Kognak (m)	['kɔnjak]
rum	Rum (m)	[ʀʊm]
coffee	Kaffee (m)	['kafe]
black coffee	schwarzer Kaffee (m)	['ʃvaʀtsɐ 'kafe]
white coffee	Milchkaffee (m)	['mɪlç·ka͵fe:]
cappuccino	Cappuccino (m)	[͵kapʊ'tʃi:no]
instant coffee	Pulverkaffee (m)	['pʊlfɐ͵kafe]
milk	Milch (f)	[mɪlç]
cocktail	Cocktail (m)	['kɔktɛɪl]
milkshake	Milchcocktail (m)	['mɪlç͵kɔktɛɪl]
juice	Saft (m)	[zaft]
tomato juice	Tomatensaft (m)	[to'ma:tən͵zaft]
orange juice	Orangensaft (m)	[o'ʀa:ŋʒən͵zaft]
freshly squeezed juice	frisch gepresster Saft (m)	[fʀɪʃ gə'pʀɛstə zaft]
beer	Bier (n)	[bi:ɐ]
lager	Helles (n)	['hɛlɛs]
bitter	Dunkelbier (n)	['dʊŋkəl͵bi:ɐ]
tea	Tee (m)	[te:]
black tea	schwarzer Tee (m)	['ʃvaʀtsɐ 'te:]
green tea	grüner Tee (m)	['gʀy:nɐ te:]

46. Vegetables

vegetables	Gemüse (n)	[gə'my:zə]
greens	grünes Gemüse (pl)	['gʀy:nəs gə'my:zə]
tomato	Tomate (f)	[to'ma:tə]
cucumber	Gurke (f)	['gʊʀkə]
carrot	Karotte (f)	[ka'ʀɔtə]
potato	Kartoffel (f)	[kaʀ'tɔfəl]
onion	Zwiebel (f)	['tsvi:bəl]

garlic	Knoblauch (m)	['kno:p,lauχ]
cabbage	Kohl (m)	[ko:l]
cauliflower	Blumenkohl (m)	['blu:mən,ko:l]
Brussels sprouts	Rosenkohl (m)	['ʀo:zən,ko:l]
broccoli	Brokkoli (m)	['bʀɔkoli]

beetroot	Rote Bete (f)	[,ʀo:tə'be:tə]
aubergine	Aubergine (f)	[,obɛʀ'ʒi:nə]
courgette	Zucchini (f)	[tsʊ'ki:ni]
pumpkin	Kürbis (m)	['kyʀbɪs]
turnip	Rübe (f)	['ʀy:bə]

parsley	Petersilie (f)	[petɐ'zi:lɪə]
dill	Dill (m)	[dɪl]
lettuce	Kopf Salat (m)	[kɔpf za'la:t]
celery	Sellerie (m)	['zɛləʀi]
asparagus	Spargel (m)	['ʃpaʀgəl]
spinach	Spinat (m)	[ʃpi'na:t]

pea	Erbse (f)	['ɛʀpsə]
beans	Bohnen (pl)	['bo:nən]
maize	Mais (m)	['maɪs]
kidney bean	weiße Bohne (f)	['vaɪsə 'bo:nə]

sweet paper	Paprika (m)	['papʀika]
radish	Radieschen (n)	[ʀa'di:sçən]
artichoke	Artischocke (f)	[aʀti'ʃɔkə]

47. Fruits. Nuts

fruit	Frucht (f)	[fʀʊχt]
apple	Apfel (m)	['apfəl]
pear	Birne (f)	['bɪʀnə]
lemon	Zitrone (f)	[tsi'tʀo:nə]
orange	Apfelsine (f)	[apfəl'zi:nə]
strawberry (garden ~)	Erdbeere (f)	['e:ɐt,be:ʀə]

tangerine	Mandarine (f)	[,manda'ʀi:nə]
plum	Pflaume (f)	['pflaumə]
peach	Pfirsich (m)	['pfɪʀzɪç]
apricot	Aprikose (f)	[,apʀi'ko:zə]
raspberry	Himbeere (f)	['hɪm,be:ʀə]
pineapple	Ananas (f)	['ananas]

banana	Banane (f)	[ba'na:nə]
watermelon	Wassermelone (f)	['vasɐme,lo:nə]
grape	Weintrauben (pl)	['vaɪn,tʀaubən]
sour cherry	Sauerkirsche (f)	['zaʊɐ,kɪʀʃə]
sweet cherry	Süßkirsche (f)	['zy:s,kɪʀʃə]
melon	Melone (f)	[me'lo:nə]

grapefruit	Grapefruit (f)	['gʀɛɪp,fʀu:t]
avocado	Avocado (f)	[avo'ka:do]
papaya	Papaya (f)	[pa'pa:ja]

| mango | Mango (f) | ['maŋgo] |
| pomegranate | Granatapfel (m) | [gʀa'na:t‚ʔapfəl] |

redcurrant	rote Johannisbeere (f)	['ʀo:tə jo:'hanɪsbe:ʀə]
blackcurrant	schwarze Johannisbeere (f)	['ʃvaʁtsə jo:'hanɪsbe:ʀə]
gooseberry	Stachelbeere (f)	['ʃtaχəl‚be:ʀə]
bilberry	Heidelbeere (f)	['haɪdəl‚be:ʀə]
blackberry	Brombeere (f)	['bʀɔm‚be:ʀə]

raisin	Rosinen (pl)	[ʀo'zi:nən]
fig	Feige (f)	['faɪgə]
date	Dattel (f)	['datəl]

peanut	Erdnuss (f)	['e:ɐt‚nʊs]
almond	Mandel (f)	['mandəl]
walnut	Walnuss (f)	['val‚nʊs]
hazelnut	Haselnuss (f)	['ha:zəl‚nʊs]
coconut	Kokosnuss (f)	['ko:kɔs‚nʊs]
pistachios	Pistazien (pl)	[pɪs'ta:tsɪən]

48. Bread. Sweets

bakers' confectionery (pastry)	Konditorwaren (pl)	[kɔn'dito:ɐ‚va:ʀən]
bread	Brot (n)	[bʀo:t]
biscuits	Keks (m, n)	[ke:ks]

chocolate (n)	Schokolade (f)	[ʃoko'la:də]
chocolate (as adj)	Schokoladen-	[ʃoko'la:dən]
candy (wrapped)	Bonbon (m, n)	[bɔŋ'bɔŋ]
cake (e.g. cupcake)	Kuchen (m)	['ku:χən]
cake (e.g. birthday ~)	Torte (f)	['tɔʁtə]

| pie (e.g. apple ~) | Kuchen (m) | ['ku:χən] |
| filling (for cake, pie) | Füllung (f) | ['fʏlʊŋ] |

jam (whole fruit jam)	Konfitüre (f)	[‚kɔnfi'ty:ʀə]
marmalade	Marmelade (f)	[‚maʁmə'la:də]
wafers	Waffeln (pl)	[vafəln]
ice-cream	Eis (n)	[aɪs]
pudding (Christmas ~)	Pudding (m)	['pʊdɪŋ]

49. Cooked dishes

course, dish	Gericht (n)	[gə'ʀɪçt]
cuisine	Küche (f)	['kʏçə]
recipe	Rezept (n)	[ʀe'tsɛpt]
portion	Portion (f)	[pɔʁ'tsjo:n]

salad	Salat (m)	[za'la:t]
soup	Suppe (f)	['zʊpə]
clear soup (broth)	Brühe (f), Bouillon (f)	['bʀy:ə], [bul'jɔŋ]
sandwich (bread)	belegtes Brot (n)	[bə'le:ktəs bʀo:t]

fried eggs	Spiegelei (n)	['ʃpiːgəl‚ʔaɪ]
hamburger (beefburger)	Hamburger (m)	['ham‚buʁgɐ]
beefsteak	Beefsteak (n)	['biːfˌʃteːk]

side dish	Beilage (f)	['baɪˌlaːgə]
spaghetti	Spaghetti (pl)	[ʃpaˈgɛti]
mash	Kartoffelpüree (n)	[kaʁˈtɔfəl·pyˌʁeː]
pizza	Pizza (f)	['pɪtsa]
porridge (oatmeal, etc.)	Brei (m)	[bʁaɪ]
omelette	Omelett (n)	[ɔmˈlɛt]

boiled (e.g. ~ beef)	gekocht	[gəˈkɔxt]
smoked (adj)	geräuchert	[gəˈʁɔɪçɐt]
fried (adj)	gebraten	[gəˈbʁaːtən]
dried (adj)	getrocknet	[gəˈtʁɔknət]
frozen (adj)	tiefgekühlt	['tiːfgəˌkyːlt]
pickled (adj)	mariniert	[maʁiˈniːɐt]

sweet (sugary)	süß	[zyːs]
salty (adj)	salzig	['zaltsɪç]
cold (adj)	kalt	[kalt]
hot (adj)	heiß	[haɪs]
bitter (adj)	bitter	['bɪtɐ]
tasty (adj)	lecker	['lɛkɐ]

to cook in boiling water	kochen (vt)	['kɔxən]
to cook (dinner)	zubereiten (vt)	['tsuːbəˌʁaɪtən]
to fry (vt)	braten (vt)	['bʁaːtən]
to heat up (food)	aufwärmen (vt)	['aʊfˌvɛʁmən]

to salt (vt)	salzen (vt)	['zaltsən]
to pepper (vt)	pfeffern (vt)	['pfɛfɐn]
to grate (vt)	reiben (vt)	['ʁaɪbən]
peel (n)	Schale (f)	['ʃaːlə]
to peel (vt)	schälen (vt)	['ʃɛːlən]

50. Spices

salt	Salz (n)	[zalts]
salty (adj)	salzig	['zaltsɪç]
to salt (vt)	salzen (vt)	['zaltsən]

black pepper	schwarzer Pfeffer (m)	['ʃvaʁtsɐ 'pfɛfɐ]
red pepper (milled ~)	roter Pfeffer (m)	['ʁoːtɐ 'pfɛfɐ]
mustard	Senf (m)	[zɛnf]
horseradish	Meerrettich (m)	['meːɐˌʁɛtɪç]

condiment	Gewürz (n)	[gəˈvyʁts]
spice	Gewürz (n)	[gəˈvyʁts]
sauce	Soße (f)	['zoːsə]
vinegar	Essig (m)	['ɛsɪç]

| anise | Anis (m) | [aˈniːs] |
| basil | Basilikum (n) | [baˈziːlikʊm] |

cloves	Nelke (f)	['nɛlkə]
ginger	Ingwer (m)	['ɪŋve]
coriander	Koriander (m)	[ko'ʀɪandɐ]
cinnamon	Zimt (m)	[tsɪmt]

sesame	Sesam (m)	['ze:zam]
bay leaf	Lorbeerblatt (n)	['lɔʁbe:ɐˌblat]
paprika	Paprika (m)	['papʁika]
caraway	Kümmel (m)	['kʏməl]
saffron	Safran (m)	['zafʀan]

51. Meals

| food | Essen (n) | ['ɛsən] |
| to eat (vi, vt) | essen (vi, vt) | ['ɛsən] |

breakfast	Frühstück (n)	['fʀyːʃtʏk]
to have breakfast	frühstücken (vi)	['fʀyːʃtʏkən]
lunch	Mittagessen (n)	['mɪtaːkˌʔɛsən]
to have lunch	zu Mittag essen	[tsu 'mɪtaːk 'ɛsən]
dinner	Abendessen (n)	['aːbəntˌʔɛsən]
to have dinner	zu Abend essen	[tsu 'aːbənt 'ɛsən]

| appetite | Appetit (m) | [ape'tiːt] |
| Enjoy your meal! | Guten Appetit! | [ˌɡutən ˌʔapə'tiːt] |

to open (~ a bottle)	öffnen (vt)	['œfnən]
to spill (liquid)	verschütten (vt)	[fɛɐ'ʃʏtən]
to spill out (vi)	verschüttet werden	[fɛɐ'ʃʏtət 've:ɐdən]

to boil (vi)	kochen (vi)	['kɔχən]
to boil (vt)	kochen (vt)	['kɔχən]
boiled (~ water)	gekocht	[ɡə'kɔχt]

| to chill, cool down (vt) | kühlen (vt) | ['kyːlən] |
| to chill (vi) | abkühlen (vi) | ['apˌkyːlən] |

| taste, flavour | Geschmack (m) | [ɡə'ʃmak] |
| aftertaste | Beigeschmack (m) | ['baɪɡəˌʃmak] |

to slim down (lose weight)	auf Diät sein	[aʊf di'ɛːt zaɪn]
diet	Diät (f)	[di'ɛːt]
vitamin	Vitamin (n)	[vita'miːn]
calorie	Kalorie (f)	[kalo'ʀiː]

| vegetarian (n) | Vegetarier (m) | [vege'taːʀɪɐ] |
| vegetarian (adj) | vegetarisch | [vege'taːʀɪʃ] |

fats (nutrient)	Fett (n)	[fɛt]
proteins	Protein (n)	[pʀote'iːn]
carbohydrates	Kohlenhydrat (n)	['koːlənhyˌdʀaːt]
slice (of lemon, ham)	Scheibchen (n)	['ʃaɪpçən]
piece (of cake, pie)	Stück (n)	[ʃtʏk]
crumb (of bread, cake, etc.)	Krümel (m)	['kʀyːməl]

52. Table setting

spoon	Löffel (m)	['lœfəl]
knife	Messer (n)	['mɛsɐ]
fork	Gabel (f)	[ga:bəl]

cup (e.g., coffee ~)	Tasse (f)	['tasə]
plate (dinner ~)	Teller (m)	['tɛlɐ]
saucer	Untertasse (f)	['ʊntɐˌtasə]
serviette	Serviette (f)	[zɛʁ'vɪɛtə]
toothpick	Zahnstocher (m)	['tsa:nˌʃtɔχɐ]

53. Restaurant

restaurant	Restaurant (n)	[ʀɛsto'ʀaŋ]
coffee bar	Kaffeehaus (n)	[ka'fe:ˌhaʊs]
pub, bar	Bar (f)	[ba:ɐ]
tearoom	Teesalon (m)	['te:·za'lɔŋ]

waiter	Kellner (m)	['kɛlnɐ]
waitress	Kellnerin (f)	['kɛlnəʀɪn]
barman	Barmixer (m)	['ba:ɐˌmɪksɐ]

menu	Speisekarte (f)	['ʃpaɪzəˌkaʁtə]
wine list	Weinkarte (f)	['vaɪnˌkaʁtə]
to book a table	einen Tisch reservieren	['aɪnən tɪʃ ʀɛzɛʁ'vi:ʀən]

course, dish	Gericht (n)	[gə'ʀɪçt]
to order (meal)	bestellen (vt)	[bə'ʃtɛlən]
to make an order	eine Bestellung aufgeben	['aɪnə bə'ʃtɛlʊŋ 'aʊfˌge:bən]

aperitif	Aperitif (m)	[apeʀi'ti:f]
starter	Vorspeise (f)	['fo:ɐˌʃpaɪzə]
dessert, pudding	Nachtisch (m)	['na:χˌtɪʃ]

bill	Rechnung (f)	['ʀɛçnʊŋ]
to pay the bill	Rechnung bezahlen	['ʀɛçnʊŋ bə'tsa:lən]
to give change	das Wechselgeld geben	[das 'vɛksəlˌgɛlt 'ge:bən]
tip	Trinkgeld (n)	['tʀɪŋkˌgɛlt]

Family, relatives and friends

54. Personal information. Forms

name (first name)	**Vorname** (m)	['fo:ɐ̯ˌnaːmə]
surname (last name)	**Name** (m)	['naːmə]
date of birth	**Geburtsdatum** (n)	[gə'buːɛtsˌdaːtʊm]
place of birth	**Geburtsort** (m)	[gə'buːɛtsˌʔɔʁt]
nationality	**Nationalität** (f)	[natsjɔnali'tɛːt]
place of residence	**Wohnort** (m)	['voːnˌʔɔʁt]
country	**Land** (n)	[lant]
profession (occupation)	**Beruf** (m)	[bə'ʁuːf]
gender, sex	**Geschlecht** (n)	[gə'ʃlɛçt]
height	**Größe** (f)	['gʁøːsə]
weight	**Gewicht** (n)	[gə'vɪçt]

55. Family members. Relatives

mother	**Mutter** (f)	['mʊtɐ]
father	**Vater** (m)	['faːtɐ]
son	**Sohn** (m)	[zoːn]
daughter	**Tochter** (f)	['tɔxtɐ]
younger daughter	**jüngste Tochter** (f)	['jʏŋstə 'tɔxtɐ]
younger son	**jüngste Sohn** (m)	['jʏŋstə 'zoːn]
eldest daughter	**ältere Tochter** (f)	['ɛltəʀə 'tɔxtɐ]
eldest son	**älterer Sohn** (m)	['ɛltəʀɐ 'zoːn]
brother	**Bruder** (m)	['bʁuːdɐ]
sister	**Schwester** (f)	['ʃvɛstɐ]
cousin (masc.)	**Cousin** (m)	[ku'zɛŋ]
cousin (fem.)	**Cousine** (f)	[ku'ziːnə]
mummy	**Mama** (f)	['mama]
dad, daddy	**Papa** (m)	['papa]
parents	**Eltern** (pl)	['ɛltɐn]
child	**Kind** (n)	[kɪnt]
children	**Kinder** (pl)	['kɪndɐ]
grandmother	**Großmutter** (f)	['gʁoːsˌmʊtɐ]
grandfather	**Großvater** (m)	['gʁoːsˌfaːtɐ]
grandson	**Enkel** (m)	['ɛŋkəl]
granddaughter	**Enkelin** (f)	['ɛŋkəlɪn]
grandchildren	**Enkelkinder** (pl)	['ɛŋkəlˌkɪndɐ]
uncle	**Onkel** (m)	['ɔŋkəl]
aunt	**Tante** (f)	['tantə]

| nephew | Neffe (m) | ['nɛfə] |
| niece | Nichte (f) | ['nɪçtə] |

mother-in-law (wife's mother)	Schwiegermutter (f)	['ʃviːgeˌmʊtə]
father-in-law (husband's father)	Schwiegervater (m)	['ʃviːgeˌfaːtə]
son-in-law (daughter's husband)	Schwiegersohn (m)	['ʃviːgeˌzoːn]
stepmother	Stiefmutter (f)	['ʃtiːfˌmʊtə]
stepfather	Stiefvater (m)	['ʃtiːfˌfaːtə]

infant	Säugling (m)	['zɔɪklɪŋ]
baby (infant)	Kleinkind (n)	['klaɪnˌkɪnt]
little boy, kid	Kleine (m)	['klaɪnə]

wife	Frau (f)	[fʀaʊ]
husband	Mann (m)	[man]
spouse (husband)	Ehemann (m)	['eːəˌman]
spouse (wife)	Gemahlin (f)	[gə'maːlɪn]

married (masc.)	verheiratet	[fɛɛ'haɪʀaːtət]
married (fem.)	verheiratet	[fɛɛ'haɪʀaːtət]
single (unmarried)	ledig	['leːdɪç]
bachelor	Junggeselle (m)	['jʊŋgəˌzɛlə]
divorced (masc.)	geschieden	[gə'ʃiːdən]
widow	Witwe (f)	['vɪtvə]
widower	Witwer (m)	['vɪtvə]

relative	Verwandte (m)	[fɛɛ'vantə]
close relative	naher Verwandter (m)	['naːɐ fɛɛ'vantə]
distant relative	entfernter Verwandter (m)	[ɛnt'fɛʀntə fɛɛ'vantə]
relatives	Verwandte (pl)	[fɛɛ'vantə]

orphan (boy or girl)	Waise (m, f)	['vaɪzə]
guardian (of a minor)	Vormund (m)	['foːɐˌmʊnt]
to adopt (a boy)	adoptieren (vt)	[adɔp'tiːʀən]
to adopt (a girl)	adoptieren (vt)	[adɔp'tiːʀən]

56. Friends. Colleagues

friend (masc.)	Freund (m)	[fʀɔɪnt]
friend (fem.)	Freundin (f)	['fʀɔɪndɪn]
friendship	Freundschaft (f)	['fʀɔɪntʃaft]
to be friends	befreundet sein	[bə'fʀɔɪndət zaɪn]

pal (masc.)	Freund (m)	[fʀɔɪnt]
pal (fem.)	Freundin (f)	['fʀɔɪndɪn]
partner	Partner (m)	['paʀtnə]

chief (boss)	Chef (m)	[ʃɛf]
superior (n)	Vorgesetzte (m)	['foːɐgəˌzɛtstə]
owner, proprietor	Besitzer (m)	[bə'zɪtsə]
subordinate (n)	Untergeordnete (m)	['ʊntegəˌʔɔʀtnətə]

colleague	Kollege (m), Kollegin (f)	[kɔ'leːgə], [kɔ'leːgɪn]
acquaintance (person)	Bekannte (m)	[bə'kantə]
fellow traveller	Reisegefährte (m)	['ʀaɪzə,gə'fɛːɐtə]
classmate	Mitschüler (m)	['mɪtʃyːlə]

neighbour (masc.)	Nachbar (m)	['naχ,baːɐ]
neighbour (fem.)	Nachbarin (f)	['naχbaːʀɪn]
neighbours	Nachbarn (pl)	['naχbaːɐn]

57. Man. Woman

woman	Frau (f)	[fʀaʊ]
girl (young woman)	Mädchen (n)	['mɛːtçən]
bride	Braut (f)	[bʀaʊt]

beautiful (adj)	schöne	['ʃøːnə]
tall (adj)	große	['gʀoːsə]
slender (adj)	schlanke	['ʃlaŋkə]
short (adj)	kleine	['klaɪnə]

| blonde (n) | Blondine (f) | [blɔn'diːnə] |
| brunette (n) | Brünette (f) | [bʀy'nɛtə] |

ladies' (adj)	Damen-	['daːmən]
virgin (girl)	Jungfrau (f)	['jʊŋfʀaʊ]
pregnant (adj)	schwangere	['ʃvaŋəʀə]

man (adult male)	Mann (m)	[man]
blonde haired man	Blonde (m)	['blɔndə]
dark haired man	Brünette (m)	[bʀy'nɛtə]
tall (adj)	hoch	[hoːχ]
short (adj)	klein	[klaɪn]

rude (rough)	grob	[gʀoːp]
stocky (adj)	untersetzt	[,untɐ'zɛtst]
robust (adj)	robust	[ʀo'bʊst]
strong (adj)	stark	[ʃtaʁk]
strength	Kraft (f)	[kʀaft]

plump, fat (adj)	dick	[dɪk]
swarthy (dark-skinned)	dunkelhäutig	['dʊŋkəl,hɔɪtɪç]
slender (well-built)	schlank	[ʃlaŋk]
elegant (adj)	elegant	[ele'gant]

58. Age

age	Alter (n)	['altə]
youth (young age)	Jugend (f)	['juːgənt]
young (adj)	jung	[jʊŋ]

| younger (adj) | jünger | ['jʏŋɐ] |
| older (adj) | älter | ['ɛltɐ] |

young man	Junge (m)	['jʊŋə]
teenager	Teenager (m)	['tiːneːdʒɐ]
guy, fellow	Bursche (m)	['bʊʁʃə]

| old man | Greis (m) | [gʀaɪs] |
| old woman | alte Frau (f) | ['altə 'fʀaʊ] |

adult (adj)	Erwachsene (f)	[ɛɐ'vaksənə]
middle-aged (adj)	in mittleren Jahren	[ɪn 'mɪtləʀən 'jaːʀən]
elderly (adj)	älterer	['ɛltəʀɐ]
old (adj)	alt	[alt]

retirement	Ruhestand (m)	['ʀuːəʃtant]
to retire (from job)	in Rente gehen	[ɪn 'ʀɛntə 'geːən]
retiree, pensioner	Rentner (m)	['ʀɛntnɐ]

59. Children

child	Kind (n)	[kɪnt]
children	Kinder (pl)	['kɪndɐ]
twins	Zwillinge (pl)	['tsvɪlɪŋə]

cradle	Wiege (f)	['viːgə]
rattle	Rassel (f)	['ʀasəl]
nappy	Windel (f)	['vɪndəl]

| dummy, comforter | Schnuller (m) | ['ʃnʊlɐ] |
| pram | Kinderwagen (m) | ['kɪndɐˌvaːgən] |

| nursery | Kindergarten (m) | ['kɪndɐˌgaʁtən] |
| babysitter | Kinderfrau (f) | ['kɪndɐˌfʀaʊ] |

| childhood | Kindheit (f) | ['kɪnthaɪt] |
| doll | Puppe (f) | ['pʊpə] |

| toy | Spielzeug (n) | ['ʃpiːlˌtsɔɪk] |
| construction set (toy) | Baukasten (m) | ['baʊˌkastən] |

well-bred (adj)	wohlerzogen	['voːlɛɐˌtsoːgən]
ill-bred (adj)	ungezogen	['ʊngəˌtsoːgən]
spoilt (adj)	verwöhnt	[fɛɐ'vøːnt]

| to be naughty | unartig sein | ['ʊnʔaʁtɪç zaɪn] |
| mischievous (adj) | unartig | ['ʊnʔaʁtɪç] |

| mischievousness | Unart (f) | ['ʊnʔaʁt] |
| mischievous child | Schelm (m) | [ʃɛlm] |

| obedient (adj) | gehorsam | [gə'hoːɐza:m] |
| disobedient (adj) | ungehorsam | ['ʊngəˌhoːɐza:m] |

docile (adj)	fügsam	[fyːksam]
clever (intelligent)	klug	[kluːk]
child prodigy	Wunderkind (n)	['vʊndɐˌkɪnt]

60. Married couples. Family life

to kiss (vt)	küssen (vt)	['kʏsən]
to kiss (vi)	sich küssen	[zɪç 'kʏsən]
family (n)	Familie (f)	[fa'miːliə]
family (as adj)	Familien-	[fa'miːliən]
couple	Paar (n)	[paːɐ̯]
marriage (state)	Ehe (f)	['eːə]
hearth (home)	Heim (n)	['haɪm]
dynasty	Dynastie (f)	[dynas'tiː]

date	Rendezvous (n)	[ʀãde'vuː]
kiss	Kuss (m)	[kʊs]

love (for sb)	Liebe (f)	['liːbə]
to love (sb)	lieben (vt)	['liːbən]
beloved	geliebt	[gə'liːpt]

tenderness	Zärtlichkeit (f)	['tsɛːɐ̯tlɪçkaɪt]
tender (affectionate)	zärtlich	['tsɛːɐ̯tlɪç]
faithfulness	Treue (f)	['tʀɔɪə]
faithful (adj)	treu	[tʀɔɪ]
care (attention)	Fürsorge (f)	['fyːɐ̯ˌzɔʀgə]
caring (~ father)	sorgsam	['zɔʀkzaːm]

newlyweds	Frischvermählte (pl)	['fʀɪʃ·fɛɐ̯'mɛːltə]
honeymoon	Flitterwochen (pl)	['flɪtɐˌvɔχən]
to get married (ab. woman)	heiraten (vi)	['haɪʀaːtən]
to get married (ab. man)	heiraten (vi)	['haɪʀaːtən]

wedding	Hochzeit (f)	['hɔχˌtsaɪt]
golden wedding	goldene Hochzeit (f)	['gɔldənə 'hɔχˌtsaɪt]
anniversary	Jahrestag (m)	['jaːʀəsˌtaːk]

lover (masc.)	Geliebte (m)	[gə'liːptə]
mistress (lover)	Geliebte (f)	[gə'liːptə]

adultery	Ehebruch (m)	['eːəˌbʀʊχ]
to cheat on ... (commit adultery)	Ehebruch begehen	['eːəˌbʀʊχ bə'geːən]
jealous (adj)	eifersüchtig	['aɪfɐˌzʏçtɪç]
to be jealous	eifersüchtig sein	['aɪfɐˌzʏçtɪç zaɪn]
divorce	Scheidung (f)	['ʃaɪdʊŋ]
to divorce (vi)	sich scheiden lassen	[zɪç 'ʃaɪdən 'lasən]

to quarrel (vi)	streiten (vi)	['ʃtʀaɪtən]
to be reconciled (after an argument)	sich versöhnen	[zɪç fɛɐ̯'zøːnən]
together (adv)	zusammen	[tsu'zamən]
sex	Sex (m)	[sɛks], [zɛks]

happiness	Glück (n)	[glʏk]
happy (adj)	glücklich	['glʏklɪç]
misfortune (accident)	Unglück (n)	['ʊnˌglʏk]
unhappy (adj)	unglücklich	['ʊnˌglʏklɪç]

Character. Feelings. Emotions

61. Feelings. Emotions

feeling (emotion)	**Gefühl** (n)	[gəˈfyːl]
feelings	**Gefühle** (pl)	[gəˈfyːlə]
to feel (vt)	**fühlen** (vt)	[ˈfyːlən]
hunger	**Hunger** (m)	[ˈhʊŋɐ]
to be hungry	**hungrig sein**	[ˈhʊŋʁɪç zaɪn]
thirst	**Durst** (m)	[dʊʁst]
to be thirsty	**Durst haben**	[ˈdʊʁst ˈhaːbən]
sleepiness	**Schläfrigkeit** (f)	[ˈʃlɛːfʁɪçkaɪt]
to feel sleepy	**schlafen wollen**	[ˈʃlaːfən ˈvɔlən]
tiredness	**Müdigkeit** (f)	[ˈmyːdɪçkaɪt]
tired (adj)	**müde**	[ˈmyːdə]
to get tired	**müde werden**	[ˈmyːdə ˈveːɐdən]
mood (humour)	**Laune** (f)	[ˈlaʊnə]
boredom	**Langeweile** (f)	[ˈlaŋəˌvaɪlə]
to be bored	**sich langweilen**	[zɪç ˈlaŋˌvaɪlən]
seclusion	**Zurückgezogenheit** (n)	[tsuˈʁʏkgəˌtsoːgənhaɪt]
to seclude oneself	**sich zurückziehen**	[zɪç tsuˈʁʏkˌtsiːən]
to worry (make anxious)	**beunruhigen** (vt)	[bəˈʔʊnˌʁuːɪgən]
to be worried	**sorgen** (vi)	[ˈzɔʁgən]
worrying (n)	**Besorgnis** (f)	[bəˈzɔʁknɪs]
anxiety	**Angst** (f)	[ˈaŋst]
preoccupied (adj)	**besorgt**	[bəˈzɔʁkt]
to be nervous	**nervös sein**	[nɛʁˈvøːs zaɪn]
to panic (vi)	**in Panik verfallen** (vi)	[ɪn ˈpaːnɪk fɛʁˈfalən]
hope	**Hoffnung** (f)	[ˈhɔfnʊŋ]
to hope (vi, vt)	**hoffen** (vi)	[ˈhɔfən]
certainty	**Sicherheit** (f)	[ˈzɪçɐhaɪt]
certain, sure (adj)	**sicher**	[ˈzɪçɐ]
uncertainty	**Unsicherheit** (f)	[ˈʊnˌzɪçɐhaɪt]
uncertain (adj)	**unsicher**	[ˈʊnˌzɪçɐ]
drunk (adj)	**betrunken**	[bəˈtʁʊŋkən]
sober (adj)	**nüchtern**	[ˈnʏçtɐn]
weak (adj)	**schwach**	[ˈʃvaχ]
happy (adj)	**glücklich**	[ˈglʏklɪç]
to scare (vt)	**erschrecken** (vt)	[ɛɐˈʃʁɛkən]
fury (madness)	**Wut** (f)	[vuːt]
rage (fury)	**Rage** (f)	[ˈʁaːʒə]
depression	**Depression** (f)	[depʁɛˈsjoːn]
discomfort (unease)	**Unbehagen** (n)	[ˈʊnbəˌhaːgən]

comfort	Komfort (m)	[kɔm'foːɐ]
to regret (be sorry)	bedauern (vt)	[bə'dauɐn]
regret	Bedauern (n)	[bə'dauɐn]
bad luck	Missgeschick (n)	['mɪsgəʃɪk]
sadness	Kummer (m)	['kumɐ]

shame (remorse)	Scham (f)	[ʃaːm]
gladness	Freude (f)	['frɔɪdə]
enthusiasm, zeal	Begeisterung (f)	[bə'gaɪstəruŋ]
enthusiast	Enthusiast (m)	[ɛntu'zɪast]
to show enthusiasm	Begeisterung zeigen	[bə'gaɪstəruŋ 'tsaɪgən]

62. Character. Personality

character	Charakter (m)	[ka'raktɐ]
character flaw	Charakterfehler (m)	[ka'raktəˌfeːlɐ]
mind	Verstand (m)	[fɛɐ'ʃtant]
reason	Vernunft (f)	[fɛɐ'nunft]

conscience	Gewissen (n)	[gə'vɪsən]
habit (custom)	Gewohnheit (f)	[gə'voːnhaɪt]
ability (talent)	Fähigkeit (f)	['fɛːɪçkaɪt]
can (e.g. ~ swim)	können (v mod)	['kœnən]

patient (adj)	geduldig	[gə'duldɪç]
impatient (adj)	ungeduldig	['ungəduldɪç]
curious (inquisitive)	neugierig	['nɔɪˌgiːrɪç]
curiosity	Neugier (f)	['nɔɪˌgiːɐ]

modesty	Bescheidenheit (f)	[bə'ʃaɪdənhaɪt]
modest (adj)	bescheiden	[bə'ʃaɪdən]
immodest (adj)	unbescheiden	['unbə'ʃaɪdən]

laziness	Faulheit (f)	['faulhaɪt]
lazy (adj)	faul	[faul]
lazy person (masc.)	Faulenzer (m)	['faulɛntsɐ]

cunning (n)	Listigkeit (f)	['lɪstɪçkaɪt]
cunning (as adj)	listig	['lɪstɪç]
distrust	Misstrauen (n)	['mɪsˌtrauən]
distrustful (adj)	misstrauisch	['mɪstrauɪʃ]

generosity	Freigebigkeit (f)	['fraɪˌgeːbɪçkaɪt]
generous (adj)	freigebig	['fraɪˌgeːbɪç]
talented (adj)	talentiert	[talɛn'tiːɐt]
talent	Talent (n)	[ta'lɛnt]

courageous (adj)	tapfer	['tapfɐ]
courage	Tapferkeit (f)	['tapfɐkaɪt]
honest (adj)	ehrlich	['eːɐlɪç]
honesty	Ehrlichkeit (f)	['eːɐlɪçkaɪt]

| careful (cautious) | vorsichtig | ['foːɐˌzɪçtɪç] |
| brave (courageous) | tapfer | ['tapfɐ] |

| serious (adj) | ernst | [ɛʀnst] |
| strict (severe, stern) | streng | [ʃtʀɛŋ] |

decisive (adj)	entschlossen	[ɛnt'ʃlɔsən]
indecisive (adj)	unentschlossen	['ʊn?ɛntʃlɔsən]
shy, timid (adj)	schüchtern	['ʃʏçten]
shyness, timidity	Schüchternheit (f)	['ʃʏçtenhaɪt]

confidence (trust)	Vertrauen (n)	[fɛɐ'tʀaʊən]
to believe (trust)	vertrauen (vi)	[fɛɐ'tʀaʊən]
trusting (credulous)	vertrauensvoll	[fɛɐ'tʀaʊəns,fɔl]

sincerely (adv)	aufrichtig	['aʊf,ʀɪçtɪç]
sincere (adj)	aufrichtig	['aʊf,ʀɪçtɪç]
sincerity	Aufrichtigkeit (f)	['aʊf,ʀɪçtɪçkaɪt]
open (person)	offen	['ɔfən]

calm (adj)	still	[ʃtɪl]
frank (sincere)	freimütig	['fʀaɪ,my:tɪç]
naïve (adj)	naiv	[na'i:f]
absent-minded (adj)	zerstreut	[tsɛɐ'ʃtʀɔɪt]
funny (odd)	drollig, komisch	['dʀɔlɪç], ['ko:mɪʃ]

greed, stinginess	Gier (f)	[gi:ɐ]
greedy, stingy (adj)	habgierig	['ha:p,gi:ʀɪç]
stingy (adj)	geizig	['gaɪtsɪç]
evil (adj)	böse	['bø:zə]
stubborn (adj)	hartnäckig	['haʀt,nɛkɪç]
unpleasant (adj)	unangenehm	['ʊn?angə,ne:m]

selfish person (masc.)	Egoist (m)	[ego'ɪst]
selfish (adj)	egoistisch	[ego'ɪstɪʃ]
coward	Feigling (m)	['faɪklɪŋ]
cowardly (adj)	feige	['faɪgə]

63. Sleep. Dreams

to sleep (vi)	schlafen (vi)	['ʃla:fən]
sleep, sleeping	Schlaf (m)	[ʃla:f]
dream	Traum (m)	[tʀaʊm]
to dream (in sleep)	träumen (vi, vt)	['tʀɔɪmən]
sleepy (adj)	verschlafen	[fɛɐ'ʃla:fən]

bed	Bett (n)	[bɛt]
mattress	Matratze (f)	[ma'tʀatsə]
blanket (eiderdown)	Decke (f)	['dɛkə]
pillow	Kissen (n)	['kɪsən]
sheet	Laken (n)	['la:kən]

insomnia	Schlaflosigkeit (f)	['ʃla:flo:zɪçkaɪt]
sleepless (adj)	schlaflos	['ʃla:flo:s]
sleeping pill	Schlafmittel (n)	['ʃla:f,mɪtəl]
to take a sleeping pill	Schlafmittel nehmen	['ʃla:f,mɪtəl 'ne:mən]
to feel sleepy	schlafen wollen	['ʃla:fən 'vɔlən]

to yawn (vi)	gähnen (vi)	['gɛ:nən]
to go to bed	schlafen gehen	['ʃla:fən 'ge:ən]
to make up the bed	das Bett machen	[das bɛt 'maxən]
to fall asleep	einschlafen (vi)	['aɪnˌʃaltən]

nightmare	Alptraum (m)	['alpˌtʀaʊm]
snore, snoring	Schnarchen (n)	['ʃnaʀçən]
to snore (vi)	schnarchen (vi)	['ʃnaʀçən]

alarm clock	Wecker (m)	['vɛkɐ]
to wake (vt)	aufwecken (vt)	['aʊfˌvɛkən]
to wake up	erwachen (vi)	[ɛɐ'vaxən]
to get up (vi)	aufstehen (vi)	['aʊfˌʃte:ən]
to have a wash	sich waschen	[zɪç 'vaʃən]

64. Humour. Laughter. Gladness

humour (wit, fun)	Humor (m)	[hu'mo:ɐ]
sense of humour	Sinn (m) für Humor	[zɪn fy:ɐ hu'mo:ɐ]
to enjoy oneself	sich amüsieren	[zɪç amy'zi:ʀən]
cheerful (merry)	froh	[fʀo:]
merriment (gaiety)	Fröhlichkeit (f)	['fʀø:lɪçˌkaɪt]

smile	Lächeln (n)	['lɛçəln]
to smile (vi)	lächeln (vi)	['lɛçəln]
to start laughing	auflachen (vi)	['aʊflaxən]
to laugh (vi)	lachen (vi)	['laxən]
laugh, laughter	Lachen (n)	['laxən]

anecdote	Anekdote, Witz (m)	[anɛk'do:tə], [vɪts]
funny (anecdote, etc.)	lächerlich	['lɛçɐlɪç]
funny (odd)	komisch	['ko:mɪʃ]

to joke (vi)	Witz machen	[vɪts 'maxən]
joke (verbal)	Spaß (m)	[ʃpa:s]
joy (emotion)	Freude (f)	['fʀɔɪdə]
to rejoice (vi)	sich freuen	[zɪç 'fʀɔɪən]
joyful (adj)	froh	[fʀo:]

65. Discussion, conversation. Part 1

| communication | Kommunikation (f) | [kɔmunika'tsɪo:n] |
| to communicate | kommunizieren (vi) | [kɔmuni'tsi:ʀən] |

conversation	Konversation (f)	[kɔnvɛʀza'tsjo:n]
dialogue	Dialog (m)	[dia'lo:k]
discussion (discourse)	Diskussion (f)	[dɪskʊ'sjo:n]
dispute (debate)	Streitgespräch (n)	['ʃtʀaɪt·gə'ʃpʀɛ:ç]
to dispute, to debate	streiten (vi)	['ʃtʀaɪtən]

| interlocutor | Gesprächspartner (m) | [gə'ʃpʀɛ:çsˌpaʀtnɐ] |
| topic (theme) | Thema (n) | ['te:ma] |

point of view	Gesichtspunkt (m)	[gə'zɪçts,pʊŋkt]
opinion (point of view)	Meinung (f)	['maɪnʊŋ]
speech (talk)	Rede (f)	['ʀeːdə]

discussion (of a report, etc.)	Besprechung (f)	[bə'ʃpʀɛçʊŋ]
to discuss (vt)	besprechen (vt)	[bə'ʃpʀɛçən]
talk (conversation)	Gespräch (n)	[gə'ʃpʀɛːç]
to talk (to chat)	Gespräche führen	[gə'ʃpʀɛːçə 'fyːʀən]
meeting (encounter)	Treffen (n)	['tʀɛfən]
to meet (vi, vt)	sich treffen	[zɪç 'tʀɛfən]

proverb	Sprichwort (n)	['ʃpʀɪç,vɔʁt]
saying	Redensart (f)	['ʀeːdəns,ʔaːʀt]
riddle (poser)	Rätsel (n)	['ʀɛːtsəl]
to pose a riddle	ein Rätsel aufgeben	[aɪn 'ʀɛːtsəl 'aʊf,geːbən]
password	Parole (f)	[pa'ʀoːlə]
secret	Geheimnis (n)	[gə'haɪmnɪs]

oath (vow)	Eid (m), Schwur (m)	[aɪt], [ʃvuːɐ]
to swear (an oath)	schwören (vi, vt)	['ʃvøːʀən]
promise	Versprechen (n)	[fɛɐ'ʃpʀɛçən]
to promise (vt)	versprechen (vt)	[fɛɐ'ʃpʀɛçən]

advice (counsel)	Rat (m)	[ʀaːt]
to advise (vt)	raten (vt)	['ʀaːtən]
to follow one's advice	einen Rat befolgen	['aɪnən ʀaːt bə'fɔlgən]
to listen to … (obey)	gehorchen (vi)	[gə'hɔʁçən]

news	Neuigkeit (f)	['nɔjɪçkaɪt]
sensation (news)	Sensation (f)	[zɛnza'tsjoːn]
information (report)	Informationen (pl)	[ɪnfɔʁma'tsjoːnən]
conclusion (decision)	Schlussfolgerung (f)	['ʃlʊs,fɔlgəʀʊŋ]
voice	Stimme (f)	['ʃtɪmə]
compliment	Kompliment (n)	[,kɔmpli'mɛnt]
kind (nice)	freundlich	['fʀɔɪntlɪç]

word	Wort (n)	[vɔʁt]
phrase	Phrase (f)	['fʀaːzə]
answer	Antwort (f)	['antvɔʁt]

| truth | Wahrheit (f) | ['vaːɐhaɪt] |
| lie | Lüge (f) | ['lyːgə] |

thought	Gedanke (m)	[gə'daŋkə]
idea (inspiration)	Idee (f)	[i'deː]
fantasy	Phantasie (f)	[fanta'ziː]

66. Discussion, conversation. Part 2

respected (adj)	angesehen	['angə,zeːən]
to respect (vt)	respektieren (vt)	[ʀɛspɛk'tiːʀən]
respect	Respekt (m)	[ʀe'spɛkt]
Dear … (letter)	Sehr geehrter …	[zeːɐ gə'leːɐtə]
to introduce (sb to sb)	bekannt machen	[bə'kant 'maxən]

to make acquaintance	kennenlernen (vt)	['kɛnənˌlɛʁnən]
intention	Absicht (f)	['apzɪçt]
to intend (have in mind)	beabsichtigen (vt)	[bə'ʔapzɪçtɪgən]
wish	Wunsch (m)	[vʊnʃ]
to wish (~ good luck)	wünschen (vt)	['vʏnʃən]

surprise (astonishment)	Staunen (n)	['ʃtaunən]
to surprise (amaze)	erstaunen (vt)	[ɛɐ'ʃtaunən]
to be surprised	staunen (vi)	['ʃtaunən]

to give (vt)	geben (vt)	['geːbən]
to take (get hold of)	nehmen (vt)	['neːmən]
to give back	herausgeben (vt)	[hɛ'ʁausˌgeːbən]
to return (give back)	zurückgeben (vt)	[tsu'ʁʏkˌgeːbən]

to apologize (vi)	sich entschuldigen	[zɪç ɛnt'ʃʊldɪgən]
apology	Entschuldigung (f)	[ɛnt'ʃʊldɪgʊŋ]
to forgive (vt)	verzeihen (vt)	[fɛɐ'tsaɪən]

to talk (speak)	sprechen (vi)	['ʃpʁɛçən]
to listen (vi)	hören (vt), zuhören (vi)	['høːʁən], ['tsuːˌhøːʁən]
to hear out	sich anhören	[zɪç 'anˌhøːʁən]
to understand (vt)	verstehen (vt)	[fɛɐ'ʃteːən]

to show (to display)	zeigen (vt)	['tsaɪgən]
to look at ...	ansehen (vt)	['anzeːən]
to call (yell for sb)	rufen (vt)	['ʁuːfən]
to distract (disturb)	belästigen (vt)	[bə'lɛstɪgən]
to disturb (vt)	stören (vt)	['ʃtøːʁən]
to pass (to hand sth)	übergeben (vt)	[yːbe'geːbən]

demand (request)	Bitte (f)	['bɪtə]
to request (ask)	bitten (vt)	['bɪtən]
demand (firm request)	Verlangen (n)	[fɛɐ'laŋən]
to demand (request firmly)	verlangen (vt)	[fɛɐ'laŋən]

to tease (call names)	necken (vt)	['nɛkən]
to mock (make fun of)	spotten (vi)	['ʃpɔtən]
mockery, derision	Spott (m)	[ʃpɔt]
nickname	Spitzname (m)	['ʃpɪtsˌnaːmə]

insinuation	Andeutung (f)	['anˌdɔɪtʊŋ]
to insinuate (imply)	andeuten (vt)	['anˌdɔɪtən]
to mean (vt)	meinen (vt)	['maɪnən]

description	Beschreibung (f)	[bə'ʃʁaɪbʊŋ]
to describe (vt)	beschreiben (vt)	[bə'ʃʁaɪbən]
praise (compliments)	Lob (n)	[loːp]
to praise (vt)	loben (vt)	['loːbən]

disappointment	Enttäuschung (f)	[ɛnt'tɔɪʃʊŋ]
to disappoint (vt)	enttäuschen (vt)	[ɛnt'tɔɪʃən]
to be disappointed	enttäuscht sein	[ɛnt'tɔɪʃt zaɪn]

supposition	Vermutung (f)	[fɛɐ'muːtʊŋ]
to suppose (assume)	vermuten (vt)	[fɛɐ'muːtən]

| warning (caution) | Warnung (f) | ['vaʁnʊŋ] |
| to warn (vt) | warnen (vt) | ['vaʁnən] |

67. Discussion, conversation. Part 3

| to talk into (convince) | überreden (vt) | [y:bɐ'ʁe:dən] |
| to calm down (vt) | beruhigen (vt) | [bə'ʁu:ɪgən] |

silence (~ is golden)	Schweigen (n)	['ʃvaɪgən]
to be silent (not speaking)	schweigen (vi)	['ʃvaɪgən]
to whisper (vi, vt)	flüstern (vt)	['flʏstɐn]
whisper	Flüstern (n)	['flʏstɐn]

| frankly, sincerely (adv) | offen | ['ɔfən] |
| in my opinion ... | meiner Meinung nach ... | ['maɪnə 'maɪnʊŋ na:χ] |

detail (of the story)	Detail (n)	[de'taɪ]
detailed (adj)	ausführlich	['aʊsˌfy:ɐlɪç]
in detail (adv)	ausführlich	['aʊsˌfy:ɐlɪç]

| hint, clue | Tipp (m) | [tɪp] |
| to give a hint | einen Tipp geben | ['aɪnən tɪp 'ge:bən] |

look (glance)	Blick (m)	[blɪk]
to have a look	anblicken (vt)	['anblikən]
fixed (look)	starr	[ʃtaʁ]
to blink (vi)	blinzeln (vi)	['blɪntsəln]
to wink (vi)	zwinkern (vi)	['tsvɪŋkɐn]
to nod (in assent)	nicken (vi)	['nɪkən]

sigh	Seufzer (m)	['zɔɪftsɐ]
to sigh (vi)	aufseufzen (vi)	['aʊfˌzɔɪftsən]
to shudder (vi)	zusammenzucken (vi)	[tsu'zamənˌtsʊkən]
gesture	Geste (f)	['gɛstə]
to touch (one's arm, etc.)	berühren (vt)	[bə'ʁy:ʁən]
to seize (e.g., ~ by the arm)	ergreifen (vt)	[ɛɐ'gʁaɪfən]
to tap (on the shoulder)	klopfen (vt)	['klɔpfən]

Look out!	Vorsicht!	['fo:ɐˌzɪçt]
Really?	Wirklich?	['vɪʁklɪç]
Good luck!	Viel Glück!	[fi:l glʏk]
I see!	Klar!	[kla:ɐ]
What a pity!	Schade!	['ʃa:də]

68. Agreement. Refusal

consent	Einverständnis (n)	['aɪnfɛɐˌʃtɛntnɪs]
to consent (vi)	zustimmen (vi)	['tsu:ˌʃtɪmən]
approval	Billigung (f)	['bɪlɪgʊŋ]
to approve (vt)	billigen (vt)	['bɪlɪgən]
refusal	Absage (f)	['apˌza:gə]
to refuse (vi, vt)	sich weigern	[zɪç 'vaɪgɐn]

Great!	Ausgezeichnet!	['aʊsgəˌtsaɪçnət]
All right!	Ganz recht!	[gants ʀɛçt]
Okay! (I agree)	Gut! Okay!	[guːt], [oˈkeː]

forbidden (adj)	verboten	[fɛɐˈboːtən]
it's forbidden	Es ist verboten	[ɛs ist fɛɐˈboːtən]
it's impossible	Es ist unmöglich	[ɛs ist ˈʊnmøːklɪç]
incorrect (adj)	falsch	[falʃ]

to reject (~ a demand)	ablehnen (vt)	['apˌleːnən]
to support (cause, idea)	unterstützen (vt)	[ˌʊntɐˈʃtʏtsən]
to accept (~ an apology)	akzeptieren (vt)	[ˌaktsɛpˈtiːʀən]

to confirm (vt)	bestätigen (vt)	[bəˈʃtɛːtɪgən]
confirmation	Bestätigung (f)	[bəˈʃtɛːtɪgʊŋ]
permission	Erlaubnis (f)	[ɛɐˈlaʊpnɪs]
to permit (vt)	erlauben (vt)	[ɛɐˈlaʊbən]
decision	Entscheidung (f)	[ɛntˈʃaɪdʊŋ]
to say nothing (hold one's tongue)	schweigen (vi)	[ˈʃvaɪgən]

condition (term)	Bedingung (f)	[bəˈdɪŋʊŋ]
excuse (pretext)	Ausrede (f)	['aʊsˌʀeːdə]
praise (compliments)	Lob (n)	[loːp]
to praise (vt)	loben (vt)	['loːbən]

69. Success. Good luck. Failure

success	Erfolg (m)	[ɛɐˈfɔlk]
successfully (adv)	erfolgreich	[ɛɐˈfɔlkʀaɪç]
successful (adj)	erfolgreich	[ɛɐˈfɔlkʀaɪç]

luck (good luck)	Glück (n)	[glʏk]
Good luck!	Viel Glück!	[fiːl glʏk]
lucky (e.g. ~ day)	Glücks-	[glʏks]
lucky (fortunate)	glücklich	['glʏklɪç]

failure	Misserfolg (m)	['mɪsʔɛɐˌfɔlk]
misfortune	Missgeschick (n)	['mɪsgəˌʃɪk]
bad luck	Unglück (n)	['ʊnˌglʏk]

unsuccessful (adj)	missglückt	[mɪsˈglʏkt]
catastrophe	Katastrophe (f)	[ˌkatasˈtʀoːfə]

pride	Stolz (m)	[ʃtɔlts]
proud (adj)	stolz	[ʃtɔlts]
to be proud	stolz sein	[ʃtɔlts zaɪn]

winner	Sieger (m)	['ziːgɐ]
to win (vi)	siegen (vi)	['ziːgən]
to lose (not win)	verlieren (vt)	[fɛɐˈliːʀən]
try	Versuch (m)	[fɛɐˈzuːχ]
to try (vi)	versuchen (vt)	[fɛɐˈzuːχən]
chance (opportunity)	Chance (f)	['ʃaŋsə]

70. Quarrels. Negative emotions

shout (scream)	Schrei (m)	[ʃʀaɪ]
to shout (vi)	schreien (vi)	[ˈʃʀaɪən]
to start to cry out	beginnen zu schreien	[bəˈɡɪnən tsu ˈʃʀaɪən]

quarrel	Zank (m)	[tsaŋk]
to quarrel (vi)	sich zanken	[zɪç ˈtsaŋkən]
fight (squabble)	Riesenkrach (m)	[ˈʀiːzənˌkʀax]
to make a scene	Krach haben	[ˈkʀax haːbən]
conflict	Konflikt (m)	[kɔnˈflɪkt]
misunderstanding	Missverständnis (n)	[ˈmɪsfɛɐˌʃtɛntnɪs]

insult	Kränkung (f)	[ˈkʀɛŋkʊŋ]
to insult (vt)	kränken (vt)	[ˈkʀɛŋkən]
insulted (adj)	gekränkt	[ɡəˈkʀɛŋkt]
resentment	Beleidigung (f)	[bəˈlaɪdɪɡʊŋ]
to offend (vt)	beleidigen (vt)	[bəˈlaɪdɪɡən]
to take offence	sich beleidigt fühlen	[zɪç bəˈlaɪdɪçt ˈfyːlən]

indignation	Empörung (f)	[ɛmˈpøːʀʊŋ]
to be indignant	sich empören	[zɪç ɛmˈpøːʀən]
complaint	Klage (f)	[ˈklaːɡə]
to complain (vi, vt)	klagen (vi)	[ˈklaːɡən]

apology	Entschuldigung (f)	[ɛntˈʃʊldɪɡʊŋ]
to apologize (vi)	sich entschuldigen	[zɪç ɛntˈʃʊldɪɡən]
to beg pardon	um Entschuldigung bitten	[ʊm ɛntˈʃʊldɪɡʊŋ ˈbɪtən]

criticism	Kritik (f)	[kʀiˈtiːk]
to criticize (vt)	kritisieren (vt)	[kʀitiˈziːʀən]
accusation (charge)	Anklage (f)	[ˈanklaːɡə]
to accuse (vt)	anklagen (vt)	[ˈanˌklaːɡən]

revenge	Rache (f)	[ˈʀaxə]
to avenge (get revenge)	rächen (vt)	[ˈʀɛçən]
to pay back	sich rächen	[zɪç ˈʀɛçən]

disdain	Verachtung (f)	[fɛɐˈʔaxtʊŋ]
to despise (vt)	verachten (vt)	[fɛɐˈʔaxtən]
hatred, hate	Hass (m)	[has]
to hate (vt)	hassen (vt)	[ˈhasən]

nervous (adj)	nervös	[nɛɐˈvøːs]
to be nervous	nervös sein	[nɛɐˈvøːs zaɪn]
angry (mad)	verärgert	[fɛɐˈɛɐɡət]
to make angry	ärgern (vt)	[ˈɛɐɡən]

humiliation	Erniedrigung (f)	[ɛɐˈniːdʀɪɡʊŋ]
to humiliate (vt)	erniedrigen (vt)	[ɛɐˈniːdʀɪɡən]
to humiliate oneself	sich erniedrigen	[zɪç ɛɐˈniːdʀɪɡən]

shock	Schock (m)	[ʃɔk]
to shock (vt)	schockieren (vt)	[ʃɔˈkiːʀən]
trouble (e.g. serious ~)	Ärger (m)	[ˈɛɐɡə]

unpleasant (adj)	unangenehm	['ʊnʔangəˌneːm]
fear (dread)	Angst (f)	['aŋst]
terrible (storm, heat)	furchtbar	['fʊʁçtbaːɐ]
scary (e.g. ~ story)	schrecklich	['ʃʁɛklɪç]
horror	Entsetzen (n)	[ɛnt'zɛtsən]
awful (crime, news)	entsetzlich	[ɛnt'zɛtslɪç]

to begin to tremble	zittern (vi)	['tsɪtən]
to cry (weep)	weinen (vi)	['vaɪnən]
to start crying	anfangen zu weinen	['anˌfaŋən tsu: 'vaɪnən]
tear	Träne (f)	['tʁɛːnə]

fault	Schuld (f)	[ʃʊlt]
guilt (feeling)	Schuldgefühl (n)	['ʃʊltgəˌfyːl]
dishonor (disgrace)	Schmach (f)	[ʃmaːχ]
protest	Protest (m)	[pʁo'tɛst]
stress	Stress (m)	[stʁɛs]

to disturb (vt)	stören (vt)	['ʃtøːʁən]
to be furious	sich ärgern	[zɪç 'ɛʁgen]
angry (adj)	ärgerlich	['ɛʁgeˌlɪç]
to end (~ a relationship)	abbrechen (vi)	['apˌbʁɛçən]
to swear (at sb)	schelten (vi)	['ʃɛltən]

to scare (become afraid)	erschrecken (vi)	[ɛɐ'ʃʁɛkən]
to hit (strike with hand)	schlagen (vt)	['ʃlaːgən]
to fight (street fight, etc.)	sich prügeln	[zɪç 'pʁyːgəln]

to settle (a conflict)	beilegen (vt)	['baɪˌleːgən]
discontented (adj)	unzufrieden	['ʊntsuˌfʁiːdən]
furious (adj)	wütend	['vyːtənt]

It's not good!	Das ist nicht gut!	[das is nɪçt guːt]
It's bad!	Das ist schlecht!	[das is ʃlɛçt]

Medicine

71. Diseases

illness	**Krankheit** (f)	['kʀaŋkhaɪt]
to be ill	**krank sein**	[kʀaŋk zaɪn]
health	**Gesundheit** (f)	[gə'zʊnthaɪt]
runny nose (coryza)	**Schnupfen** (m)	['ʃnʊpfən]
tonsillitis	**Angina** (f)	[aŋ'giːna]
cold (illness)	**Erkältung** (f)	[ɛɐ'kɛltʊŋ]
to catch a cold	**sich erkälten**	[zɪç ɛɐ'kɛltən]
bronchitis	**Bronchitis** (f)	[bʀɔn'çiːtɪs]
pneumonia	**Lungenentzündung** (f)	['lʊŋən?ɛnt,tsʏndʊŋ]
flu, influenza	**Grippe** (f)	['gʀɪpə]
shortsighted (adj)	**kurzsichtig**	['kʊɐts,zɪçtɪç]
longsighted (adj)	**weitsichtig**	['vaɪt,zɪçtɪç]
strabismus (crossed eyes)	**Schielen** (n)	['ʃiːlən]
squint-eyed (adj)	**schielend**	['ʃiːlənt]
cataract	**grauer Star** (m)	['gʀaʊɐ ʃtaːɐ]
glaucoma	**Glaukom** (n)	[glau'koːm]
stroke	**Schlaganfall** (m)	['ʃlaːk?an,fal]
heart attack	**Infarkt** (m)	[ɪn'faɐkt]
myocardial infarction	**Herzinfarkt** (m)	['hɛɐts?ɪn,faɐkt]
paralysis	**Lähmung** (f)	['lɛːmʊŋ]
to paralyse (vt)	**lähmen** (vt)	['lɛːmən]
allergy	**Allergie** (f)	[,alɛɐ'giː]
asthma	**Asthma** (n)	['astma]
diabetes	**Diabetes** (m)	[dia'beːtɛs]
toothache	**Zahnschmerz** (m)	['tsaːnʃmɛɐts]
caries	**Karies** (f)	['kaːʀɪɛs]
diarrhoea	**Durchfall** (m)	['dʊɐçfal]
constipation	**Verstopfung** (f)	[fɛɐ'ʃtɔpfʊŋ]
stomach upset	**Magenverstimmung** (f)	['maːgən·fɛɐʃtɪmʊŋ]
food poisoning	**Vergiftung** (f)	[fɛɐ'gɪftʊŋ]
to get food poisoning	**Vergiftung bekommen**	[fɛɐ'gɪftʊŋ bə'kɔmən]
arthritis	**Arthritis** (f)	[aɐ'tʀiːtɪs]
rickets	**Rachitis** (f)	[ʀa'xiːtɪs]
rheumatism	**Rheumatismus** (m)	[ʀɔɪma'tɪsmʊs]
atherosclerosis	**Atherosklerose** (f)	[atɛɐɔskle'ʀoːzə]
gastritis	**Gastritis** (f)	[gas'tʀiːtɪs]
appendicitis	**Blinddarmentzündung** (f)	['blɪntdaɐm?ɛnt,tsʏndʊŋ]

| cholecystitis | Cholezystitis (f) | [çoletsʏs'ti:tɪs] |
| ulcer | Geschwür (n) | [gə'ʃvy:ɐ] |

measles	Masern (pl)	['ma:zen]
rubella (German measles)	Röteln (pl)	['ʀø:təln]
jaundice	Gelbsucht (f)	['gɛlp͜zuχt]
hepatitis	Hepatitis (f)	[ˌhepa'ti:tɪs]

schizophrenia	Schizophrenie (f)	[ʃitsofʀe'ni:]
rabies (hydrophobia)	Tollwut (f)	['tɔlˌvu:t]
neurosis	Neurose (f)	[nɔɪ'ʀo:zə]
concussion	Gehirnerschütterung (f)	[gə'hɪʀn͜ʔɛɐʃʏtɐʀʊŋ]

cancer	Krebs (m)	[kʀe:ps]
sclerosis	Sklerose (f)	[skle'ʀo:zə]
multiple sclerosis	multiple Sklerose (f)	[mʊl'ti:plə skle'ʀo:zə]

alcoholism	Alkoholismus (m)	[ˌalkoho'lɪsmʊs]
alcoholic (n)	Alkoholiker (m)	[alko'ho:likɐ]
syphilis	Syphilis (f)	['zy:filɪs]
AIDS	AIDS	['eɪts]

tumour	Tumor (m)	['tu:mo:ɐ]
malignant (adj)	bösartig	['bø:sˌʔa:ɐtɪç]
benign (adj)	gutartig	['gu:tˌʔa:ɐtɪç]
fever	Fieber (n)	['fi:bɐ]
malaria	Malaria (f)	[ma'la:ʀɪa]
gangrene	Gangrän (f, n)	[gaŋ'gʀɛ:n]
seasickness	Seekrankheit (f)	['ze:ˌkʀaŋkhaɪt]
epilepsy	Epilepsie (f)	[epilɛ'psi:]

epidemic	Epidemie (f)	[epide'mi:]
typhus	Typhus (m)	['ty:fʊs]
tuberculosis	Tuberkulose (f)	[tubɛʀku'lo:zə]
cholera	Cholera (f)	['ko:leʀa]
plague (bubonic ~)	Pest (f)	[pɛst]

72. Symptoms. Treatments. Part 1

symptom	Symptom (n)	[zʏmp'to:m]
temperature	Temperatur (f)	[tɛmpəʀa'tu:ɐ]
high temperature (fever)	Fieber (n)	['fi:bɐ]
pulse (heartbeat)	Puls (m)	[pʊls]

dizziness (vertigo)	Schwindel (m)	['ʃvɪndəl]
hot (adj)	heiß	[haɪs]
shivering	Schüttelfrost (m)	['ʃʏtəlˌfʀɔst]
pale (e.g. ~ face)	blass	[blas]

cough	Husten (m)	['hu:stən]
to cough (vi)	husten (vi)	['hu:stən]
to sneeze (vi)	niesen (vi)	['ni:zən]
faint	Ohnmacht (f)	['o:nˌmaχt]
to faint (vi)	ohnmächtig werden	['o:nˌmɛçtɪç 've:ɐdən]

bruise (hématome)	**blauer Fleck** (m)	['blaʊə flɛk]
bump (lump)	**Beule** (f)	['bɔɪlə]
to bang (bump)	**sich stoßen**	[zɪç 'ʃtoːsən]
contusion (bruise)	**Prellung** (f)	['pʀɛlʊŋ]
to get a bruise	**sich stoßen**	[zɪç 'ʃtoːsən]

to limp (vi)	**hinken** (vi)	['hɪŋkən]
dislocation	**Verrenkung** (f)	[fɛɐ'ʀɛnkʊŋ]
to dislocate (vt)	**ausrenken** (vt)	['aʊs‚ʀɛŋkən]
fracture	**Fraktur** (f)	[fʀak'tuːɐ]
to have a fracture	**brechen** (vt)	['bʀɛçən]

cut (e.g. paper ~)	**Schnittwunde** (f)	['ʃnɪt‚vʊndə]
to cut oneself	**sich schneiden**	[zɪç 'ʃnaɪdən]
bleeding	**Blutung** (f)	['bluːtʊŋ]

burn (injury)	**Verbrennung** (f)	[fɛɐ'bʀɛnʊŋ]
to get burned	**sich verbrennen**	[zɪç fɛɐ'bʀɛnən]

to prick (vt)	**stechen** (vt)	['ʃtɛçən]
to prick oneself	**sich stechen**	[zɪç 'ʃtɛçən]
to injure (vt)	**verletzen** (vt)	[fɛɐ'lɛtsən]
injury	**Verletzung** (f)	[fɛɐ'lɛtsʊŋ]
wound	**Wunde** (f)	['vʊndə]
trauma	**Trauma** (n)	['tʀaʊma]

to be delirious	**irrereden** (vi)	['ɪʀə‚ʀeːdən]
to stutter (vi)	**stottern** (vi)	['ʃtɔtən]
sunstroke	**Sonnenstich** (m)	['zɔnən‚ʃtɪç]

73. Symptoms. Treatments. Part 2

pain, ache	**Schmerz** (m)	[ʃmɛʁts]
splinter (in foot, etc.)	**Splitter** (m)	['ʃplɪtə]

sweat (perspiration)	**Schweiß** (m)	[ʃvaɪs]
to sweat (perspire)	**schwitzen** (vi)	['ʃvɪtsən]
vomiting	**Erbrechen** (n)	[ɛɐ'bʀɛçən]
convulsions	**Krämpfe** (pl)	['kʀɛmpfə]

pregnant (adj)	**schwanger**	['ʃvaŋɐ]
to be born	**geboren sein**	[gə'boːʀən zaɪn]
delivery, labour	**Geburt** (f)	[gə'buːɐt]
to deliver (~ a baby)	**gebären** (vt)	[gə'bɛːʀən]
abortion	**Abtreibung** (f)	['ap‚tʀaɪbʊŋ]

breathing, respiration	**Atem** (m)	['aːtəm]
in-breath (inhalation)	**Atemzug** (m)	['aːtəm‚tsuːk]
out-breath (exhalation)	**Ausatmung** (f)	['aʊsʔaːtmʊŋ]
to exhale (breathe out)	**ausatmen** (vt)	['aʊs‚ʔaːtmən]
to inhale (vi)	**einatmen** (vt)	['aɪn‚ʔaːtmən]

disabled person	**Invalide** (m)	[ɪnva'liːdə]
cripple	**Krüppel** (m)	['kʀʏpəl]

drug addict	Drogenabhängiger (m)	['dʀoːgən‿ʔaphɛŋɪgə]
deaf (adj)	taub	[taʊp]
mute (adj)	stumm	[ʃtʊm]
deaf mute (adj)	taubstumm	['taʊpʃtʊm]
mad, insane (adj)	verrückt	[fɛɐ'ʀʏkt]
madman	Irre (m)	['ɪʀə]
(demented person)		
madwoman	Irre (f)	['ɪʀə]
to go insane	den Verstand verlieren	[den fɛɐ'ʃtant fɛɐ'liːʀən]
gene	Gen (n)	[geːn]
immunity	Immunität (f)	[ɪmuni'tɛːt]
hereditary (adj)	erblich	['ɛʀplɪç]
congenital (adj)	angeboren	['angə‿boːʀən]
virus	Virus (m, n)	['viːʀʊs]
microbe	Mikrobe (f)	[mi'kʀoːbə]
bacterium	Bakterie (f)	[bak'teːʀɪə]
infection	Infektion (f)	[ɪnfɛk'tsjoːn]

74. Symptoms. Treatments. Part 3

hospital	Krankenhaus (n)	['kʀaŋkən‿haʊs]
patient	Patient (m)	[pa'tsɪɛnt]
diagnosis	Diagnose (f)	[dia'gnoːzə]
cure	Heilung (f)	['haɪlʊŋ]
medical treatment	Behandlung (f)	[bə'handlʊŋ]
to get treatment	Behandlung bekommen	[bə'handlʊŋ bə'kɔmən]
to treat (~ a patient)	behandeln (vt)	[bə'handəln]
to nurse (look after)	pflegen (vt)	['pfleːgən]
care (nursing ~)	Pflege (f)	['pfleːgə]
operation, surgery	Operation (f)	[opəʀa'tsjoːn]
to bandage (head, limb)	verbinden (vt)	[fɛɐ'bɪndən]
bandaging	Verband (m)	[fɛɐ'bant]
vaccination	Impfung (f)	['ɪmpfʊŋ]
to vaccinate (vt)	impfen (vt)	['ɪmpfən]
injection	Spritze (f)	['ʃpʀɪtsə]
to give an injection	eine Spritze geben	['aɪnə 'ʃpʀɪtsə 'geːbən]
attack	Anfall (m)	['an‿fal]
amputation	Amputation (f)	[amputa'tsjoːn]
to amputate (vt)	amputieren (vt)	[ampu'tiːʀən]
coma	Koma (n)	['koːma]
to be in a coma	im Koma liegen	[ɪm 'koːma 'liːgən]
intensive care	Reanimation (f)	[ʀeʔanima'tsjoːn]
to recover (~ from flu)	genesen von ...	[gə'neːzən fɔn]
condition (patient's ~)	Zustand (m)	['tsuː‿ʃtant]
consciousness	Bewusstsein (n)	[bə'vʊstzaɪn]
memory (faculty)	Gedächtnis (n)	[gə'dɛçtnɪs]

to pull out (tooth)	ziehen (vt)	['tsi:ən]
filling	Plombe (f)	['plɔmbə]
to fill (a tooth)	plombieren (vt)	[plɔm'bi:ʀən]

| hypnosis | Hypnose (f) | [hʏp'no:zə] |
| to hypnotize (vt) | hypnotisieren (vt) | [hʏpnoti'zi:ʀən] |

75. Doctors

doctor	Arzt (m)	[aʁtst]
nurse	Krankenschwester (f)	[kʀaŋkənˌʃvɛstə]
personal doctor	Privatarzt (m)	[pʀi'va:tˌʔaʁtst]

dentist	Zahnarzt (m)	['tsa:nˌʔaʁtst]
optician	Augenarzt (m)	['auɡənˌʔaʁtst]
general practitioner	Internist (m)	[ɪntɐ'nɪst]
surgeon	Chirurg (m)	[çi'ʀuʁk]

psychiatrist	Psychiater (m)	[psy'çɪa:tɐ]
paediatrician	Kinderarzt (m)	['kɪndɐˌʔaʁtst]
psychologist	Psychologe (m)	[psyço'lo:ɡə]
gynaecologist	Frauenarzt (m)	['fʀauənˌʔaʁtst]
cardiologist	Kardiologe (m)	[kaʁdɪo'lo:ɡə]

76. Medicine. Drugs. Accessories

medicine, drug	Arznei (f)	[aʁts'naɪ]
remedy	Heilmittel (n)	['haɪlˌmɪtəl]
to prescribe (vt)	verschreiben (vt)	[fɛɐ'ʃʀaɪbən]
prescription	Rezept (n)	[ʀe'tsɛpt]

tablet, pill	Tablette (f)	[tab'letə]
ointment	Salbe (f)	['zalbə]
ampoule	Ampulle (f)	[am'pʊlə]
mixture, solution	Mixtur (f)	[mɪks'tu:ɐ]
syrup	Sirup (m)	['zi:ʀʊp]
capsule	Pille (f)	['pɪlə]
powder	Pulver (n)	['pʊlfɐ]

gauze bandage	Verband (m)	[fɛɐ'bant]
cotton wool	Watte (f)	['vatə]
iodine	Jod (n)	[jo:t]

plaster	Pflaster (n)	['pflastɐ]
eyedropper	Pipette (f)	[pi'pɛtə]
thermometer	Thermometer (n)	[tɛʁmo'me:tɐ]
syringe	Spritze (f)	['ʃpʀɪtsə]

wheelchair	Rollstuhl (m)	['ʀɔlˌʃtu:l]
crutches	Krücken (pl)	['kʀʏkən]
painkiller	Betäubungsmittel (n)	[bə'tɔɪbʊŋsˌmɪtəl]
laxative	Abführmittel (n)	['apfy:ɐˌmɪtəl]

spirits (ethanol)	Spiritus (m)	['spi:ʀitʊs]
medicinal herbs	Heilkraut (n)	['haɪlˌkʀaʊt]
herbal (~ tea)	Kräuter-	['kʀɔɪtɐ]

77. Smoking. Tobacco products

tobacco	Tabak (m)	['taːbak]
cigarette	Zigarette (f)	[tsiga'ʀɛtə]
cigar	Zigarre (f)	[tsi'gaʀə]
pipe	Pfeife (f)	['pfaɪfə]
packet (of cigarettes)	Packung (f)	['pakʊŋ]

matches	Streichhölzer (pl)	['ʃtʀaɪçˌhœltsɐ]
matchbox	Streichholzschachtel (f)	['ʃtʀaɪç·hɔltsˌʃaχtəl]
lighter	Feuerzeug (n)	['fɔɪɐˌtsɔɪk]
ashtray	Aschenbecher (m)	['aʃən·bɛçɐ]
cigarette case	Zigarettenetui (n)	[tsiga'ʀɛtənʔɛtˌviː]

| cigarette holder | Mundstück (n) | ['mʊntʃtʏk] |
| filter (cigarette tip) | Filter (n) | ['fɪltɐ] |

to smoke (vi, vt)	rauchen (vi, vt)	['ʀaʊχən]
to light a cigarette	anrauchen (vt)	['anˌʀaʊχən]
smoking	Rauchen (n)	['ʀaʊχən]
smoker	Raucher (m)	['ʀaʊχɐ]

cigarette end	Stummel (m)	['ʃtʊməl]
smoke, fumes	Rauch (m)	[ʀaʊχ]
ash	Asche (f)	['aʃə]

75

HUMAN HABITAT

City

78. City. Life in the city

city, town	**Stadt** (f)	[ʃtat]
capital city	**Hauptstadt** (f)	['haʊptˌʃtat]
village	**Dorf** (n)	[dɔʁf]
city map	**Stadtplan** (m)	['ʃtatˌpla:n]
city centre	**Stadtzentrum** (n)	['ʃtatˌtsɛntʀʊm]
suburb	**Vorort** (m)	['fo:ɐˌʔɔʁt]
suburban (adj)	**Vorort-**	['fo:ɐˌʔɔʁt]
outskirts	**Stadtrand** (m)	['ʃtatˌʀant]
environs (suburbs)	**Umgebung** (f)	[ʊm'ge:bʊŋ]
city block	**Stadtviertel** (n)	['ʃtatˌfɪʁtəl]
residential block (area)	**Wohnblock** (m)	['vo:nˌblɔk]
traffic	**Straßenverkehr** (m)	['ʃtʀa:sən·fɛɐˌke:ɐ]
traffic lights	**Ampel** (f)	['ampəl]
public transport	**Stadtverkehr** (m)	['ʃtat·fɛɐ'ke:ɐ]
crossroads	**Straßenkreuzung** (f)	['ʃtʀa:sənˌkʀɔɪtsʊŋ]
zebra crossing	**Übergang** (m)	['y:bɐˌgaŋ]
pedestrian subway	**Fußgängerunterführung** (f)	['fu:sˌgɛŋɐ·ʊntɐ'fy:ʀʊŋ]
to cross (~ the street)	**überqueren** (vt)	[y:bɐ'kve:ʀən]
pedestrian	**Fußgänger** (m)	['fu:sˌgɛŋɐ]
pavement	**Gehweg** (m)	['ge:ˌve:k]
bridge	**Brücke** (f)	['bʀʏkə]
embankment (river walk)	**Kai** (m)	[kaɪ]
fountain	**Springbrunnen** (m)	['ʃpʀɪŋˌbʀʊnən]
allée (garden walkway)	**Allee** (f)	[a'le:]
park	**Park** (m)	[paʁk]
boulevard	**Boulevard** (m)	[bulə'va:ɐ]
square	**Platz** (m)	[plats]
avenue (wide street)	**Avenue** (f)	[avə'ny:]
street	**Straße** (f)	['ʃtʀa:sə]
side street	**Gasse** (f)	['gasə]
dead end	**Sackgasse** (f)	['zakˌgasə]
house	**Haus** (n)	[haʊs]
building	**Gebäude** (n)	[gə'bɔɪdə]
skyscraper	**Wolkenkratzer** (m)	['vɔlkənˌkʀatsɐ]
facade	**Fassade** (f)	[fa'sa:də]
roof	**Dach** (n)	[daχ]

window	Fenster (n)	['fɛnstɐ]
arch	Bogen (m)	['boːgən]
column	Säule (f)	['zɔɪlə]
corner	Ecke (f)	['ɛkə]

shop window	Schaufenster (n)	['ʃaʊˌfɛnstɐ]
signboard (store sign, etc.)	Firmenschild (n)	['fɪʁmənˌʃɪlt]
poster (e.g., playbill)	Anschlag (m)	['anˌʃlaːk]
advertising poster	Werbeposter (m)	['vɛʁbəˌpoːstɐ]
hoarding	Werbeschild (n)	['vɛʁbəˌʃɪlt]

rubbish	Müll (m)	[mʏl]
rubbish bin	Mülleimer (m)	['mʏlˌʔaɪmɐ]
to litter (vi)	Abfall wegwerfen	['apfal 'vɛkˌvɛʁfən]
rubbish dump	Mülldeponie (f)	['mʏlˈdepoˌniː]

telephone box	Telefonzelle (f)	[teleˈfoːnˌtsɛlə]
lamppost	Straßenlaterne (f)	['ʃtʁaːsənˈlaˌtɛʁnə]
bench (park ~)	Bank (f)	[baŋk]

police officer	Polizist (m)	[poliˈtsɪst]
police	Polizei (f)	[ˌpoliˈtsaɪ]
beggar	Bettler (m)	['bɛtlɐ]
homeless (n)	Obdachlose (m)	['ɔpdaxˌloːzə]

79. Urban institutions

shop	Laden (m)	['laːdən]
chemist, pharmacy	Apotheke (f)	[apoˈteːkə]
optician (spectacles shop)	Optik (f)	['ɔptɪk]
shopping centre	Einkaufszentrum (n)	['aɪnkaʊfsˌtsɛntʁʊm]
supermarket	Supermarkt (m)	['zuːpɐˌmaʁkt]

bakery	Bäckerei (f)	[ˌbɛkəˈʁaɪ]
baker	Bäcker (m)	['bɛkɐ]
cake shop	Konditorei (f)	[ˌkɔnditoˈʁaɪ]
grocery shop	Lebensmittelladen (m)	['leːbənsˌmɪtəlˈlaːdən]
butcher shop	Metzgerei (f)	[mɛtsgəˈʁaɪ]

| greengrocer | Gemüseladen (m) | [gəˈmyːzəˌlaːdən] |
| market | Markt (m) | [maʁkt] |

coffee bar	Kaffeehaus (n)	[kaˈfeːˌhaʊs]
restaurant	Restaurant (n)	[ʁɛstoˈʁaŋ]
pub, bar	Bierstube (f)	['biːɐˌʃtuːbə]
pizzeria	Pizzeria (f)	[pɪtseˈʁiːa]

hairdresser	Friseursalon (m)	[fʁiˈzøːɐˈzaˌlɔŋ]
post office	Post (f)	[pɔst]
dry cleaners	chemische Reinigung (f)	[çeːmɪʃə 'ʁaɪnɪgʊŋ]
photo studio	Fotostudio (n)	['fotoˌʃtuːdɪo]

| shoe shop | Schuhgeschäft (n) | ['ʃuːgəˌʃɛft] |
| bookshop | Buchhandlung (f) | ['buːxˌhandlʊŋ] |

sports shop	Sportgeschäft (n)	['ʃpɔʁt·gə'ʃɛft]
clothes repair shop	Kleiderreparatur (f)	['klaɪde‚ʁepaʁa'tu:ɐ]
formal wear hire	Bekleidungsverleih (m)	[bə'klaɪdʊŋs·fɛɐ'laɪ]
video rental shop	Videothek (f)	[video'te:k]
circus	Zirkus (m)	['tsɪʁkʊs]
zoo	Zoo (m)	['tso:]
cinema	Kino (n)	['ki:no]
museum	Museum (n)	[mu'ze:ʊm]
library	Bibliothek (f)	[biblio'te:k]
theatre	Theater (n)	[te'a:tɐ]
opera (opera house)	Opernhaus (n)	['o:pɐn‚haʊs]
nightclub	Nachtklub (m)	['naχt‚klʊp]
casino	Kasino (n)	[ka'zi:no]
mosque	Moschee (f)	[mɔ'ʃe:]
synagogue	Synagoge (f)	[zyna'go:gə]
cathedral	Kathedrale (f)	[kate'dʁa:lə]
temple	Tempel (m)	['tɛmpəl]
church	Kirche (f)	['kɪʁçə]
college	Institut (n)	[ɪnsti'tu:t]
university	Universität (f)	[univɛʁzi'tɛ:t]
school	Schule (f)	['ʃu:lə]
prefecture	Präfektur (f)	[pʁɛfɛk'tu:ɐ]
town hall	Rathaus (n)	['ʁa:t‚haʊs]
hotel	Hotel (n)	[ho'tɛl]
bank	Bank (f)	[baŋk]
embassy	Botschaft (f)	['bo:tʃaft]
travel agency	Reisebüro (n)	['ʁaɪzə·by‚ʁo:]
information office	Informationsbüro (n)	[ɪnfoʁma'tsjo:ns·by‚ʁo:]
currency exchange	Wechselstube (f)	['vɛksəl‚ʃtu:bə]
underground, tube	U-Bahn (f)	['u:ba:n]
hospital	Krankenhaus (n)	['kʁaŋkən‚haʊs]
petrol station	Tankstelle (f)	['taŋk‚ʃtɛlə]
car park	Parkplatz (m)	['paʁk‚plats]

80. Signs

signboard (store sign, etc.)	Firmenschild (n)	['fɪʁmən‚ʃɪlt]
notice (door sign, etc.)	Aufschrift (f)	['aʊf‚ʃʁɪft]
poster	Plakat (n)	[pla'ka:t]
direction sign	Wegweiser (m)	['vɛk‚vaɪzɐ]
arrow (sign)	Pfeil (m)	[pfaɪl]
caution	Vorsicht (f)	['fo:ɐ‚zɪçt]
warning sign	Warnung (f)	['vaʁnʊŋ]
to warn (vt)	warnen (vt)	['vaʁnən]
rest day (weekly ~)	freier Tag (m)	['fʁaɪɐ ta:k]

| timetable (schedule) | Fahrplan (m) | ['faːeˌplaːn] |
| opening hours | Öffnungszeiten (pl) | ['œfnʊŋsˌtsaɪtən] |

WELCOME!	HERZLICH WILLKOMMEN!	['hɛʁtslɪç vɪl'kɔmən]
ENTRANCE	EINGANG	['aɪnˌgaŋ]
WAY OUT	AUSGANG	['aʊsˌgaŋ]

PUSH	DRÜCKEN	['dʀʏkən]
PULL	ZIEHEN	['tsiːən]
OPEN	GEÖFFNET	[gə'ʔœfnət]
CLOSED	GESCHLOSSEN	[gə'ʃlɔsən]

| WOMEN | DAMEN, FRAUEN | ['daːmən], ['fʀaʊən] |
| MEN | HERREN, MÄNNER | ['hɛʀən], ['mɛnɐ] |

DISCOUNTS	AUSVERKAUF	['aʊsfɛɐˌkaʊf]
SALE	REDUZIERT	[ʀedu'tsiːɐt]
NEW!	NEU!	[nɔɪ]
FREE	GRATIS	['gʀaːtɪs]

ATTENTION!	ACHTUNG!	['aχtʊŋ]
NO VACANCIES	ZIMMER BELEGT	['tsɪmɐ bə'leːkt]
RESERVED	RESERVIERT	[ʀezɛʁ'viːɐt]

| ADMINISTRATION | VERWALTUNG | [fɛɐ'valtʊŋ] |
| STAFF ONLY | NUR FÜR PERSONAL | [nuːɐ fyːɐ pɛʁzo'naːl] |

BEWARE OF THE DOG!	VORSICHT BISSIGER HUND	['foːeˌzɪçt 'bɪsɪgɐ hʊnt]
NO SMOKING	RAUCHEN VERBOTEN!	['ʀaʊχən fɛɐ'boːtən]
DO NOT TOUCH!	BITTE NICHT BERÜHREN	['bɪtə nɪçt bə'ʀyːʀən]

DANGEROUS	GEFÄHRLICH	[gə'fɛːɐlɪç]
DANGER	VORSICHT!	['foːeˌzɪçt]
HIGH VOLTAGE	HOCHSPANNUNG	['hoːχˌʃpanʊŋ]
NO SWIMMING!	BADEN VERBOTEN	['baːdən fɛɐ'boːtən]
OUT OF ORDER	AUßER BETRIEB	[ˌaʊsɐ bə'tʀiːp]

FLAMMABLE	LEICHTENTZÜNDLICH	['laɪçtʔɛn'tsʏntlɪç]
FORBIDDEN	VERBOTEN	[fɛɐ'boːtən]
NO TRESPASSING!	DURCHGANG VERBOTEN	['dʊʁçˌgaŋ fɛɐ'boːtən]
WET PAINT	FRISCH GESTRICHEN	[fʀɪʃ gə'ʃtʀɪçən]

81. Urban transport

bus, coach	Bus (m)	[bʊs]
tram	Straßenbahn (f)	['ʃtʀaːsənˌbaːn]
trolleybus	Obus (m)	['oːbʊs]
route (bus ~)	Linie (f)	['liːniə]
number (e.g. bus ~)	Nummer (f)	['nʊmɐ]

to go by ...	mit ... fahren	[mɪt ... 'faːʀən]
to get on (~ the bus)	einsteigen (vi)	['aɪnˌʃtaɪgən]
to get off ...	aussteigen (vi)	['aʊsˌʃtaɪgən]

stop (e.g. bus ~)	Haltestelle (f)	['haltəˌʃtɛlə]
next stop	nächste Haltestelle (f)	['nɛːçstə 'haltəˌʃtɛlə]
terminus	Endhaltestelle (f)	['ɛntˌhaltəʃtɛlə]
timetable	Fahrplan (m)	['faːɐˌplaːn]
to wait (vt)	warten (vi, vt)	['vaʁtən]

ticket	Fahrkarte (f)	['faːɐˌkaʁtə]
fare	Fahrpreis (m)	['faːɐˌpʀaɪs]

cashier (ticket seller)	Kassierer (m)	[ka'siːʀɐ]
ticket inspection	Fahrkartenkontrolle (f)	['faːɐˌkaʁtən·kɔn'tʀɔlə]
ticket inspector	Kontrolleur (m)	[kɔntʀɔ'løːɐ]

to be late (for ...)	sich verspäten	[zɪç fɛɐ'ʃpɛːtən]
to miss (~ the train, etc.)	versäumen (vt)	[fɛɐ'zɔɪmən]
to be in a hurry	sich beeilen	[zɪç bə'ʔaɪlən]

taxi, cab	Taxi (n)	['taksi]
taxi driver	Taxifahrer (m)	['taksiˌfaːʀɐ]
by taxi	mit dem Taxi	[mɪt dem 'taksi]
taxi rank	Taxistand (m)	['taksiˌʃtant]
to call a taxi	ein Taxi rufen	[aɪn 'taksi 'ʀuːfən]
to take a taxi	ein Taxi nehmen	[aɪn 'taksi 'neːmən]

traffic	Straßenverkehr (m)	['ʃtʀaːsən·fɛɐˌkeːɐ]
traffic jam	Stau (m)	[ʃtaʊ]
rush hour	Hauptverkehrszeit (f)	['haʊpt·fɛɐ'keːɐsˌtsaɪt]
to park (vi)	parken (vi)	['paʁkən]
to park (vt)	parken (vt)	['paʁkən]
car park	Parkplatz (m)	['paʁkˌplats]

underground, tube	U-Bahn (f)	['uːbaːn]
station	Station (f)	[ʃta'tsjoːn]
to take the tube	mit der U-Bahn fahren	[mɪt deːɐ 'uːbaːn 'faːʀən]
train	Zug (m)	[tsuːk]
train station	Bahnhof (m)	['baːnˌhoːf]

82. Sightseeing

monument	Denkmal (n)	['dɛŋkˌmaːl]
fortress	Festung (f)	['fɛstʊŋ]
palace	Palast (m)	[pa'last]
castle	Schloss (n)	[ʃlɔs]
tower	Turm (m)	[tʊʁm]
mausoleum	Mausoleum (n)	[ˌmaʊzo'leːʊm]

architecture	Architektur (f)	[aʁçitɛk'tuːɐ]
medieval (adj)	mittelalterlich	['mɪtəlˌʔaltɐlɪç]
ancient (adj)	alt	[alt]
national (adj)	national	[natsjo'naːl]
famous (monument, etc.)	berühmt	[bə'ʀyːmt]

tourist	Tourist (m)	[tu'ʀɪst]
guide (person)	Fremdenführer (m)	['fʀɛmdənˌfyːʀɐ]

excursion, sightseeing tour	Ausflug (m)	['aʊsˌfluːk]
to show (vt)	zeigen (vt)	['tsaɪɡən]
to tell (vt)	erzählen (vt)	[ɛɐ'tsɛːlən]

to find (vt)	finden (vt)	['fɪndən]
to get lost (lose one's way)	sich verlieren	[zɪç fɛɐ'liːbən]
map (e.g. underground ~)	Karte (f)	['kaʁtə]
map (e.g. city ~)	Karte (f)	['kaʁtə]

souvenir, gift	Souvenir (n)	[zuvəˌniːɐ]
gift shop	Souvenirladen (m)	[zuvəˌniːɐ'laːdən]
to take pictures	fotografieren (vt)	[fotoɡʁa'fiːʁən]
to have one's picture taken	sich fotografieren	[zɪç fotoɡʁa'fiːʁən]

83. Shopping

to buy (purchase)	kaufen (vt)	['kaʊfən]
shopping	Einkauf (m)	['aɪnˌkaʊf]
to go shopping	einkaufen gehen	['aɪnˌkaʊfən 'ɡeːən]
shopping	Einkaufen (n)	['aɪnˌkaʊfən]

to be open (ab. shop)	offen sein	['ɔfən zaɪn]
to be closed	zu sein	[tsu zaɪn]

footwear, shoes	Schuhe (pl)	['ʃuːə]
clothes, clothing	Kleidung (f)	['klaɪdʊŋ]
cosmetics	Kosmetik (f)	[kɔs'meːtɪk]
food products	Lebensmittel (pl)	['leːbənsˌmɪtəl]
gift, present	Geschenk (n)	[ɡə'ʃɛŋk]

shop assistant (masc.)	Verkäufer (m)	[fɛɐ'kɔɪfɐ]
shop assistant (fem.)	Verkäuferin (f)	[fɛɐ'kɔɪfəʁɪn]

cash desk	Kasse (f)	['kasə]
mirror	Spiegel (m)	['ʃpiːɡəl]
counter (shop ~)	Ladentisch (m)	['laːdənˌtɪʃ]
fitting room	Umkleidekabine (f)	['ʊmklaɪdə·kaˌbiːnə]

to try on	anprobieren (vt)	['anpʁoˌbiːʁən]
to fit (ab. dress, etc.)	passen (vi)	['pasən]
to fancy (vt)	gefallen (vi)	[ɡə'falən]

price	Preis (m)	[pʁaɪs]
price tag	Preisschild (n)	['pʁaɪsˌʃɪlt]
to cost (vt)	kosten (vt)	['kɔstən]
How much?	Wie viel?	['viː fiːl]
discount	Rabatt (m)	[ʁa'bat]

inexpensive (adj)	preiswert	['pʁaɪsˌveːɐt]
cheap (adj)	billig	['bɪlɪç]
expensive (adj)	teuer	['tɔɪɐ]
It's expensive	Das ist teuer	[das is 'tɔɪɐ]
hire (n)	Verleih (m)	[fɛɐ'laɪ]
to hire (~ a dinner jacket)	ausleihen (vt)	['aʊsˌlaɪən]

| credit (trade credit) | Kredit (m), Darlehen (n) | [kʀe'di:t], ['daʀˌle:ən] |
| on credit (adv) | auf Kredit | [aʊf kʀe'di:t] |

84. Money

money	Geld (n)	[gɛlt]
currency exchange	Austausch (m)	['aʊsˌtaʊʃ]
exchange rate	Kurs (m)	[kʊʀs]
cashpoint	Geldautomat (m)	['gɛlt?aʊtoˌma:t]
coin	Münze (f)	['mʏntsə]

| dollar | Dollar (m) | ['dɔlaʀ] |
| euro | Euro (m) | ['ɔɪʀo] |

lira	Lira (f)	['li:ʀa]
Deutschmark	Mark (f)	[maʀk]
franc	Franken (m)	['fʀaŋkən]
pound sterling	Pfund Sterling (n)	[pfʊnt 'ʃtɛʀlɪŋ]
yen	Yen (m)	[jɛn]

debt	Schulden (pl)	['ʃʊldən]
debtor	Schuldner (m)	['ʃʊldnɐ]
to lend (money)	leihen (vt)	['laɪən]
to borrow (vi, vt)	ausleihen (vt)	['aʊsˌlaɪən]

bank	Bank (f)	[baŋk]
account	Konto (n)	['kɔnto]
to deposit (vt)	einzahlen (vt)	['aɪnˌtsa:lən]
to deposit into the account	auf ein Konto einzahlen	[aʊf aɪn 'kɔnto 'aɪnˌtsa:lən]
to withdraw (vt)	abheben (vt)	['apˌhe:bən]

credit card	Kreditkarte (f)	[kʀe'di:tˌkaʀtə]
cash	Bargeld (n)	['ba:ɐ̯ˌgɛlt]
cheque	Scheck (m)	[ʃɛk]
to write a cheque	einen Scheck schreiben	['aɪnən ʃɛk 'ʃʀaɪbn]
chequebook	Scheckbuch (n)	['ʃɛkˌbu:x]

wallet	Geldtasche (f)	['gɛltˌtaʃə]
purse	Geldbeutel (m)	['gɛltˌbɔɪtəl]
safe	Safe (m)	[sɛɪf]

heir	Erbe (m)	['ɛʀbə]
inheritance	Erbschaft (f)	['ɛʀpʃaft]
fortune (wealth)	Vermögen (n)	[fɛʀ'mø:gən]

lease	Pacht (f)	[paxt]
rent (money)	Miete (f)	['mi:tə]
to rent (sth from sb)	mieten (vt)	['mi:tən]

price	Preis (m)	[pʀaɪs]
cost	Kosten (pl)	['kɔstən]
sum	Summe (f)	['zʊmə]
to spend (vt)	ausgeben (vt)	['aʊsˌge:bən]
expenses	Ausgaben (pl)	['aʊsˌga:bən]

| to economize (vi, vt) | sparen (vt) | ['ʃpaːʀən] |
| economical | sparsam | ['ʃpaːɛzaːm] |

to pay (vi, vt)	zahlen (vt)	['tsaːlən]
payment	Lohn (m)	[loːn]
change (give the ~)	Wechselgeld (n)	['vɛksəlˌgɛlt]

tax	Steuer (f)	['ʃtɔɪɐ]
fine	Geldstrafe (f)	['gɛltˌʃtʀaːfə]
to fine (vt)	bestrafen (vt)	[bə'ʃtʀaːfən]

85. Post. Postal service

post office	Post (f)	[pɔst]
post (letters, etc.)	Post (f)	[pɔst]
postman	Briefträger (m)	['bʀiːfˌtʀɛːgɐ]
opening hours	Öffnungszeiten (pl)	['œfnʊŋsˌtsaɪtən]

letter	Brief (m)	[bʀiːf]
registered letter	Einschreibebrief (m)	['aɪnʃʀaɪbəˌbʀiːf]
postcard	Postkarte (f)	['pɔstˌkaʁtə]
telegram	Telegramm (n)	[tele'gʀam]
parcel	Postpaket (n)	['pɔstˌpaˈkeːt]
money transfer	Geldanweisung (f)	['gɛltˌanvaɪzʊŋ]

to receive (vt)	bekommen (vt)	[bə'kɔmən]
to send (vt)	abschicken (vt)	['apˌʃɪkən]
sending	Absendung (f)	['apˌzɛndʊŋ]

address	Postanschrift (f)	['pɔstˌanʃʀɪft]
postcode	Postleitzahl (f)	['pɔstlaɪtˌtsaːl]
sender	Absender (m)	['apˌzɛndɐ]
receiver	Empfänger (m)	[ɛm'pfɛŋɐ]

| name (first name) | Vorname (m) | ['foːɐˌnaːmə] |
| surname (last name) | Nachname (m) | ['naːχˌnaːmə] |

postage rate	Tarif (m)	[ta'ʀiːf]
standard (adj)	Standard-	['standaʁt]
economical (adj)	Spar-	['ʃpaːɐ]

weight	Gewicht (n)	[gə'vɪçt]
to weigh (~ letters)	abwiegen (vt)	['apˌviːgən]
envelope	Briefumschlag (m)	['bʀiːfʔʊmˌʃlaːk]
postage stamp	Briefmarke (f)	['bʀiːfˌmaʁkə]
to stamp an envelope	Briefmarke aufkleben	['bʀiːfˌmaʁkə 'aʊfˌkleːbən]

83

Dwelling. House. Home

86. House. Dwelling

house	Haus (n)	[haʊs]
at home (adv)	zu Hause	[tsu 'haʊzə]
yard	Hof (m)	[hoːf]
fence (iron ~)	Zaun (m)	[tsaʊn]

brick (n)	Ziegel (m)	['tsiːgəl]
brick (as adj)	Ziegel-	['tsiːgəl]
stone (n)	Stein (m)	[ʃtaɪn]
stone (as adj)	Stein-	[ʃtaɪn]
concrete (n)	Beton (m)	[be'tɔŋ]
concrete (as adj)	Beton-	[be'tɔŋ]

new (new-built)	neu	[nɔɪ]
old (adj)	alt	[alt]
decrepit (house)	baufällig	['baʊˌfɛlɪç]
modern (adj)	modern	[mo'dɛʁn]
multistorey (adj)	mehrstöckig	['meːɐ̯ˌʃtœkɪç]
tall (~ building)	hoch	[hoːχ]

| floor, storey | Stock (m) | [ʃtɔk] |
| single-storey (adj) | einstöckig | ['aɪnˌʃtœkɪç] |

| ground floor | Erdgeschoß (n) | ['eːɐ̯t·gəˌʃoːs] |
| top floor | oberster Stock (m) | ['obɐstɐ ʃtɔk] |

| roof | Dach (n) | [daχ] |
| chimney | Schlot (m) | [ʃloːt] |

roof tiles	Dachziegel (m)	['daχˌtsiːgəl]
tiled (adj)	Dachziegel-	['daχˌtsiːgəl]
loft (attic)	Dachboden (m)	['daχˌboːdən]

| window | Fenster (n) | ['fɛnstɐ] |
| glass | Glas (n) | [glaːs] |

| window ledge | Fensterbrett (n) | ['fɛnstɐˌbʁɛt] |
| shutters | Fensterläden (pl) | ['fɛnstɐˌlɛːdən] |

wall	Wand (f)	[vant]
balcony	Balkon (m)	[bal'koːn]
downpipe	Regenfallrohr (n)	['ʁeːgənˌfalʁoːɐ̯]

upstairs (to be ~)	nach oben	[naːχ 'oːbən]
to go upstairs	hinaufgehen (vi)	[hɪ'naʊfˌgeːən]
to come down (the stairs)	herabsteigen (vi)	[hɛ'ʁapˌʃtaɪgən]
to move (to new premises)	umziehen (vi)	['ʊmtsiːən]

87. House. Entrance. Lift

entrance	Eingang (m)	['aɪnˌgaŋ]
stairs (stairway)	Treppe (f)	['tʀɛpə]
steps	Stufen (pl)	['ʃtuːfən]
banisters	Geländer (n)	[gə'lɛndɐ]
lobby (hotel ~)	Halle (f)	['halə]

postbox	Briefkasten (m)	['bʀiːfˌkastən]
waste bin	Müllkasten (m)	['mʏlˌkastən]
refuse chute	Müllschlucker (m)	['mʏlˌʃlʊkɐ]

lift	Aufzug (m), Fahrstuhl (m)	['aʊfˌtsuːk], ['faːɐʃtuːl]
goods lift	Lastenaufzug (m)	['lastən·'aʊfˌtsuːk]
lift cage	Aufzugkabine (f)	['aʊfˌtsuːk·ka'biːnə]
to take the lift	Aufzug nehmen	['aʊfˌtsuːk 'neːmən]

flat	Wohnung (f)	['voːnʊŋ]
residents (~ of a building)	Mieter (pl)	['miːtɐ]
neighbour (masc.)	Nachbar (m)	['naχˌbaːɐ]
neighbour (fem.)	Nachbarin (f)	['naχbaːʀɪn]
neighbours	Nachbarn (pl)	['naχbaːɐn]

88. House. Electricity

electricity	Elektrizität (f)	[elɛktʀitsi'tɛːt]
light bulb	Glühbirne (f)	['glyːˌbɪʀnə]
switch	Schalter (m)	['ʃaltɐ]
fuse (plug fuse)	Sicherung (f)	['zɪçəʀʊŋ]

cable, wire (electric ~)	Draht (m)	[dʀaːt]
wiring	Leitung (f)	['laɪtʊŋ]
electricity meter	Stromzähler (m)	['ʃtʀoːmˌtsɛːlɐ]
readings	Zählerstand (m)	['tsɛːlɐˌʃtant]

89. House. Doors. Locks

door	Tür (f)	[tyːɐ]
gate (vehicle ~)	Tor (n)	[toːɐ]
handle, doorknob	Griff (m)	[gʀɪf]
to unlock (unbolt)	aufschließen (vt)	['aʊfˌʃliːsən]
to open (vt)	öffnen (vt)	['œfnən]
to close (vt)	schließen (vt)	['ʃliːsən]

key	Schlüssel (m)	['ʃlʏsəl]
bunch (of keys)	Bündel (n)	['bʏndəl]
to creak (door, etc.)	knarren (vi)	['knaʀən]
creak	Knarren (n)	['knaʀən]
hinge (door ~)	Türscharnier (n)	['tyːɐʃaʀ'niːɐ]
doormat	Fußmatte (f)	['fuːsˌmatə]
door lock	Schloss (n)	[ʃlɔs]

keyhole	Schlüsselloch (n)	['ʃlʏsəlˌlɔx]
crossbar (sliding bar)	Türriegel (m)	['ty:ɐˌʀi:gəl]
door latch	Riegel (m)	['ʀi:gəl]
padlock	Vorhängeschloss (n)	['fo:ɛhɛŋəˌʃlɔs]

to ring (~ the door bell)	klingeln (vi)	['klɪŋəln]
ringing (sound)	Klingel (f)	['klɪŋəl]
doorbell	Türklingel (f)	['ty:ɐˌklɪŋəl]
doorbell button	Knopf (m)	[knɔpf]
knock (at the door)	Klopfen (n)	['klɔpfən]
to knock (vi)	anklopfen (vi)	['anˌklɔpfən]

code	Code (m)	[ko:t]
combination lock	Zahlenschloss (n)	['tsa:lənˌʃlɔs]
intercom	Sprechanlage (f)	['ʃpʀɛçʔanˌla:gə]
number (on the door)	Nummer (f)	['nʊmɐ]
doorplate	Türschild (n)	['ty:ɐʃɪlt]
peephole	Türspion (m)	['ty:ɐˈʃpiˌo:n]

90. Country house

village	Dorf (n)	[dɔʁf]
vegetable garden	Gemüsegarten (m)	[gə'my:zəˌgaʁtən]
fence	Zaun (m)	[tsaʊn]
picket fence	Lattenzaun (m)	['latənˌtsaʊn]
wicket gate	Zauntür (f)	['tsaʊŋˌty:ɐ]

granary	Speicher (m)	['ʃpaɪçɐ]
cellar	Keller (m)	['kɛlɐ]
shed (garden ~)	Schuppen (m)	['ʃʊpən]
water well	Brunnen (m)	['bʀʊnən]

stove (wood-fired ~)	Ofen (m)	['o:fən]
to stoke the stove	heizen (vt)	['haɪtsən]
firewood	Holz (n)	[hɔlts]
log (firewood)	Holzscheit (n)	['hɔltsˌʃaɪt]

veranda	Veranda (f)	[ve'ʀanda]
deck (terrace)	Terrasse (f)	[tɛ'ʀasə]
stoop (front steps)	Außentreppe (f)	['aʊsənˌtʀɛpə]
swing (hanging seat)	Schaukel (f)	['ʃaʊkəl]

91. Villa. Mansion

country house	Landhaus (n)	['lantˌhaʊs]
country-villa	Villa (f)	['vɪla]
wing (~ of a building)	Flügel (m)	['fly:gəl]

garden	Garten (m)	['gaʁtən]
park	Park (m)	[paʁk]
conservatory (greenhouse)	Orangerie (f)	[oʀaŋʒə'ʀi:]
to look after (garden, etc.)	pflegen (vt)	['pfle:gən]

swimming pool	Schwimmbad (n)	['ʃvɪmbaːt]
gym (home gym)	Kraftraum (m)	['kʀaftˌʀaʊm]
tennis court	Tennisplatz (m)	['tɛnɪsˌplats]
home theater (room)	Heimkinoraum (m)	['haɪmkiːnoˌʀaʊm]
garage	Garage (f)	[gaˈʀaːʒə]

| private property | Privateigentum (n) | [pʀiˈvaːtˌʔaɪgəntuːm] |
| private land | Privatgrundstück (n) | [pʀiˈvaːtˌgʀʊntʃtʏk] |

| warning (caution) | Warnung (f) | ['vaʀnʊŋ] |
| warning sign | Warnschild (n) | ['vaʀnʃɪlt] |

security	Bewachung (f)	[bəˈvaxʊŋ]
security guard	Wächter (m)	['vɛçtə]
burglar alarm	Alarmanlage (f)	[aˈlaʀmˈanˌlaːgə]

92. Castle. Palace

castle	Schloss (n)	[ʃlɔs]
palace	Palast (m)	[paˈlast]
fortress	Festung (f)	['fɛstʊŋ]
wall (round castle)	Mauer (f)	['maʊə]
tower	Turm (m)	[tʊʀm]
keep, donjon	Bergfried (m)	['bɛʀkˌfʀiːt]

portcullis	Fallgatter (n)	['falˌgatə]
subterranean passage	Tunnel (n)	['tʊnəl]
moat	Graben (m)	['gʀaːbən]
chain	Kette (f)	['kɛtə]
arrow loop	Schießscharte (f)	['ʃiːsˌʃaʀtə]

magnificent (adj)	großartig, prächtig	['gʀoːsˌʔaːʀtɪç], ['pʀɛçtɪç]
majestic (adj)	majestätisch	[majɛsˈtɛːtɪʃ]
impregnable (adj)	unnahbar	[ʊnˈnaːbaːɐ]
medieval (adj)	mittelalterlich	['mɪtəlˌʔaltəlɪç]

93. Flat

flat	Wohnung (f)	['voːnʊŋ]
room	Zimmer (n)	['tsɪmə]
bedroom	Schlafzimmer (n)	['ʃlaːfˌtsɪmə]
dining room	Esszimmer (n)	['ɛsˌtsɪmə]
living room	Wohnzimmer (n)	['voːnˌtsɪmə]
study (home office)	Arbeitszimmer (n)	['aʀbaɪtsˌtsɪmə]

entry room	Vorzimmer (n)	['foːɐˌtsɪmə]
bathroom	Badezimmer (n)	['baːdəˌtsɪmə]
water closet	Toilette (f)	[toaˈlɛtə]

ceiling	Decke (f)	['dɛkə]
floor	Fußboden (m)	['fuːsˌboːdən]
corner	Ecke (f)	['ɛkə]

94. Flat. Cleaning

to clean (vi, vt)	aufräumen (vt)	['aʊfˌʀɔɪmən]
to put away (to stow)	weglegen (vt)	['vɛkˌleːgən]
dust	Staub (m)	[ʃtaʊp]
dusty (adj)	staubig	['ʃtaʊbɪç]
to dust (vt)	Staub abwischen	[ʃtaʊp 'apˌvɪʃən]
vacuum cleaner	Staubsauger (m)	['ʃtaʊpˌzaʊgɐ]
to vacuum (vt)	Staub saugen	[ʃtaʊp 'zaʊgən]

to sweep (vi, vt)	kehren, fegen (vt)	['keːʀən], ['feːgən]
sweepings	Kehricht (m, n)	['keːʀɪçt]
order	Ordnung (f)	['ɔʁdnʊŋ]
disorder, mess	Unordnung (f)	['ʊnˌʔɔʁdnʊŋ]

mop	Schrubber (m)	['ʃʀʊbɐ]
duster	Lappen (m)	['lapən]
short broom	Besen (m)	['beːzən]
dustpan	Kehrichtschaufel (f)	['keːʀɪçtˌʃaʊfəl]

95. Furniture. Interior

furniture	Möbel (n)	['møːbəl]
table	Tisch (m)	[tɪʃ]
chair	Stuhl (m)	[ʃtuːl]
bed	Bett (n)	[bɛt]
sofa, settee	Sofa (n)	['zoːfa]
armchair	Sessel (m)	['zɛsəl]

bookcase	Bücherschrank (m)	['byːçɐˌʃʀaŋk]
shelf	Regal (n)	[ʀeˈgaːl]

wardrobe	Schrank (m)	[ʃʀaŋk]
coat rack (wall-mounted ~)	Hakenleiste (f)	['haːkənˌlaɪstə]
coat stand	Kleiderständer (m)	['klaɪdɐˌʃtɛndɐ]

chest of drawers	Kommode (f)	[kɔˈmoːdə]
coffee table	Couchtisch (m)	['kaʊtʃˌtɪʃ]

mirror	Spiegel (m)	['ʃpiːgəl]
carpet	Teppich (m)	['tɛpɪç]
small carpet	Matte (f)	['matə]

fireplace	Kamin (m)	[kaˈmiːn]
candle	Kerze (f)	['kɛʁtsə]
candlestick	Kerzenleuchter (m)	['kɛʁtsənˌlɔɪçtɐ]

drapes	Vorhänge (pl)	['foːɐhɛŋə]
wallpaper	Tapete (f)	[taˈpeːtə]
blinds (jalousie)	Jalousie (f)	[ʒaluˈziː]

table lamp	Tischlampe (f)	['tɪʃˌlampə]
wall lamp (sconce)	Leuchte (f)	['lɔɪçtə]

| standard lamp | Stehlampe (f) | ['ʃteː,lampə] |
| chandelier | Kronleuchter (m) | ['kʀoːnˌlɔɪçtɐ] |

leg (of a chair, table)	Bein (n)	[baɪn]
armrest	Armlehne (f)	['aʁmˌleːnə]
back (backrest)	Lehne (f)	['leːnə]
drawer	Schublade (f)	['ʃuːpˌlaːdə]

96. Bedding

bedclothes	Bettwäsche (f)	['bɛtˌvɛʃə]
pillow	Kissen (n)	['kɪsən]
pillowslip	Kissenbezug (m)	['kɪsən·bəˌtsuːk]
duvet	Bettdecke (f)	['bɛtˌdɛkə]
sheet	Laken (n)	['laːkən]
bedspread	Tagesdecke (f)	['taːgəsˌdɛkə]

97. Kitchen

kitchen	Küche (f)	['kʏçə]
gas	Gas (n)	[gaːs]
gas cooker	Gasherd (m)	['gaːsˌheːɐt]
electric cooker	Elektroherd (m)	[e'lɛktʀoˌheːɐt]
oven	Backofen (m)	['bakˌʔoːfən]
microwave oven	Mikrowellenherd (m)	['mikʀovɛlənˌheːɐt]

refrigerator	Kühlschrank (m)	['kyːlˌʃʀaŋk]
freezer	Tiefkühltruhe (f)	['tiːfkyːlˌtʀuːə]
dishwasher	Geschirrspülmaschine (f)	[gə'ʃɪʁ·ʃpyːl·maˌʃiːnə]

mincer	Fleischwolf (m)	['flaɪ ʃvɔlf]
juicer	Saftpresse (f)	['zaftˌpʀɛsə]
toaster	Toaster (m)	['toːstɐ]
mixer	Mixer (m)	['mɪksɐ]

coffee machine	Kaffeemaschine (f)	['kafe·maˌʃiːnə]
coffee pot	Kaffeekanne (f)	['kafeˌkanə]
coffee grinder	Kaffeemühle (f)	['kafeˌmyːlə]

kettle	Wasserkessel (m)	['vasɐˌkɛsəl]
teapot	Teekanne (f)	['teːˌkanə]
lid	Deckel (m)	['dɛkəl]
tea strainer	Teesieb (n)	['teːˌziːp]

spoon	Löffel (m)	['lœfəl]
teaspoon	Teelöffel (m)	['teːˌlœfəl]
soup spoon	Esslöffel (m)	['ɛsˌlœfəl]
fork	Gabel (f)	[gaːbəl]
knife	Messer (n)	['mɛsɐ]

| tableware (dishes) | Geschirr (n) | [gə'ʃɪʁ] |
| plate (dinner ~) | Teller (m) | ['tɛlɐ] |

saucer	Untertasse (f)	['ʊntɛˌtasə]
shot glass	Schnapsglas (n)	['ʃnapsˌglaːs]
glass (tumbler)	Glas (n)	[glaːs]
cup	Tasse (f)	['tasə]

sugar bowl	Zuckerdose (f)	['tsʊkɛˌdoːzə]
salt cellar	Salzstreuer (m)	['zaltsˌʃtʁɔɪɐ]
pepper pot	Pfefferstreuer (m)	['pfɛfɛˌʃtʁɔɪɐ]
butter dish	Butterdose (f)	['bʊtɛˌdoːzə]

stock pot (soup pot)	Kochtopf (m)	['kɔχˌtɔpf]
frying pan (skillet)	Pfanne (f)	['pfanə]
ladle	Schöpflöffel (m)	['ʃœpfˌlœfəl]
colander	Durchschlag (m)	['dʊʁçˌʃlaːk]
tray (serving ~)	Tablett (n)	[taˈblɛt]

bottle	Flasche (f)	['flaʃə]
jar (glass)	Einmachglas (n)	['aɪnmaχˌglaːs]
tin (can)	Dose (f)	['doːzə]

bottle opener	Flaschenöffner (m)	['flaʃənˌʔœfnɐ]
tin opener	Dosenöffner (m)	['doːzənˌʔœfnɐ]
corkscrew	Korkenzieher (m)	['kɔʁkənˌtsiːɐ]
filter	Filter (n)	['fɪltɐ]
to filter (vt)	filtern (vt)	['fɪltɐn]

| waste (food ~, etc.) | Müll (m) | [mʏl] |
| waste bin (kitchen ~) | Mülleimer (m) | ['mʏlˌʔaɪmɐ] |

98. Bathroom

bathroom	Badezimmer (n)	['baːdəˌtsɪmɐ]
water	Wasser (n)	['vasɐ]
tap	Wasserhahn (m)	['vasɛˌhaːn]
hot water	Warmwasser (n)	['vaʁmˌvasɐ]
cold water	Kaltwasser (n)	['kaltˌvasɐ]

toothpaste	Zahnpasta (f)	['tsaːnˌpasta]
to clean one's teeth	Zähne putzen	['tsɛːnə 'pʊtsən]
toothbrush	Zahnbürste (f)	['tsaːnˌbʏʁstə]

to shave (vi)	sich rasieren	[zɪç ʁaˈziːʁən]
shaving foam	Rasierschaum (m)	[ʁaˈziːɐˌʃaʊm]
razor	Rasierer (m)	[ʁaˈziːɐ]

to wash (one's hands, etc.)	waschen (vt)	['vaʃən]
to have a bath	sich waschen	[zɪç 'vaʃən]
shower	Dusche (f)	['duːʃə]
to have a shower	sich duschen	[zɪç 'duːʃən]

bath	Badewanne (f)	['baːdəˌvanə]
toilet (toilet bowl)	Klosettbecken (n)	[kloˈzɛtˌbɛkən]
sink (washbasin)	Waschbecken (n)	['vaʃˌbɛkən]
soap	Seife (f)	['zaɪfə]

soap dish	Seifenschale (f)	['zaɪfənˌʃaːlə]
sponge	Schwamm (m)	[ʃvam]
shampoo	Shampoo (n)	['ʃampu]
towel	Handtuch (n)	['hantˌtuːx]
bathrobe	Bademantel (m)	['baːdəˌmantəl]

laundry (laundering)	Wäsche (f)	['vɛʃə]
washing machine	Waschmaschine (f)	['vaʃˈmaˌʃiːnə]
to do the laundry	waschen (vt)	['vaʃən]
washing powder	Waschpulver (n)	['vaʃˌpʊlvɐ]

99. Household appliances

TV, telly	Fernseher (m)	['fɛɐnˌzeːɐ]
tape recorder	Tonbandgerät (n)	['toːnbantˈɡəˌʀɛːt]
video	Videorekorder (m)	['videoˈʀeˌkɔɐdɐ]
radio	Empfänger (m)	[ɛm'pfɛŋɐ]
player (CD, MP3, etc.)	Player (m)	['plɛɪɐ]

video projector	Videoprojektor (m)	['viːdeoˈpʀoˌjɛktoːɐ]
home cinema	Heimkino (n)	['haɪmkiːno]
DVD player	DVD-Player (m)	[defaʊˈdeːˌplɛɪɐ]
amplifier	Verstärker (m)	[fɛɐˈʃtɛɐkɐ]
video game console	Spielkonsole (f)	['ʃpiːlˈkɔnˌzoːlə]

video camera	Videokamera (f)	['viːdeoˌkaməʀa]
camera (photo)	Kamera (f)	['kaməʀa]
digital camera	Digitalkamera (f)	[digiˈtaːlˌkaməʀa]

vacuum cleaner	Staubsauger (m)	['ʃtaʊpˌzaʊɡɐ]
iron (e.g. steam ~)	Bügeleisen (n)	['byːɡəlˌʔaɪzən]
ironing board	Bügelbrett (n)	['byːɡəlˌbʀɛt]

telephone	Telefon (n)	[teleˈfoːn]
mobile phone	Mobiltelefon (n)	[moˈbiːlˈteleˌfoːn]
typewriter	Schreibmaschine (f)	['ʃʀaɪpˈmaˌʃiːnə]
sewing machine	Nähmaschine (f)	['nɛːˈmaˌʃiːnə]

microphone	Mikrophon (n)	[mikʀoˈfoːn]
headphones	Kopfhörer (m)	['kɔpfˌhøːʀɐ]
remote control (TV)	Fernbedienung (f)	['fɛɐnbəˌdiːnʊŋ]

CD, compact disc	CD (f)	[tseːˈdeː]
cassette, tape	Kassette (f)	[ka'sɛtə]
vinyl record	Schallplatte (f)	['ʃalˌplatə]

100. Repairs. Renovation

renovations	Renovierung (f)	[ʀenoˈviːʀʊŋ]
to renovate (vt)	renovieren (vt)	[ʀenoˈviːʀən]
to repair, to fix (vt)	reparieren (vt)	[ʀepaˈʀiːʀən]
to put in order	in Ordnung bringen	[ɪn 'ɔɐdnʊŋ 'bʀɪŋən]

to redo (do again)	noch einmal machen	[nɔx 'aɪnmaːl 'maxən]
paint	Farbe (f)	['faʁbə]
to paint (~ a wall)	streichen (vt)	['ʃtʁaɪçən]
house painter	Anstreicher (m)	['anˌʃtʁaɪçɐ]
paintbrush	Pinsel (m)	['pɪnzəl]

| whitewash | Kalkfarbe (f) | ['kalkˌfaʁbə] |
| to whitewash (vt) | weißen (vt) | ['vaɪsən] |

wallpaper	Tapete (f)	[ta'peːtə]
to wallpaper (vt)	tapezieren (vt)	[tape'tsiːʀən]
varnish	Lack (m)	['lak]
to varnish (vt)	lackieren (vt)	[la'kiːʀən]

101. Plumbing

water	Wasser (n)	['vasɐ]
hot water	Warmwasser (n)	['vaʁmˌvasɐ]
cold water	Kaltwasser (n)	['kaltˌvasɐ]
tap	Wasserhahn (m)	['vasɐˌhaːn]

drop (of water)	Tropfen (m)	['tʀɔpfən]
to drip (vi)	tropfen (vi)	['tʀɔpfən]
to leak (ab. pipe)	durchsickern (vi)	['dʊʁçˌzɪkɐn]
leak (pipe ~)	Leck (n)	[lɛk]
puddle	Lache (f)	['laːxə]

pipe	Rohr (n)	[ʀoːɐ]
valve (e.g., ball ~)	Ventil (n)	[vɛn'tiːl]
to be clogged up	sich verstopfen	[zɪç fɛɐ'ʃtɔpfən]

tools	Werkzeuge (pl)	['vɛʁkˌtsɔɪɡə]
adjustable spanner	Engländer (m)	['ɛŋlɛndɐ]
to unscrew (lid, filter, etc.)	abdrehen (vt)	['apˌdʀeːən]
to screw (tighten)	zudrehen (vt)	[tsuː'dʀeːən]

to unclog (vt)	reinigen (vt)	['ʀaɪnɪɡən]
plumber	Klempner (m)	['klɛmpnɐ]
basement	Keller (m)	['kɛlɐ]
sewerage (system)	Kanalisation (f)	[kanaliza'tsjoːn]

102. Fire. Conflagration

fire (accident)	Feuer (n)	['fɔɪɐ]
flame	Flamme (f)	['flamə]
spark	Funke (m)	['fʊŋkə]
smoke (from fire)	Rauch (m)	[ʀaʊx]
torch (flaming stick)	Fackel (f)	['fakəl]
campfire	Lagerfeuer (n)	['laːɡɐˌfɔɪɐ]

| petrol | Benzin (n) | [bɛn'tsiːn] |
| paraffin | Kerosin (n) | [keʀo'ziːn] |

flammable (adj)	brennbar	['brɛnbaːɐ]
explosive (adj)	explosiv	[ɛksploˈziːf]
NO SMOKING	RAUCHEN VERBOTEN!	['rauχən fɛɐˈboːtən]

safety	Sicherheit (f)	['zɪçɐhaɪt]
danger	Gefahr (f)	[gəˈfaːɐ]
dangerous (adj)	gefährlich	[gəˈfɛːəlɪç]

to catch fire	sich entflammen	[zɪç ɛntˈflamən]
explosion	Explosion (f)	[ɛksploˈzjoːn]
to set fire	in Brand stecken	[ɪn brant ˈʃtɛkən]
arsonist	Brandstifter (m)	['brantˌʃtɪftɐ]
arson	Brandstiftung (f)	['brantˌʃtɪftʊŋ]

to blaze (vi)	flammen (vi)	['flamən]
to burn (be on fire)	brennen (vi)	['brɛnən]
to burn down	verbrennen (vi)	[fɛɐ'brɛnən]

to call the fire brigade	die Feuerwehr rufen	[di ˈfɔɪɐˌveːɐ ˈruːfən]
firefighter, fireman	Feuerwehrmann (m)	['fɔɪɐveːɐˌman]
fire engine	Feuerwehrauto (n)	['fɔɪɐveːɐˌʔauto]
fire brigade	Feuerwehr (f)	['fɔɪɐˌveːɐ]
fire engine ladder	Drehleiter (f)	['dreːˌlaɪtɐ]

fire hose	Schlauch (m)	[ʃlauχ]
fire extinguisher	Feuerlöscher (m)	['fɔɪɐˌlœʃɐ]
helmet	Helm (m)	[hɛlm]
siren	Sirene (f)	[ˌziˈreːnə]

to cry (for help)	schreien (vi)	['ʃraɪən]
to call for help	um Hilfe rufen	[ʊm 'hɪlfə 'ruːfən]
rescuer	Retter (m)	['rɛtɐ]
to rescue (vt)	retten (vt)	['rɛtən]

to arrive (vi)	ankommen (vi)	['anˌkɔmən]
to extinguish (vt)	löschen (vt)	['lœʃən]
water	Wasser (n)	['vasɐ]
sand	Sand (m)	[zant]

ruins (destruction)	Trümmer (pl)	['trʏmɐ]
to collapse (building, etc.)	zusammenbrechen (vi)	[tsuˈzamənˌbrɛçən]
to fall down (vi)	einfallen (vi)	['aɪnˌfalən]
to cave in (ceiling, floor)	einstürzen (vi)	['aɪnˌʃtʏʁtsən]

| piece of debris | Bruchstück (n) | ['bruχˌʃtʏk] |
| ash | Asche (f) | ['aʃə] |

| to suffocate (die) | ersticken (vi) | [ɛɐˈʃtɪkən] |
| to be killed (perish) | ums Leben kommen | [ʊms 'leːbən 'kɔmən] |

HUMAN ACTIVITIES

Job. Business. Part 1

103. Office. Working in the office

office (company ~)	Büro (n)	[by'ʀo:]
office (director's ~)	Büro (n)	[by'ʀo:]
reception desk	Rezeption (f)	[ʀɛtsɛp'tsjo:n]
secretary	Sekretär (m)	[zekʀe'tɛ:ɐ]
secretary (fem.)	Sekretärin (f)	[zekʀe'tɛ:ʀɪn]
director	Direktor (m)	[di'ʀɛkto:ɐ]
manager	Manager (m)	['mɛnɪdʒɐ]
accountant	Buchhalter (m)	['bu:χˌhaltɐ]
employee	Mitarbeiter (m)	['mɪtʔaʁˌbaɪtɐ]
furniture	Möbel (n)	['mø:bəl]
desk	Tisch (m)	[tɪʃ]
desk chair	Schreibtischstuhl (m)	['ʃʀaɪptɪʃˌʃtu:l]
drawer unit	Rollcontainer (m)	['ʀɔl·kɔnˌte:nɐ]
coat stand	Kleiderständer (m)	['klaɪdɐˌʃtɛndɐ]
computer	Computer (m)	[kɔm'pju:tɐ]
printer	Drucker (m)	['dʀʊkɐ]
fax machine	Fax (m, n)	[faks]
photocopier	Kopierer (m)	[ko'pi:ʀɐ]
paper	Papier (n)	[pa'pi:ɐ]
office supplies	Büromaterial (n)	[by'ʀo:mateˌʀɪa:l]
mouse mat	Mousepad (n)	['maʊspɛt]
sheet of paper	Blatt (n) Papier	[blat pa'pi:ɐ]
binder	Ordner (m)	['ɔʁdnɐ]
catalogue	Katalog (m)	[kata'lo:k]
phone directory	Adressbuch (n)	[a'dʀɛsˌbu:χ]
documentation	Dokumentation (f)	[dokumɛnta'tsjo:n]
brochure (e.g. 12 pages ~)	Broschüre (f)	[bʀo'ʃy:ʀə]
leaflet (promotional ~)	Flugblatt (n)	['flu:kˌblat]
sample	Muster (n)	['mʊstɐ]
training meeting	Training (n)	['tʀɛ:nɪŋ]
meeting (of managers)	Meeting (n)	['mi:tɪŋ]
lunch time	Mittagspause (f)	['mɪta:ksˌpaʊzə]
to make a copy	eine Kopie machen	['aɪnə ko'pi: 'maχən]
to make multiple copies	vervielfältigen (vt)	[fɛɐ'fi:lˌfɛltɪgən]
to receive a fax	ein Fax bekommen	[aɪn faks bə'kɔmən]
to send a fax	ein Fax senden	[aɪn faks 'zɛndən]

to call (by phone)	anrufen (vt)	['an͵ʀuːfən]
to answer (vt)	antworten (vi)	['ant͵vɔʁtən]
to put through	verbinden (vt)	[fɛɐ'bɪndən]
to arrange, to set up	ausmachen (vt)	['aʊs͵maχən]
to demonstrate (vt)	demonstrieren (vt)	[demɔn'stʀiːʀən]
to be absent	fehlen (vi)	['feːlən]
absence	Abwesenheit (f)	['ap͵veːzən·haɪt]

104. Business processes. Part 1

business	Geschäft (n)	[gə'ʃɛft]
occupation	Angelegenheit (f)	['angə͵leːgənhaɪt]
firm	Firma (f)	['fɪʁma]
company	Gesellschaft (f)	[gə'zɛlʃaft]
corporation	Konzern (m)	[kɔn'tsɛʁn]
enterprise	Unternehmen (n)	[͵ʊntɐ'neːmən]
agency	Agentur (f)	[agɛn'tuːɐ]
agreement (contract)	Vereinbarung (f)	[fɛɐ'ʔaɪnbaːʀʊŋ]
contract	Vertrag (m)	[fɛɐ'tʀaːk]
deal	Geschäft (n)	[gə'ʃɛft]
order (to place an ~)	Auftrag (m)	['aʊf͵tʀaːk]
terms (of the contract)	Bedingung (f)	[bə'dɪŋʊŋ]
wholesale (adv)	en gros	[ɛn 'gʁo]
wholesale (adj)	Großhandels-	['gʁoːs͵handəls]
wholesale (n)	Großhandel (m)	['gʁoːs͵handəl]
retail (adj)	Einzelhandels-	['aɪntsəl͵handəls]
retail (n)	Einzelhandel (m)	['aɪntsəl͵handəl]
competitor	Konkurrent (m)	[kɔnkʊ'ʀɛnt]
competition	Konkurrenz (f)	[͵kɔnkʊ'ʀɛnts]
to compete (vi)	konkurrieren (vi)	[kɔŋkʊ'ʀiːʀən]
partner (associate)	Partner (m)	['paʁtnɐ]
partnership	Partnerschaft (f)	['paʁtnɐʃaft]
crisis	Krise (f)	['kʀiːzə]
bankruptcy	Bankrott (m)	[baŋ'kʀɔt]
to go bankrupt	Bankrott machen	[baŋ'kʀɔt 'maχən]
difficulty	Schwierigkeit (f)	['ʃviːʀɪçkaɪt]
problem	Problem (n)	[pʀo'bleːm]
catastrophe	Katastrophe (f)	[͵katas'tʀoːfə]
economy	Wirtschaft (f)	['vɪʁtʃaft]
economic (~ growth)	wirtschaftlich	['vɪʁtʃaftlɪç]
economic recession	Rezession (f)	[ʀetsɛ'sjoːn]
goal (aim)	Ziel (n)	[tsiːl]
task	Aufgabe (f)	['aʊf͵gaːbə]
to trade (vi)	handeln (vi)	['handəln]
network (distribution ~)	Netz (n)	[nɛts]

| inventory (stock) | Lager (n) | ['la:gə] |
| range (assortment) | Sortiment (n) | [zɔʁti'mɛnt] |

leader (leading company)	führende Unternehmen (n)	['fy:ʁəndə ʊntɐ'ne:mən]
large (~ company)	groß	[gʁo:s]
monopoly	Monopol (n)	[mono'po:l]

theory	Theorie (f)	[teo'ʁi:]
practice	Praxis (f)	['pʁaksɪs]
experience (in my ~)	Erfahrung (f)	[ɛɐ'fa:ʁʊŋ]
trend (tendency)	Tendenz (f)	[tɛn'dɛnts]
development	Entwicklung (f)	[ɛnt'vɪklʊŋ]

105. Business processes. Part 2

| profit (foregone ~) | Vorteil (m) | ['foʁ‚taɪl] |
| profitable (~ deal) | vorteilhaft | ['foʁtaɪl‚haft] |

delegation (group)	Delegation (f)	[delega'tsjo:n]
salary	Lohn (m)	[lo:n]
to correct (an error)	korrigieren (vt)	[kɔʁi'gi:ʁən]
business trip	Dienstreise (f)	['di:nst‚ʁaɪzə]
commission	Kommission (f)	[kɔmɪ'sjo:n]

to control (vt)	kontrollieren (vt)	[kɔntʁo'li:ʁən]
conference	Konferenz (f)	[‚kɔnfe'ʁɛnts]
licence	Lizenz (f)	[li'tsɛnts]
reliable (~ partner)	zuverlässig	['tsu:fɛɐ‚lɛsɪç]

initiative (undertaking)	Initiative (f)	[initsɪa'ti:və]
norm (standard)	Norm (f)	[nɔʁm]
circumstance	Umstand (m)	['ʊmʃtant]
duty (of an employee)	Pflicht (f)	[pflɪçt]

organization (company)	Unternehmen (n)	[‚ʊntɐ'ne:mən]
organization (process)	Organisation (f)	[‚ɔʁganiza'tsjo:n]
organized (adj)	organisiert	[ɔʁgani'zi:ɐt]
cancellation	Abschaffung (f)	['ap‚ʃafʊŋ]
to cancel (call off)	abschaffen (vt)	['ap‚ʃafən]
report (official ~)	Bericht (m)	[bə'ʁɪçt]

patent	Patent (n)	[pa'tɛnt]
to patent (obtain patent)	patentieren (vt)	[patɛn'ti:ʁən]
to plan (vt)	planen (vt)	['pla:nən]

bonus (money)	Prämie (f)	['pʁɛ:mɪə]
professional (adj)	professionell	[pʁofɛsjɔ'nɛl]
procedure	Prozedur (f)	[‚pʁotse'du:ɐ]

to examine (contract, etc.)	prüfen (vt)	['pʁy:fən]
calculation	Berechnung (f)	[bə'ʁɛçnʊŋ]
reputation	Ruf (m)	[ʁu:f]
risk	Risiko (n)	['ʁi:ziko]
to manage, to run	leiten (vt)	['laɪtən]

information (report)	Informationen (pl)	[ɪnfoʁma'tsjo:nən]
property	Eigentum (n)	['aɪgəntu:m]
union	Bund (m)	[bʊnt]

life insurance	Lebensversicherung (f)	['le:bəns·fɛɐ̯ˌzɪçəʁʊŋ]
to insure (vt)	versichern (vt)	[fɛɐ̯'zɪçən]
insurance	Versicherung (f)	[fɛɐ̯'zɪçəʁʊŋ]

auction (~ sale)	Auktion (f)	[aʊk'tsjo:n]
to notify (inform)	benachrichtigen (vt)	[bə'na:χˌʁɪçtɪgən]
management (process)	Verwaltung (f)	[fɛɐ̯'valtʊŋ]
service (~ industry)	Dienst (m)	[di:nst]

forum	Forum (n)	['fo:ʁʊm]
to function (vi)	funktionieren (vi)	[fʊŋktsjo'ni:ʁən]
stage (phase)	Etappe (f)	[e'tapə]
legal (~ services)	juristisch	[ju'ʁɪstɪʃ]
lawyer (legal advisor)	Jurist (m)	[ju'ʁɪst]

106. Production. Works

plant	Werk (n)	[vɛʁk]
factory	Fabrik (f)	[fa'bʁi:k]
workshop	Werkstatt (f)	['vɛʁkʃtat]
works, production site	Betrieb (m)	[bə'tʁi:p]

industry (manufacturing)	Industrie (f)	[ɪndʊs'tʁi:]
industrial (adj)	Industrie-	[ɪndʊs'tʁi:]
heavy industry	Schwerindustrie (f)	['ʃveːɐ̯ʔɪndʊsˌtʁi:]
light industry	Leichtindustrie (f)	['laɪçtʔɪndʊsˌtʁi:]

products	Produktion (f)	[pʁodʊk'tsjo:n]
to produce (vt)	produzieren (vt)	[pʁodu'tsi:ʁən]
raw materials	Rohstoff (m)	['ʁo:ˌʃtɔf]

foreman (construction ~)	Vorarbeiter (m), Meister (m)	[fo:ʁ'ʔaʁbaɪtə], ['maɪstə]
workers team (crew)	Arbeitsteam (n)	['aʁbaɪtsˌti:m]
worker	Arbeiter (m)	['aʁbaɪtə]

working day	Arbeitstag (m)	['aʁbaɪtsˌta:k]
pause (rest break)	Pause (f)	['paʊzə]
meeting	Versammlung (f)	[fɛɐ̯'zamlʊŋ]
to discuss (vt)	besprechen (vt)	[bə'ʃpʁɛçən]

plan	Plan (m)	[pla:n]
to fulfil the plan	den Plan erfüllen	[den pla:n ɛɐ̯'fʏlən]
rate of output	Arbeitsertrag (m)	['aʁbaɪtsˌɛɐ̯'tʁa:k]
quality	Qualität (f)	[kvali'tɛ:t]
control (checking)	Prüfung, Kontrolle (f)	['pʁy:fʊŋ], [kɔn'tʁɔlə]
quality control	Gütekontrolle (f)	['gy:tə·kɔn'tʁɔlə]

workplace safety	Arbeitsplatzsicherheit (f)	['aʁbaɪts·platsˌzɪçehaɪt]
discipline	Disziplin (f)	[dɪstsi'pli:n]
violation (of safety rules, etc.)	Übertretung (f)	[y:bɐ'tʁe:tʊŋ]

to violate (rules)	übertreten (vt)	[yːbɐˈtʀeːtən]
strike	Streik (m)	[ʃtʀaɪk]
striker	Streikender (m)	[ˈʃtʀaɪkəndɐ]
to be on strike	streiken (vi)	[ˈʃtʀaɪkən]
trade union	Gewerkschaft (f)	[ɡəˈvɛʀkʃaft]

to invent (machine, etc.)	erfinden (vt)	[ɛɐˈfɪndən]
invention	Erfindung (f)	[ɛɐˈfɪndʊŋ]
research	Erforschung (f)	[ɛɐˈfɔʀʃʊŋ]
to improve (make better)	verbessern (vt)	[fɛɐˈbɛsən]
technology	Technologie (f)	[tɛçnoloˈɡiː]
technical drawing	Zeichnung (f)	[ˈtsaɪçnʊŋ]

load, cargo	Ladung (f)	[ˈlaːdʊŋ]
loader (person)	Ladearbeiter (m)	[ˈlaːdəˌaʀbaɪtɐ]
to load (vehicle, etc.)	laden (vt)	[ˈlaːdən]
loading (process)	Beladung (f)	[bəˈlaːdʊŋ]
to unload (vi, vt)	entladen (vt)	[ɛntˈlaːdən]
unloading	Entladung (f)	[ɛntˈlaːdʊŋ]

transport	Transport (m)	[tʀansˈpɔʀt]
transport company	Transportunternehmen (n)	[tʀansˈpɔʀtˈʊntɐˈneːmən]
to transport (vt)	transportieren (vt)	[ˌtʀanspɔʀˈtiːʀən]

wagon	Güterwagen (m)	[ˈɡyːtɐˌvaːɡən]
tank (e.g., oil ~)	Zisterne (f)	[tsɪsˈtɛʀnə]
lorry	Lastkraftwagen (m)	[ˈlastkʀaftˌvaːɡən]

machine tool	Werkzeugmaschine (f)	[ˈvɛʀktsɔɪkˈmaˌʃiːnə]
mechanism	Mechanismus (m)	[meçaˈnɪsmʊs]

industrial waste	Industrieabfälle (pl)	[ɪndʊsˈtʀiːʔapˌfɛlə]
packing (process)	Verpacken (n)	[fɛɐˈpakən]
to pack (vt)	verpacken (vt)	[fɛɐˈpakən]

107. Contract. Agreement

contract	Vertrag (m)	[fɛɐˈtʀaːk]
agreement	Vereinbarung (f)	[fɛɐˈʔaɪnbaːʀʊŋ]
addendum	Anhang (m)	[ˈanhaŋ]

to sign a contract	einen Vertrag abschließen	[ˈaɪnən fɛɐˈtʀaːk ˈapˌʃliːsən]
signature	Unterschrift (f)	[ˈʊntɐˌʃʀɪft]
to sign (vt)	unterschreiben (vt)	[ˌʊntɐˈʃʀaɪbən]
seal (stamp)	Stempel (m)	[ˈʃtɛmpəl]

subject of the contract	Vertragsgegenstand (m)	[fɛɐˈtʀaːksˈɡeːɡənʃtant]
clause	Punkt (m)	[pʊŋkt]
parties (in contract)	Parteien (pl)	[paʀˈtaɪən]
legal address	rechtmäßige Anschrift (f)	[ˈʀɛçtˌmɛːsɪɡə ˈanʃʀɪft]

to violate the contract	Vertrag brechen	[fɛɐˈtʀaːk ˈbʀɛçən]
commitment (obligation)	Verpflichtung (f)	[fɛɐˈpflɪçtʊŋ]
responsibility	Verantwortlichkeit (f)	[fɛɐˈʔantvɔʀtlɪçkaɪt]

force majeure	Force majeure (f)	[fɔʁs·ma'ʒœ:r]
dispute	Streit (m)	[ʃtʁaɪt]
penalties	Strafsanktionen (pl)	['ʃtʁa:f·zaŋk'tsjo:nən]

108. Import & Export

import	Import (m)	[ˌɪm'pɔʁt]
importer	Importeur (m)	[ɪmpɔʁ'tø:ɐ]
to import (vt)	importieren (vt)	[ɪmpɔʁ'ti:ʁən]
import (as adj.)	Import-	[ˌɪm'pɔʁt]

export (exportation)	Export (m)	[ɛks'pɔʁt]
exporter	Exporteur (m)	[ɛkspɔʁ'tø:ɐ]
to export (vt)	exportieren (vt)	[ˌɛkspɔʁ'ti:ʁən]
export (as adj.)	Export-	[ɛks'pɔʁt]

| goods (merchandise) | Waren (pl) | ['va:ʁən] |
| consignment, lot | Partie (f), Ladung (f) | [paʁ'ti:], ['la:dʊŋ] |

weight	Gewicht (n)	[gə'vɪçt]
volume	Volumen (n)	[vo'lu:mən]
cubic metre	Kubikmeter (m)	[ku'bi:kˌme:tɐ]

manufacturer	Hersteller (m)	['he:ɐˌʃtɛlɐ]
transport company	Transportunternehmen (n)	[tʁans'pɔʁt·ʊntɐ'ne:mən]
container	Container (m)	[ˌkɔn'tɛɪnɐ]

border	Grenze (f)	['gʁɛntsə]
customs	Zollamt (n)	['tsɔlˌʔamt]
customs duty	Zoll (m)	[tsɔl]
customs officer	Zollbeamter (m)	['tsɔl·bəˌʔamtɐ]
smuggling	Schmuggel (m)	['ʃmʊgəl]
contraband (smuggled goods)	Schmuggelware (f)	['ʃmʊgəlˌva:ʁə]

109. Finances

share, stock	Aktie (f)	['aktsiə]
bond (certificate)	Obligation (f)	[ɔbliga'tsjo:n]
promissory note	Wechsel (m)	['vɛksəl]

| stock exchange | Börse (f) | ['bœʁzə] |
| stock price | Aktienkurs (m) | ['aktsiən·kʊʁs] |

| to go down (become cheaper) | billiger werden | ['bɪlɪgɐ 've:ɐdən] |
| to go up (become more expensive) | teuer werden | ['tɔɪɐ 've:ɐdən] |

share	Anteil (m)	['anˌtaɪl]
controlling interest	Mehrheitsbeteiligung (f)	['me:ɐhaɪts·bə'taɪlɪgʊŋ]
investment	Investitionen (pl)	[ɪnvɛsti'tsjo:nən]

to invest (vt)	investieren (vt)	[ɪnvɛs'tiːʀən]
percent	Prozent (n)	[pʀo'tsɛnt]
interest (on investment)	Zinsen (pl)	['tsɪnzən]

profit	Gewinn (m)	[gə'vɪn]
profitable (adj)	gewinnbringend	[gə'vɪn‚bʀɪŋənt]
tax	Steuer (f)	['ʃtɔɪɐ]

currency (foreign ~)	Währung (f)	['vɛːʀʊŋ]
national (adj)	Landes-	['landəs]
exchange (currency ~)	Geldumtausch (m)	['gɛlt‚umtauʃ]

| accountant | Buchhalter (m) | ['buːχ‚haltɐ] |
| accounting | Buchhaltung (f) | ['buːχ‚haltʊŋ] |

bankruptcy	Bankrott (m)	[baŋ'kʀɔt]
collapse, ruin	Zusammenbruch (m)	[tsu'zamən‚bʀʊχ]
ruin	Pleite (f)	['plaɪtə]
to be ruined (financially)	pleite gehen	['plaɪtə 'geːən]
inflation	Inflation (f)	[ɪnfla'tsjoːn]
devaluation	Abwertung (f)	['ap‚veːɐtʊŋ]

capital	Kapital (n)	[kapi'taːl]
income	Einkommen (n)	['aɪn‚kɔmən]
turnover	Umsatz (m)	['ʊm‚zats]
resources	Mittel (pl)	['mɪtəl]
monetary resources	Geldmittel (pl)	['gɛlt‚mɪtəl]

| overheads | Gemeinkosten (pl) | [gə'maɪn‚kɔstən] |
| to reduce (expenses) | reduzieren (vt) | [ʀedu'tsiːʀən] |

110. Marketing

marketing	Marketing (n)	['maʀkətɪŋ]
market	Markt (m)	[maʀkt]
market segment	Marktsegment (n)	['maʀkt·zɛ'gmɛnt]
product	Produkt (n)	[pʀo'dʊkt]
goods (merchandise)	Waren (pl)	['vaːʀən]

brand	Schutzmarke (f)	['ʃuts‚maʀkə]
trademark	Handelsmarke (f)	['handəls‚maʀkə]
logotype	Firmenzeichen (n)	['fɪʀmən‚tsaɪçən]
logo	Logo (m, n)	['loːgɔ]

demand	Nachfrage (f)	['naːχ‚fʀaːgə]
supply	Angebot (n)	['angə‚boːt]
need	Bedürfnis (n)	[bə'dʏʀfnɪs]
consumer	Verbraucher (m)	[fɛɐ'bʀauχɐ]

analysis	Analyse (f)	[ana'lyːzə]
to analyse (vt)	analysieren (vt)	[‚analy'ziːʀən]
positioning	Positionierung (f)	[pozitsjo'niːʀʊŋ]
to position (vt)	positionieren (vt)	[pozitsjo'niːʀən]
price	Preis (m)	[pʀaɪs]

| pricing policy | Preispolitik (f) | ['pʀaɪs·poli'tɪk] |
| price formation | Preisbildung (f) | ['pʀaɪs͵bɪlduŋ] |

111. Advertising

advertising	Werbung (f)	['vɛʁbuŋ]
to advertise (vt)	werben (vt)	['vɛʁbən]
budget	Budget (n)	[by'dʒe:]

ad, advertisement	Werbeanzeige (f)	['vɛʁbə?an͵tsaɪɡə]
TV advertising	Fernsehwerbung (f)	['fɛʁnze:͵vɛʁbuŋ]
radio advertising	Radiowerbung (f)	['ʀa:dɪo͵vɛʁbuŋ]
outdoor advertising	Außenwerbung (f)	['ausən͵vɛʁbuŋ]

mass medias	Massenmedien (pl)	['masən͵me:dɪən]
periodical (n)	Zeitschrift (f)	['tsaɪtʃʀɪft]
image (public appearance)	Image (n)	['ɪmɪdʒ]

| slogan | Losung (f) | ['lo:zuŋ] |
| motto (maxim) | Motto (n) | ['mɔto] |

campaign	Kampagne (f)	[kam'panjə]
advertising campaign	Werbekampagne (f)	['vɛʁbə·kam'panjə]
target group	Zielgruppe (f)	['tsi:l͵gʀupə]

business card	Visitenkarte (f)	[vi'zi:tən͵kaʁtə]
leaflet (promotional ~)	Flugblatt (n)	['flu:k͵blat]
brochure (e.g. 12 pages ~)	Broschüre (f)	[bʀɔ'ʃy:ʀə]
pamphlet	Faltblatt (n)	['falt͵blat]
newsletter	Informationsblatt (n)	[ɪnfɔʁma'tsjo:ns͵blat]

signboard (store sign, etc.)	Firmenschild (n)	['fɪʁmənʃɪlt]
poster	Plakat (n)	[pla'ka:t]
hoarding	Werbeschild (n)	['vɛʁbəʃɪlt]

112. Banking

| bank | Bank (f) | [baŋk] |
| branch (of a bank) | Filiale (f) | [fi'lɪa:lə] |

| consultant | Berater (m) | [bə'ʀa:tɐ] |
| manager (director) | Leiter (m) | ['laɪtɐ] |

bank account	Konto (n)	['kɔnto]
account number	Kontonummer (f)	['kɔnto͵numɐ]
current account	Kontokorrent (n)	[kɔnto·kɔ'ʀɛnt]
deposit account	Sparkonto (n)	['ʃpa:ɐ͵kɔnto]

to open an account	ein Konto eröffnen	[aɪn 'kɔnto ɛɐ'?œfnən]
to close the account	das Konto schließen	[das 'kɔnto 'ʃli:sən]
to deposit into the account	auf ein Konto einzahlen	[auf aɪn 'kɔnto 'aɪn͵tsa:lən]
to withdraw (vt)	abheben (vt)	['ap͵he:bən]

deposit	Einzahlung (f)	['aɪnˌtsaːlʊŋ]
to make a deposit	eine Einzahlung machen	['aɪnə 'aɪnˌtsaːlʊŋ 'maχən]
wire transfer	Überweisung (f)	[ˌyːbɐ'vaɪzən]
to wire, to transfer	überweisen (vt)	[ˌyːbɐ'vaɪzən]

| sum | Summe (f) | ['zʊmə] |
| How much? | Wie viel? | ['viː fiːl] |

| signature | Unterschrift (f) | ['ʊntɐˌʃrɪft] |
| to sign (vt) | unterschreiben (vt) | [ˌʊntɐ'ʃraɪbən] |

credit card	Kreditkarte (f)	[kʀe'diːtˌkaʁtə]
code (PIN code)	Code (m)	[koːt]
credit card number	Kreditkartennummer (f)	[kʀe'diːtˌkaʁtə'nʊmɐ]
cashpoint	Geldautomat (m)	['gɛltʔaʊtoˌmaːt]

cheque	Scheck (m)	[ʃɛk]
to write a cheque	einen Scheck schreiben	['aɪnən ʃɛk 'ʃraɪbn]
chequebook	Scheckbuch (n)	['ʃɛkˌbuːχ]

loan (bank ~)	Darlehen (m)	['daʁˌleːən]
to apply for a loan	ein Darlehen beantragen	[aɪn 'daʁˌleːən bə'ʔantʀaːgən]
to get a loan	ein Darlehen aufnehmen	[aɪn daʁˌleːən 'aʊfˌneːmən]
to give a loan	ein Darlehen geben	[aɪn 'daʁˌleːən 'geːbən]
guarantee	Sicherheit (f)	['zɪçɐhaɪt]

113. Telephone. Phone conversation

telephone	Telefon (n)	[tele'foːn]
mobile phone	Mobiltelefon (n)	[mo'biːl·teleˌfoːn]
answerphone	Anrufbeantworter (m)	['anʀuːfbə·antˌvɔʁtɐ]

| to call (by phone) | anrufen (vt) | ['anˌʀuːfən] |
| call, ring | Anruf (m) | ['anˌʀuːf] |

to dial a number	eine Nummer wählen	['aɪnə 'nʊmɐ 'vɛːlən]
Hello!	Hallo!	[ha'loː]
to ask (vt)	fragen (vt)	['fʀaːgən]
to answer (vi, vt)	antworten (vi)	['antˌvɔʁtən]

to hear (vt)	hören (vt)	['høːʀən]
well (adv)	gut	[guːt]
not well (adv)	schlecht	[ʃlɛçt]
noises (interference)	Störungen (pl)	['ʃtøːʀʊŋən]

receiver	Hörer (m)	['høːʀɐ]
to pick up (~ the phone)	den Hörer abnehmen	[den 'høːʀɐ 'apˌneːmən]
to hang up (~ the phone)	auflegen (vt)	['aʊfˌleːgən]

busy (engaged)	besetzt	[bə'zɛtst]
to ring (ab. phone)	läuten (vi)	['lɔɪtən]
telephone book	Telefonbuch (n)	[tele'foːnˌbuːχ]
local (adj)	Orts-	[ɔʁts]
local call	Ortsgespräch	[ɔʁts·gə'ʃpʀɛːç]

trunk (e.g. ~ call)	Fern-	['fɛʁn]
trunk call	Ferngespräch	['fɛʁn·ɡə'ʃpʁɛ:ç]
international (adj)	Auslands-	['aʊslants]
international call	Auslandsgespräch	['aʊslants·ɡə'ʃpʁɛ:ç]

114. Mobile telephone

mobile phone	Mobiltelefon (n)	[mo'bi:l·tele͡fo:n]
display	Display (n)	[dɪs'ple:]
button	Knopf (m)	[knɔpf]
SIM card	SIM-Karte (f)	['zɪm͡kaʁtə]

battery	Batterie (f)	[batə'ʁi:]
to be flat (battery)	leer sein	[le:ɐ zaɪn]
charger	Ladegerät (n)	['la:də·ɡə'ʁɛ:t]

menu	Menü (n)	[me'ny:]
settings	Einstellungen (pl)	['aɪnʃtɛlʊŋən]
tune (melody)	Melodie (f)	[melo'di:]
to select (vt)	auswählen (vt)	['aʊs͡vɛ:lən]

calculator	Rechner (m)	['ʁɛçnɐ]
voice mail	Anrufbeantworter (m)	['anʁu:fbə·ant͡vɔʁtɐ]
alarm clock	Wecker (m)	['vɛkɐ]
contacts	Kontakte (pl)	[kɔn'taktə]

SMS (text message)	SMS-Nachricht (f)	[ɛsʔɛm'ʔɛs 'na:χͅʁɪçt]
subscriber	Teilnehmer (m)	['taɪl͡ne:mɐ]

115. Stationery

ballpoint pen	Kugelschreiber (m)	['ku:ɡəlͅʃʁaɪbɐ]
fountain pen	Federhalter (m)	['fe:dɐͅhaltɐ]

pencil	Bleistift (m)	['blaɪ͡ʃtɪft]
highlighter	Faserschreiber (m)	['fa:zɐͅʃʁaɪbɐ]
felt-tip pen	Filzstift (m)	['fɪlts͡ʃtɪft]

notepad	Notizblock (m)	[no'ti:tsͅblɔk]
diary	Terminkalender (m)	[tɛʁ'mi:n·kaͅlɛndɐ]

ruler	Lineal (n)	[line'a:l]
calculator	Rechner (m)	['ʁɛçnɐ]
rubber	Radiergummi (m)	[ʁa'di:ɐͅɡumi]

drawing pin	Reißzwecke (f)	['ʁaɪs·tsvɛkə]
paper clip	Heftklammer (f)	['hɛftͅklamɐ]

glue	Klebstoff (m)	['kle:pͅʃtɔf]
stapler	Hefter (m)	['hɛftɐ]
hole punch	Locher (m)	['lɔχɐ]
pencil sharpener	Bleistiftspitzer (m)	['blaɪʃtɪftͅʃpɪtsɐ]

116. Various kinds of documents

account (report)	Bericht (m)	[bə'rɪçt]
agreement	Abkommen (n)	['ap͜kɔmən]
application form	Anmeldeformular (n)	['anmɛldə·fɔʁmu͜laːɐ]
authentic (adj)	Original-	[ɔrigi'naːl]
badge (identity tag)	Namensschild (n)	['naːmənsʃɪlt]
business card	Visitenkarte (f)	[vi'ziːtən͜kaʁtə]

certificate (~ of quality)	Zertifikat (n)	[tsɛʁtifi'kaːt]
cheque (e.g. draw a ~)	Scheck (m)	[ʃɛk]
bill (in restaurant)	Rechnung (f)	['rɛçnʊŋ]
constitution	Verfassung (f)	[fɛɐ'fasʊŋ]

contract (agreement)	Vertrag (m)	[fɛɐ'traːk]
copy	Kopie (f)	[ko'piː]
copy (of a contract, etc.)	Kopie (f)	[ko'piː]

customs declaration	Zolldeklaration (f)	['tsɔl·deklaʁa'tsjoːn]
document	Dokument (n)	[͜doku'mɛnt]
driving licence	Führerschein (m)	['fyːʁɐ͜ʃaɪn]
addendum	Anlage (f)	['an͜laːgə]
form	Fragebogen (m)	['fraːgə͜boːgən]

ID card (e.g., warrant card)	Ausweis (m)	['aʊs͜vaɪs]
inquiry (request)	Anfrage (f)	['an͜fraːgə]
invitation card	Einladungskarte (f)	['aɪnlaːdʊŋs͜kaʁtə]
invoice	Rechnung (f)	['rɛçnʊŋ]

law	Gesetz (n)	[gə'zɛts]
letter (mail)	Brief (m)	[briːf]
letterhead	Briefbogen (n)	['briːf͜boːgən]
list (of names, etc.)	Liste (f)	['lɪstə]
manuscript	Manuskript (n)	[manu'skrɪpt]
newsletter	Informationsblatt (n)	[ɪnfɔʁma'tsjoːns͜blat]
note (short letter)	Zettel (m)	['tsɛtəl]

pass (for worker, visitor)	Passierschein (m)	[pa'siːɐ͜ʃaɪn]
passport	Pass (m)	[pas]
permit	Erlaubnis (f)	[ɛɐ'laʊpnɪs]
curriculum vitae, CV	Lebenslauf (m)	['leːbəns͜laʊf]
debt note, IOU	Schuldschein (m)	['ʃʊltʃaɪn]
receipt (for purchase)	Quittung (f)	['kvɪtʊŋ]
till receipt	Kassenzettel (m)	['kasən͜tsɛtəl]
report (mil.)	Bericht (m)	[bə'rɪçt]

to show (ID, etc.)	vorzeigen (vt)	['foː͜ɐ͜tsaɪgən]
to sign (vt)	unterschreiben (vt)	[͜ʊntɐ'ʃraɪbən]
signature	Unterschrift (f)	['ʊntɐʃrɪft]
seal (stamp)	Stempel (m)	['ʃtɛmpəl]
text	Text (m)	[tɛkst]
ticket (for entry)	Eintrittskarte (f)	['aɪntrɪts͜kaʁtə]

to cross out	streichen (vt)	['ʃtraɪçən]
to fill in (~ a form)	ausfüllen (vt)	['aʊs͜fʏlən]

| waybill (shipping invoice) | Frachtbrief (m) | ['fʀaχt͵bʀi:f] |
| will (testament) | Testament (n) | [tɛsta'mɛnt] |

117. Kinds of business

accounting services	Buchführung (f)	['bu:χ͵fy:ʀʊŋ]
advertising	Werbung (f)	['vɛʀbʊŋ]
advertising agency	Werbeagentur (f)	['vɛʀbə?agɛn͵tu:ɐ]
air-conditioners	Klimaanlagen (pl)	['kli:ma͵?anla:gən]
airline	Fluggesellschaft (f)	['flu:kgə͵zɛlʃaft]

alcoholic beverages	Spirituosen (pl)	[ʃpiʀi'tʊo:zən]
antiques (antique dealers)	Antiquitäten (pl)	[antikvi'tɛ:tən]
art gallery (contemporary ~)	Kunstgalerie (f)	['kʊnst͵galə'ʀi:]
audit services	Rechnungsprüfung (f)	['ʀɛçnʊŋs͵pʀy:fʊŋ]

banking industry	Bankwesen (n)	['baŋk͵ve:zən]
beauty salon	Schönheitssalon (m)	['ʃø:nhaɪts͵za'lɔŋ]
bookshop	Buchhandlung (f)	['bu:χ͵handlʊŋ]
brewery	Bierbrauerei (f)	['bi:ɐ·bʀaʊə͵ʀaɪ]
business centre	Bürogebäude (n)	[by'ʀo:gə͵bɔɪdə]
business school	Business-Schule (f)	['bɪznɛs·'ʃu:lə]

casino	Kasino (n)	[ka'zi:no]
chemist, pharmacy	Apotheke (f)	[apo'te:kə]
cinema	Kino (n)	['ki:no]
construction	Bau (m)	['baʊ]
consulting	Beratung (f)	[bə'ʀa:tʊŋ]

dental clinic	Stomatologie (f)	[ʃtomatolo'gi:]
design	Design (n)	[di'zaɪn]
dry cleaners	chemische Reinigung (f)	[çe:miʃə 'ʀaɪnɪgʊŋ]

employment agency	Personalagentur (f)	[pɛʀzo'na:l·agɛn'tu:ɐ]
financial services	Finanzdienstleistungen (pl)	[fi'nants·'di:nst͵laɪstʊŋən]
food products	Nahrungsmittel (pl)	['na:ʀʊŋs͵mɪtəl]
furniture (e.g. house ~)	Möbel (n)	['mø:bəl]
clothing, garment	Kleidung (f)	['klaɪdʊŋ]
hotel	Hotel (n)	[ho'tɛl]

ice-cream	Eis (n)	[aɪs]
industry (manufacturing)	Industrie (f)	[ɪndʊs'tʀi:]
insurance	Versicherung (f)	[fɛɐ'zɪçəʀʊŋ]
Internet	Internet (n)	['ɪntɐnɛt]
investments (finance)	Investitionen (pl)	[ɪnvɛsti'tsjo:nən]
jeweller	Juwelier (m)	[juve'li:ɐ]
jewellery	Juwelierwaren (pl)	[juve'li:ɐ͵va:ʀən]

laundry (shop)	Wäscherei (f)	[vɛʃə'ʀaɪ]
legal adviser	Rechtsberatung (f)	['ʀɛçts·bə'ʀa:tʊŋ]
light industry	Leichtindustrie (f)	['laɪçt?ɪndʊs͵tʀi:]

| magazine | Zeitschrift (f) | ['tsaɪt͵ʃʀɪft] |
| mail order selling | Versandhandel (m) | [fɛɐ'zant͵handəl] |

105

medicine	**Medizin** (f)	[medi'tsi:n]
museum	**Museum** (n)	[mu'ze:ʊm]
news agency	**Nachrichtenagentur** (f)	['na:χrɪçtən?agɛnˌtu:ɐ]
newspaper	**Zeitung** (f)	['tsaɪtʊŋ]
nightclub	**Nachtklub** (m)	['naχtˌklʊp]
oil (petroleum)	**Erdöl** (n)	['e:ɐtˌ?ø:l]
courier services	**Kurierdienst** (m)	[ku'ri:ɐˌdi:nst]
pharmaceutics	**Pharmaindustrie** (f)	['faʁma?ɪndʊsˌtri:]
printing (industry)	**Druckindustrie** (f)	[dʁʊk·ɪndʊs'tri:]
pub	**Bar** (f)	[ba:ɐ]
publishing house	**Verlag** (m)	[fɛɐ'la:k]
radio (~ station)	**Rundfunk** (m)	['ʁʊntfʊŋk]
real estate	**Immobilien** (pl)	[ɪmo'bi:lɪən]
restaurant	**Restaurant** (n)	[ʁɛsto'ʁaŋ]
security company	**Sicherheitsagentur** (f)	['zɪçɐhaɪts·agɛn'tu:ɐ]
shop	**Laden** (m)	['la:dən]
sport	**Sport** (m)	[ʃpɔʁt]
stock exchange	**Börse** (f)	['bœʁzə]
supermarket	**Supermarkt** (m)	['zu:pɐˌmaʁkt]
swimming pool (public ~)	**Schwimmbad** (n)	['ʃvɪmba:t]
tailor shop	**Atelier** (n)	[ate'lie:]
television	**Fernsehen** (n)	['fɛʁnˌze:ən]
theatre	**Theater** (n)	[te'a:tɐ]
trade (commerce)	**Handel** (m)	['handəl]
transport companies	**Transporte** (pl)	[tʁans'pɔʁtə]
travel	**Reisen** (pl)	['ʁaɪzən]
undertakers	**Bestattungsinstitut** (n)	[bə'ʃtatʊŋs?ɪnstiˌtu:t]
veterinary surgeon	**Tierarzt** (m)	['ti:ɐˌ?aʁtst]
warehouse	**Warenlager** (n)	['va:ʁənˌla:gɐ]
waste collection	**Müllabfuhr** (f)	['mʏlˌ?apfu:ɐ]

Job. Business. Part 2

118. Show. Exhibition

exhibition, show	Ausstellung (f)	['aʊsˌʃtɛlʊŋ]
trade show	Handelsausstellung (f)	['handəlsˌaʊsʃtɛlʊŋ]
participation	Teilnahme (f)	['taɪlˌna:mə]
to participate (vi)	teilnehmen (vi)	['taɪlˌne:mən]
participant (exhibitor)	Teilnehmer (m)	['taɪlˌne:mɐ]
director	Direktor (m)	[di'ʀɛkto:ɐ]
organizers' office	Messeverwaltung (f)	['mɛsə·fɛɐ'valtʊŋ]
organizer	Organisator (m)	[ɔʁgani'za:to:ɐ]
to organize (vt)	veranstalten (vt)	[fɛɐ'ʔanʃtaltən]
participation form	Anmeldeformular (n)	['anmɛldə·fɔʁmuˌla:ɐ]
to fill in (vt)	ausfüllen (vt)	['aʊsˌfʏlən]
details	Details (pl)	[de'taɪs]
information	Information (f)	[ɪnfɔʁma'tsjo:n]
price (cost, rate)	Preis (m)	[pʀaɪs]
including	einschließlich	['aɪnʃli:slɪç]
to include (vt)	einschließen (vt)	['aɪnˌʃli:sən]
to pay (vi, vt)	zahlen (vt)	['tsa:lən]
registration fee	Anmeldegebühr (f)	['anmɛldə·gəˌby:ɐ]
entrance	Eingang (m)	['aɪnˌgaŋ]
pavilion, hall	Pavillon (m)	['pavɪljɔn]
to register (vt)	registrieren (vt)	[ʀegɪs'tʀi:ʀən]
badge (identity tag)	Namensschild (n)	['na:mənsˌʃɪlt]
stand	Stand (m)	[ʃtant]
to reserve, to book	reservieren (vt)	[ʀezɛʁ'vi:ʀən]
display case	Vitrine (f)	[vi'tʀi:nə]
spotlight	Strahler (m)	['ʃtʀa:lɐ]
design	Design (n)	[di'zaɪn]
to place (put, set)	stellen (vt)	['ʃtɛlən]
to be placed	gelegen sein	[gə'le:gən zaɪn]
distributor	Distributor (m)	[dɪstʀi'bu:to:ɐ]
supplier	Lieferant (m)	[ˌli:fə'ʀant]
to supply (vt)	liefern (vt)	['li:fɐn]
country	Land (n)	[lant]
foreign (adj)	ausländisch	['aʊsˌlɛndɪʃ]
product	Produkt (n)	[pʀo'dʊkt]
association	Assoziation (f)	[asɔtsia'tsjo:n]
conference hall	Konferenzraum (m)	[kɔnfe'ʀɛntsˌʀaʊm]

congress	Kongress (m)	[kɔŋ'grɛs]
contest (competition)	Wettbewerb (m)	['vɛtbə‚vɛʁp]

visitor (attendee)	Besucher (m)	[bə'zuːχɐ]
to visit (attend)	besuchen (vt)	[bə'zuːχən]
customer	Auftraggeber (m)	['aʊftʀaːk‚geːbɐ]

119. Mass Media

newspaper	Zeitung (f)	['tsaɪtʊŋ]
magazine	Zeitschrift (f)	['tsaɪtʃʀɪft]
press (printed media)	Presse (f)	['pʀɛsə]
radio	Rundfunk (m)	['ʀʊntfʊŋk]
radio station	Rundfunkstation (f)	['ʀʊntfʊŋk‚ʃtaˈtsjoːn]
television	Fernsehen (n)	['fɛʁn‚zeːən]

presenter, host	Moderator (m)	[modeˈʀaːtoːɐ]
newsreader	Sprecher (m)	['ʃpʀɛçɐ]
commentator	Kommentator (m)	[kɔmən'tatoːɐ]

journalist	Journalist (m)	[ʒʊʁnaˈlɪst]
correspondent (reporter)	Korrespondent (m)	[kɔʀɛspɔn'dɛnt]
press photographer	Bildberichterstatter (m)	['bɪlt‚bə'ʀɪçtʔɛɐ‚ʃtatɐ]
reporter	Reporter (m)	[ʀe'pɔʁtɐ]

editor	Redakteur (m)	[ʀedak'tøːɐ]
editor-in-chief	Chefredakteur (m)	['ʃɛf‚ʀedak‚tøːɐ]

to subscribe (to ...)	abonnieren (vt)	[abɔ'niːʀən]
subscription	Abonnement (n)	[abɔnə'maːŋ]
subscriber	Abonnent (m)	[abo'nɛnt]
to read (vi, vt)	lesen (vi, vt)	['leːzən]
reader	Leser (m)	['leːzɐ]

circulation (of a newspaper)	Auflage (f)	['aʊf‚laːgə]
monthly (adj)	monatlich	['moːnatlɪç]
weekly (adj)	wöchentlich	['vœçəntlɪç]
issue (edition)	Ausgabe (f)	['aʊs‚gaːbə]
new (~ issue)	neueste (~ Ausgabe)	['nɔɪstə]

headline	Titel (m)	['tiːtəl]
short article	Notiz (f)	[no'tiːts]
column (regular article)	Rubrik (f)	[ʀu'bʀiːk]
article	Artikel (m)	[‚aʁ'tiːkl]
page	Seite (f)	['zaɪtə]

reportage, report	Reportage (f)	[ʀepɔʁ'taːʒə]
event (happening)	Ereignis (n)	[ɛɐ'ʔaɪgnɪs]
sensation (news)	Sensation (f)	[zɛnza'tsjoːn]
scandal	Skandal (m)	[skan'daːl]
scandalous (adj)	skandalös	[skanda'løːs]
great (~ scandal)	groß	[gʀoːs]
programme (e.g. cooking ~)	Sendung (f)	['zɛndʊŋ]
interview	Interview (n)	['ɪntɐvjuː]

| live broadcast | Live-Übertragung (f) | ['laɪfʔyːbəˌtʁaːgʊŋ] |
| channel | Kanal (m) | [ka'naːl] |

120. Agriculture

agriculture	Landwirtschaft (f)	['lantvɪʁtʃaft]
peasant (masc.)	Bauer (m)	['bauɐ]
peasant (fem.)	Bäuerin (f)	['bɔɪəʁɪn]
farmer	Farmer (m)	['faʁmɐ]

| tractor | Traktor (m) | ['tʁaktoːɐ] |
| combine, harvester | Mähdrescher (m) | ['mɛːˌdʁɛʃɐ] |

plough	Pflug (m)	[pfluːk]
to plough (vi, vt)	pflügen (vt)	['pflyːgən]
ploughland	Acker (m)	['akɐ]
furrow (in field)	Furche (f)	['fuʁçə]

to sow (vi, vt)	säen (vt)	['zɛːən]
seeder	Sämaschine (f)	['zɛːˑmaˈʃiːnə]
sowing (process)	Saat (f)	['zaːt]

| scythe | Sense (f) | ['zɛnzə] |
| to mow, to scythe | mähen (vt) | ['mɛːən] |

| spade (tool) | Schaufel (f) | ['ʃaufəl] |
| to till (vt) | graben (vt) | ['gʁaːbən] |

hoe	Hacke (f)	['hakə]
to hoe, to weed	jäten (vt)	['jɛːtən]
weed (plant)	Unkraut (n)	['ʊnˌkʁaut]

watering can	Gießkanne (f)	['giːsˌkanə]
to water (plants)	gießen (vt)	['giːsən]
watering (act)	Bewässerung (f)	[bə'vɛsəʁʊŋ]

| pitchfork | Heugabel (f) | ['hɔɪˌgaːbəl] |
| rake | Rechen (m) | [ʁɛçən] |

fertiliser	Dünger (m)	['dʏŋɐ]
to fertilise (vt)	düngen (vt)	['dʏŋən]
manure (fertiliser)	Mist (m)	[mɪst]

field	Feld (n)	[fɛlt]
meadow	Wiese (f)	['viːzə]
vegetable garden	Gemüsegarten (m)	[gə'myːzəˌgaʁtən]
orchard (e.g. apple ~)	Obstgarten (m)	['oːpstˌgaʁtən]

to graze (vt)	weiden (vt)	['vaɪdən]
herdsman	Hirt (m)	[hɪʁt]
pasture	Weide (f)	['vaɪdə]

| cattle breeding | Viehzucht (f) | ['fiːˌtsʊxt] |
| sheep farming | Schafzucht (f) | ['ʃaːfˌtsʊxt] |

plantation	**Plantage** (f)	[plan'taːʒə]
row (garden bed ~s)	**Beet** (n)	['beːt]
hothouse	**Treibhaus** (n)	['tʀaɪp̩ˌhaʊs]

drought (lack of rain)	**Dürre** (f)	['dʏʀə]
dry (~ summer)	**dürr, trocken**	[dʏʀ], 'tʀɔkən]

grain	**Getreide** (n)	[gə'tʀaɪdə]
cereal crops	**Getreidepflanzen** (pl)	[gə'tʀaɪdəˌpflantsən]
to harvest, to gather	**ernten** (vt)	['ɛʀntən]

miller (person)	**Müller** (m)	['mʏlɐ]
mill (e.g. gristmill)	**Mühle** (f)	['myːlə]
to grind (grain)	**mahlen** (vt)	['maːlən]
flour	**Mehl** (n)	[meːl]
straw	**Stroh** (n)	[ʃtʀoː]

121. Building. Building process

building site	**Baustelle** (f)	['baʊʃtɛlə]
to build (vt)	**bauen** (vt)	['baʊən]
building worker	**Bauarbeiter** (m)	['baʊʔaʁˌbaɪtɐ]

project	**Projekt** (n)	[pʀo'jɛkt]
architect	**Architekt** (m)	[aʁçi'tɛkt]
worker	**Arbeiter** (m)	['aʁbaɪtɐ]

foundations (of a building)	**Fundament** (n)	[fʊnda'mɛnt]
roof	**Dach** (n)	[daχ]
foundation pile	**Pfahl** (m)	[pfaːl]
wall	**Wand** (f)	[vant]

reinforcing bars	**Bewehrungsstahl** (m)	[bə've:ʀʊŋsˌʃtaːl]
scaffolding	**Gerüst** (n)	[gə'ʀʏst]

concrete	**Beton** (m)	[be'tɔŋ]
granite	**Granit** (m)	[gʀa'niːt]
stone	**Stein** (m)	[ʃtaɪn]
brick	**Ziegel** (m)	['tsiːgəl]

sand	**Sand** (m)	[zant]
cement	**Zement** (m, n)	[tse'mɛnt]
plaster (for walls)	**Putz** (m)	[pʊts]
to plaster (vt)	**verputzen** (vt)	[fɛʀ'pʊtsən]

paint	**Farbe** (f)	['faʁbə]
to paint (~ a wall)	**färben** (vt)	['fɛʀbən]
barrel	**Fass** (n), **Tonne** (f)	[fas], ['tɔnə]

crane	**Kran** (m)	[kʀaːn]
to lift, to hoist (vt)	**aufheben** (vt)	['aʊfˌheːbən]
to lower (vt)	**herunterlassen** (vt)	[hɛ'ʀʊntəˌlasən]
bulldozer	**Planierraupe** (f)	[pla'niːɐˌʀaʊpə]
excavator	**Bagger** (m)	['bagɐ]

scoop, bucket	Baggerschaufel (f)	['bagəˌʃaʊfəl]
to dig (excavate)	graben (vt)	['ɡʀaːbən]
hard hat	Schutzhelm (m)	['ʃʊtsˌhɛlm]

122. Science. Research. Scientists

science	Wissenschaft (f)	['vɪsənˌʃaft]
scientific (adj)	wissenschaftlich	['vɪsənˌʃaftlɪç]
scientist	Wissenschaftler (m)	['vɪsənˌʃaftlɐ]
theory	Theorie (f)	[teo'ʀiː]

axiom	Axiom (n)	[a'ksɪoːm]
analysis	Analyse (f)	[ana'lyːzə]
to analyse (vt)	analysieren (vt)	[ˌanaly:'ziːʀən]
argument (strong ~)	Argument (n)	[aʁɡu'mɛnt]
substance (matter)	Substanz (f)	[zʊps'tants]

hypothesis	Hypothese (f)	[ˌhypo'teːzə]
dilemma	Dilemma (n)	[ˌdi'lɛma]
dissertation	Dissertation (f)	[dɪsɛʁta'tsjoːn]
dogma	Dogma (n)	['dɔgma]

doctrine	Doktrin (f)	[dɔk'tʀiːn]
research	Forschung (f)	['fɔʁʃʊŋ]
to research (vt)	forschen (vi)	['fɔʁʃən]
tests (laboratory ~)	Kontrolle (f)	[kɔn'tʀɔlə]
laboratory	Labor (n)	[la'boːɐ]

method	Methode (f)	[me'toːdə]
molecule	Molekül (n)	[mole'kyːl]
monitoring	Monitoring (n)	['mɔːnitoːʀɪŋ]
discovery (act, event)	Entdeckung (f)	[ɛnt'dɛkʊŋ]

postulate	Postulat (n)	[pɔstu'laːt]
principle	Prinzip (n)	[pʀɪn'tsiːp]
forecast	Prognose (f)	[pʀo'gnoːzə]
to forecast (vt)	prognostizieren (vt)	[pʀognɔsti'tsiːʀən]

synthesis	Synthese (f)	[zʏn'teːzə]
trend (tendency)	Tendenz (f)	[tɛn'dɛnts]
theorem	Theorem (n)	[teo'ʀeːm]

| teachings | Lehre (f) | ['leːʀə] |
| fact | Tatsache (f) | ['taːtˌzaxə] |

| expedition | Expedition (f) | [ɛkspedi'tsjoːn] |
| experiment | Experiment (n) | [ɛkspeʀi'mɛnt] |

academician	Akademiemitglied (n)	[akade'miːˌmɪtˌgliːt]
bachelor (e.g. ~ of Arts)	Bachelor (m)	['bɛtʃəlɐ]
doctor (PhD)	Doktor (m)	['dɔktoːɐ]
Associate Professor	Dozent (m)	[do'tsɛnt]
Master (e.g. ~ of Arts)	Magister (m)	[ma'gɪstɐ]
professor	Professor (m)	[pʀo'fɛsoːɐ]

Professions and occupations

job	Arbeit (f), Stelle (f)	['aʁbaɪt], ['ʃtɛlə]
staff (work force)	Belegschaft (f)	[bə'le:kʃaft]
personnel	Personal (n)	[pɛʁzo'na:l]
career	Karriere (f)	[ka'ʀɪe:ʀə]
prospects (chances)	Perspektive (f)	[pɛʁspɛk'ti:və]
skills (mastery)	Können (n)	['kœnən]
selection (screening)	Auswahl (f)	['aʊsva:l]
employment agency	Personalagentur (f)	[pɛʁzo'na:l·agɛn'tu:ɐ]
curriculum vitae, CV	Lebenslauf (m)	['le:bəns,laʊf]
job interview	Vorstellungsgespräch (n)	['fo:ɐʃtɛlʊŋs·gəʃpʀɛ:ç]
vacancy	Vakanz (f)	[va'kants]
salary, pay	Gehalt (n)	[gə'halt]
fixed salary	festes Gehalt (n)	['fɛstəs gə'halt]
pay, compensation	Arbeitslohn (m)	['aʁbaɪts,lo:n]
position (job)	Stellung (f)	['ʃtɛlʊŋ]
duty (of an employee)	Pflicht (f), Aufgabe (f)	[pflɪçt], ['aʊf,ga:bə]
range of duties	Aufgabenspektrum (n)	['aʊf,ga:bən'ʃpɛktʀʊm]
busy (I'm ~)	beschäftigt	[ˌbə'ʃɛftɪçt]
to fire (dismiss)	kündigen (vt)	['kʏndɪgən]
dismissal	Kündigung (f)	['kʏndɪgʊŋ]
unemployment	Arbeitslosigkeit (f)	['aʁbaɪts,lo:zɪçkaɪt]
unemployed (n)	Arbeitslose (m)	['aʁbaɪts,lo:zə]
retirement	Rente (f), Ruhestand (m)	['ʀɛntə], ['ʀu:əʃtant]
to retire (from job)	in Rente gehen	[ɪn 'ʀɛntə 'ge:ən]

director	Direktor (m)	[di'ʀɛkto:ɐ]
manager (director)	Leiter (m)	['laɪtə]
boss	Boss (m)	[bɔs]
superior	Vorgesetzte (m)	['fo:ɐgə,zɛtstə]
superiors	Vorgesetzten (pl)	['fo:ɐgə,zɛtstən]
president	Präsident (m)	[pʀɛzi'dɛnt]
chairman	Vorsitzende (m)	['fo:ɐ,zɪtsəndə]
deputy (substitute)	Stellvertreter (m)	['ʃtɛlfɛɐ,tʀe:tɐ]
assistant	Helfer (m)	['hɛlfɐ]

| secretary | Sekretär (m) | [zekʀe'tɛːɐ] |
| personal assistant | Privatsekretär (m) | [pʀi'vaːt·zekʀe'tɛːɐ] |

businessman	Geschäftsmann (m)	[gə'ʃɛfts,man]
entrepreneur	Unternehmer (m)	[,unte'neːmɐ]
founder	Gründer (m)	['gʀʏndɐ]
to found (vt)	gründen (vt)	['gʀʏndən]

founding member	Gründungsmitglied (n)	['gʀʏndʊŋs,mɪtgliːt]
partner	Partner (m)	['paʁtnɐ]
shareholder	Aktionär (m)	[aktsjo'nɛːɐ]

millionaire	Millionär (m)	[mɪljo'nɛːɐ]
billionaire	Milliardär (m)	[,mɪlɪaʁ'dɛːɐ]
owner, proprietor	Besitzer (m)	[bə'zɪtsɐ]
landowner	Landbesitzer (m)	['lantbə,zɪtsɐ]

client	Kunde (m)	['kʊndə]
regular client	Stammkunde (m)	['ʃtam,kʊndə]
buyer (customer)	Käufer (m)	['kɔɪfɐ]
visitor	Besucher (m)	[bə'zuːχɐ]

professional (n)	Fachmann (m)	['faχ,man]
expert	Experte (m)	[ɛks'pɛʁtə]
specialist	Spezialist (m)	[ʃpetsɪa'lɪst]

| banker | Bankier (m) | [baŋ'kɪeː] |
| broker | Makler (m) | ['maːklɐ] |

cashier	Kassierer (m)	[ka'siːʀɐ]
accountant	Buchhalter (m)	['buːχ,haltɐ]
security guard	Wächter (m)	['vɛçtɐ]

investor	Investor (m)	[ɪn'vɛstoːɐ]
debtor	Schuldner (m)	['ʃʊldnɐ]
creditor	Gläubiger (m)	['glɔɪbɪgɐ]
borrower	Kreditnehmer (m)	[kʀe'diːt,neːmɐ]

| importer | Importeur (m) | [ɪmpoʁ'tøːɐ] |
| exporter | Exporteur (m) | [ɛkspoʁ'tøːɐ] |

manufacturer	Hersteller (m)	['heːɐ,ʃtɛlɐ]
distributor	Distributor (m)	[dɪstʀi'buːtoːɐ]
middleman	Vermittler (m)	[fɛɐ'mɪtlɐ]

consultant	Berater (m)	[bə'ʀaːtɐ]
sales representative	Vertreter (m)	[fɛɐ'tʀeːtɐ]
agent	Agent (m)	[agɛnt]
insurance agent	Versicherungsagent (m)	[fɛɐ'zɪçəʀʊŋs·a'gɛnt]

125. Service professions

| cook | Koch (m) | [kɔχ] |
| chef (kitchen chef) | Chefkoch (m) | ['ʃɛf,kɔχ] |

113

baker	Bäcker (m)	['bɛkɐ]
barman	Barmixer (m)	['baːɐˌmɪksɐ]
waiter	Kellner (m)	['kɛlnɐ]
waitress	Kellnerin (f)	['kɛlnərɪn]

lawyer, barrister	Rechtsanwalt (m)	['rɛçtsʔanˌvalt]
lawyer (legal expert)	Jurist (m)	[juˈrɪst]
notary public	Notar (m)	[noˈtaːɐ]

electrician	Elektriker (m)	[ˌeˈlɛktrikɐ]
plumber	Klempner (m)	['klɛmpnɐ]
carpenter	Zimmermann (m)	['tsɪmɐˌman]

masseur	Masseur (m)	[maˈsøːɐ]
masseuse	Masseurin (f)	[maˈsøːrɪn]
doctor	Arzt (m)	[aʁtst]

taxi driver	Taxifahrer (m)	['taksiˌfaːʁɐ]
driver	Fahrer (m)	['faːʁɐ]
delivery man	Ausfahrer (m)	['aʊsˌfaːʁɐ]

chambermaid	Zimmermädchen (n)	['tsɪmɐˌmɛːtçən]
security guard	Wächter (m)	['vɛçtɐ]
flight attendant (fem.)	Flugbegleiterin (f)	['fluːkˌbəˌglaɪtərɪn]

schoolteacher	Lehrer (m)	['leːʁɐ]
librarian	Bibliothekar (m)	[biblioteˌkaːɐ]
translator	Übersetzer (m)	[ˌyːbɐˈzɛtsɐ]
interpreter	Dolmetscher (m)	['dɔlmɛtʃɐ]
guide	Fremdenführer (m)	['frɛmdənˌfyːʁɐ]

hairdresser	Friseur (m)	[friˈzøːɐ]
postman	Briefträger (m)	['briːfˌtrɛːgɐ]
salesman (store staff)	Verkäufer (m)	[fɛɐˈkɔɪfɐ]

gardener	Gärtner (m)	['gɛʁtnɐ]
domestic servant	Diener (m)	['diːnɐ]
maid (female servant)	Magd (f)	[maːkt]
cleaner (cleaning lady)	Putzfrau (f)	['pʊtsˌfraʊ]

126. Military professions and ranks

private	einfacher Soldat (m)	['aɪnfaxɐ zɔlˈdaːt]
sergeant	Feldwebel (m)	['fɛltˌveːbəl]
lieutenant	Leutnant (m)	['lɔɪtnant]
captain	Hauptmann (m)	['haʊptman]

major	Major (m)	[maˈjoːɐ]
colonel	Oberst (m)	['oːbɛst]
general	General (m)	[genəˈraːl]
marshal	Marschall (m)	['maʁʃal]
admiral	Admiral (m)	[ˌatmiˈraːl]
military (n)	Militärperson (f)	[miliˈtɛːɐˌpɛʁˈzoːn]
soldier	Soldat (m)	[zɔlˈdaːt]

officer	Offizier (m)	[ɔfi'tsi:ɐ]
commander	Kommandeur (m)	[kɔman'dø:ɐ]

border guard	Grenzsoldat (m)	['gʀɛnts·zɔl‚da:t]
radio operator	Funker (m)	['fuŋkɐ]
scout (searcher)	Aufklärer (m)	['aʊf‚klɛ:ʀɐ]
pioneer (sapper)	Pionier (m)	[pɪo'ni:ɐ]
marksman	Schütze (m)	['ʃʏtsə]
navigator	Steuermann (m)	['ʃtɔɪɐ‚man]

127. Officials. Priests

king	König (m)	['kø:nɪç]
queen	Königin (f)	['kø:nɪgɪn]

prince	Prinz (m)	[pʀɪnts]
princess	Prinzessin (f)	[pʀɪn'tsɛsɪn]

czar	Zar (m)	[tsa:ɐ]
czarina	Zarin (f)	['tsa:ʀɪn]

president	Präsident (m)	[pʀɛzi'dɛnt]
Secretary (minister)	Minister (m)	[mi'nɪstɐ]
prime minister	Ministerpräsident (m)	[mi'nɪstɐ·pʀɛzi‚dɛnt]
senator	Senator (m)	[ze'na:to:ɐ]

diplomat	Diplomat (m)	[‚diplo'ma:t]
consul	Konsul (m)	['kɔnzʊl]
ambassador	Botschafter (m)	['bo:tʃaftɐ]
counselor (diplomatic officer)	Ratgeber (m)	['ʀa:t‚ge:bɐ]

official, functionary (civil servant)	Beamte (m)	[bə'ʔamtə]
prefect	Präfekt (m)	[pʀɛ'fɛkt]
mayor	Bürgermeister (m)	['bʏʁgɐ‚maɪstɐ]

judge	Richter (m)	['ʀɪçtɐ]
prosecutor	Staatsanwalt (m)	['ʃta:ts?an‚valt]

missionary	Missionar (m)	[‚mɪsjo'na:ɐ]
monk	Mönch (m)	[mœnç]
abbot	Abt (m)	[apt]
rabbi	Rabbiner (m)	[ʀa'bi:nɐ]

vizier	Wesir (m)	[ve'zi:ɐ]
shah	Schah (n)	[ʃaχ]
sheikh	Scheich (m)	[ʃaɪç]

128. Agricultural professions

beekeeper	Bienenzüchter (m)	['bi:nən‚tsʏçtɐ]
shepherd	Hirt (m)	[hɪʁt]

agronomist	Agronom (m)	[agʀoˈnoːm]
cattle breeder	Viehzüchter (m)	[ˈfiːˌtsʏçtɐ]
veterinary surgeon	Tierarzt (m)	[ˈtiːɐˌʔaʁtst]

farmer	Farmer (m)	[ˈfaʁmɐ]
winemaker	Winzer (m)	[ˈvɪntsɐ]
zoologist	Zoologe (m)	[tsooˈloːgə]
cowboy	Cowboy (m)	[ˈkaʊbɔɪ]

129. Art professions

| actor | Schauspieler (m) | [ˈʃaʊˌʃpiːlɐ] |
| actress | Schauspielerin (f) | [ˈʃaʊˌʃpiːləʀɪn] |

| singer (masc.) | Sänger (m) | [ˈzɛŋɐ] |
| singer (fem.) | Sängerin (f) | [ˈzɛŋəʀɪn] |

| dancer (masc.) | Tänzer (m) | [ˈtɛntsɐ] |
| dancer (fem.) | Tänzerin (f) | [ˈtɛntsəʀɪn] |

| performer (masc.) | Künstler (m) | [ˈkʏnstlɐ] |
| performer (fem.) | Künstlerin (f) | [ˈkʏnstləʀɪn] |

musician	Musiker (m)	[ˈmuːzikɐ]
pianist	Pianist (m)	[pɪaˈnɪst]
guitar player	Gitarrist (m)	[gitaˈʀɪst]

conductor (orchestra ~)	Dirigent (m)	[ˌdiʀiˈgɛnt]
composer	Komponist (m)	[ˌkɔmpoˈnɪst]
impresario	Manager (m)	[ˈmɛnɪdʒɐ]

film director	Regisseur (m)	[ʀeʒɪˈsøːɐ]
producer	Produzent (m)	[pʀoduˈtsɛnt]
scriptwriter	Drehbuchautor (m)	[ˈdʀeːbuːxˌʔaʊtoːɐ]
critic	Kritiker (m)	[ˈkʀiːtɪkɐ]

writer	Schriftsteller (m)	[ˈʃʀɪftˌʃtɛlɐ]
poet	Dichter (m)	[ˈdɪçtɐ]
sculptor	Bildhauer (m)	[ˈbɪltˌhaʊɐ]
artist (painter)	Maler (m)	[ˈmaːlɐ]

juggler	Jongleur (m)	[ʒɔŋˈgløːɐ]
clown	Clown (m)	[klaʊn]
acrobat	Akrobat (m)	[akʀoˈbaːt]
magician	Zauberkünstler (m)	[ˈtsaʊbɐˌkʏnstlɐ]

130. Various professions

doctor	Arzt (m)	[aʁtst]
nurse	Krankenschwester (f)	[kʀaŋkənˌʃvɛstɐ]
psychiatrist	Psychiater (m)	[psyˈçiaːtɐ]
dentist	Zahnarzt (m)	[ˈtsaːnˌʔaʁtst]

surgeon	Chirurg (m)	[çi'ʁuʁk]
astronaut	Astronaut (m)	[astʁo'naʊt]
astronomer	Astronom (m)	[astʁo'noːm]
pilot	Pilot (m)	[pi'loːt]

driver (of a taxi, etc.)	Fahrer (m)	['faːʁɐ]
train driver	Lokführer (m)	['lɔkˌfyːʁɐ]
mechanic	Mechaniker (m)	[me'çaːnikɐ]

miner	Bergarbeiter (m)	['bɛʁkʔaʁˌbaɪtɐ]
worker	Arbeiter (m)	['aʁbaɪtɐ]
locksmith	Schlosser (m)	['ʃlɔsɐ]
joiner (carpenter)	Tischler (m)	['tɪʃlɐ]
turner (lathe operator)	Dreher (m)	['dʁeːɐ]
building worker	Bauarbeiter (m)	['baʊʔaʁˌbaɪtɐ]
welder	Schweißer (m)	['ʃvaɪsɐ]

professor (title)	Professor (m)	[pʁo'fɛsoːɐ]
architect	Architekt (m)	[aʁçi'tɛkt]
historian	Historiker (m)	[hɪs'toːʁikɐ]
scientist	Wissenschaftler (m)	['vɪsənˌʃaftlɐ]
physicist	Physiker (m)	['fyːzikɐ]
chemist (scientist)	Chemiker (m)	['çeːmikɐ]

archaeologist	Archäologe (m)	[aʁçɛo'loːgə]
geologist	Geologe (m)	[geo'loːgə]
researcher (scientist)	Forscher (m)	['fɔʁʃɐ]

| babysitter | Kinderfrau (f) | ['kɪndɐˌfʁaʊ] |
| teacher, educator | Lehrer (m) | ['leːʁɐ] |

editor	Redakteur (m)	[ʁedak'tøːɐ]
editor-in-chief	Chefredakteur (m)	['ʃɛf·ʁedakˌtøːɐ]
correspondent	Korrespondent (m)	[kɔʁɛspɔn'dɛnt]
typist (fem.)	Schreibkraft (f)	['ʃʁaɪpˌkʁaft]

designer	Designer (m)	[di'zaɪnɐ]
computer expert	Computerspezialist (m)	[kɔm'pjuːtɐ·ʃpetsɪa'lɪst]
programmer	Programmierer (m)	[pʁogʁa'miːʁɐ]
engineer (designer)	Ingenieur (m)	[ɪnʒe'nɪøːɐ]

sailor	Seemann (m)	['zeːman]
seaman	Matrose (m)	[ma'tʁoːzə]
rescuer	Retter (m)	['ʁɛtɐ]

firefighter	Feuerwehrmann (m)	['fɔɪveːɐˌman]
police officer	Polizist (m)	[poli'tsɪst]
watchman	Nachtwächter (m)	['naxtˌvɛçtɐ]
detective	Detektiv (m)	[detɛk'tiːf]

customs officer	Zollbeamter (m)	['tsɔl·bəˌʔamtɐ]
bodyguard	Leibwächter (m)	['laɪpˌvɛçtɐ]
prison officer	Gefängniswärter (m)	[gə'fɛŋnɪs·vɛʁtɐ]
inspector	Inspektor (m)	[ɪn'spɛktoːɐ]
sportsman	Sportler (m)	['ʃpɔʁtlɐ]
trainer, coach	Trainer (m)	['tʁɛːnɐ]

butcher	**Fleischer** (m)	['flaɪʃɐ]
cobbler (shoe repairer)	**Schuster** (m)	['ʃuːstɐ]
merchant	**Geschäftsmann** (m)	[gə'ʃɛfts͵man]
loader (person)	**Ladearbeiter** (m)	['laːdə͵aʁbaɪtɐ]

fashion designer	**Modedesigner** (m)	['moːdə·di'zaɪnɐ]
model (fem.)	**Modell** (n)	[mo'dɛl]

131. Occupations. Social status

schoolboy	**Schüler** (m)	['ʃyːlɐ]
student (college ~)	**Student** (m)	[ʃtu'dɛnt]

philosopher	**Philosoph** (m)	[filo'zoːf]
economist	**Ökonom** (m)	[øko'noːm]
inventor	**Erfinder** (m)	[ɛɐ'fɪndɐ]

unemployed (n)	**Arbeitslose** (m)	['aʁbaɪts͵loːzə]
retiree, pensioner	**Rentner** (m)	['ʀɛntnɐ]
spy, secret agent	**Spion** (m)	[ʃpi'oːn]

prisoner	**Gefangene** (m)	[gə'faŋənə]
striker	**Streikender** (m)	['ʃtʀaɪkəndɐ]
bureaucrat	**Bürokrat** (m)	[͵byʀo'kʀaːt]
traveller (globetrotter)	**Reisende** (m)	['ʀaɪzəndə]

gay, homosexual (n)	**Homosexuelle** (m)	[homozɛ'ksuɛlə]
hacker	**Hacker** (m)	['hɛkɐ]
hippie	**Hippie** (m)	['hɪpi]

bandit	**Bandit** (m)	[ban'diːt]
hit man, killer	**Killer** (m)	['kɪlɐ]
drug addict	**Drogenabhängiger** (m)	['dʀoːgən͵ʔaphɛŋɪgɐ]
drug dealer	**Drogenhändler** (m)	['dʀoːgən͵hɛndlɐ]
prostitute (fem.)	**Prostituierte** (f)	[͵pʀostitu'iːɐtə]
pimp	**Zuhälter** (m)	['tsuː͵hɛltɐ]

sorcerer	**Zauberer** (m)	['tsaʊbəʀɐ]
sorceress (evil ~)	**Zauberin** (f)	['tsaʊbəʀɪn]
pirate	**Seeräuber** (m)	['zeː͵ʀɔɪbɐ]
slave	**Sklave** (m)	['sklaːvə]
samurai	**Samurai** (m)	[zamu'ʀaɪ]
savage (primitive)	**Wilde** (m)	['vɪldə]

Sports

sportsman	**Sportler** (m)	['ʃpɔʁtlɐ]
kind of sport	**Sportart** (f)	['ʃpɔʁtʔaːɐt]
basketball	**Basketball** (m)	['baːskətbal]
basketball player	**Basketballspieler** (m)	['baːskətbalˌʃpiːlɐ]
baseball	**Baseball** (m, n)	['bɛɪsbɔːl]
baseball player	**Baseballspieler** (m)	['beɪsbɔːlˌʃpiːlɐ]
football	**Fußball** (m)	['fuːsbal]
football player	**Fußballspieler** (m)	['fuːsbalˌʃpiːlɐ]
goalkeeper	**Torwart** (m)	['toːɐˌvaʁt]
ice hockey	**Eishockey** (n)	['aɪsˌhɔki]
ice hockey player	**Eishockeyspieler** (m)	['aɪshɔkiˌʃpiːlɐ]
volleyball	**Volleyball** (m)	['vɔliˌbal]
volleyball player	**Volleyballspieler** (m)	['vɔlibalˌʃpiːlɐ]
boxing	**Boxen** (n)	['bɔksən]
boxer	**Boxer** (m)	['bɔksɐ]
wrestling	**Ringen** (n)	['ʁɪŋən]
wrestler	**Ringkämpfer** (m)	['ʁɪŋˌkɛmpfɐ]
karate	**Karate** (n)	[ka'ʁaːtə]
karate fighter	**Karatekämpfer** (m)	[ka'ʁaːtəˌkɛmpfɐ]
judo	**Judo** (n)	['juːdɔ]
judo athlete	**Judoka** (m)	[ju'doːka]
tennis	**Tennis** (n)	['tɛnɪs]
tennis player	**Tennisspieler** (m)	['tɛnɪsˌʃpiːlɐ]
swimming	**Schwimmen** (n)	['ʃvɪmən]
swimmer	**Schwimmer** (m)	['ʃvɪmɐ]
fencing	**Fechten** (n)	['fɛçtən]
fencer	**Fechter** (m)	['fɛçtɐ]
chess	**Schach** (n)	[ʃax]
chess player	**Schachspieler** (m)	['ʃaxˌʃpiːlɐ]
alpinism	**Bergsteigen** (n)	['bɛʁkˌʃtaɪgən]
alpinist	**Bergsteiger** (m)	['bɛʁkˌʃtaɪgɐ]
running	**Lauf** (m)	[laʊf]

runner	Läufer (m)	['lɔɪfɐ]
athletics	Leichtathletik (f)	['laɪçt?at͜le:tik]
athlete	Athlet (m)	[at'le:t]

| horse riding | Pferdesport (m) | ['pfe:ɐdəʃpɔɐt] |
| horse rider | Reiter (m) | ['ʀaɪtɐ] |

figure skating	Eiskunstlauf (m)	['aɪskʊnst͜laʊf]
figure skater (masc.)	Eiskunstläufer (m)	['aɪskʊnst͜lɔɪfɐ]
figure skater (fem.)	Eiskunstläuferin (f)	['aɪskʊnst͜lɔɪfəʀɪn]

| powerlifting | Gewichtheben (n) | [gə'vɪçt͜he:bən] |
| powerlifter | Gewichtheber (m) | [gə'vɪçt͜he:bɐ] |

| car racing | Autorennen (n) | ['aʊtoʀɛnən] |
| racer (driver) | Rennfahrer (m) | ['ʀɛn͜fa:ʀɐ] |

| cycling | Radfahren (n) | ['ʀa:t͜fa:ʀən] |
| cyclist | Radfahrer (m) | ['ʀa:t͜fa:ʀɐ] |

long jump	Weitsprung (m)	['vaɪtʃpʀʊŋ]
pole vaulting	Stabhochsprung (m)	['ʃta:pho:χʃpʀʊŋ]
jumper	Springer (m)	['ʃpʀɪŋɐ]

133. Kinds of sports. Miscellaneous

American football	American Football (m)	[ɛ'mɛʀɪkən 'fʊtbo:l]
badminton	Federballspiel (n)	['fe:dɐˌbal·ʃpi:l]
biathlon	Biathlon (n)	['bi:atlɔn]
billiards	Billard (n)	['bɪljaɐt]

bobsleigh	Bob (m)	[bɔp]
bodybuilding	Bodybuilding (n)	['bɔdiˌbɪldɪŋ]
water polo	Wasserballspiel (n)	['vasɐbalʃpi:l]
handball	Handball (m)	['hant͜bal]
golf	Golf (n)	[gɔlf]

rowing	Rudern (n)	['ʀu:dɐn]
scuba diving	Tauchen (n)	['taʊχən]
cross-country skiing	Skilanglauf (m)	['ʃi:ˌlantlɔɪf]
table tennis (ping-pong)	Tischtennis (n)	[tɪʃtɛnɪs]

sailing	Segelsport (m)	['ze:gəlʃpɔɐt]
rally	Rallye (f, n)	['ʀali]
rugby	Rugby (n)	['ʀakbi]
snowboarding	Snowboard (n)	['sno:ˌbo:ɐt]
archery	Bogenschießen (n)	['bo:gənˌʃi:sən]

134. Gym

| barbell | Hantel (f) | ['hantəl] |
| dumbbells | Hanteln (pl) | ['hantəln] |

training machine	Trainingsgerät (n)	['trɛ:nɪŋs·gə'rɛ:t]
exercise bicycle	Fahrradtrainer (m)	['faːɐra:ˌtrɛ:nɐ]
treadmill	Laufband (n)	['lauf͜bant]

horizontal bar	Reck (n)	[rɛk]
parallel bars	Barren (m)	['barən]
vault (vaulting horse)	Sprungpferd (n)	['ʃprɪŋˌpfe:ɐt]
mat (exercise ~)	Matte (f)	['matə]

skipping rope	Sprungseil (n)	['ʃprʊŋˌzaɪl]
aerobics	Aerobic (n)	[ɛ'ro:bɪk]
yoga	Yoga (m, n)	['jo:ga]

135. Ice hockey

ice hockey	Eishockey (n)	['aɪsˌhɔki]
ice hockey player	Eishockeyspieler (m)	['aɪshɔkiˌʃpi:lɐ]
to play ice hockey	Hockey spielen	['hɔki 'ʃpi:lən]
ice	Eis (n)	[aɪs]

puck	Puck (m)	[pʊk]
ice hockey stick	Hockeyschläger (m)	['hɔkiˌʃlɛ:gɐ]
ice skates	Schlittschuhe (pl)	['ʃlɪtˌʃu:ə]

| board (ice hockey rink ~) | Bord (m) | [bɔɐt] |
| shot | Schuss (m) | [ʃʊs] |

goaltender	Torwart (m)	['to:ɐˌvaɐt]
goal (score)	Tor (n)	[to:ɐ]
to score a goal	ein Tor schießen	[aɪn 'to:ɐ 'ʃi:sən]

period	Drittel (n)	['drɪtəl]
second period	zweites Drittel (n)	['tsvaɪtəs 'drɪtəl]
substitutes bench	Ersatzbank (f)	[ɛɐ'zatsˌbaŋk]

136. Football

football	Fußball (m)	['fu:sbal]
football player	Fußballspieler (m)	['fu:sbalˌʃpi:lɐ]
to play football	Fußball spielen	['fu:sbal 'ʃpi:lən]

major league	Oberliga (f)	['o:bɐˌli:ga]
football club	Fußballclub (m)	['fu:sbalˌklʊp]
coach	Trainer (m)	['trɛ:nɐ]
owner, proprietor	Besitzer (m)	[bə'zɪtsɐ]

team	Mannschaft (f)	['manʃaft]
team captain	Mannschaftskapitän (m)	['manʃafts·kapiˌtɛ:n]
player	Spieler (m)	['ʃpi:lɐ]
substitute	Ersatzspieler (m)	[ɛɐ'zatsˌʃpi:lɐ]
forward	Stürmer (m)	['ʃtʏrmɐ]
centre forward	Mittelstürmer (m)	['mɪtəlˌʃtʏrmɐ]

scorer	Torjäger (m)	['toːɐˌjɛːgɐ]
defender, back	Verteidiger (m)	[fɛɐ'taɪdɪgɐ]
midfielder, halfback	Läufer (m)	['lɔɪfɐ]

match	Spiel (n)	[ʃpiːl]
to meet (vi, vt)	sich begegnen	[zɪç bə'geːgnən]
final	Finale (n)	[fi'naːlə]
semi-final	Halbfinale (n)	['halpˌfiˌnaːlə]
championship	Meisterschaft (f)	['maɪstɐˌʃaft]

period, half	Halbzeit (f)	['halpˌtsaɪt]
first period	erste Halbzeit (f)	['ɛɐstə 'halpˌtsaɪt]
half-time	Halbzeit (f)	['halpˌtsaɪt]

goal	Tor (n)	[toːɐ]
goalkeeper	Torwart (m)	['toːɐˌvaɐt]
goalpost	Torpfosten (m)	['toːɐˌpfɔstən]
crossbar	Torlatte (f)	['toːɐˌlatə]
net	Netz (n)	[nɛts]
to concede a goal	ein Tor zulassen	[aɪn 'toːɐ 'tsuːˌlasn]

ball	Ball (m)	[bal]
pass	Pass (m)	[pas]
kick	Schuss (m)	[ʃʊs]
to kick (~ the ball)	schießen (vi)	['ʃiːsən]
free kick (direct ~)	Freistoß (m)	['fʀaɪˌʃtoːs]
corner kick	Eckball (m)	['ɛkˌbal]

attack	Attacke (f)	[a'takə]
counterattack	Gegenangriff (m)	['geːgənˌʔangʀɪf]
combination	Kombination (f)	[kɔmbina'tsjoːn]

referee	Schiedsrichter (m)	['ʃiːtsˌʀɪçtɐ]
to blow the whistle	pfeifen (vi)	['pfaɪfən]
whistle (sound)	Pfeife (f)	['pfaɪfə]
foul, misconduct	Foul (n)	[faʊl]
to commit a foul	foulen (vt)	['faʊlən]
to send off	vom Platz verweisen	[fɔm plats fɛɐ'vaɪzən]

yellow card	gelbe Karte (f)	['gɛlbə 'kaɐtə]
red card	rote Karte (f)	['ʀoːtə 'kaɐtə]
disqualification	Disqualifizierung (f)	[dɪskvalifi'tsiːʀʊŋ]
to disqualify (vt)	disqualifizieren (vt)	[dɪskvalifi'tsiːʀən]

penalty kick	Elfmeter (m)	[ɛlf'meːtɐ]
wall	Mauer (f)	['maʊɐ]
to score (vi, vt)	ein Tor schießen	[aɪn 'toːɐ 'ʃiːsən]
goal (score)	Tor (n)	[toːɐ]
to score a goal	ein Tor schießen	[aɪn 'toːɐ 'ʃiːsən]

substitution	Wechsel (m)	['vɛksəl]
to replace (a player)	ersetzen (vt)	[ɛɐ'zɛtsən]
rules	Regeln (pl)	['ʀeːgəln]
tactics	Taktik (f)	['taktɪk]
stadium	Stadion (n)	['ʃtaːdjɔn]
terrace	Tribüne (f)	[tʀi'byːnə]

| fan, supporter | Anhänger (m) | ['an‚hɛŋɐ] |
| to shout (vi) | schreien (vi) | ['ʃʀaɪən] |

| scoreboard | Anzeigetafel (f) | ['antsaɪgə‚ta:fəl] |
| score | Ergebnis (n) | [ɛɐ'ge:pnɪs] |

| defeat | Niederlage (f) | ['ni:dɐ‚la:gə] |
| to lose (not win) | verlieren (vt) | [fɛɐ'li:ʀən] |

| draw | Unentschieden (n) | ['ʊnʔɛntʃi:dən] |
| to draw (vi) | unentschieden spielen | ['ʊnʔɛntʃi:dən 'ʃpi:lən] |

victory	Sieg (m)	[zi:k]
to win (vi, vt)	gewinnen (vt)	[gə'vɪnən]
champion	Meister (m)	['maɪstɐ]
best (adj)	der beste	[de:ɐ 'bɛstə]
to congratulate (vt)	gratulieren (vi)	[gʀatu'li:ʀən]

commentator	Kommentator (m)	[kɔmən'tato:ɐ]
to commentate (vt)	kommentieren (vt)	[kɔmɛn'ti:ʀən]
broadcast	Übertragung (f)	[‚y:bɐ'tʀa:gʊŋ]

137. Alpine skiing

skis	Ski (pl)	[ʃi:]
to ski (vi)	Ski laufen	['ʃi: 'laʊfən]
mountain-ski resort	Skiort (m)	['ʃi:‚ʔɔʁt]
ski lift	Skilift (m)	['ʃi:‚lɪft]

ski poles	Skistöcke (pl)	['ʃi:‚ʃtœkə]
slope	Abhang (m)	['ap‚haŋ]
slalom	Slalom (m)	['sla:lɔm]

138. Tennis. Golf

golf	Golf (n)	[gɔlf]
golf club	Golfklub (m)	['gɔlf‚klʊp]
golfer	Golfspieler (m)	['gɔlfʃpi:lɐ]

hole	Loch (n)	[lɔχ]
club	Schläger (m)	['ʃlɛ:gɐ]
golf trolley	Golfwagen (m)	['gɔlf‚va:gən]

| tennis | Tennis (n) | ['tɛnɪs] |
| tennis court | Tennisplatz (m) | ['tɛnɪs‚plats] |

| serve | Aufschlag (m) | ['aʊfʃla:k] |
| to serve (vt) | angeben (vt) | ['an‚ge:bən] |

racket	Tennisschläger (m)	['tɛnɪsʃlɛ:gɐ]
net	Netz (n)	[nɛts]
ball	Ball (m)	[bal]

139. Chess

chess	Schach (n)	[ʃaχ]
chessmen	Schachfiguren (pl)	[ˈʃaχˌfiˌguːʀən]
chess player	Schachspieler (m)	[ˈʃaχˌʃpiːlɐ]
chessboard	Schachbrett (n)	[ˈʃaχˌbʀɛt]
chessman	Figur (f)	[fiˈguːɐ]
White (white pieces)	Weißen (pl)	[ˈvaɪsən]
Black (black pieces)	Schwarze (pl)	[ˈʃvaʁtsə]
pawn	Bauer (m)	[ˈbaʊɐ]
bishop	Läufer (m)	[ˈlɔɪfɐ]
knight	Springer (m)	[ˈʃpʀɪŋɐ]
rook	Turm (m)	[tʊʁm]
queen	Königin (f)	[ˈkøːnɪɡɪn]
king	König (m)	[ˈkøːnɪç]
move	Zug (m)	[tsuːk]
to move (vi, vt)	einen Zug machen	[ˈaɪnən tsuːk ˈmaχən]
to sacrifice (vt)	opfern (vt)	[ˈɔpfɐn]
castling	Rochade (f)	[ʀɔˈχaːdə]
check	Schach (n)	[ʃaχ]
checkmate	Matt (n)	[mat]
chess tournament	Schachturnier (n)	[ˈʃaχˌtʊʁˌniːɐ]
Grand Master	Großmeister (m)	[ˈɡʀoːsˌmaɪstɐ]
combination	Kombination (f)	[kɔmbinaˈtsjoːn]
game (in chess)	Partie (f)	[paʁˈtiː]
draughts	Damespiel (n)	[ˈdaːməˌʃpiːl]

140. Boxing

boxing	Boxen (n)	[ˈbɔksən]
fight (bout)	Boxkampf (m)	[ˈbɔksˌkampf]
boxing match	Zweikampf (m)	[ˈtsvaɪˌkampf]
round (in boxing)	Runde (f)	[ˈʀʊndə]
ring	Ring (m)	[ʀɪŋ]
gong	Gong (m, n)	[ɡɔŋ]
punch	Schlag (m)	[ʃlaːk]
knockdown	Knockdown (m)	[nɔkˈdaʊn]
knockout	Knockout (m)	[nɔkˈʔaʊt]
to knock out	k.o. schlagen (vt)	[kaːˈʔoː ˈʃlaːɡən]
boxing glove	Boxhandschuh (m)	[ˈbɔksˌhantˌʃuː]
referee	Schiedsrichter (m)	[ˈʃiːtsˌʀɪçtɐ]
lightweight	Leichtgewicht (n)	[ˈlaɪçtˌɡəˌvɪçt]
middleweight	Mittelgewicht (n)	[ˈmɪtəlˌɡəˌvɪçt]
heavyweight	Schwergewicht (n)	[ˈʃveːɐˌɡəˌvɪçt]

141. Sports. Miscellaneous

Olympic Games	Olympische Spiele (pl)	[o'lʏmpɪʃə 'ʃpi:lə]
winner	Sieger (m)	['zi:gɐ]
to be winning	siegen (vi)	['zi:gən]
to win (vi)	gewinnen (vt)	[gə'vɪnən]
leader	Tabellenführer (m)	[ta'bɛlən‚fy:ʁɐ]
to lead (vi)	führen (vi)	['fy:ʁən]
first place	der erste Platz	[de:ɐ 'ɛʁstə plats]
second place	der zweite Platz	[de:ɐ 'tsvaɪtə plats]
third place	der dritte Platz	[de:ɐ 'dʁɪtə plats]
medal	Medaille (f)	[me'daljə]
trophy	Trophäe (f)	[tʁo'fɛ:ə]
prize cup (trophy)	Pokal (m)	[pɔ'ka:l]
prize (in game)	Preis (m)	[pʁaɪs]
main prize	Hauptpreis (m)	['haʊpt‚pʁaɪs]
record	Rekord (m)	[ʁe'kɔʁt]
to set a record	einen Rekord aufstellen	['aɪnən ʁe'kɔʁt 'aʊfʃtɛlən]
final	Finale (n)	[fi'na:lə]
final (adj)	Final-	[fi'na:l]
champion	Meister (m)	['maɪstɐ]
championship	Meisterschaft (f)	['maɪstɐʃaft]
stadium	Stadion (n)	['ʃta:djɔn]
terrace	Tribüne (f)	[tʁi'by:nə]
fan, supporter	Fan (m)	[fɛn]
opponent, rival	Gegner (m)	['ge:gnɐ]
start (start line)	Start (m)	[ʃtaʁt]
finish line	Ziel (n), Finish (n)	[tsi:l], ['fɪnɪʃ]
defeat	Niederlage (f)	['ni:dɐ‚la:gə]
to lose (not win)	verlieren (vt)	[fɛɐ'li:ʁən]
referee	Schiedsrichter (m)	['ʃi:ts‚ʁɪçtɐ]
jury (judges)	Jury (f)	['ʒy:ʁi]
score	Ergebnis (n)	[ɛɐ'ge:pnɪs]
draw	Unentschieden (n)	['ʊn?ɛntʃi:dən]
to draw (vi)	unentschieden spielen	['ʊn?ɛntʃi:dən 'ʃpi:lən]
point	Punkt (m)	[pʊŋkt]
result (final score)	Ergebnis (n)	[ɛɐ'ge:pnɪs]
period	Spielabschnitt (m)	['ʃpi:l‚?apʃnɪt]
half-time	Halbzeit (f), Pause (f)	['halp‚tsaɪt], ['paʊzə]
doping	Doping (n)	['do:pɪŋ]
to penalise (vt)	bestrafen (vt)	[bə'ʃtʁa:fən]
to disqualify (vt)	disqualifizieren (vt)	[dɪskvalifi'tsi:ʁən]
apparatus	Sportgerät (n)	['ʃpɔʁt·gə‚ʁɛ:t]
javelin	Speer (m)	[ʃpe:ɐ]

shot (metal ball)	**Kugel** (f)	['ku:gəl]
ball (snooker, etc.)	**Kugel** (f)	['ku:gəl]
aim (target)	**Ziel** (n)	[tsi:l]
target	**Zielscheibe** (f)	['tsi:l ʃaɪbə]
to shoot (vi)	**schießen** (vi)	['ʃi:sən]
accurate (~ shot)	**genau**	[gə'naʊ]
trainer, coach	**Trainer** (m)	['tʀɛ:nɐ]
to train (sb)	**trainieren** (vt)	[tʀɛ'ni:ʀən]
to train (vi)	**trainieren** (vi)	[tʀɛ'ni:ʀən]
training	**Training** (n)	['tʀɛ:nɪŋ]
gym	**Turnhalle** (f)	['tʊʀn halə]
exercise (physical)	**Übung** (f)	['y:bʊŋ]
warm-up (athlete ~)	**Aufwärmen** (n)	['aʊf vɛʀmən]

Education

142. School

school	**Schule** (f)	['ʃuːlə]
headmaster	**Schulleiter** (m)	['ʃuːlˌlaɪtə]
student (m)	**Schüler** (m)	['ʃyːlɐ]
student (f)	**Schülerin** (f)	['ʃyːlərɪn]
schoolboy	**Schuljunge** (m)	['ʃuːlˌjʊŋə]
schoolgirl	**Schulmädchen** (f)	['ʃuːlˌmɛːtçən]
to teach (sb)	**lehren** (vt)	['leːʀən]
to learn (language, etc.)	**lernen** (vt)	['lɛʀnən]
to learn by heart	**auswendig lernen**	['aʊsˌvɛndɪç 'lɛʀnən]
to learn (~ to count, etc.)	**lernen** (vi)	['lɛʀnən]
to be at school	**in der Schule sein**	[ɪn deːɐ 'ʃuːlə zaɪn]
to go to school	**die Schule besuchen**	[di 'ʃuːlə bə'zuːχən]
alphabet	**Alphabet** (n)	[alfa'beːt]
subject (at school)	**Fach** (n)	[faχ]
classroom	**Klassenraum** (m)	['klasənˌʀaʊm]
lesson	**Stunde** (f)	['ʃtʊndə]
playtime, break	**Pause** (f)	['paʊzə]
school bell	**Schulglocke** (f)	['ʃuːlˌglɔkə]
school desk	**Schulbank** (f)	['ʃuːlˌbaŋk]
blackboard	**Tafel** (f)	['taːfəl]
mark	**Note** (f)	['noːtə]
good mark	**gute Note** (f)	['guːtə 'noːtə]
bad mark	**schlechte Note** (f)	['ʃlɛçtə 'noːtə]
to give a mark	**eine Note geben**	['aɪnə 'noːtə 'geːbən]
mistake, error	**Fehler** (m)	['feːlɐ]
to make mistakes	**Fehler machen**	['feːlɐ 'maχən]
to correct (an error)	**korrigieren** (vt)	[kɔʀi'giːʀən]
crib	**Spickzettel** (m)	['ʃpɪkˌtsɛtəl]
homework	**Hausaufgabe** (f)	['haʊsʔaʊfˌgaːbə]
exercise (in education)	**Übung** (f)	['yːbʊŋ]
to be present	**anwesend sein**	['anˌveːzənt zaɪn]
to be absent	**fehlen** (vi)	['feːlən]
to miss school	**versäumen** (vt)	[fɛɐ'zɔɪmən]
to punish (vt)	**bestrafen** (vt)	[bə'ʃtʀaːfən]
punishment	**Strafe** (f)	['ʃtʀaːfə]
conduct (behaviour)	**Benehmen** (n)	[bə'neːmən]

school report	Zeugnis (n)	['tsɔɪknɪs]
pencil	Bleistift (m)	['blaɪˌʃtɪft]
rubber	Radiergummi (m)	[ʀa'di:ɐˌɡʊmi]
chalk	Kreide (f)	['kʀaɪdə]
pencil case	Federkasten (m)	['fe:dɐˌkastən]

schoolbag	Schulranzen (m)	['ʃu:lˌʀantsən]
pen	Kugelschreiber, Stift (m)	['ku:ɡəlˌʃʀaɪbɐ], [ʃtɪft]
exercise book	Heft (n)	[hɛft]
textbook	Lehrbuch (n)	['le:ɐˌbu:χ]
compasses	Zirkel (m)	['tsɪʀkəl]

to make technical drawings	zeichnen (vt)	['tsaɪçnən]
technical drawing	Zeichnung (f)	['tsaɪçnʊŋ]

poem	Gedicht (n)	[ɡə'dɪçt]
by heart (adv)	auswendig	['aʊsˌvɛndɪç]
to learn by heart	auswendig lernen	['aʊsˌvɛndɪç 'lɛʀnən]

school holidays	Ferien (pl)	['fe:ʀɪən]
to be on holiday	in den Ferien sein	[ɪn den 'fe:ʀɪən zaɪn]
to spend holidays	Ferien verbringen	['fe:ʀɪən fɛɐ'bʀɪŋən]

test (at school)	Test (m), Prüfung (f)	[tɛst], ['pʀy:fʊŋ]
essay (composition)	Aufsatz (m)	['aʊfˌzats]
dictation	Diktat (n)	[dɪk'ta:t]
exam (examination)	Prüfung (f)	['pʀy:fʊŋ]
to do an exam	Prüfungen ablegen	['pʀy:fʊŋən 'apˌle:ɡən]
experiment (e.g., chemistry ~)	Experiment (n)	[ɛkspeʀi'mɛnt]

143. College. University

academy	Akademie (f)	[akade'mi:]
university	Universität (f)	[univɛʀzi'tɛ:t]
faculty (e.g., ~ of Medicine)	Fakultät (f)	[fakʊl'tɛ:t]

student (masc.)	Student (m)	[ʃtu'dɛnt]
student (fem.)	Studentin (f)	[ʃtu'dɛntɪn]
lecturer (teacher)	Lehrer (m)	['le:ʀɐ]

lecture hall, room	Hörsaal (m)	['hø:ɐˌza:l]
graduate	Hochschulabsolvent (m)	['ho:χʃu:l?apzɔlˌvɛnt]

diploma	Diplom (n)	[di'plo:m]
dissertation	Dissertation (f)	[dɪsɛʀta'tsjo:n]

study (report)	Forschung (f)	['fɔʀʃʊŋ]
laboratory	Labor (n)	[la'bo:ɐ]

lecture	Vorlesung (f)	['fo:ɐˌle:zʊŋ]
coursemate	Kommilitone (m)	[ˌkɔmili'to:nə]
scholarship, bursary	Stipendium (n)	[ʃti'pɛndɪʊm]
academic degree	akademischer Grad (m)	[aka'de:mɪʃɐ ɡʀa:t]

144. Sciences. Disciplines

mathematics	Mathematik (f)	[matema'ti:k]
algebra	Algebra (f)	['algebʀa]
geometry	Geometrie (f)	[ˌgeome'tʀi:]
astronomy	Astronomie (f)	[astʀono'mi:]
biology	Biologie (f)	[ˌbiolo'gi:]
geography	Erdkunde (f)	['e:ɐtˌkʊndə]
geology	Geologie (f)	[ˌgeolo'gi:]
history	Geschichte (f)	[gə'ʃɪçtə]
medicine	Medizin (f)	[medi'tsi:n]
pedagogy	Pädagogik (f)	[pɛda'go:gɪk]
law	Recht (n)	[ʀɛçt]
physics	Physik (f)	[fy'zi:k]
chemistry	Chemie (f)	[çe'mi:]
philosophy	Philosophie (f)	[filozo'fi:]
psychology	Psychologie (f)	[psyçolo'gi:]

145. Writing system. Orthography

grammar	Grammatik (f)	[gʀa'matɪk]
vocabulary	Lexik (f)	['lɛksɪk]
phonetics	Phonetik (f)	[fo:'ne:tɪk]
noun	Substantiv (n)	['zʊpstanti:f]
adjective	Adjektiv (n)	['atjɛkti:f]
verb	Verb (n)	[vɛʁp]
adverb	Adverb (n)	[at'vɛʁp]
pronoun	Pronomen (n)	[pʀo'no:mən]
interjection	Interjektion (f)	[ˌɪntejɛk'tsjo:n]
preposition	Präposition (f)	[pʀɛpozi'tsjo:n]
root	Wurzel (f)	['vʊʁtsəl]
ending	Endung (f)	['ɛndʊŋ]
prefix	Vorsilbe (f)	['fo:ɐˌzɪlbə]
syllable	Silbe (f)	['zɪlbə]
suffix	Suffix (n), Nachsilbe (f)	['zʊfɪks], ['na:χˌzɪlbə]
stress mark	Betonung (f)	[bə'to:nʊŋ]
apostrophe	Apostroph (m)	[apo'stʀo:f]
full stop	Punkt (m)	[pʊŋkt]
comma	Komma (n)	['kɔma]
semicolon	Semikolon (n)	[zemi'ko:lɔn]
colon	Doppelpunkt (m)	['dɔpəlˌpʊŋkt]
ellipsis	Auslassungspunkte (pl)	['aʊslasʊŋsˌpʊŋktə]
question mark	Fragezeichen (n)	['fʀa:gəˌtsaɪçən]
exclamation mark	Ausrufezeichen (n)	['aʊsʀu:fəˌtsaɪçən]

inverted commas	**Anführungszeichen** (pl)	['anfy:ʀʊŋsˌtsaɪçən]
in inverted commas	**in Anführungszeichen**	[ɪn 'anfy:ʀʊŋsˌtsaɪçən]
parenthesis	**runde Klammern** (pl)	['ʀʊndə 'klamɐn]
in parenthesis	**in Klammern**	[ɪn 'klamɐn]

hyphen	**Bindestrich** (m)	['bɪndəˌʃtʀɪç]
dash	**Gedankenstrich** (m)	[gə'daŋkənˌʃtʀɪç]
space (between words)	**Leerzeichen** (n)	['leːɐˌtsaɪçən]

letter	**Buchstabe** (m)	['buːχˌʃtaːbə]
capital letter	**Großbuchstabe** (m)	['gʀoːsbuːχˌʃtaːbə]

vowel (n)	**Vokal** (m)	[vo'kaːl]
consonant (n)	**Konsonant** (m)	[ˌkɔnzo'nant]

sentence	**Satz** (m)	[zats]
subject	**Subjekt** (n)	['zʊpjɛkt]
predicate	**Prädikat** (n)	[pʀɛdi'kaːt]

line	**Zeile** (f)	['tsaɪlə]
on a new line	**in einer neuen Zeile**	[ɪn 'aɪnɐ 'nɔɪən 'tsaɪlə]
paragraph	**Absatz** (m)	['apˌzats]

word	**Wort** (n)	[vɔʀt]
group of words	**Wortverbindung** (f)	['vɔʀtfɛɐˌbɪndʊŋ]
expression	**Redensart** (f)	['ʀeːdənsˌʔaːɐt]
synonym	**Synonym** (n)	[zyno'nyːm]
antonym	**Antonym** (n)	[anto'nyːm]

rule	**Regel** (f)	['ʀeːgəl]
exception	**Ausnahme** (f)	['aʊsˌnaːmə]
correct (adj)	**richtig**	['ʀɪçtɪç]

conjugation	**Konjugation** (f)	[ˌkɔnjuga'tsjoːn]
declension	**Deklination** (f)	[ˌdeklina'tsjoːn]
nominal case	**Kasus** (m)	['kaːzʊs]
question	**Frage** (f)	['fʀaːgə]
to underline (vt)	**unterstreichen** (vt)	[ˌʊnte'ʃtʀaɪçən]
dotted line	**punktierte Linie** (f)	[pʊŋk'tiːɐtə 'liːnɪə]

146. Foreign languages

language	**Sprache** (f)	['ʃpʀaːχə]
foreign (adj)	**Fremd-**	['fʀɛmt]
foreign language	**Fremdsprache** (f)	['fʀɛmtˌʃpʀaːχə]
to study (vt)	**studieren** (vt)	[ʃtu'diːʀən]
to learn (language, etc.)	**lernen** (vt)	['lɛʀnən]

to read (vi, vt)	**lesen** (vi, vt)	['leːzən]
to speak (vi, vt)	**sprechen** (vi, vt)	['ʃpʀɛçən]
to understand (vt)	**verstehen** (vt)	[fɛɐ'ʃteːən]
to write (vt)	**schreiben** (vi, vt)	['ʃʀaɪbən]
fast (adv)	**schnell**	[ʃnɛl]
slowly (adv)	**langsam**	['laŋzaːm]

fluently (adv)	**fließend**	['fli:sənt]
rules	**Regeln** (pl)	['ʀe:gəln]
grammar	**Grammatik** (f)	[gʀa'matɪk]
vocabulary	**Vokabular** (n)	[vokabu'la:ɐ]
phonetics	**Phonetik** (f)	[fo:'ne:tɪk]
textbook	**Lehrbuch** (n)	['le:ɐˌbu:χ]
dictionary	**Wörterbuch** (n)	['vœʁteˌbu:χ]
teach-yourself book	**Selbstlernbuch** (n)	['zɛlpstˌlɛʁnbu:χ]
phrasebook	**Sprachführer** (m)	['ʃpʀa:χˌfy:ʀe]
cassette, tape	**Kassette** (f)	[ka'sɛtə]
videotape	**Videokassette** (f)	['vi:deo·ka'sɛtə]
CD, compact disc	**CD** (f)	[tse:'de:]
DVD	**DVD** (f)	[defaʊ'de:]
alphabet	**Alphabet** (n)	[alfa'be:t]
to spell (vt)	**buchstabieren** (vt)	[ˌbu:χʃta'bi:ʀən]
pronunciation	**Aussprache** (f)	['aʊsˌʃpʀa:χə]
accent	**Akzent** (m)	[ak'tsɛnt]
with an accent	**mit Akzent**	[mɪt ak'tsɛnt]
without an accent	**ohne Akzent**	['o:nə ak'tsɛnt]
word	**Wort** (n)	[vɔʁt]
meaning	**Bedeutung** (f)	[bə'dɔɪtʊŋ]
course (e.g. a French ~)	**Kurse** (pl)	['kʊʁzə]
to sign up	**sich einschreiben**	[zɪç 'aɪnˌʃʀaɪbən]
teacher	**Lehrer** (m)	['le:ʀɐ]
translation (process)	**Übertragung** (f)	[ˌy:bɐ'tʀa:gʊŋ]
translation (text, etc.)	**Übersetzung** (f)	[ˌy:bɐ'zɛtsʊŋ]
translator	**Übersetzer** (m)	[ˌy:bɐ'zɛtsɐ]
interpreter	**Dolmetscher** (m)	['dɔlmɛtʃe]
polyglot	**Polyglott** (m, f)	[poly'glɔt]
memory	**Gedächtnis** (n)	[gə'dɛçtnɪs]

147. Fairy tale characters

Father Christmas	**Weihnachtsmann** (m)	['vaɪnaχtsˌman]
Cinderella	**Aschenputtel** (n)	['aʃənpʊtəl]
mermaid	**Nixe** (f)	['nɪksə]
Neptune	**Neptun** (m)	[nɛp'tu:n]
magician, wizard	**Zauberer** (m)	['tsaʊbəʀɐ]
fairy	**Zauberin** (f)	['tsaʊbəʀɪn]
magic (adj)	**magisch, Zauber-**	['ma:gɪʃ], ['tsaʊbɐ]
magic wand	**Zauberstab** (m)	['tsaʊbɐˌʃta:p]
fairy tale	**Märchen** (n)	['mɛ:ɐçən]
miracle	**Wunder** (n)	['vʊndɐ]
dwarf	**Zwerg** (m)	[tsvɛʁk]

131

to turn into ...	sich verwandeln in ...	[zɪç fɛɛ'vandəln ɪn]
ghost	Geist (m)	[gaɪst]
phantom	Gespenst (n)	[gə'ʃpɛnst]
monster	Ungeheuer (n)	['ʊngə,hɔɪɐ]
dragon	Drache (m)	['dʀaχə]
giant	Riese (m)	['ʀiːzə]

148. Zodiac Signs

Aries	Widder (m)	['vɪdɐ]
Taurus	Stier (m)	[ʃtiːɐ]
Gemini	Zwillinge (pl)	['tsvɪlɪŋə]
Cancer	Krebs (m)	[kʀeːps]
Leo	Löwe (m)	['løːvə]
Virgo	Jungfrau (f)	['jʊŋfʀaʊ]

Libra	Waage (f)	['vaːgə]
Scorpio	Skorpion (m)	[skɔʁ'pjoːn]
Sagittarius	Schütze (m)	['ʃʏtsə]
Capricorn	Steinbock (m)	['ʃtaɪn,bɔk]
Aquarius	Wassermann (m)	['vasɐ,man]
Pisces	Fische (pl)	['fɪʃə]

character	Charakter (m)	[ka'ʀaktɐ]
character traits	Charakterzüge (pl)	[ka'ʀaktɐ,tsyːgə]
behaviour	Benehmen (n)	[bə'neːmən]
to tell fortunes	wahrsagen (vt)	['vaːɐ,zaːgən]
fortune-teller	Wahrsagerin (f)	['vaːɐ,zaːgəʀɪn]
horoscope	Horoskop (n)	[hoʀo'skoːp]

Arts

theatre	Theater (n)	[te'a:tɐ]
opera	Oper (f)	['o:pɐ]
operetta	Operette (f)	[opə'ʀɛtə]
ballet	Ballett (n)	[ba'lɛt]
theatre poster	Theaterplakat (n)	[te'a:tɐ·pla'ka:t]
theatre company	Truppe (f)	['tʀʊpə]
tour	Tournee (f)	[tʊʁ'ne:]
to be on tour	auf Tournee sein	[aʊf tʊʁ'ne: zaɪn]
to rehearse (vi, vt)	proben (vt)	['pʀo:bən]
rehearsal	Probe (f)	['pʀo:bə]
repertoire	Spielplan (m)	['ʃpi:l‚pla:n]
performance	Aufführung (f)	['aʊffy:ʀʊŋ]
theatrical show	Vorstellung (f)	['fo:ɐ‚ʃtɛlʊŋ]
play	Theaterstück (n)	[te'a:tɐ‚ʃtʏk]
ticket	Karte (f)	['kaʁtə]
booking office	Theaterkasse (f)	[te'a:tɐ‚'kasə]
lobby, foyer	Halle (f)	['halə]
coat check (cloakroom)	Garderobe (f)	[gaʁdə'ʀo:bə]
cloakroom ticket	Garderobennummer (f)	[gaʁdə'ʀobən‚nʊmɐ]
binoculars	Opernglas (n)	['o:pen‚gla:s]
usher	Platzanweiser (m)	['plats?an‚vaɪzɐ]
stalls (orchestra seats)	Parkett (n)	[paʁ'kɛt]
balcony	Balkon (m)	[bal'ko:n]
dress circle	der erste Rang	[de:ɐ 'ɛʁstə ʀaŋ]
box	Loge (f)	['lo:ʒə]
row	Reihe (f)	['ʀaɪə]
seat	Platz (m)	[plats]
audience	Publikum (n)	['pu:blikʊm]
spectator	Zuschauer (m)	['tsu:‚ʃaʊɐ]
to clap (vi, vt)	klatschen (vi)	['klatʃən]
applause	Applaus (m)	[a'plaʊs]
ovation	Ovation (f)	[ova'tsjo:n]
stage	Bühne (f)	['by:nə]
curtain	Vorhang (m)	['fo:ɐ‚haŋ]
scenery	Dekoration (f)	[dekoʀa'tsjo:n]
backstage	Kulissen (pl)	[ku'lɪsən]
scene (e.g. the last ~)	Szene (f)	['stse:nə]
act	Akt (m)	[akt]
interval	Pause (f)	['paʊzə]

150. Cinema

| actor | Schauspieler (m) | [ˈʃauˌʃpiːlɐ] |
| actress | Schauspielerin (f) | [ˈʃauˌʃpiːlərɪn] |

cinema (industry)	Kino (n)	[ˈkiːno]
film	Film (m)	[fɪlm]
episode	Folge (f)	[ˈfɔlgə]

detective film	Krimi (m)	[ˈkʀɪmi]
action film	Actionfilm (m)	[ˈɛkʃənˌfilm]
adventure film	Abenteuerfilm (m)	[ˈaːbəntɔɪɐˌfɪlm]
science fiction film	Science-Fiction-Film (m)	[ˌsaɪənsˈfɪkʃənˌfɪlm]
horror film	Horrorfilm (m)	[ˈhɔʀoːɐˌfɪlm]

comedy film	Komödie (f)	[koˈmøːdɪə]
melodrama	Melodrama (n)	[meloˈdʀaːma]
drama	Drama (n)	[ˈdʀaːma]

fictional film	Spielfilm (m)	[ˈʃpiːlˌfɪlm]
documentary	Dokumentarfilm (m)	[dokumɛnˈtaːɐˌfɪlm]
cartoon	Zeichentrickfilm (m)	[ˈtsaɪçənˌtʀɪkˌfɪlm]
silent films	Stummfilm (m)	[ˈʃtʊmˌfɪlm]

role (part)	Rolle (f)	[ˈʀɔlə]
leading role	Hauptrolle (f)	[ˈhauptˌʀɔlə]
to play (vi, vt)	spielen (vi)	[ˈʃpiːlən]

film star	Filmstar (m)	[ˈfɪlmˌʃtaːɐ]
well-known (adj)	bekannt	[bəˈkant]
famous (adj)	berühmt	[bəˈʀyːmt]
popular (adj)	populär	[popuˈlɛːɐ]

script (screenplay)	Drehbuch (n)	[ˈdʀeːˌbuːχ]
scriptwriter	Drehbuchautor (m)	[ˈdʀeːbuːχˌʔautoːɐ]
film director	Regisseur (m)	[ʀeʒɪˈsøːɐ]
producer	Produzent (m)	[pʀoduˈtsɛnt]
assistant	Assistent (m)	[asɪsˈtɛnt]
cameraman	Kameramann (m)	[ˈkaməʀaˌman]
stuntman	Stuntman (m)	[ˈstantmɛn]
double (body double)	Double (n)	[ˈduːbəl]

to shoot a film	einen Film drehen	[ˈaɪnən fɪlm ˈdʀeːən]
audition, screen test	Probe (f)	[ˈpʀoːbə]
shooting	Dreharbeiten (pl)	[ˈdʀeːʔaʁˌbaɪtən]
film crew	Filmteam (n)	[ˈfɪlmˌtiːm]
film set	Filmset (m)	[ˈfɪlmsɛt]
camera	Filmkamera (f)	[ˈfɪlmˌkaməʀa]

cinema	Kino (n)	[ˈkiːno]
screen (e.g. big ~)	Leinwand (f)	[ˈlaɪnˌvant]
to show a film	einen Film zeigen	[ˈaɪnən fɪlm ˈtsaɪgən]

| soundtrack | Tonspur (f) | [ˈtoːnˌʃpuːɐ] |
| special effects | Spezialeffekte (pl) | [ʃpeˈtsɪaːlˌʔɛˈfɛktə] |

subtitles	Untertitel (pl)	['ʊntɐˌtiːtəl]
credits	Abspann (m)	['apˌʃpan]
translation	Übersetzung (f)	[ˌyːbɐ'zɛtsʊŋ]

151. Painting

art	Kunst (f)	[kʊnst]
fine arts	schönen Künste (pl)	['ʃøːnən 'kʏnstə]
art gallery	Kunstgalerie (f)	['kʊnstˌgaleˈʁiː]
art exhibition	Kunstausstellung (f)	['kʊnstˑ'aʊsˌʃtɛlʊŋ]

painting (art)	Malerei (f)	[ˌmaːlə'ʁaɪ]
graphic art	Graphik (f)	['gʁaːfɪk]
abstract art	abstrakte Kunst (f)	[ap'stʁaktə kʊnst]
impressionism	Impressionismus (m)	[ɪmpʁɛsjo'nɪsmʊs]

picture (painting)	Bild (n)	[bɪlt]
drawing	Zeichnung (f)	['tsaɪçnʊŋ]
poster	Plakat (n)	[pla'kaːt]

illustration (picture)	Illustration (f)	[ɪlustʁa'tsjoːn]
miniature	Miniatur (f)	[minɪa'tuːɐ]
copy (of painting, etc.)	Kopie (f)	[ko'piː]
reproduction	Reproduktion (f)	[ʁepʁodʊk'tsjoːn]

mosaic	Mosaik (n)	[moza'iːk]
stained glass window	Glasmalerei (f)	[glaːsˌmaːlə'ʁaɪ]
fresco	Fresko (n)	['fʁɛsko]
engraving	Gravüre (f)	[gʁa'vyːʁə]

bust (sculpture)	Büste (f)	['byːstə]
sculpture	Skulptur (f)	[skʊlp'tuːɐ]
statue	Statue (f)	['ʃtaːtuə]
plaster of Paris	Gips (m)	[gɪps]
plaster (as adj)	aus Gips	[ˌaʊs 'gɪps]

portrait	Porträt (n)	[pɔʁ'tʁɛː]
self-portrait	Selbstporträt (n)	['zɛlpstˑpɔʁˌtʁɛː]
landscape painting	Landschaftsbild (n)	['lantʃaftsˌbɪlt]
still life	Stillleben (n)	['ʃtɪlˌleːbən]
caricature	Karikatur (f)	[kaʁika'tuːɐ]
sketch	Entwurf (m)	[ɛnt'vʊʁf]

paint	Farbe (f)	['faʁbə]
watercolor paint	Aquarellfarbe (f)	[akva'ʁɛlˌfaʁbə]
oil (paint)	Öl (n)	[øːl]
pencil	Bleistift (m)	['blaɪˌʃtɪft]
Indian ink	Tusche (f)	['tʊʃə]
charcoal	Kohle (f)	['koːlə]

to draw (vi, vt)	zeichnen (vt)	['tsaɪçnən]
to paint (vi, vt)	malen (vi, vt)	['maːlən]
to pose (vi)	Modell stehen	[mo'dɛl 'ʃteːən]
artist's model (masc.)	Modell (n)	[mo'dɛl]

artist's model (fem.)	Modell (n)	[mo'dɛl]
artist (painter)	Maler (m)	['maːlɐ]
work of art	Kunstwerk (n)	['kʊnst‚vɛʁk]
masterpiece	Meisterwerk (n)	['maɪstɐ‚vɛʁk]
studio (artist's workroom)	Atelier (n), Werkstatt (f)	[ate'liːe:], ['vɛʁkʃtat]

canvas (cloth)	Leinwand (f)	['laɪn‚vant]
easel	Staffelei (f)	[ʃtafə'laɪ]
palette	Palette (f)	[pa'lɛtə]

frame (picture ~, etc.)	Rahmen (m)	['ʁaːmən]
restoration	Restauration (f)	[ʁɛstaʊʁa'tsjoːn]
to restore (vt)	restaurieren (vt)	[ʁɛstaʊ'ʁiːʁən]

152. Literature & Poetry

literature	Literatur (f)	[lɪtəʁa'tuːɐ]
author (writer)	Autor (m)	['aʊtoːɐ]
pseudonym	Pseudonym (n)	[psɔɪdo'nyːm]

book	Buch (n)	[buːχ]
volume	Band (m)	[bant]
table of contents	Inhaltsverzeichnis (n)	['ɪnhalts·fɛɐ‚tsaɪçnɪs]
page	Seite (f)	['zaɪtə]
main character	Hauptperson (f)	['haʊpt‚pɛʁ'zoːn]
autograph	Autogramm (n)	[aʊto'gʁam]

short story	Kurzgeschichte (f)	['kʊʁts·gə‚ʃɪçtə]
story (novella)	Erzählung (f)	[ɛɐ'tsɛːlʊŋ]
novel	Roman (m)	[ʁo'maːn]
work (writing)	Werk (n)	[vɛʁk]
fable	Fabel (f)	['faːbəl]
detective novel	Krimi (m)	['kʁɪmi]

poem (verse)	Gedicht (n)	[gə'dɪçt]
poetry	Dichtung (f), Poesie (f)	['dɪçtʊŋ], [‚poe'ziː]
poem (epic, ballad)	Gedicht (n)	[gə'dɪçt]
poet	Dichter (m)	['dɪçtɐ]

fiction	schöne Literatur (f)	['ʃøːnə lɪtəʁa'tuːɐ]
science fiction	Science-Fiction (f)	[‚saɪəns'fɪkʃən]
adventures	Abenteuer (n)	['aːbəntɔɪɐ]
educational literature	Schülerliteratur (pl)	['ʃyːlɐ·lɪtəʁa‚tuːɐ]
children's literature	Kinderliteratur (f)	['kɪndɐ·lɪtəʁa‚tuːɐ]

153. Circus

circus	Zirkus (m)	['tsɪʁkʊs]
travelling circus	Wanderzirkus (m)	['vandɐ‚tsɪʁkʊs]
programme	Programm (n)	[pʁo'gʁam]
performance	Vorstellung (f)	['foːɐ‚ʃtɛlʊŋ]
act (circus ~)	Nummer (f)	['nʊmɐ]

circus ring	Manege (f)	[ma'ne:ʒə]
pantomime (act)	Pantomime (f)	[ˌpanto'mi:mə]
clown	Clown (m)	[klaʊn]

acrobat	Akrobat (m)	[akʀo'ba:t]
acrobatics	Akrobatik (f)	[akʀo'ba:tɪk]
gymnast	Turner (m)	['tʊʁnɐ]
acrobatic gymnastics	Turnen (n)	['tʊʁnən]
somersault	Salto (m)	['zalto]

strongman	Kraftmensch (m)	['kʀaftˌmɛnʃ]
tamer (e.g., lion ~)	Bändiger, Dompteur (m)	['bɛndɪgə], [dɔmp'tø:ɐ]
rider (circus horse ~)	Reiter (m)	['ʀaɪtɐ]
assistant	Assistent (m)	[asɪs'tɛnt]

stunt	Trick (m)	[tʀɪk]
magic trick	Zaubertrick (m)	['tsaʊbeˌtʀɪk]
conjurer, magician	Zauberkünstler (m)	['tsaʊbeˌkʏnstlɐ]

juggler	Jongleur (m)	[ʒɔŋ'glø:ɐ]
to juggle (vi, vt)	jonglieren (vi)	[ʒɔŋ'gli:ʀən]
animal trainer	Dresseur (m)	[dʀɛ'sø:ɐ]
animal training	Dressur (f)	[dʀɛ'su:ɐ]
to train (animals)	dressieren (vt)	[dʀɛ'si:ʀən]

154. Music. Pop music

music	Musik (f)	[mu'zi:k]
musician	Musiker (m)	['mu:zikɐ]
musical instrument	Musikinstrument (n)	[mu'zi:kʔɪnstʀuˌmɛnt]
to play ...	spielen (vt)	['ʃpi:lən]

guitar	Gitarre (f)	[ˌgi'ʀafə]
violin	Geige (f)	['gaɪgə]
cello	Cello (n)	['tʃɛlo]
double bass	Kontrabass (m)	['kɔntʀaˌbas]
harp	Harfe (f)	['haʁfə]

piano	Klavier (n)	[kla'vi:ɐ]
grand piano	Flügel (m)	['fly:gəl]
organ	Orgel (f)	['ɔʁgəl]

wind instruments	Blasinstrumente (pl)	['bla:sʔɪnstʀuˌmɛntə]
oboe	Oboe (f)	[o'bo:e]
saxophone	Saxophon (n)	[ˌzakso'fo:n]
clarinet	Klarinette (f)	[klaʀi'nɛtə]
flute	Flöte (f)	['flø:tə]
trumpet	Trompete (f)	[tʀɔm'pe:tə]

| accordion | Akkordeon (n) | [a'kɔʁdeˌɔn] |
| drum | Trommel (f) | ['tʀɔməl] |

| duo | Duo (n) | ['du:o] |
| trio | Trio (n) | ['tʀi:o] |

quartet	**Quartett** (n)	[kvaʁ'tɛt]
choir	**Chor** (m)	[koːɐ]
orchestra	**Orchester** (n)	[ɔʁ'kɛstɐ]
pop music	**Popmusik** (f)	['pɔp·muˌziːk]
rock music	**Rockmusik** (f)	['ʀɔk·muˌziːk]
rock group	**Rockgruppe** (f)	['ʀɔkˌgʀʊpə]
jazz	**Jazz** (m)	[dʒɛs]
idol	**Idol** (n)	[i'doːl]
admirer, fan	**Verehrer** (m)	[fɛɐ'ʔeːʀɐ]
concert	**Konzert** (n)	[kɔn'tsɛʁt]
symphony	**Sinfonie** (f)	[zɪnfo'niː]
composition	**Komposition** (f)	[kɔmpozi'tsjoːn]
to compose (write)	**komponieren** (vt)	[kɔmpo'niːʀən]
singing (n)	**Gesang** (m)	[gə'zaŋ]
song	**Lied** (n)	[liːt]
tune (melody)	**Melodie** (f)	[melo'diː]
rhythm	**Rhythmus** (m)	['ʀʏtmʊs]
blues	**Blues** (m)	[bluːs]
sheet music	**Noten** (pl)	['noːtən]
baton	**Taktstock** (m)	['taktˌʃtɔk]
bow	**Bogen** (m)	['boːgən]
string	**Saite** (f)	['zaɪtə]
case (e.g. guitar ~)	**Koffer** (m)	['kɔfɐ]

Rest. Entertainment. Travel

155. Trip. Travel

English	German	IPA
tourism, travel	Tourismus (m)	[tuˈrɪsmʊs]
tourist	Tourist (m)	[tuˈrɪst]
trip, voyage	Reise (f)	[ˈraɪzə]
adventure	Abenteuer (n)	[ˈaːbəntɔɪe]
trip, journey	Fahrt (f)	[faːet]
holiday	Urlaub (m)	[ˈuːeˌlaʊp]
to be on holiday	auf Urlaub sein	[aʊf ˈuːeˌlaʊp zaɪn]
rest	Erholung (f)	[ɛeˈhoːlʊŋ]
train	Zug (m)	[tsuːk]
by train	mit dem Zug	[mɪt dem tsuːk]
aeroplane	Flugzeug (n)	[ˈfluːkˌtsɔɪk]
by aeroplane	mit dem Flugzeug	[mɪt dem ˈfluːkˌtsɔɪk]
by car	mit dem Auto	[mɪt dem ˈaʊto]
by ship	mit dem Schiff	[mɪt dem ʃɪf]
luggage	Gepäck (n)	[gəˈpɛk]
suitcase	Koffer (m)	[ˈkɔfe]
luggage trolley	Gepäckwagen (m)	[gəˈpɛkˌvaːgən]
passport	Pass (m)	[pas]
visa	Visum (n)	[ˈviːzʊm]
ticket	Fahrkarte (f)	[ˈfaːeˌkaʁtə]
air ticket	Flugticket (n)	[ˈfluːkˌtɪkət]
guidebook	Reiseführer (m)	[ˈraɪzəˌfyːre]
map (tourist ~)	Landkarte (f)	[ˈlantˌkaʁtə]
area (rural ~)	Gegend (f)	[ˈgeːgənt]
place, site	Ort (m)	[ɔʁt]
exotica (n)	Exotika (pl)	[ɛˈksoːtika]
exotic (adj)	exotisch	[ɛˈksoːtɪʃ]
amazing (adj)	erstaunlich	[ɛeˈʃtaʊnlɪç]
group	Gruppe (f)	[ˈgrʊpə]
excursion, sightseeing tour	Ausflug (m)	[ˈaʊsˌfluːk]
guide (person)	Reiseleiter (m)	[ˈraɪzəˌlaɪte]

156. Hotel

English	German	IPA
hotel	Hotel (n)	[hoˈtɛl]
motel	Motel (n)	[moˈtɛl]
three-star (~ hotel)	drei Sterne	[draɪ ˈʃtɛʁnə]

| five-star | fünf Sterne | [fʏnf 'ʃtɛʁnə] |
| to stay (in a hotel, etc.) | absteigen (vi) | ['apˌʃtaɪɡən] |

room	Hotelzimmer (n)	[ho'tɛlˌtsɪmɐ]
single room	Einzelzimmer (n)	['aɪntsəlˌtsɪmɐ]
double room	Zweibettzimmer (n)	['tsvaɪbɛtˌtsɪmɐ]
to book a room	reservieren (vt)	[ʀezɛʁ'viːʀən]

| half board | Halbpension (f) | ['halpˌpanˌzjoːn] |
| full board | Vollpension (f) | ['fɔlˌpanˌzjoːn] |

with bath	mit Bad	[mɪt 'baːt]
with shower	mit Dusche	[mɪt 'duːʃə]
satellite television	Satellitenfernsehen (n)	[zatɛ'liːtənˌfɛʁnzeːən]
air-conditioner	Klimaanlage (f)	['kliːmaˌʔanlaːɡə]
towel	Handtuch (n)	['hantˌtuːχ]
key	Schlüssel (m)	['ʃlʏsəl]

administrator	Verwalter (m)	[fɛɐ'valtɐ]
chambermaid	Zimmermädchen (n)	['tsɪmɐˌmɛːtçən]
porter	Träger (m)	['tʀɛːɡɐ]
doorman	Portier (m)	[pɔʁ'tɪeː]

restaurant	Restaurant (n)	[ʀɛsto'ʀaŋ]
pub, bar	Bar (f)	[baːɐ]
breakfast	Frühstück (n)	['fʀyːʃtʏk]
dinner	Abendessen (n)	['aːbəntˌʔɛsən]
buffet	Buffet (n)	[bʏ'feː]

| lobby | Foyer (n) | [foa'jeː] |
| lift | Aufzug (m), Fahrstuhl (m) | ['aʊfˌtsuːk], ['faːɐˌʃtuːl] |

| DO NOT DISTURB | BITTE NICHT STÖREN! | ['bɪtə nɪçt 'ʃtøːʀən] |
| NO SMOKING | RAUCHEN VERBOTEN! | ['ʀaʊχən fɛɐ'boːtən] |

157. Books. Reading

book	Buch (n)	[buːχ]
author	Autor (m)	['aʊtoːɐ]
writer	Schriftsteller (m)	['ʃʀɪftˌʃtɛlɐ]
to write (~ a book)	verfassen (vt)	[fɛɐ'fasən]

reader	Leser (m)	['leːzɐ]
to read (vi, vt)	lesen (vi, vt)	['leːzən]
reading (activity)	Lesen (n)	['leːzən]

| silently (to oneself) | still | [ʃtɪl] |
| aloud (adv) | laut | [laʊt] |

to publish (vt)	verlegen (vt)	[fɛɐ'leːɡən]
publishing (process)	Ausgabe (f)	['aʊsˌɡaːbə]
publisher	Herausgeber (m)	[hə'ʀaʊsˌɡeːbɐ]
publishing house	Verlag (m)	[fɛɐ'laːk]
to come out (be released)	erscheinen (vi)	[ɛɐ'ʃaɪnən]

| release (of a book) | Erscheinen (n) | [ɛɐ'ʃaɪnən] |
| print run | Auflage (f) | ['aʊfˌlaːɡə] |

| bookshop | Buchhandlung (f) | ['buːχˌhandlʊŋ] |
| library | Bibliothek (f) | [biblio'teːk] |

story (novella)	Erzählung (f)	[ɛɐ'tsɛːlʊŋ]
short story	Kurzgeschichte (f)	['kʊɐts·ɡəˌʃɪçtə]
novel	Roman (m)	[ʀo'maːn]
detective novel	Krimi (m)	['kʀɪmi]

memoirs	Memoiren (pl)	[me'moaːʀən]
legend	Legende (f)	[le'ɡɛndə]
myth	Mythos (m)	['myːtɔs]

poetry, poems	Gedichte (pl)	[ɡə'dɪçtə]
autobiography	Autobiographie (f)	[aʊtobioɡʀa'fiː]
selected works	ausgewählte Werke (pl)	['aʊsɡəˌvɛːltə 'vɛʀkə]
science fiction	Science-Fiction (f)	[ˌsaɪəns'fɪkʃən]

title	Titel (m)	['tiːtəl]
introduction	Einleitung (f)	['aɪnlaɪtʊŋ]
title page	Titelseite (f)	['tiːtəlˌzaɪtə]

chapter	Kapitel (n)	[ka'pɪtəl]
extract	Auszug (m)	['aʊstsuːk]
episode	Episode (f)	[epi'zoːdə]

plot (storyline)	Sujet (n)	[zy'ʒeː]
contents	Inhalt (m)	['ɪnˌhalt]
table of contents	Inhaltsverzeichnis (n)	['ɪnhalts·fɛɐˌtsaɪçnɪs]
main character	Hauptperson (f)	['haʊptˌpɛʀ'zoːn]

volume	Band (m)	[bant]
cover	Buchdecke (f)	['buːχˌdɛkə]
binding	Einband (m)	['aɪnˌbant]
bookmark	Lesezeichen (n)	['leːzəˌtsaɪçən]

page	Seite (f)	['zaɪtə]
to page through	blättern (vi)	['blɛtən]
margins	Ränder (pl)	['ʀɛndɐ]
annotation	Notiz (f)	[no'tiːts]
(marginal note, etc.)		
footnote	Anmerkung (f)	['anmɛʀkʊŋ]

text	Text (m)	[tɛkst]
type, fount	Schrift (f)	[ʃʀɪft]
misprint, typo	Druckfehler (m)	['dʀʊkˌfeːlɐ]

translation	Übersetzung (f)	[ˌyːbɐ'zɛtsʊŋ]
to translate (vt)	übersetzen (vt)	[ˌyːbɐ'zɛtsən]
original (n)	Original (n)	[oʀiɡi'naːl]

famous (adj)	berühmt	[bə'ʀyːmt]
unknown (not famous)	unbekannt	['ʊnbəkant]
interesting (adj)	interessant	[ɪntəʀɛ'sant]

bestseller	Bestseller (m)	['bɛstˌzɛlɐ]
dictionary	Wörterbuch (n)	['vœʁtɐˌbuːχ]
textbook	Lehrbuch (n)	['leːɐˌbuːχ]
encyclopedia	Enzyklopädie (f)	[ˌɛntsyklopɛ'diː]

158. Hunting. Fishing

hunting	Jagd (f)	[jaːkt]
to hunt (vi, vt)	jagen (vi)	['jagən]
hunter	Jäger (m)	['jɛːgɐ]

to shoot (vi)	schießen (vi)	['ʃiːsən]
rifle	Gewehr (n)	[gə'veːɐ]
bullet (shell)	Patrone (f)	[pa'tʀoːnə]
shot (lead balls)	Schrot (n)	[ʃʀoːt]

steel trap	Falle (f)	['falə]
snare (for birds, etc.)	Schlinge (f)	['ʃlɪŋə]
to fall into the steel trap	in die Falle gehen	[ɪn di 'falə 'geːən]
to lay a steel trap	eine Falle stellen	['aɪnə 'falə 'ʃtɛlən]

poacher	Wilddieb (m)	['vɪltˌdiːp]
game (in hunting)	Wild (n)	[vɪlt]
hound dog	Jagdhund (m)	['jaːktˌhʊnt]
safari	Safari (f)	[za'faːʀi]
mounted animal	ausgestopftes Tier (n)	['aʊsˌgə'ʃtɔpftəs 'tiːɐ]

fisherman	Fischer (m)	['fɪʃɐ]
fishing (angling)	Fischen (n)	['fɪʃən]
to fish (vi)	angeln, fischen (vt)	['aŋəln], ['fɪʃən]

fishing rod	Angel (f)	['aŋl]
fishing line	Angelschnur (f)	['aŋlˌʃnuːɐ]
hook	Haken (m)	['haːkən]
float	Schwimmer (m)	['ʃvɪmɐ]
bait	Köder (m)	['køːdɐ]

| to cast a line | die Angel auswerfen | [di 'aŋl 'aʊsˌvɛʁfən] |
| to bite (ab. fish) | anbeißen (vi) | ['anbaɪsən] |

| catch (of fish) | Fang (m) | [faŋ] |
| ice-hole | Eisloch (n) | ['aɪsˌlɔχ] |

fishing net	Netz (n)	[nɛts]
boat	Boot (n)	['boːt]
to net (to fish with a net)	mit dem Netz fangen	[mɪt dem 'nɛts 'faŋən]
to cast[throw] the net	das Netz hineinwerfen	[das nɛts hɪ'naɪnˌvɛʁfən]

| to haul the net in | das Netz einholen | [das nɛts 'aɪnˌhoːlən] |
| to fall into the net | ins Netz gehen | [ɪns nɛts 'geːən] |

whaler (person)	Walfänger (m)	['vaːlˌfɛŋɐ]
whaleboat	Walfangschiff (n)	['vaːlfaŋˌʃɪf]
harpoon	Harpune (f)	[haʁ'puːnə]

159. Games. Billiards

billiards	**Billard** (n)	['bɪljaʁt]
billiard room, hall	**Billardzimmer** (n)	['bɪljaʁt͜tsɪmɐ]
ball (snooker, etc.)	**Billardkugel** (f)	['bɪljaʁt͜kuːgəl]
to pocket a ball	**eine Kugel einlochen**	['aɪnə 'kuːgəl 'aɪnlɔχən]
cue	**Queue** (n)	[køː]
pocket	**Tasche** (f), **Loch** (n)	['taʃə], [lɔχ]

160. Games. Playing cards

diamonds	**Karo** (n)	['kaːʀo]
spades	**Pik** (n)	[piːk]
hearts	**Herz** (n)	[hɛʁts]
clubs	**Kreuz** (n)	[kʀɔɪts]
ace	**As** (n)	[as]
king	**König** (m)	['køːnɪç]
queen	**Dame** (f)	['daːmə]
jack, knave	**Bube** (m)	['buːbə]
playing card	**Spielkarte** (f)	['ʃpiːl͜kaʁtə]
cards	**Karten** (pl)	['kaʁtən]
trump	**Trumpf** (m)	[tʀʊmpf]
pack of cards	**Kartenspiel** (n)	['kaʁtənʃpiːl]
point	**Punkt** (m)	[pʊŋkt]
to deal (vi, vt)	**ausgeben** (vt)	['aʊsˌgeːbən]
to shuffle (cards)	**mischen** (vt)	['mɪʃən]
lead, turn (n)	**Zug** (m)	[tsuːk]
cardsharp	**Falschspieler** (m)	['falʃʃpiːlɐ]

161. Casino. Roulette

casino	**Kasino** (n)	[ka'ziːno]
roulette (game)	**Roulette** (n)	[ʀu'lɛt]
bet	**Einsatz** (m)	['aɪnˌzats]
to place bets	**setzen** (vt)	['zɛtsən]
red	**Rot** (n)	[ʀoːt]
black	**Schwarz** (n)	['ʃvaʁts]
to bet on red	**auf Rot setzen**	[aʊf ʀoːt 'zɛtsən]
to bet on black	**auf Schwarz setzen**	[aʊf ʃvaʁts 'zɛtsən]
croupier (dealer)	**Croupier** (m)	[kʀu'pie]
to spin the wheel	**das Rad drehen**	[das ʀaːt 'dʀeːən]
rules (~ of the game)	**Spielregeln** (pl)	['ʃpiːlˌʀeːgəln]
chip	**Spielmarke** (f)	['ʃpiːlˌmaʁkə]
to win (vi, vt)	**gewinnen** (vt)	[gə'vɪnən]
win (winnings)	**Gewinn** (m)	[gə'vɪn]

to lose (~ 100 dollars)	verlieren (vt)	[fɛɐ'liːʀən]
loss (losses)	Verlust (m)	[fɛɐ'lʊst]

player	Spieler (m)	['ʃpiːlɐ]
blackjack (card game)	Blackjack (n)	['blɛk͜ˌdʒɛk]
craps (dice game)	Würfelspiel (n)	['vʏɐfəlˌʃpiːl]
dice (a pair of ~)	Würfeln (pl)	['vʏɐfəln]
fruit machine	Spielautomat (m)	['ʃpiːlʔautoˌmaːt]

162. Rest. Games. Miscellaneous

to stroll (vi, vt)	spazieren gehen (vi)	[ʃpa'tsiːʀən 'geːən]
stroll (leisurely walk)	Spaziergang (m)	[ʃpa'tsiːɐˌgaŋ]
car ride	Fahrt (f)	[faːɐt]
adventure	Abenteuer (n)	['aːbəntɔɪɐ]
picnic	Picknick (n)	['pɪkˌnɪk]

game (chess, etc.)	Spiel (n)	[ʃpiːl]
player	Spieler (m)	['ʃpiːlɐ]
game (one ~ of chess)	Partie (f)	[paʀ'tiː]

collector (e.g. philatelist)	Sammler (m)	['zamlɐ]
to collect (stamps, etc.)	sammeln (vt)	['zaməln]
collection	Sammlung (f)	['zamlʊŋ]

crossword puzzle	Kreuzworträtsel (n)	['kʀɔɪtsvɔɐtˌʀɛːtsəl]
racecourse (hippodrome)	Rennbahn (f)	['ʀɛnˌbaːn]
disco (discotheque)	Diskothek (f)	[dɪsko'teːk]

sauna	Sauna (f)	['zauna]
lottery	Lotterie (f)	[lɔtə'ʀiː]

camping trip	Wanderung (f)	['vandəʀʊŋ]
camp	Lager (n)	['laːgɐ]
tent (for camping)	Zelt (n)	[tsɛlt]
compass	Kompass (m)	['kɔmpas]
camper	Tourist (m)	[tu'ʀɪst]

to watch (film, etc.)	fernsehen (vi)	['fɛɐnˌzeːən]
viewer	Fernsehzuschauer (m)	['fɛɐnzeːˌtsuːʃauɐ]
TV show (TV program)	Fernsehsendung (f)	['fɛɐnzeːˌzɛndʊŋ]

163. Photography

camera (photo)	Kamera (f)	['kaməʀa]
photo, picture	Foto (n)	['foːto]

photographer	Fotograf (m)	[foto'gʀaːf]
photo studio	Fotostudio (n)	['fotoˌʃtuːdɪo]
photo album	Fotoalbum (n)	['fotoˌʔalbʊm]
camera lens	Objektiv (n)	[ɔpjɛk'tiːf]
telephoto lens	Teleobjektiv (n)	['teleʔɔpjɛkˌtiːf]

| filter | Filter (n) | ['fɪltɐ] |
| lens | Linse (f) | ['lɪnzə] |

optics (high-quality ~)	Optik (f)	['ɔptɪk]
diaphragm (aperture)	Blende (f)	['blɛndə]
exposure time (shutter speed)	Belichtungszeit (f)	[bə'lɪçtʊŋsˌtsaɪt]
viewfinder	Sucher (m)	['zuːχɐ]

digital camera	Digitalkamera (f)	[digi'taːlˌkaməʀa]
tripod	Stativ (n)	[ʃta'tiːf]
flash	Blitzgerät (n)	['blɪtsˌgəˌʀɛːt]

to photograph (vt)	fotografieren (vt)	[fotogʀa'fiːʀən]
to take pictures	aufnehmen (vt)	['aʊfˌneːmən]
to have one's picture taken	sich fotografieren lassen	[zɪç fotogʀa'fiːʀən 'lasən]

focus	Fokus (m)	['foːkʊs]
to focus	den Fokus einstellen	[den 'foːkʊs 'aɪnˌʃtɛlən]
sharp, in focus (adj)	scharf	[ʃaʀf]
sharpness	Schärfe (f)	['ʃɛʀfə]

| contrast | Kontrast (m) | [kɔn'tʀast] |
| contrast (as adj) | kontrastreich | [kɔn'tʀastˌʀaɪç] |

picture (photo)	Aufnahme (f)	['aʊfˌnaːmə]
negative (n)	Negativ (n)	['neːgatiːf]
film (a roll of ~)	Film (m)	[fɪlm]
frame (still)	Einzelbild (n)	['aintsəlˌbilt]
to print (photos)	drucken (vt)	['dʀʊkən]

164. Beach. Swimming

beach	Strand (m)	[ʃtʀant]
sand	Sand (m)	[zant]
deserted (beach)	menschenleer	['mɛnʃənˌleːɐ]

suntan	Bräune (f)	['bʀɔɪnə]
to get a tan	sich bräunen	[zɪç 'bʀɔɪnən]
tanned (adj)	gebräunt	[gə'bʀɔɪnt]
sunscreen	Sonnencreme (f)	['zɔnənˌkʀɛːm]

bikini	Bikini (m)	[bi'kiːni]
swimsuit, bikini	Badeanzug (m)	['baːdəˌʔantsuːk]
swim trunks	Badehose (f)	['baːdəˌhoːzə]

swimming pool	Schwimmbad (n)	['ʃvɪmbaːt]
to swim (vi)	schwimmen (vi)	['ʃvɪmən]
shower	Dusche (f)	['duːʃə]
to change (one's clothes)	sich umkleiden	[zɪç 'ʊmklaɪdən]
towel	Handtuch (n)	['hantˌtuːχ]

| boat | Boot (n) | ['boːt] |
| motorboat | Motorboot (n) | ['moːtoːɐˌboːt] |

water ski	**Wasserski** (m)	['vasɐˌʃiː]
pedalo	**Tretboot** (n)	['tʀeːtˌboːt]
surfing	**Surfen** (n)	['sœːɐfən]
surfer	**Surfer** (m)	['sœɐfɐ]
scuba set	**Tauchgerät** (n)	['taʊχˈɡəˈʀɛːt]
flippers (swim fins)	**Schwimmflossen** (pl)	['ʃvɪmˌflɔsən]
mask (diving ~)	**Maske** (f)	['maskə]
diver	**Taucher** (m)	['taʊχɐ]
to dive (vi)	**tauchen** (vi)	['taʊχən]
underwater (adv)	**unter Wasser**	['ʊntɐ 'vasɐ]
beach umbrella	**Sonnenschirm** (m)	['zɔnənˌʃɪʁm]
beach chair (sun lounger)	**Liege** (f)	['liːɡə]
sunglasses	**Sonnenbrille** (f)	['zɔnənˌbʀɪlə]
air mattress	**Schwimmmatratze** (f)	['ʃvɪmˈmaˈtʀatsə]
to play (amuse oneself)	**spielen** (vi, vt)	['ʃpiːlən]
to go for a swim	**schwimmen gehen**	['ʃvɪmən 'ɡeːən]
beach ball	**Ball** (m)	[bal]
to inflate (vt)	**aufblasen** (vt)	['aʊfˌblaːzən]
inflatable, air (adj)	**aufblasbar**	['aʊfˌblaːsbaːɐ]
wave	**Welle** (f)	['vɛlə]
buoy (line of ~s)	**Boje** (f)	['boːjə]
to drown (ab. person)	**ertrinken** (vi)	[ɛɐˈtʀɪŋkən]
to save, to rescue	**retten** (vt)	['ʀɛtən]
life jacket	**Schwimmweste** (f)	['ʃvɪmˌvɛstə]
to observe, to watch	**beobachten** (vt)	[bəˈʔoːbaχtən]
lifeguard	**Bademeister** (m)	['baːdəˌmaɪstɐ]

TECHNICAL EQUIPMENT. TRANSPORT

Technical equipment

165. Computer

computer	**Computer** (m)	[kɔm'pjuːtɐ]
notebook, laptop	**Laptop** (m), **Notebook** (n)	['lɛptɔp], ['nɔutbʊk]
to turn on	**einschalten** (vt)	['aɪnʃaltən]
to turn off	**abstellen** (vt)	['apʃtɛlən]
keyboard	**Tastatur** (f)	[tasta'tuːɐ]
key	**Taste** (f)	['tastə]
mouse	**Maus** (f)	[maʊs]
mouse mat	**Mousepad** (n)	['maʊspɛt]
button	**Knopf** (m)	[knɔpf]
cursor	**Cursor** (m)	['køːɐzɐ]
monitor	**Monitor** (m)	['moːnitoːɐ]
screen	**Schirm** (m)	[ʃɪʁm]
hard disk	**Festplatte** (f)	['fɛstplatə]
hard disk capacity	**Festplattengröße** (f)	['fɛstplatən‚gʁøːsə]
memory	**Speicher** (m)	['ʃpaɪçɐ]
random access memory	**Arbeitsspeicher** (m)	['aʁbaɪts‚ʃpaɪçɐ]
file	**Datei** (f)	[da'taɪ]
folder	**Ordner** (m)	['ɔʁdnɐ]
to open (vt)	**öffnen** (vt)	['œfnən]
to close (vt)	**schließen** (vt)	['ʃliːsən]
to save (vt)	**speichern** (vt)	['ʃpaɪçɐn]
to delete (vt)	**löschen** (vt)	['lœʃən]
to copy (vt)	**kopieren** (vt)	[ko'piːʁən]
to sort (vt)	**sortieren** (vt)	[zɔʁ'tiːʁən]
to transfer (copy)	**transferieren** (vt)	[tʁansfə'ʁiːʁən]
programme	**Programm** (n)	[pʁo'gʁam]
software	**Software** (f)	['sɔftwɛːɐ]
programmer	**Programmierer** (m)	[pʁogʁa'miːʁɐ]
to program (vt)	**programmieren** (vt)	[pʁogʁa'miːʁən]
hacker	**Hacker** (m)	['hɛkɐ]
password	**Kennwort** (n)	['kɛn‚vɔʁt]
virus	**Virus** (m, n)	['viːʁʊs]
to find, to detect	**entdecken** (vt)	[ɛnt'dɛkən]
byte	**Byte** (n)	[baɪt]

megabyte	Megabyte (n)	['me:gaˌbaɪt]
data	Daten (pl)	['da:tən]
database	Datenbank (f)	['da:tənˌbaŋk]

cable (USB, etc.)	Kabel (n)	['ka:bəl]
to disconnect (vt)	trennen (vt)	['tʀɛnən]
to connect (sth to sth)	anschließen (vt)	['anˌʃli:sən]

166. Internet. E-mail

Internet	Internet (n)	['ɪntenɛt]
browser	Browser (m)	['bʀauzɐ]
search engine	Suchmaschine (f)	['zu:χˌmaʃi:nə]
provider	Provider (m)	[ˌpʀo'vaɪdɐ]

webmaster	Webmaster (m)	['vɛpˌma:stɐ]
website	Website (f)	['vɛpˌsaɪt]
web page	Webseite (f)	['vɛpˌzaɪtə]

| address (e-mail ~) | Adresse (f) | [a'dʀɛsə] |
| address book | Adressbuch (n) | [a'dʀɛsˌbu:χ] |

postbox	Mailbox (f)	['mɛjlˌbɔks]
post	Post (f)	[pɔst]
full (adj)	überfüllt	[y:bɐ'fʏlt]

message	Mitteilung (f)	['mɪtˌtaɪlʊŋ]
incoming messages	eingehenden Nachrichten	['aɪnˌge:əndən 'na:χʀɪçtən]
outgoing messages	ausgehenden Nachrichten	['ausˌge:əndən 'na:χʀɪçtən]

sender	Absender (m)	['apˌzɛndɐ]
to send (vt)	senden (vt)	['zɛndən]
sending (of mail)	Absendung (f)	['apˌzɛndʊŋ]

| receiver | Empfänger (m) | [ɛm'pfɛŋɐ] |
| to receive (vt) | empfangen (vt) | [ɛm'pfaŋən] |

| correspondence | Briefwechsel (m) | ['bʀi:fˌvɛksəl] |
| to correspond (vi) | im Briefwechsel stehen | [ɪm 'bʀi:fˌvɛksəl 'ʃte:ən] |

file	Datei (f)	[da'taɪ]
to download (vt)	herunterladen (vt)	[hɛ'ʀʊntɐˌla:dən]
to create (vt)	schaffen (vt)	['ʃafən]
to delete (vt)	löschen (vt)	['lœʃən]
deleted (adj)	gelöscht	[gə'lœʃt]

connection (ADSL, etc.)	Verbindung (f)	[fɛɐ'bɪndʊŋ]
speed	Geschwindigkeit (f)	[gə'ʃvɪndɪç·kaɪt]
modem	Modem (m, n)	['mo:dɛm]
access	Zugang (m)	['tsu:gaŋ]
port (e.g. input ~)	Port (m)	[pɔʁt]
connection (make a ~)	Anschluss (m)	['anʃlʊs]

to connect to ... (vi)	sich anschließen	[zɪç 'anʃliːsən]
to select (vt)	auswählen (vt)	['aʊsˌvɛːlən]
to search (for ...)	suchen (vt)	['zuːχən]

167. Electricity

electricity	Elektrizität (f)	[elɛktʀitsi'tɛːt]
electric, electrical (adj)	elektrisch	[e'lɛktʀɪʃ]
electric power station	Elektrizitätswerk (n)	[elɛktʀitsi'tɛːtsˌvɛʀk]
energy	Energie (f)	[enɛʀ'giː]
electric power	Strom (m)	[ʃtʀoːm]

light bulb	Glühbirne (f)	['glyːˌbɪʀnə]
torch	Taschenlampe (f)	['taʃənˌlampə]
street light	Straßenlaterne (f)	['ʃtʀaːsən·laˌtɛʀnə]

light	Licht (n)	[lɪçt]
to turn on	einschalten (vt)	['aɪnʃaltən]
to turn off	ausschalten (vt)	['aʊsʃaltən]
to turn off the light	das Licht ausschalten	[das lɪçt 'aʊsʃaltən]

to burn out (vi)	durchbrennen (vi)	['dʊʀçˌbʀɛnən]
short circuit	Kurzschluss (m)	['kʊʀtsʃlʊs]
broken wire	Riß (m)	[ʀɪs]
contact (electrical ~)	Kontakt (m)	[kɔn'takt]

light switch	Schalter (m)	['ʃaltɐ]
socket outlet	Steckdose (f)	['ʃtɛkˌdoːzə]
plug	Stecker (m)	['ʃtɛkɐ]
extension lead	Verlängerung (f)	[fɛʀ'lɛŋəʀʊŋ]

fuse	Sicherung (f)	['zɪçəʀʊŋ]
cable, wire	Draht (m)	[dʀaːt]
wiring	Verdrahtung (f)	[fɛʀ'dʀaːtʊŋ]

ampere	Ampere (n)	[am'peːɐ]
amperage	Stromstärke (f)	['ʃtʀoːmʃtɛʀkə]
volt	Volt (n)	[vɔlt]
voltage	Voltspannung (f)	['vɔltʃpanʊŋ]

| electrical device | Elektrogerät (n) | [e'lɛktʀo·gəˌʀɛːt] |
| indicator | Indikator (m) | [ɪndi'kaːtoːɐ] |

electrician	Elektriker (m)	[ˌe'lɛktʀikɐ]
to solder (vt)	löten (vt)	['løːtən]
soldering iron	Lötkolben (m)	['løːtˌkɔlbən]
electric current	Strom (m)	[ʃtʀoːm]

168. Tools

| tool, instrument | Werkzeug (n) | ['vɛʀkˌtsɔɪk] |
| tools | Werkzeuge (pl) | ['vɛʀkˌtsɔɪgə] |

equipment (factory ~)	Ausrüstung (f)	['aʊsˌʀʏstʊŋ]
hammer	Hammer (m)	['hamɐ]
screwdriver	Schraubenzieher (m)	['ʃʀaʊbəntsiːɐ]
axe	Axt (f)	[akst]

saw	Säge (f)	['zɛːgə]
to saw (vt)	sägen (vt)	['zɛːgən]
plane (tool)	Hobel (m)	['hoːbl]
to plane (vt)	hobeln (vt)	['hoːbəln]
soldering iron	Lötkolben (m)	['løːtˌkɔlbən]
to solder (vt)	löten (vt)	['løːtən]

file (tool)	Feile (f)	['faɪlə]
carpenter pincers	Kneifzange (f)	['knaɪfˌtsaŋə]
combination pliers	Flachzange (f)	['flaxˌtsaŋə]
chisel	Stemmeisen (n)	['ʃtɛmˌʔaɪzən]

drill bit	Bohrer (m)	['boːʀɐ]
electric drill	Bohrmaschine (f)	['boːɐˌmaʃiːnə]
to drill (vi, vt)	bohren (vt)	['boːʀən]

knife	Messer (n)	['mɛsɐ]
blade	Klinge (f)	['klɪŋə]

sharp (blade, etc.)	scharf	[ʃaʁf]
dull, blunt (adj)	stumpf	[ʃtʊmpf]
to get blunt (dull)	stumpf werden (vi)	[ʃtʊmpf 'veːɐdən]
to sharpen (vt)	schärfen (vt)	['ʃɛʁfən]

bolt	Bolzen (m)	['bɔltsən]
nut	Mutter (f)	['mʊtɐ]
thread (of a screw)	Gewinde (n)	[gə'vɪndə]
wood screw	Holzschraube (f)	['hɔltsˌʃʀaʊbə]

nail	Nagel (m)	['naːgəl]
nailhead	Nagelkopf (m)	['naːgəlˌkɔpf]

ruler (for measuring)	Lineal (n)	[line'aːl]
tape measure	Metermaß (n)	['meːtɐˌmaːs]
spirit level	Wasserwaage (f)	['vasɐˌvaːgə]
magnifying glass	Lupe (f)	['luːpə]

measuring instrument	Messinstrument (n)	['mɛsʔɪnstʀuˌmɛnt]
to measure (vt)	messen (vt)	['mɛsən]
scale (temperature ~, etc.)	Skala (f)	['skaːla]
readings	Ablesung (f)	['apleːzʊŋ]

compressor	Kompressor (m)	[kɔm'pʀɛsoːɐ]
microscope	Mikroskop (n)	[mikʀo'skoːp]

pump (e.g. water ~)	Pumpe (f)	['pʊmpə]
robot	Roboter (m)	['ʀɔbotɐ]
laser	Laser (m)	['leːzɐ]

spanner	Schraubenschlüssel (m)	['ʃʀaʊbənˌʃlʏsəl]
adhesive tape	Klebeband (n)	['kleːbəˌbant]

glue	Klebstoff (m)	['kle:pʃtɔf]
sandpaper	Sandpapier (n)	['zant·paˌpiːɐ]
spring	Sprungfeder (f)	['ʃpʀʊŋˌfeːdɐ]
magnet	Magnet (m)	[ma'gneːt]
gloves	Handschuhe (pl)	['hantʃuːə]

rope	Leine (f)	['laɪnə]
cord	Schnur (f)	[ʃnuːɐ]
wire (e.g. telephone ~)	Draht (m)	[dʀaːt]
cable	Kabel (n)	['kaːbəl]

sledgehammer	schwerer Hammer (m)	['ʃveːʀɐ 'hamɐ]
prybar	Brecheisen (n)	['bʀɛçˌʔaɪzən]
ladder	Leiter (f)	['laɪtɐ]
stepladder	Trittleiter (f)	['tʀɪtˌlaɪtɐ]

to screw (tighten)	zudrehen (vt)	[tsuː'dʀeːən]
to unscrew (lid, filter, etc.)	abdrehen (vt)	['apˌdʀeːən]
to tighten (e.g. with a clamp)	zusammendrücken (vt)	[tsu'zamənˌdʀʏkən]
to glue, to stick	ankleben (vt)	['anˌkleːbən]
to cut (vt)	schneiden (vt)	['ʃnaɪdən]

malfunction (fault)	Störung (f)	['ʃtøːʀʊŋ]
repair (mending)	Reparatur (f)	[ʀepaʀa'tuːɐ]
to repair, to fix (vt)	reparieren (vt)	[ʀepa'ʀiːʀən]
to adjust (machine, etc.)	einstellen (vt)	['aɪnˌʃtɛlən]

to check (to examine)	prüfen (vt)	['pʀyːfən]
checking	Prüfung (f)	['pʀyːfʊŋ]
readings	Ablesung (f)	['apleːzʊŋ]

| reliable, solid (machine) | sicher | ['zɪçɐ] |
| complex (adj) | kompliziert | [kompli'tsiːɐt] |

to rust (get rusted)	verrosten (vi)	[fɛɐ'ʀɔstən]
rusty (adj)	rostig	['ʀɔstɪç]
rust	Rost (m)	[ʀɔst]

Transport

169. Aeroplane

aeroplane	**Flugzeug** (n)	['flu:k͵tsɔɪk]
air ticket	**Flugticket** (n)	['flu:k͵tɪkət]
airline	**Fluggesellschaft** (f)	['flu:kgə͵zɛlʃaft]
airport	**Flughafen** (m)	['flu:k͵ha:fən]
supersonic (adj)	**Überschall-**	['y:bə͵ʃal]
captain	**Flugkapitän** (m)	['flu:k·kapi͵tɛ:n]
crew	**Besatzung** (f)	[bə'zatsʊŋ]
pilot	**Pilot** (m)	[pi'lo:t]
stewardess	**Flugbegleiterin** (f)	['flu:k·bə͵glaɪtəʀɪn]
navigator	**Steuermann** (m)	['ʃtɔɪɐ͵man]
wings	**Flügel** (pl)	['fly:gəl]
tail	**Schwanz** (m)	[ʃvants]
cockpit	**Kabine** (f)	[ka'bi:nə]
engine	**Motor** (m)	['mo:to:ɐ]
undercarriage (landing gear)	**Fahrgestell** (n)	['fa:ɐ·gə͵ʃtɛl]
turbine	**Turbine** (f)	[tʊʀ'bi:nə]
propeller	**Propeller** (m)	[pʀo'pɛlɐ]
black box	**Flugschreiber** (m)	['flu:k͵ʃʀaɪbɐ]
yoke (control column)	**Steuerrad** (n)	['ʃtɔɪɐ͵ʀa:t]
fuel	**Treibstoff** (m)	['tʀaɪpʃtɔf]
safety card	**Sicherheitskarte** (f)	['zɪçɐhaɪts͵kaʀtə]
oxygen mask	**Sauerstoffmaske** (f)	['zaʊɐʃtɔf͵maskə]
uniform	**Uniform** (f)	['ʊni͵fɔʀm]
lifejacket	**Rettungsweste** (f)	['ʀɛtʊŋs͵vɛstə]
parachute	**Fallschirm** (m)	['fal͵ʃɪʀm]
takeoff	**Abflug, Start** (m)	['ap͵flu:k], [ʃtaʀt]
to take off (vi)	**starten** (vi)	['ʃtaʀtən]
runway	**Startbahn** (f)	['ʃtaʀtba:n]
visibility	**Sicht** (f)	[zɪçt]
flight (act of flying)	**Flug** (m)	[flu:k]
altitude	**Höhe** (f)	['hø:ə]
air pocket	**Luftloch** (n)	['lʊft͵lɔχ]
seat	**Platz** (m)	[plats]
headphones	**Kopfhörer** (m)	['kɔpf͵hø:ʀɐ]
folding tray (tray table)	**Klapptisch** (m)	['klap͵tɪʃ]
airplane window	**Bullauge** (n)	['bʊl͵ʔaʊgə]
aisle	**Durchgang** (m)	['dʊʀç͵gaŋ]

170. Train

train	**Zug** (m)	[tsu:k]
commuter train	**elektrischer Zug** (m)	[e'lɛktrɪʃɐ tsu:k]
express train	**Schnellzug** (m)	['ʃnɛl͜tsu:k]
diesel locomotive	**Diesellok** (f)	['di:zəl͜lɔk]
steam locomotive	**Dampflok** (f)	['dampf͜lɔk]

coach, carriage	**Personenwagen** (m)	[pɛʁ'zo:nən͜va:gən]
buffet car	**Speisewagen** (m)	['ʃpaɪzə͜va:gən]

rails	**Schienen** (pl)	['ʃi:nən]
railway	**Eisenbahn** (f)	['aɪzən·ba:n]
sleeper (track support)	**Bahnschwelle** (f)	['ba:n͜ʃvɛlə]

platform (railway ~)	**Bahnsteig** (m)	['ba:n͜ʃtaɪk]
platform (~ 1, 2, etc.)	**Gleis** (n)	['glaɪs]
semaphore	**Eisenbahnsignal** (n)	['aɪzənba:n·zɪ'gna:l]
station	**Station** (f)	[ʃta'tsjo:n]

train driver	**Lokführer** (m)	['lɔk͜fy:ʁɐ]
porter (of luggage)	**Träger** (m)	['trɛ:gɐ]
carriage attendant	**Schaffner** (m)	['ʃafnɐ]
passenger	**Fahrgast** (m)	['fa:ɐ͜gast]
ticket inspector	**Kontrolleur** (m)	[kɔntrɔ'lø:ɐ]

corridor (in train)	**Flur** (m)	[flu:ɐ]
emergency brake	**Notbremse** (f)	['no:t͜bʁɛmzə]

compartment	**Abteil** (n)	[ap'taɪl]
berth	**Liegeplatz** (m), **Schlafkoje** (f)	['li:gə͜plats], ['ʃla:f͜ko:jə]
upper berth	**oberer Liegeplatz** (m)	['o:bɐʁ 'li:gə͜plats]
lower berth	**unterer Liegeplatz** (m)	['ʊntɐʁ 'li:gə͜plats]
bed linen, bedding	**Bettwäsche** (f)	['bɛt͜vɛʃə]

ticket	**Fahrkarte** (f)	['fa:ɐ͜kaʁtə]
timetable	**Fahrplan** (m)	['fa:ɐ͜pla:n]
information display	**Anzeigetafel** (f)	['antsaɪgə͜ta:fəl]

to leave, to depart	**abfahren** (vi)	['ap͜fa:ʁən]
departure (of a train)	**Abfahrt** (f)	['ap͜fa:ɐt]
to arrive (ab. train)	**ankommen** (vi)	['an͜kɔmən]
arrival	**Ankunft** (f)	['ankʊnft]

to arrive by train	**mit dem Zug kommen**	[mɪt dem tsu:k 'kɔmən]
to get on the train	**in den Zug einsteigen**	[ɪn den tsu:k 'aɪn͜ʃtaɪgən]
to get off the train	**aus dem Zug aussteigen**	['aʊs dem tsu:k 'aʊs͜ʃtaɪgən]

train crash	**Zugunglück** (n)	['tsu:k?ʊn͜glʏk]
to derail (vi)	**entgleisen** (vi)	[ɛnt'glaɪzən]

steam locomotive	**Dampflok** (f)	['dampf͜lɔk]
stoker, fireman	**Heizer** (m)	['haɪtsɐ]
firebox	**Feuerbuchse** (f)	['fɔɪɐ͜bʊksə]
coal	**Kohle** (f)	['ko:lə]

153

171. Ship

ship	Schiff (n)	[ʃɪf]
vessel	Fahrzeug (n)	['faːɐ̯ˌtsɔɪk]
steamship	Dampfer (m)	['dampfɐ]
riverboat	Motorschiff (n)	['moːtoːɐ̯ˌʃɪf]
cruise ship	Kreuzfahrtschiff (n)	['kʀɔɪtsfaːɐ̯tʃɪf]
cruiser	Kreuzer (m)	['kʀɔɪtsɐ]
yacht	Jacht (f)	[jaχt]
tugboat	Schlepper (m)	['ʃlɛpɐ]
barge	Lastkahn (m)	[lastˌkaːn]
ferry	Fähre (f)	['fɛːʀə]
sailing ship	Segelschiff (n)	['zeːgəlˌʃɪf]
brigantine	Brigantine (f)	[bʀigan'tiːnə]
ice breaker	Eisbrecher (m)	['aɪsˌbʀɛçɐ]
submarine	U-Boot (n)	['uːboːt]
boat (flat-bottomed ~)	Boot (n)	['boːt]
dinghy (lifeboat)	Dingi (n)	['dɪŋgi]
lifeboat	Rettungsboot (n)	['ʀɛtʊŋsˌboːt]
motorboat	Motorboot (n)	['moːtoːɐ̯ˌboːt]
captain	Kapitän (m)	[kapi'tɛn]
seaman	Matrose (m)	[ma'tʀoːzə]
sailor	Seemann (m)	['zeːman]
crew	Besatzung (f)	[bə'zatsʊŋ]
boatswain	Bootsmann (m)	['boːtsman]
ship's boy	Schiffsjunge (m)	['ʃɪfsˌjʊŋə]
cook	Schiffskoch (m)	['ʃɪfsˌkɔχ]
ship's doctor	Schiffsarzt (m)	['ʃɪfsˌʔaʀtst]
deck	Deck (n)	[dɛk]
mast	Mast (m)	[mast]
sail	Segel (n)	[zeːgəl]
hold	Schiffsraum (m)	['ʃɪfsˌʀaʊm]
bow (prow)	Bug (m)	[buːk]
stern	Heck (n)	[hɛk]
oar	Ruder (n)	['ʀuːdɐ]
screw propeller	Schraube (f)	['ʃʀaʊbə]
cabin	Kajüte (f)	[ka'jyːtə]
wardroom	Messe (f)	['mɛsə]
engine room	Maschinenraum (m)	[ma'ʃiːnənˌʀaʊm]
bridge	Brücke (f)	['bʀʏkə]
radio room	Funkraum (m)	['fʊŋkˌʀaʊm]
wave (radio)	Radiowelle (f)	['ʀaːdɪoˌvɛlə]
logbook	Schiffstagebuch (n)	['ʃɪfsˈtaːgəbuːχ]
spyglass	Fernrohr (n)	['fɛʀnˌʀoːɐ̯]
bell	Glocke (f)	['glɔkə]

flag	Fahne (f)	['fa:nə]
hawser (mooring ~)	Seil (n)	[zaɪl]
knot (bowline, etc.)	Knoten (m)	['kno:tən]

deckrails	Geländer (n)	[gə'lɛndɐ]
gangway	Treppe (f)	['tRɛpə]

anchor	Anker (m)	['aŋkɐ]
to weigh anchor	den Anker lichten	[den 'aŋkɐ 'lɪçtən]
to drop anchor	Anker werfen	['aŋkɐ ˌvɛʁfən]
anchor chain	Ankerkette (f)	['ankɐˌkɛtə]

port (harbour)	Hafen (m)	['ha:fən]
quay, wharf	Anlegestelle (f)	['anleːgəˌʃtɛlə]
to berth (moor)	anlegen (vi)	['anˌleːgən]
to cast off	abstoßen (vt)	['apˌʃto:sən]

trip, voyage	Reise (f)	['Raɪzə]
cruise (sea trip)	Kreuzfahrt (f)	['kRɔɪtsˌfaːɐt]
course (route)	Kurs (m)	[kuʁs]
route (itinerary)	Reiseroute (f)	['RaɪzəˌRuːtə]

fairway (safe water channel)	Fahrwasser (n)	['faːɐˌvasɐ]
shallows	Untiefe (f)	['ʊnˌtiːfə]
to run aground	stranden (vi)	['ʃtRandən]

storm	Sturm (m)	[ʃtʊʁm]
signal	Signal (n)	[zɪ'gnaːl]
to sink (vi)	untergehen (vi)	['ʊntɐˌgeːən]
Man overboard!	Mann über Bord!	[man 'yːbɐ bɔʁt]
SOS (distress signal)	SOS	[ɛso:'ʔɛs]
ring buoy	Rettungsring (m)	['RɛtʊŋsˌRɪŋ]

172. Airport

airport	Flughafen (m)	['fluːkˌhaːfən]
aeroplane	Flugzeug (n)	['fluːkˌtsɔɪk]
airline	Fluggesellschaft (f)	['fluːkgəˌzɛlʃaft]
air traffic controller	Fluglotse (m)	['fluːkˌloːtsə]

departure	Abflug (m)	['apˌfluːk]
arrival	Ankunft (f)	['ankʊnft]
to arrive (by plane)	anfliegen (vi)	['anˌfliːgən]

departure time	Abflugzeit (f)	['apfluːkˌtsaɪt]
arrival time	Ankunftszeit (f)	['ankʊnftsˌtsaɪt]

to be delayed	sich verspäten	[zɪç fɛɐ'ʃpɛːtən]
flight delay	Abflugverspätung (f)	['apfluːk·fɛɐ'ʃpɛːtʊŋ]

information board	Anzeigetafel (f)	['antsaɪgəˌtaːfəl]
information	Information (f)	[ɪnfɔʁma'tsjoːn]
to announce (vt)	ankündigen (vt)	['ankʏndɪgən]
flight (e.g. next ~)	Flug (m)	[fluːk]

| customs | Zollamt (n) | ['tsɔl,ʔamt] |
| customs officer | Zollbeamter (m) | ['tsɔl·bə,ʔamtɐ] |

customs declaration	Zolldeklaration (f)	['tsɔl·deklaʀa'tsjoːn]
to fill in (vt)	ausfüllen (vt)	['aʊs,fʏlən]
to fill in the declaration	die Zollerklärung ausfüllen	[di 'tsɔl·ɛɐ'klɛːʀʊŋ 'aʊs,fʏlən]
passport control	Passkontrolle (f)	['pas·kɔn,tʀɔlə]

luggage	Gepäck (n)	[gə'pɛk]
hand luggage	Handgepäck (n)	['hant·gə,pɛk]
luggage trolley	Kofferkuli (m)	['kɔfɐ,kuːli]

landing	Landung (f)	['landʊŋ]
landing strip	Landebahn (f)	['landə,baːn]
to land (vi)	landen (vi)	['landən]
airstair (passenger stair)	Fluggasttreppe (f)	['fluːkgast,tʀɛpə]

check-in	Check-in (n)	[tʃɛk?in]
check-in counter	Check-in-Schalter (m)	[tʃɛk?in 'ʃaltɐ]
to check-in (vi)	sich registrieren lassen	[zɪç ʀeɡɪs'tʀiːʀən 'lasən]
boarding card	Bordkarte (f)	['boɐt,kaɐtə]
departure gate	Abfluggate (n)	['apfluː k,ɡeɪt]

transit	Transit (m)	[tʀan'ziːt]
to wait (vt)	warten (vi)	['vaɐtən]
departure lounge	Wartesaal (m)	['vaɐtə,zaːl]
to see off	begleiten (vt)	[bə'ɡlaɪtən]
to say goodbye	sich verabschieden	[zɪç fɛɐ'apʃiːdən]

173. Bicycle. Motorcycle

bicycle	Fahrrad (n)	['faːɐ,ʀaːt]
scooter	Motorroller (m)	['moːtoːɐ,ʀɔlɐ]
motorbike	Motorrad (n)	['moːtoːɐ,ʀaːt]

to go by bicycle	Rad fahren	[ʀaːt 'faːʀən]
handlebars	Lenkstange (f)	['lɛŋkʃtaŋə]
pedal	Pedal (n)	[pe'daːl]
brakes	Bremsen (pl)	['bʀɛmzən]
bicycle seat (saddle)	Sattel (m)	['zatəl]

pump	Pumpe (f)	['pʊmpə]
pannier rack	Gepäckträger (m)	[gə'pɛk,tʀɛːgɐ]
front lamp	Scheinwerfer (m)	['ʃaɪn,vɛɐfɐ]
helmet	Helm (m)	[hɛlm]

wheel	Rad (n)	[ʀaːt]
mudguard	Schutzblech (n)	['ʃʊts,blɛç]
rim	Felge (f)	['fɛlgə]
spoke	Speiche (f)	['ʃpaɪçə]

Cars

car	Auto (n)	['aʊto]
sports car	Sportwagen (m)	['ʃpɔʁtˌvaːgən]
limousine	Limousine (f)	[limu'ziːnə]
off-road vehicle	Geländewagen (m)	[gə'lɛndəˌvaːgən]
drophead coupé (convertible)	Kabriolett (n)	[kabʁio'lɛt]
minibus	Kleinbus (m)	['klaɪnˌbʊs]
ambulance	Krankenwagen (m)	['kʁaŋkənˌvaːgən]
snowplough	Schneepflug (m)	['ʃneːˌpfluːk]
lorry	Lastkraftwagen (m)	['lastkʁaftˌvaːgən]
road tanker	Tankwagen (m)	['taŋkˌvaːgən]
van (small truck)	Kastenwagen (m)	['kastənˌvaːgən]
tractor unit	Sattelzug (m)	['zatəlˌtsuːk]
trailer	Anhänger (m)	['anˌhɛŋɐ]
comfortable (adj)	komfortabel	[kɔmfɔʁ'taːbəl]
used (adj)	gebraucht	[gə'bʁaʊxt]

bonnet	Motorhaube (f)	['moːtoːɐˌhaʊbə]
wing	Kotflügel (m)	['koːtflyːgəl]
roof	Dach (n)	[daχ]
windscreen	Windschutzscheibe (f)	['vɪntʃʊtsˌʃaɪbə]
rear-view mirror	Rückspiegel (m)	['ʁʏkˌʃpiːgəl]
windscreen washer	Scheibenwaschanlage (f)	['ʃaɪbən·'vaʃʔanˌlaːgə]
windscreen wipers	Scheibenwischer (m)	['ʃaɪbənˌvɪʃɐ]
side window	Seitenscheibe (f)	['zaɪtənˌʃaɪbə]
electric window	Fensterheber (m)	['fɛnstɐˌheːbɐ]
aerial	Antenne (f)	[an'tɛnə]
sunroof	Schiebedach (n)	['ʃiːbəˌdaχ]
bumper	Stoßstange (f)	['ʃtoːsˌʃtaŋə]
boot	Kofferraum (m)	['kɔfɐˌʁaʊm]
roof luggage rack	Dachgepäckträger (m)	['daχ·gəpɛkˌtʁɛːgɐ]
door	Wagenschlag (m)	['vaːgənˌʃlaːk]
door handle	Türgriff (m)	['tyːɐˌgʁɪf]
door lock	Türschloss (n)	['tyːɐˌʃlɔs]
number plate	Nummernschild (n)	['nʊmɐnˌʃɪlt]
silencer	Auspufftopf (m)	['aʊspʊfˌtɔpf]

157

| petrol tank | Benzintank (m) | [bɛn'tsiːnˌtaŋk] |
| exhaust pipe | Auspuffrohr (n) | ['aʊspʊfˌʀoːɐ] |

accelerator	Gas (n)	[gaːs]
pedal	Pedal (n)	[pe'daːl]
accelerator pedal	Gaspedal (n)	['gasˑpe'daːl]

brake	Bremse (f)	['bʀɛmzə]
brake pedal	Bremspedal (n)	['bʀɛmzˑpe'daːl]
to brake (use the brake)	bremsen (vi)	['bʀɛmzən]
handbrake	Handbremse (f)	['hantˌbʀɛmzə]

clutch	Kupplung (f)	['kʊplʊŋ]
clutch pedal	Kupplungspedal (n)	['kʊplʊŋsˑpe'daːl]
clutch disc	Kupplungsscheibe (f)	['kʊplʊŋsˌʃaɪbə]
shock absorber	Stoßdämpfer (m)	['ʃtoːsˑdɛmpfɐ]

wheel	Rad (n)	[ʀaːt]
spare tyre	Reserverad (n)	[ʀe'zɛʁvəˌʀaːt]
tyre	Reifen (m)	['ʀaɪfən]
wheel cover (hubcap)	Radkappe (f)	['ʀaːtˌkapə]

driving wheels	Triebräder (pl)	['tʀiːpˌʀɛːdɐ]
front-wheel drive (as adj)	mit Vorderantrieb	[mɪt 'foːɐdeːɐˌʔantʀiːp]
rear-wheel drive (as adj)	mit Hinterradantrieb	[mɪt 'hɪntɐʀaːtˌʔantʀiːp]
all-wheel drive (as adj)	mit Allradantrieb	[mɪt 'alʀaːtˌʔantʀiːp]

gearbox	Getriebe (n)	[gə'tʀiːbə]
automatic (adj)	Automatik-	[aʊto'maːtɪk]
mechanical (adj)	Schalt-	['ʃalt]
gear lever	Schalthebel (m)	['ʃaltˌheːbəl]

| headlamp | Scheinwerfer (m) | ['ʃaɪnˌvɛʁfɐ] |
| headlights | Scheinwerfer (pl) | ['ʃaɪnˌvɛʁfɐ] |

dipped headlights	Abblendlicht (n)	['apblɛntˌlɪçt]
full headlights	Fernlicht (n)	['fɛʁnˌlɪçt]
brake light	Stopplicht (n)	['ʃtɔpˌlɪçt]

sidelights	Standlicht (n)	['ʃtantˌlɪçt]
hazard lights	Warnblinker (m)	['vaʁnˌblɪŋkɐ]
fog lights	Nebelscheinwerfer (pl)	['neːbəlˌʃaɪnvɛʁfɐ]
turn indicator	Blinker (m)	['blɪŋkɐ]
reversing light	Rückfahrscheinwerfer (m)	['ʀʏkfaːɐˌʃaɪnvɛʁfɐ]

176. Cars. Passenger compartment

car interior	Wageninnere (n)	['vaːgənˌʔɪnəʀə]
leather (as adj)	Leder-	['leːdɐ]
velour (as adj)	aus Velours	[aʊs və'luːɐ]
upholstery	Polster (n)	['pɔlstɐ]

| instrument (gage) | Instrument (n) | [ˌɪnstʀu'mɛnt] |
| dashboard | Armaturenbrett (n) | [aʁma'tuːʁənˌbʀɛt] |

| speedometer | Tachometer (m) | [taxo'me:tɐ] |
| needle (pointer) | Nadel (f) | ['na:dəl] |

mileometer	Kilometerzähler (m)	[kilo'me:tɐ͵tsɛ:lɐ]
indicator (sensor)	Anzeige (f)	['an͵tsaɪgə]
level	Pegel (m)	['pe:gəl]
warning light	Kontrollleuchte (f)	[kɔn'tʀɔl͵lɔɪçtə]

steering wheel	Steuerrad (n)	['ʃtɔɪɐ͵ʀa:t]
horn	Hupe (f)	['hu:pə]
button	Knopf (m)	[knɔpf]
switch	Umschalter (m)	['ʊm͵ʃaltɐ]

seat	Sitz (m)	[zɪts]
backrest	Rückenlehne (f)	['ʀʏkən͵le:nə]
headrest	Kopfstütze (f)	['kɔpf͵ʃtʏtsə]
seat belt	Sicherheitsgurt (m)	['zɪçɐhaɪts͵gʊʀt]
to fasten the belt	sich anschnallen	[zɪç 'an͵ʃnalən]
adjustment (of seats)	Einstellung (f)	['aɪn͵ʃtɛlʊŋ]

| airbag | Airbag (m) | ['ɛ:ɐ·bak] |
| air-conditioner | Klimaanlage (f) | ['kli:ma͵ʔanla:gə] |

radio	Radio (n)	['ʀa:dɪo]
CD player	CD-Spieler (m)	[tse:'de: 'ʃpi:lɐ]
to turn on	einschalten (vt)	['aɪnʃaltən]
aerial	Antenne (f)	[an'tɛnə]
glove box	Handschuhfach (n)	['hantʃu:͵faχ]
ashtray	Aschenbecher (m)	['aʃən·bɛçɐ]

177. Cars. Engine

engine	Triebwerk (n)	['tʀi:p͵vɛʀk]
motor	Motor (m)	['mo:to:ɐ]
diesel (as adj)	Diesel-	['di:zəl]
petrol (as adj)	Benzin-	[bɛn'tsi:n]

engine volume	Hubraum (m)	['hu:p͵ʀaʊm]
power	Leistung (f)	['laɪstʊŋ]
horsepower	Pferdestärke (f)	['pfe:ɐdə͵ʃtɛʀkə]
piston	Kolben (m)	[kɔlbən]
cylinder	Zylinder (m)	[tsy'lɪndɐ]
valve	Ventil (n)	[vɛn'ti:l]

injector	Injektor (m)	[ɪn'jɛktɔ:ɐ]
generator (alternator)	Generator (m)	[genə'ʀa:to:ɐ]
carburettor	Vergaser (m)	[fɛɐ'ga:zɐ]
motor oil	Motoröl (n)	['mo:to:ɐ͵ʔø:l]

radiator	Kühler (m)	['ky:lɐ]
coolant	Kühlflüssigkeit (f)	[ky:l'flʏsɪç͵kaɪt]
cooling fan	Ventilator (m)	[vɛnti'la:to:ɐ]
battery (accumulator)	Autobatterie (f)	['aʊtobatə͵ʀi:]
starter	Anlasser (m)	['an͵lasɐ]

ignition	Zündung (f)	['tsʏndʊŋ]
sparking plug	Zündkerze (f)	['tsʏnt‚kɛʁtsə]
terminal (battery ~)	Klemme (f)	['klɛmə]
positive terminal	Pluspol (m)	['plʊs‚poːl]
negative terminal	Minuspol (m)	['miːnʊs‚poːl]
fuse	Sicherung (f)	['zɪçəʁʊŋ]
air filter	Luftfilter (m, n)	['lʊft‚fɪltɐ]
oil filter	Ölfilter (m)	['øːl‚fɪltɐ]
fuel filter	Treibstofffilter (m)	['tʁaɪpʃtɔf‚fɪltɐ]

178. Cars. Crash. Repair

car crash	Unfall (m)	['ʊnfal]
traffic accident	Verkehrsunfall (m)	[fɛɐ'keːɐsʔʊn‚fal]
to crash (into the wall, etc.)	fahren gegen ...	['faːʁən 'geːgən]
to get smashed up	verunglücken (vi)	[fɛɐ'ʔʊnglʏkən]
damage	Schaden (m)	['ʃaːdən]
intact (unscathed)	heil	['haɪl]
breakdown	Panne (f)	['panə]
to break down (vi)	kaputtgehen (vi)	[ka'pʊt‚geːən]
towrope	Abschleppseil (n)	['apʃlɛp‚zaɪl]
puncture	Reifenpanne (f)	['ʁaɪfən‚panə]
to have a puncture	platt sein	[plat zaɪn]
to pump up	pumpen (vt)	['pʊmpən]
pressure	Druck (m)	[dʁʊk]
to check (to examine)	prüfen (vt)	['pʁyːfən]
repair	Reparatur (f)	[ʁepaʁa'tuːɐ]
garage (auto service shop)	Reparaturwerkstatt (f)	[ʁepaʁa‚tuːɐ'vɛʁkʃtat]
spare part	Ersatzteil (m, n)	[ɛɐ'zats‚taɪl]
part	Einzelteil (m, n)	['aɪntsəl‚taɪl]
bolt (with nut)	Bolzen (m)	['bɔltsən]
screw (fastener)	Schraube (f)	['ʃʁaʊbə]
nut	Mutter (f)	['mʊtɐ]
washer	Scheibe (f)	['ʃaɪbə]
bearing (e.g. ball ~)	Lager (n)	['laːgɐ]
tube	Rohr (n)	[ʁoːɐ]
gasket (head ~)	Dichtung (f)	['dɪçtʊŋ]
cable, wire	Draht (m)	[dʁaːt]
jack	Wagenheber (m)	['vaːgən‚heːbɐ]
spanner	Schraubenschlüssel (m)	['ʃʁaʊbənʃlʏsəl]
hammer	Hammer (m)	['hamɐ]
pump	Pumpe (f)	['pʊmpə]
screwdriver	Schraubenzieher (m)	['ʃʁaʊbəntsiːɐ]
fire extinguisher	Feuerlöscher (m)	['fɔɪɐ‚lœʃɐ]
warning triangle	Warndreieck (n)	['vaʁn‚dʁaɪɛk]

to stall (vi)	**abwürgen** (vi)	['ap͵vʏʁɡən]
stall (n)	**Anhalten** (n)	['anhaltən]
to be broken	**kaputt sein**	[ka'pʊt zaɪn]

to overheat (vi)	**überhitzt werden**	[y:bɐ'hɪtst 've:ɐdən]
to be clogged up	**verstopft sein**	[fɛɐ'ʃtɔpft zaɪn]
to freeze up (pipes, etc.)	**einfrieren** (vi)	['aɪn͵fʁi:ʁən]
to burst (vi, ab. tube)	**zerplatzen** (vi)	[tsɛɐ'platsən]

pressure	**Druck** (m)	[dʁʊk]
level	**Pegel** (m)	['pe:ɡəl]
slack (~ belt)	**schlaff**	[ʃlaf]

dent	**Delle** (f)	['dɛlə]
knocking noise (engine)	**Klopfen** (n)	['klɔpfən]
crack	**Riß** (m)	[ʁɪs]
scratch	**Kratzer** (m)	['kʁatsɐ]

179. Cars. Road

road	**Fahrbahn** (f)	['fa:ɐ͵ba:n]
motorway	**Schnellstraße** (f)	['ʃnɛl͵ʃtʁa:sə]
highway	**Autobahn** (f)	['aʊto͵ba:n]
direction (way)	**Richtung** (f)	['ʁɪçtʊŋ]
distance	**Entfernung** (f)	[ɛnt'fɛʁnʊŋ]

bridge	**Brücke** (f)	['bʁʏkə]
car park	**Parkplatz** (m)	['paʁk͵plats]
square	**Platz** (m)	[plats]
road junction	**Autobahnkreuz** (n)	['aʊtoba:n͵kʁɔɪts]
tunnel	**Tunnel** (m)	['tʊnəl]

petrol station	**Tankstelle** (f)	['taŋkʃtɛlə]
car park	**Parkplatz** (m)	['paʁk͵plats]
petrol pump	**Zapfsäule** (f)	['tsapf͵zɔɪlə]
auto repair shop	**Reparaturwerkstatt** (f)	[ʁepaʁa͵tu:ɐ'vɛʁk͵ʃtat]
to fill up	**tanken** (vt)	['taŋkən]
fuel	**Treibstoff** (m)	['tʁaɪp͵ʃtɔf]
jerrycan	**Kanister** (m)	[ka'nɪstɐ]

asphalt, tarmac	**Asphalt** (m)	[as'falt]
road markings	**Markierung** (f)	[maʁ'ki:ʁʊŋ]
kerb	**Bordstein** (m)	['bɔʁt͵ʃtaɪn]
crash barrier	**Leitplanke** (f)	['laɪt͵plaŋkə]
ditch	**Graben** (m)	['ɡʁa:bən]
roadside (shoulder)	**Straßenrand** (m)	['ʃtʁa:sən͵ʁant]
lamppost	**Straßenlaterne** (f)	['ʃtʁa:sən·la͵tɛʁnə]

to drive (a car)	**fahren** (vt)	['fa:ʁən]
to turn (e.g., ~ left)	**abbiegen** (vi)	['ap͵bi:ɡən]
to make a U-turn	**umkehren** (vi)	['ʊm͵ke:ʁən]
reverse (~ gear)	**Rückwärtsgang** (m)	['ʁʏkvɛʁts͵ɡaŋ]
to honk (vi)	**hupen** (vi)	['hu:pən]
honk (sound)	**Hupe** (f)	['hu:pə]

to get stuck (in the mud, etc.)	stecken (vi)	['ʃtɛkən]
to spin the wheels	durchdrehen (vi)	['dʊʁçˌdʁeːən]
to cut, to turn off (vt)	abstellen (vt)	['apʃtɛlən]

speed	Geschwindigkeit (f)	[gəˈʃvɪndɪçˌkaɪt]
to exceed the speed limit	Geschwindigkeit überschreiten	[gəˈʃvɪndɪçˌkaɪt ˌyːbɐˈʃʁaɪtən]
to give a ticket	bestrafen (vt)	[bəˈʃtʁaːfən]
traffic lights	Ampel (f)	['ampəl]
driving licence	Führerschein (m)	['fyːʁɐˌʃaɪn]

level crossing	Bahnübergang (m)	['baːnʔyːbɐˌgaŋ]
crossroads	Straßenkreuzung (f)	['ʃtʁaːsənˌkʁɔɪtsʊŋ]
zebra crossing	Fußgängerüberweg (m)	['fuːsˌgɛŋɐ·yːbɐˈveːk]
bend, curve	Kehre (f)	['keːʁə]
pedestrian precinct	Fußgängerzone (f)	['fuːsgɛŋɐˌtsoːnə]

180. Signs

Highway Code	Verkehrsregeln (pl)	[fɛɐˈkeːɐsˌʁeːgəln]
road sign (traffic sign)	Verkehrszeichen (n)	[fɛɐˈkeːɐsˌtsaɪçən]
overtaking	Überholen (n)	[yːbɐˈhoːlən]
curve	Kurve (f)	['kʊʁvə]
U-turn	Wende (f)	['vɛndə]
roundabout	Kreisverkehr (m)	['kʁaɪs·fɛɐˌkeːɐ]

No entry	Einfahrt verboten	['aɪnˌfaːɐt fɛɐˈboːtən]
All vehicles prohibited	Verkehr verboten	[fɛɐˈkeːɐ fɛɐˈboːtən]
No overtaking	Überholverbot	[yːbɐˈhoːlˌfɛɐˌboːt]
No parking	Parken verboten	['paʁkən fɛɐˈboːtən]
No stopping	Halteverbot	['haltə·fɛɐˌboːt]

dangerous curve	gefährliche Kurve (f)	[gəˈfɛːɐlɪçə 'kʊʁvə]
steep descent	Gefälle (n)	[gəˈfɛlə]
one-way traffic	Einbahnstraße (f)	['aɪnbaːnˌʃtʁaːsə]
zebra crossing	Fußgängerüberweg (m)	['fuːsˌgɛŋɐ·yːbɐˈveːk]
slippery road	Schleudergefahr	['ʃlɔɪdɐˌgəˈfaːɐ]
GIVE WAY	Vorfahrt gewähren!	['foːɐfaɐt gəˈvɛːʁən]

PEOPLE. LIFE EVENTS

181. Holidays. Event

celebration, holiday	**Fest** (n)	[fɛst]
national day	**Nationalfeiertag** (m)	[natsjɔ'na:lˌfaɪeta:k]
public holiday	**Feiertag** (m)	['faɪeˌta:k]
to commemorate (vt)	**feiern** (vt)	['faɪɐn]
event (happening)	**Ereignis** (n)	[ɛɐ'ʔaɪgnɪs]
event (organized activity)	**Veranstaltung** (f)	[fɛɐ'ʔanʃtaltʊŋ]
banquet (party)	**Bankett** (n)	[baŋ'kɛt]
reception (formal party)	**Empfang** (m)	[ɛm'pfaŋ]
feast	**Festmahl** (n)	['fɛstˌma:l]
anniversary	**Jahrestag** (m)	['ja:ʀəsˌta:k]
jubilee	**Jubiläumsfeier** (f)	[jubi'lɛːʊmsˌfaɪe]
to celebrate (vt)	**begehen** (vt)	[bə'ge:ən]
New Year	**Neujahr** (n)	['nɔɪjaːɐ]
Happy New Year!	**Frohes Neues Jahr!**	[ˌfʀoːəs 'nɔɪəs jaːɐ]
Christmas	**Weihnachten** (n)	['vaɪnaxtən]
Merry Christmas!	**Frohe Weihnachten!**	[ˌfʀoːə 'vaɪnaxtən]
Christmas tree	**Tannenbaum** (m)	['tanənˌbaʊm]
fireworks (fireworks show)	**Feuerwerk** (n)	['fɔɪeˌvɛʁk]
wedding	**Hochzeit** (f)	['hɔxˌtsaɪt]
groom	**Bräutigam** (m)	['bʀɔɪtɪgam]
bride	**Braut** (f)	[bʀaʊt]
to invite (vt)	**einladen** (vt)	['aɪnˌla:dən]
invitation card	**Einladung** (f)	['aɪnˌla:dʊŋ]
guest	**Gast** (m)	[gast]
to visit (~ your parents, etc.)	**besuchen** (vt)	[bə'zu:xən]
to meet the guests	**Gäste empfangen**	['gɛstə ɛm'pfaŋən]
gift, present	**Geschenk** (n)	[gə'ʃɛŋk]
to give (sth as present)	**schenken** (vt)	['ʃɛŋkən]
to receive gifts	**Geschenke bekommen**	[gə'ʃɛŋkə bə'kɔmən]
bouquet (of flowers)	**Blumenstrauß** (m)	['blu:mənˌʃtʀaʊs]
congratulations	**Glückwunsch** (m)	['glʏkˌvʊnʃ]
to congratulate (vt)	**gratulieren** (vi)	[gʀatu'li:ʀən]
greetings card	**Glückwunschkarte** (f)	['glʏkvʊnʃˌkaʁtə]
to send a postcard	**eine Karte abschicken**	['aɪnə 'kaʁtə 'apˌʃɪkən]
to get a postcard	**eine Karte erhalten**	['aɪnə 'kaʁtə ɛɐ'haltən]
toast	**Trinkspruch** (m)	['tʀɪŋkˌʃpʀʊx]

to offer (a drink, etc.)	anbieten (vt)	['anbi:tən]
champagne	Champagner (m)	[ʃam'panjɐ]
to enjoy oneself	sich amüsieren	[zɪç amy'zi:ʀən]
merriment (gaiety)	Fröhlichkeit (f)	['fʀø:lɪç͵kaɪt]
joy (emotion)	Freude (f)	['fʀɔɪdə]
dance	Tanz (m)	[tants]
to dance (vi, vt)	tanzen (vi, vt)	['tantsən]
waltz	Walzer (m)	['valtsɐ]
tango	Tango (m)	['taŋgo]

182. Funerals. Burial

cemetery	Friedhof (m)	['fʀi:t͵ho:f]
grave, tomb	Grab (n)	[gʀa:p]
cross	Kreuz (n)	[kʀɔɪts]
gravestone	Grabstein (m)	['gʀa:p͵ʃtaɪn]
fence	Zaun (m)	[tsaʊn]
chapel	Kapelle (f)	[ka'pɛlə]
death	Tod (m)	[to:t]
to die (vi)	sterben (vi)	['ʃtɛʀbən]
the deceased	Verstorbene (m)	[fɛɐ'ʃtɔʀbənɐ]
mourning	Trauer (f)	['tʀaʊɐ]
to bury (vt)	begraben (vt)	[bə'gʀa:bən]
undertakers	Bestattungsinstitut (n)	[bə'ʃtatʊŋs?ɪnsti͵tu:t]
funeral	Begräbnis (n)	[bə'gʀɛ:pnɪs]
wreath	Kranz (m)	[kʀants]
coffin	Sarg (m)	[zaʀk]
hearse	Katafalk (m)	[kata'falk]
shroud	Totenhemd (n)	['to:tən͵hɛmt]
funeral procession	Trauerzug (m)	['tʀaʊɐ͵tsu:k]
funerary urn	Urne (f)	['ʊʀnə]
crematorium	Krematorium (n)	[kʀema'to:ʀiʊm]
obituary	Nachruf (m)	['na:χʀu:f]
to cry (weep)	weinen (vi)	['vaɪnən]
to sob (vi)	schluchzen (vi)	['ʃlʊχtsən]

183. War. Soldiers

platoon	Zug (m)	[tsu:k]
company	Kompanie (f)	[kɔmpa'ni:]
regiment	Regiment (n)	[ʀegi'mɛnt]
army	Armee (f)	[aʀ'me:]
division	Division (f)	[divi'zjo:n]
section, squad	Abteilung (f)	[ap'taɪlʊŋ]

host (army)	Heer (n)	[heːɐ]
soldier	Soldat (m)	[zɔl'daːt]
officer	Offizier (m)	[ɔfi'tsiːɐ]

private	Soldat (m)	[zɔl'daːt]
sergeant	Feldwebel (m)	['fɛlt‚veːbəl]
lieutenant	Leutnant (m)	['lɔɪtnant]
captain	Hauptmann (m)	['haʊptman]
major	Major (m)	[ma'joːɐ]
colonel	Oberst (m)	['oːbɐst]
general	General (m)	[genə'ʀaːl]

sailor	Matrose (m)	[ma'tʀoːzə]
captain	Kapitän (m)	[kapi'tɛn]
boatswain	Bootsmann (m)	['boːtsman]

artilleryman	Artillerist (m)	['aʁtɪləʀɪst]
paratrooper	Fallschirmjäger (m)	['falʃɪʁmˌjɛːgɐ]
pilot	Pilot (m)	[pi'loːt]
navigator	Steuermann (m)	['ʃtɔɪɐˌman]
mechanic	Mechaniker (m)	[me'çaːnikɐ]

pioneer (sapper)	Pionier (m)	[pɪo'niːɐ]
parachutist	Fallschirmspringer (m)	['falʃɪʁmˌʃpʀɪŋɐ]
reconnaissance scout	Aufklärer (m)	['aʊfˌklɛːʀɐ]
sniper	Scharfschütze (m)	['ʃaʁfʃʏtsə]

patrol (group)	Patrouille (f)	[pa'tʀʊljə]
to patrol (vt)	patrouillieren (vi)	[patʀʊl'jiːʀən]
sentry, guard	Wache (f)	['vaxə]

warrior	Krieger (m)	['kʀiːgɐ]
patriot	Patriot (m)	[patʀi'oːt]
hero	Held (m)	[hɛlt]
heroine	Heldin (f)	['hɛldɪn]

| traitor | Verräter (m) | [fɛɐ'ʀɛːtɐ] |
| to betray (vt) | verraten (vt) | [fɛɐ'ʀaːtən] |

| deserter | Deserteur (m) | [dezɛʁ'tøːɐ] |
| to desert (vi) | desertieren (vi) | [dezɛʁ'tiːʀən] |

mercenary	Söldner (m)	['zœldnɐ]
recruit	Rekrut (m)	[ʀe'kʀuːt]
volunteer	Freiwillige (m)	[ˌfʀaɪvɪlɪgə]

dead (n)	Getoetete (m)	[gə'tøːtətə]
wounded (n)	Verwundete (m)	[fɛɐ'vʊndətə]
prisoner of war	Kriegsgefangene (m)	['kʀiːks·gəˌfaŋənə]

184. War. Military actions. Part 1

| war | Krieg (m) | [kʀiːk] |
| to be at war | Krieg führen | [kʀiːk 'fyːʀən] |

civil war	**Bürgerkrieg** (m)	['bʏʁgəˌkʀiːk]
treacherously (adv)	**heimtückisch**	['haɪmˌtʏkɪʃ]
declaration of war	**Kriegserklärung** (f)	['kʀiːksʔɛɐˌklɛːʀʊŋ]
to declare (~ war)	**erklären** (vt)	[ɛɐ'klɛːʀən]
aggression	**Aggression** (f)	[agʀɛ'sjoːn]
to attack (invade)	**einfallen** (vt)	['aɪnˌfalən]

to invade (vt)	**einfallen** (vi)	['aɪnˌfalən]
invader	**Invasoren** (pl)	[ɪnva'zoːʀən]
conqueror	**Eroberer** (m)	[ɛɐ'ʔoːbəʀɐ]

defence	**Verteidigung** (f)	[fɛɐ'taɪdɪgʊŋ]
to defend (a country, etc.)	**verteidigen** (vt)	[fɛɐ'taɪdɪgən]
to defend (against …)	**sich verteidigen**	[zɪç fɛɐ'taɪdɪgən]

enemy	**Feind** (m)	[faɪnt]
foe, adversary	**Gegner** (m)	['geːgnɐ]
enemy (as adj)	**Feind-**	[faɪnt]

strategy	**Strategie** (f)	[ʃtʀate'giː]
tactics	**Taktik** (f)	['taktɪk]

order	**Befehl** (m)	[bə'feːl]
command (order)	**Anordnung** (f)	['anˌʔoʁdnʊŋ]
to order (vt)	**befehlen** (vt)	[ˌbə'feːlən]
mission	**Auftrag** (m)	['aʊfˌtʀaːk]
secret (adj)	**geheim**	[gə'haɪm]

battle	**Gefecht** (n)	[gə'fɛçt]
combat	**Kampf** (m)	[kampf]

attack	**Angriff** (m)	['anˌgʀɪf]
charge (assault)	**Sturm** (m)	[ʃtʊʁm]
to storm (vt)	**stürmen** (vt)	['ʃtʏʁmən]
siege (to be under ~)	**Belagerung** (f)	[bə'laːgəʀʊŋ]

offensive (n)	**Angriff** (m)	['anˌgʀɪf]
to go on the offensive	**angreifen** (vt)	['anˌgʀaɪfən]

retreat	**Rückzug** (m)	['ʀʏkˌtsuːk]
to retreat (vi)	**sich zurückziehen**	[zɪç tsu'ʀʏkˌtsiːən]

encirclement	**Einkesselung** (f)	['aɪnˌkɛsəlʊŋ]
to encircle (vt)	**einkesseln** (vt)	['aɪnˌkɛsəln]

bombing (by aircraft)	**Bombenangriff** (m)	['bɔmbənˌʔangʀɪf]
to drop a bomb	**eine Bombe abwerfen**	['aɪnə 'bɔmbə 'apˌvɛʁfən]
to bomb (vt)	**bombardieren** (vt)	[bɔmbaʁ'diːʀən]
explosion	**Explosion** (f)	[ɛksplo'zjoːn]

shot	**Schuss** (m)	[ʃʊs]
to fire (~ a shot)	**schießen** (vt)	['ʃiːsən]
firing (burst of ~)	**Schießerei** (f)	[ʃiːsə'ʀaɪ]

to aim (to point a weapon)	**zielen auf …**	['tsiːlən aʊf]
to point (a gun)	**richten** (vt)	['ʀɪçtən]

to hit (the target)	treffen (vt)	['tRɛfən]
to sink (~ a ship)	versenken (vt)	[fɛɐ'zɛŋkən]
hole (in a ship)	Loch (n)	[lɔx]
to founder, to sink (vi)	versinken (vi)	[fɛɐ'zɪŋkən]

front (war ~)	Front (f)	[fRɔnt]
evacuation	Evakuierung (f)	[evaku'i:Rʊŋ]
to evacuate (vt)	evakuieren (vt)	[evaku'i:Rən]

trench	Schützengraben (m)	['ʃʏtsən,gRa:bən]
barbed wire	Stacheldraht (m)	['ʃtaχəl,dRa:t]
barrier (anti tank ~)	Sperre (f)	['ʃpɛRə]
watchtower	Wachtturm (m)	['vaχt,tuɐm]

military hospital	Lazarett (n)	[latsa'Rɛt]
to wound (vt)	verwunden (vt)	[fɛɐ'vʊndən]
wound	Wunde (f)	['vʊndə]
wounded (n)	Verwundete (m)	[fɛɐ'vʊndətə]
to be wounded	verletzt sein	[fɛɐ'lɛtst zaɪn]
serious (wound)	schwer	[ʃve:ɐ]

185. War. Military actions. Part 2

captivity	Gefangenschaft (f)	[gə'faŋənʃaft]
to take captive	gefangen nehmen (vt)	[gə'faŋən 'ne:mən]
to be held captive	in Gefangenschaft sein	[ɪn gə'faŋənʃaft zaɪn]
to be taken captive	in Gefangenschaft geraten	[ɪn gə'faŋənʃaft gə'Ra:tən]

concentration camp	Konzentrationslager (n)	[kɔntsɛntRa'tsjo:ns,la:gə]
prisoner of war	Kriegsgefangene (m)	['kRi:ks·gə,faŋənə]
to escape (vi)	fliehen (vi)	['fli:ən]

to betray (vt)	verraten (vt)	[fɛɐ'Ra:tən]
betrayer	Verräter (m)	[fɛɐ'Rɛ:tɐ]
betrayal	Verrat (m)	[fɛɐ'Ra:t]

| to execute (by firing squad) | erschießen (vt) | [ɛɐ'ʃi:sən] |
| execution (by firing squad) | Erschießung (f) | [ɛɐ'ʃi:sʊŋ] |

equipment (military gear)	Ausrüstung (f)	['aʊs,Rʏstʊŋ]
shoulder board	Schulterstück (n)	['ʃʊltɐˌʃtʏk]
gas mask	Gasmaske (f)	['ga:s,maskə]

field radio	Funkgerät (n)	['fʊŋk·gə,Rɛ:t]
cipher, code	Chiffre (f)	['ʃɪfRə]
secrecy	Geheimhaltung (f)	[gə'haɪm,haltʊŋ]
password	Kennwort (n)	['kɛn,vɔɐt]

land mine	Mine (f)	['mi:nə]
to mine (road, etc.)	Minen legen	['mi:nən 'le:gən]
minefield	Minenfeld (n)	['mi:nən,fɛlt]

| air-raid warning | Luftalarm (m) | ['lʊftʔa,laɐm] |
| alarm (alert signal) | Alarm (m) | [a'laɐm] |

signal	Signal (n)	[zɪ'gna:l]
signal flare	Signalrakete (f)	[zɪ'gna:l·ʀaˌke:tə]
headquarters	Hauptquartier (n)	['haʊpt·kvaʀˌti:ɐ]
reconnaissance	Aufklärung (f)	['aʊfˌklɛ:ʀʊn]
situation	Lage (f)	['la:gə]
report	Bericht (m)	[bə'ʀɪçt]
ambush	Hinterhalt (m)	['hɪntɐˌhalt]
reinforcement (army)	Verstärkung (f)	[fɛɐ'ʃtɛʀkʊn]
target	Zielscheibe (f)	['tsi:lˌʃaɪbə]
training area	Schießplatz (m)	['ʃi:sˌplats]
military exercise	Manöver (n)	[ma'nø:vɐ]
panic	Panik (f)	['pa:nɪk]
devastation	Verwüstung (f)	[fɛɐ'vy:stʊn]
destruction, ruins	Trümmer (pl)	['tʀʏmɐ]
to destroy (vt)	zerstören (vt)	[tsɛɐ'ʃtø:ʀən]
to survive (vi, vt)	überleben (vi)	[ˌy:bɐ'le:bən]
to disarm (vt)	entwaffnen (vt)	[ɛnt'vafnən]
to handle (~ a gun)	handhaben (vt)	['hantˌha:bən]
Attention!	Stillgestanden!	['ʃtɪlgəˌʃtandən]
At ease!	Rühren!	['ʀy:ʀən]
feat, act of courage	Heldentat (f)	['hɛldənˌta:t]
oath (vow)	Eid (m), Schwur (m)	[aɪt], [ʃvu:ɐ]
to swear (an oath)	schwören (vi, vt)	['ʃvø:ʀən]
decoration (medal, etc.)	Lohn (m)	[lo:n]
to award (give a medal to)	auszeichnen (vt)	['aʊsˌtsaɪçnən]
medal	Medaille (f)	[me'daljə]
order (e.g. ~ of Merit)	Orden (m)	['ɔʀdən]
victory	Sieg (m)	[zi:k]
defeat	Niederlage (f)	['ni:dɐˌla:gə]
armistice	Waffenstillstand (m)	['vafənˌʃtɪlʃtant]
standard (battle flag)	Fahne (f)	['fa:nə]
glory (honour, fame)	Ruhm (m)	[ʀu:m]
parade	Parade (f)	[pa'ʀa:də]
to march (on parade)	marschieren (vi)	[maʀ'ʃi:ʀən]

186. Weapons

weapons	Waffe (f)	['vafə]
firearms	Schusswaffe (f)	['ʃʊsˌvafə]
cold weapons (knives, etc.)	blanke Waffe (f)	['blankə 'vafə]
chemical weapons	chemischen Waffen (pl)	[çe:miʃən 'vafən]
nuclear (adj)	Kern-, Atom-	[kɛʀn], [a'to:m]
nuclear weapons	Kernwaffe (f)	['kɛʀnˌvafə]
bomb	Bombe (f)	['bɔmbə]

atomic bomb	Atombombe (f)	[a'to:m‚bɔmbə]
pistol (gun)	Pistole (f)	[pɪs'to:lə]
rifle	Gewehr (n)	[gə've:ɐ]
submachine gun	Maschinenpistole (f)	[ma'ʃi:nən·pɪs‚to:lə]
machine gun	Maschinengewehr (n)	[ma'ʃi:nən·gə‚ve:ɐ]

muzzle	Mündung (f)	['mʏndʊŋ]
barrel	Lauf (m)	[laʊf]
calibre	Kaliber (n)	[‚ka'li:bɐ]

trigger	Abzug (m)	['ap‚tsu:k]
sight (aiming device)	Visier (n)	[vi'zi:ɐ]
magazine	Magazin (n)	[maga'tsi:n]
butt (shoulder stock)	Kolben (m)	[kɔlbən]

| hand grenade | Handgranate (f) | ['hant·gʀa‚na:tə] |
| explosive | Sprengstoff (m) | ['ʃpʀɛŋ‚ʃtɔf] |

bullet	Kugel (f)	['ku:gəl]
cartridge	Patrone (f)	[pa'tʀo:nə]
charge	Ladung (f)	['la:dʊŋ]
ammunition	Munition (f)	[muni'tsjo:n]

bomber (aircraft)	Bomber (m)	['bɔmbɐ]
fighter	Kampfflugzeug (n)	['kampfflu:k‚tsɔɪk]
helicopter	Hubschrauber (m)	['hu:p‚ʃʀaʊbɐ]

anti-aircraft gun	Flugabwehrkanone (f)	[flu:k'ʔapve:ɐka‚no:nə]
tank	Panzer (m)	['pantsɐ]
tank gun	Panzerkanone (f)	['pantsɐ‚ka'no:nə]

artillery	Artillerie (f)	['aʁtɪləʀi:]
gun (cannon, howitzer)	Haubitze (f), Kanone (f)	[haʊ'bɪtsə], [ka'no:nə]
to lay (a gun)	richten (vt)	['ʀɪçtən]

shell (projectile)	Geschoß (n)	[gə'ʃo:s]
mortar bomb	Wurfgranate (f)	['vʊʁf·gʀa'na:tə]
mortar	Granatwerfer (m)	[gʀa'na:t‚vɛʁfɐ]
splinter (shell fragment)	Splitter (m)	['ʃplɪtɐ]

submarine	U-Boot (n)	['u:bo:t]
torpedo	Torpedo (m)	[tɔʁ'pe:do]
missile	Rakete (f)	[ʀa'ke:tə]

to load (gun)	laden (vt)	['la:dən]
to shoot (vi)	schießen (vi)	['ʃi:sən]
to point at (the cannon)	zielen auf ...	['tsi:lən aʊf]
bayonet	Bajonett (n)	[‚bajo'nɛt]

rapier	Degen (m)	['de:gən]
sabre (e.g. cavalry ~)	Säbel (m)	['zɛ:bəl]
spear (weapon)	Speer (m)	[ʃpe:ɐ]
bow	Bogen (m)	['bo:gən]
arrow	Pfeil (m)	[pfaɪl]
musket	Muskete (f)	[mʊs'ke:tə]
crossbow	Armbrust (f)	['aʁm‚bʀʊst]

187. Ancient people

primitive (prehistoric)	vorzeitlich	['fo:ɐˌtsaɪtlɪç]
prehistoric (adj)	prähistorisch	[ˌpʀɛhɪs'to:ʀɪʃ]
ancient (~ civilization)	alt	[alt]
Stone Age	Steinzeit (f)	['ʃtaɪnˌtsaɪt]
Bronze Age	Bronzezeit (f)	['bʀɔŋsəˌtsaɪt]
Ice Age	Eiszeit (f)	['aɪsˌtsaɪt]
tribe	Stamm (m)	[ʃtam]
cannibal	Kannibale (m)	[kani'ba:lə]
hunter	Jäger (m)	['jɛ:gɐ]
to hunt (vi, vt)	jagen (vi)	['jagən]
mammoth	Mammut (n)	['mamʊt]
cave	Höhle (f)	['hø:lə]
fire	Feuer (n)	['fɔɪɐ]
campfire	Lagerfeuer (n)	['la:gɐˌfɔɪɐ]
cave painting	Höhlenmalerei (f)	['hø:lən·ma:ləˌʀaɪ]
tool (e.g. stone axe)	Werkzeug (n)	['vɛʀkˌtsɔɪk]
spear	Speer (m)	[ʃpe:ɐ]
stone axe	Steinbeil (n), Steinaxt (f)	['ʃtaɪnˌbaɪl], ['ʃtaɪnˌakst]
to be at war	Krieg führen	[kʀi:k 'fy:ʀən]
to domesticate (vt)	domestizieren (vt)	[domɛsti'tsi:ʀən]
idol	Idol (n)	[i'do:l]
to worship (vt)	anbeten (vt)	['anˌbe:tən]
superstition	Aberglaube (m)	['a:bɐˌglaʊbə]
rite	Ritus (m), Ritual (n)	['ʀi:tʊs], [ʀi'tua:l]
evolution	Evolution (f)	[evolu'tsjo:n]
development	Entwicklung (f)	[ɛnt'vɪklʊŋ]
disappearance (extinction)	Verschwinden (n)	[fɛɐ'ʃvɪndən]
to adapt oneself	sich anpassen	[zɪç 'anˌpasən]
archaeology	Archäologie (f)	[aʀçɛolo'gi:]
archaeologist	Archäologe (m)	[aʀçɛo'lo:gə]
archaeological (adj)	archäologisch	[aʀçɛo'lo:gɪʃ]
excavation site	Ausgrabungsstätte (f)	['aʊsgʀa:bʊŋsˌʃtɛtə]
excavations	Ausgrabungen (pl)	['aʊsgʀa:bʊŋən]
find (object)	Fund (m)	[fʊnt]
fragment	Fragment (n)	[fʀa'gmɛnt]

188. Middle Ages

people (ethnic group)	Volk (n)	[fɔlk]
peoples	Völker (pl)	['fœlkɐ]
tribe	Stamm (m)	[ʃtam]
tribes	Stämme (pl)	['ʃtɛmə]
barbarians	Barbaren (pl)	[baʀ'ba:ʀən]

Gauls	Gallier (pl)	['galɐe]
Goths	Goten (pl)	['go:tən]
Slavs	Slawen (pl)	['slaːvən]
Vikings	Wikinger (pl)	['viːkɪŋe]

| Romans | Römer (pl) | ['ʀøːme] |
| Roman (adj) | römisch | ['ʀøːmɪʃ] |

Byzantines	Byzantiner (pl)	[bytsan'tiːne]
Byzantium	Byzanz (n)	[by'tsants]
Byzantine (adj)	byzantinisch	[bytsan'tiːnɪʃ]

emperor	Kaiser (m)	['kaɪze]
leader, chief (tribal ~)	Häuptling (m)	['hɔɪptlɪŋ]
powerful (~ king)	mächtig	['mɛçtɪç]
king	König (m)	['køːnɪç]
ruler (sovereign)	Herrscher (m)	['hɛʁʃe]

knight	Ritter (m)	['ʀɪte]
feudal lord	Feudalherr (m)	[fɔɪ'daːlˌhɛʁ]
feudal (adj)	feudal, Feudal-	[fɔɪ'daːl]
vassal	Vasall (m)	[va'zal]

duke	Herzog (m)	['hɛʁtsoːk]
earl	Graf (m)	[gʀaːf]
baron	Baron (m)	[ba'ʀoːn]
bishop	Bischof (m)	['bɪʃɔf]

armour	Rüstung (f)	['ʀʏstʊŋ]
shield	Schild (m)	[ʃɪlt]
sword	Schwert (n)	[ʃveːɐt]
visor	Visier (n)	[vi'ziːɐ]
chainmail	Panzerhemd (n)	['pantseˌhɛmt]

| Crusade | Kreuzzug (m) | ['kʀɔɪtsˌtsuːk] |
| crusader | Kreuzritter (m) | ['kʀɔɪtsˌʀɪte] |

territory	Territorium (n)	[tɛʀi'toːʀiʊm]
to attack (invade)	einfallen (vt)	['aɪnˌfalən]
to conquer (vt)	erobern (vt)	[ɛɐ'ʔoːben]
to occupy (invade)	besetzen (vt)	[bə'zɛtsən]

siege (to be under ~)	Belagerung (f)	[bə'laːgəʀʊŋ]
besieged (adj)	belagert	[bə'laːget]
to besiege (vt)	belagern (vt)	[bə'laːgen]

inquisition	Inquisition (f)	[ɪnkvizi'tsjoːn]
inquisitor	Inquisitor (m)	[ɪnkvi'ziːtoːɐ]
torture	Folter (f)	['fɔlte]
cruel (adj)	grausam	['gʀaʊˌzaːm]
heretic	Häretiker (m)	[hɛ'ʀetike]
heresy	Häresie (f)	[hɛʀe'ziː]

seafaring	Seefahrt (f)	['zeːˌfaːɐt]
pirate	Seeräuber (m)	['zeːˌʀɔɪbe]
piracy	Seeräuberei (f)	['zeːˌʀɔɪbəʀaɪ]

boarding (attack)	Enterung (f)	['ɛnteʁʊŋ]
loot, booty	Beute (f)	['bɔɪtə]
treasure	Schätze (pl)	['ʃɛtsə]

discovery	Entdeckung (f)	[ɛnt'dɛkʊŋ]
to discover (new land, etc.)	entdecken (vt)	[ɛnt'dɛkən]
expedition	Expedition (f)	[ɛkspedi'tsjo:n]

musketeer	Musketier (m)	[mʊske'ti:ɐ]
cardinal	Kardinal (m)	[ˌkaʁdi'na:l]
heraldry	Heraldik (f)	[he'ʁaldɪk]
heraldic (adj)	heraldisch	[he'ʁaldɪʃ]

189. Leader. Chief. Authorities

king	König (m)	['kø:nɪç]
queen	Königin (f)	['kø:nɪgɪn]
royal (adj)	königlich	['kø:nɪklɪç]
kingdom	Königreich (n)	['kø:nɪkˌʁaɪç]

| prince | Prinz (m) | [pʁɪnts] |
| princess | Prinzessin (f) | [pʁɪn'tsɛsɪn] |

president	Präsident (m)	[pʁɛzi'dɛnt]
vice-president	Vizepräsident (m)	['fi:tsə·pʁɛziˌdɛnt]
senator	Senator (m)	[ze'na:to:ɐ]

monarch	Monarch (m)	[mo'naʁç]
ruler (sovereign)	Herrscher (m)	['hɛʁʃɐ]
dictator	Diktator (m)	[dɪk'ta:to:ɐ]
tyrant	Tyrann (m)	[ty'ʁan]
magnate	Magnat (m)	[ma'gna:t]

director	Direktor (m)	[di'ʁɛkto:ɐ]
chief	Chef (m)	[ʃɛf]
manager (director)	Leiter (m)	['laɪtɐ]
boss	Boss (m)	[bɔs]
owner	Eigentümer (m)	['aɪgənty:mɐ]

head (~ of delegation)	Leiter (m)	['laɪtɐ]
authorities	Behörden (pl)	[bə'hø:ədən]
superiors	Vorgesetzten (pl)	['fo:ɐgəˌzɛtstən]

governor	Gouverneur (m)	[guvɛʁ'nø:ɐ]
consul	Konsul (m)	['kɔnzʊl]
diplomat	Diplomat (m)	[ˌdiplo'ma:t]

| mayor | Bürgermeister (m) | ['byʁgɐˌmaɪstɐ] |
| sheriff | Sheriff (m) | ['ʃɛʁɪf] |

emperor	Kaiser (m)	['kaɪzɐ]
tsar, czar	Zar (m)	[tsa:ɐ]
pharaoh	Pharao (m)	['fa:ʁao]
khan	Khan (m)	[ka:n]

190. Road. Way. Directions

road	**Fahrbahn** (f)	['faːɐ̯ˌbaːn]
way (direction)	**Weg** (m)	[veːk]
highway	**Autobahn** (f)	['aʊtoˌbaːn]
motorway	**Schnellstraße** (f)	['ʃnɛlˌʃtʀaːsə]
trunk road	**Bundesstraße** (f)	['bʊndəsˌʃtʀaːsə]
main road	**Hauptstraße** (f)	['haʊptˌʃtʀaːsə]
dirt road	**Feldweg** (m)	['fɛltˌveːk]
pathway	**Pfad** (m)	[pfaːt]
footpath (troddenpath)	**Fußweg** (m)	['fuːsˌveːk]
Where?	**Wo?**	[voː]
Where (to)?	**Wohin?**	[vo'hɪn]
From where?	**Woher?**	[vo'heːɐ̯]
direction (way)	**Richtung** (f)	['ʀɪçtʊŋ]
to point (~ the way)	**zeigen** (vt)	['tsaɪɡən]
to the left	**nach links**	[naːχ lɪŋks]
to the right	**nach rechts**	[naːχ ʀɛçts]
straight ahead (adv)	**geradeaus**	[ɡəʀaːdə'ʔaʊs]
back (e.g. to turn ~)	**zurück**	[tsu'ʀʏk]
bend, curve	**Kurve** (f)	['kʊʁvə]
to turn (e.g., ~ left)	**abbiegen** (vi)	['apˌbiːɡən]
to make a U-turn	**umkehren** (vi)	['ʊmˌkeːʀən]
to be visible	**sichtbar sein**	['zɪçtbaːɐ̯ zaɪn]
(mountains, castle, etc.)		
to appear (come into view)	**erscheinen** (vi)	[ɛɐ̯'ʃaɪnən]
stop, halt (e.g., during a trip)	**Aufenthalt** (m)	['aʊfʔɛnthalt]
to rest, to pause (vi)	**sich erholen**	[zɪç ɛɐ̯'hoːlən]
rest (pause)	**Erholung** (f)	[ɛɐ̯'hoːlʊŋ]
to lose one's way	**sich verirren**	[zɪç fɛɐ̯'ʔɪʀən]
to lead to … (ab. road)	**führen (in …, nach …)**	['fyːʀən]
to came out	**ankommen in …**	['anˌkɔmən in]
(e.g., on the highway)		
stretch (of the road)	**Strecke** (f)	['ʃtʀɛkə]
asphalt	**Asphalt** (m)	[as'falt]
kerb	**Bordstein** (m)	['bɔʁtˌʃtaɪn]
ditch	**Graben** (m)	['ɡʀaːbən]
manhole	**Gully** (m, n)	['ɡʊli]
roadside (shoulder)	**Straßenrand** (m)	['ʃtʀaːsənˌʀant]
pit, pothole	**Schlagloch** (n)	['ʃlaːkˌlɔχ]
to go (on foot)	**gehen** (vi)	['ɡeːən]
to overtake (vt)	**überholen** (vt)	[ˌyːbɐ'hoːlən]
step (footstep)	**Schritt** (m)	[ʃʀɪt]

on foot (adv)	zu Fuß	[tsu 'fu:s]
to block (road)	blockieren (vt)	[blɔ'ki:rən]
boom gate	Schlagbaum (m)	['ʃla:k,baʊm]
dead end	Sackgasse (f)	['zak,gasə]

191. Breaking the law. Criminals. Part 1

bandit	Bandit (m)	[ban'di:t]
crime	Verbrechen (n)	[fɛɐ'bʀɛçən]
criminal (person)	Verbrecher (m)	[fɛɐ'bʀɛçɐ]

thief	Dieb (m)	[di:p]
to steal (vi, vt)	stehlen (vt)	['ʃte:lən]
stealing (larceny)	Diebstahl (m)	['di:pʃta:l]
theft	Stehlen (n)	['ʃte:lən]

to kidnap (vt)	kidnappen (vt)	['kɪt,nɛpən]
kidnapping	Kidnapping (n)	['kɪt,nɛpɪŋ]
kidnapper	Kidnapper (m)	['kɪt,nɛpɐ]

| ransom | Lösegeld (n) | ['lø:zə,gɛlt] |
| to demand ransom | Lösegeld verlangen | ['lø:zə,gɛlt fɛɐ'laŋən] |

to rob (vt)	rauben (vt)	['ʀaʊbən]
robbery	Raub (m)	['ʀaʊp]
robber	Räuber (m)	['ʀɔɪbɐ]

to extort (vt)	erpressen (vt)	[ɛɐ'pʀɛsən]
extortionist	Erpresser (m)	[ɛɐ'pʀɛsɐ]
extortion	Erpressung (f)	[ɛɐ'pʀɛsʊŋ]

to murder, to kill	morden (vt)	['mɔʁdən]
murder	Mord (m)	[mɔʁt]
murderer	Mörder (m)	['mœʁdɐ]

gunshot	Schuss (m)	[ʃʊs]
to fire (~ a shot)	schießen (vt)	['ʃi:sən]
to shoot to death	erschießen (vt)	[ɛɐ'ʃi:sən]
to shoot (vi)	feuern (vi)	['fɔɪɐn]
shooting	Schießerei (f)	[ʃi:sə'ʀaɪ]

incident (fight, etc.)	Vorfall (m)	['fo:ɐfal]
fight, brawl	Schlägerei (f)	[ʃlɛ:gə'ʀaɪ]
Help!	Hilfe!	['hɪlfə]
victim	Opfer (n)	['ɔpfɐ]

to damage (vt)	beschädigen (vt)	[bə'ʃɛ:dɪgən]
damage	Schaden (m)	['ʃa:dən]
dead body, corpse	Leiche (f)	['laɪçə]
grave (~ crime)	schwer	[ʃve:ɐ]

to attack (vt)	angreifen (vt)	['an,gʀaɪfən]
to beat (to hit)	schlagen (vt)	['ʃla:gən]
to beat up	verprügeln (vt)	[fɛɐ'pʀy:gəln]

to take (rob of sth)	wegnehmen (vt)	['vɛkˌne:mən]
to stab to death	erstechen (vt)	[ɛɐ̯'ʃtɛçən]
to maim (vt)	verstümmeln (vt)	[fɛɐ̯'ʃtʏməln]
to wound (vt)	verwunden (vt)	[fɛɐ̯'vʊndən]

blackmail	Erpressung (f)	[ɛɐ̯'pʀɛsʊŋ]
to blackmail (vt)	erpressen (vt)	[ɛɐ̯'pʀɛsən]
blackmailer	Erpresser (m)	[ɛɐ̯'pʀɛsɐ]

protection racket	Schutzgelderpressung (f)	['ʃʊtsgɛlt?ɛɐ̯ˌpʀɛsʊŋ]
racketeer	Erpresser (m)	[ɛɐ̯'pʀɛsɐ]
gangster	Gangster (m)	['gɛŋstɐ]
mafia	Mafia (f)	['mafɪa]

pickpocket	Taschendieb (m)	['taʃənˌdi:p]
burglar	Einbrecher (m)	['aɪnˌbʀɛçɐ]
smuggling	Schmuggel (m)	['ʃmʊgəl]
smuggler	Schmuggler (m)	['ʃmʊglɐ]

forgery	Fälschung (f)	['fɛlʃʊŋ]
to forge (counterfeit)	fälschen (vt)	['fɛlʃən]
fake (forged)	gefälscht	[gə'fɛlʃt]

192. Breaking the law. Criminals. Part 2

rape	Vergewaltigung (f)	[fɛɐ̯gə'valtɪgʊŋ]
to rape (vt)	vergewaltigen (vt)	[fɛɐ̯gə'valtɪgən]
rapist	Gewalttäter (m)	[gə'valtˌtɛ:tɐ]
maniac	Besessene (m)	[bə'zɛsənə]

prostitute (fem.)	Prostituierte (f)	[ˌpʀostitu'i:ɐtə]
prostitution	Prostitution (f)	[pʀostitu'tsjo:n]
pimp	Zuhälter (m)	['tsu:ˌhɛltɐ]

| drug addict | Drogenabhängiger (m) | ['dʀo:gənˌʔaphɛŋɪgɐ] |
| drug dealer | Drogenhändler (m) | ['dʀo:gənˌhɛndlɐ] |

to blow up (bomb)	sprengen (vt)	['ʃpʀɛŋən]
explosion	Explosion (f)	[ɛksplo'zjo:n]
to set fire	in Brand stecken	[ɪn bʀant 'ʃtɛkən]
arsonist	Brandstifter (m)	['bʀantˌʃtɪftɐ]

terrorism	Terrorismus (m)	[tɛʀo'ʀɪsmʊs]
terrorist	Terrorist (m)	[tɛʀo'ʀɪst]
hostage	Geisel (m, f)	['gaɪzəl]

to swindle (deceive)	betrügen (vt)	[bə'tʀy:gən]
swindle, deception	Betrug (m)	[bə'tʀu:k]
swindler	Betrüger (m)	[bə'tʀy:gɐ]

to bribe (vt)	bestechen (vt)	[bə'ʃtɛçən]
bribery	Bestechlichkeit (f)	[bə'ʃtɛçlɪçkaɪt]
bribe	Bestechungsgeld (n)	[bə'ʃtɛçʊŋsˌgɛlt]
poison	Gift (n)	[gɪft]

175

| to poison (vt) | vergiften (vt) | [fɛɐ'gɪftən] |
| to poison oneself | sich vergiften | [zɪç fɛɐ'gɪftən] |

| suicide (act) | Selbstmord (m) | ['zɛlpst‚mɔʁt] |
| suicide (person) | Selbstmörder (m) | ['zɛlpst‚mœʁdɐ] |

to threaten (vt)	drohen (vi)	['dʀoːən]
threat	Drohung (f)	['dʀoːʊŋ]
to make an attempt	versuchen (vt)	[fɛɐ'zuːχən]
attempt (attack)	Attentat (n)	['atəntaːt]

| to steal (a car) | stehlen (vt) | ['ʃteːlən] |
| to hijack (a plane) | entführen (vt) | [ɛnt'fyːʀən] |

| revenge | Rache (f) | ['ʀaχə] |
| to avenge (get revenge) | sich rächen | [zɪç 'ʀɛçən] |

to torture (vt)	foltern (vt)	['fɔltɐn]
torture	Folter (f)	['fɔltɐ]
to torment (vt)	quälen (vt)	['kvɛːlən]

pirate	Seeräuber (m)	['zeː‚ʀɔɪbɐ]
hooligan	Rowdy (m)	['ʀaʊdi]
armed (adj)	bewaffnet	[bə'vafnət]
violence	Gewalt (f)	[gə'valt]
illegal (unlawful)	ungesetzlich	['ʊngə‚zɛtslɪç]

| spying (espionage) | Spionage (f) | [ʃpio'naːʒə] |
| to spy (vi) | spionieren (vi) | [ʃpɪo'niːʀən] |

193. Police. Law. Part 1

| justice | Justiz (f) | [jʊs'tiːts] |
| court (see you in ~) | Gericht (n) | [gə'ʀɪçt] |

judge	Richter (m)	['ʀɪçtɐ]
jurors	Geschworenen (pl)	[gə'ʃvoːʀənən]
jury trial	Geschworenengericht (n)	[gə'ʃvoːʀənən·gə‚ʀɪçt]
to judge, to try (vt)	richten (vt)	['ʀɪçtən]

lawyer, barrister	Rechtsanwalt (m)	['ʀɛçtsʔan‚valt]
defendant	Angeklagte (m)	['angə‚klaːktə]
dock	Anklagebank (f)	['anklaːgə·baŋk]

| charge | Anklage (f) | ['anklaːgə] |
| accused | Beschuldigte (m) | [bə'ʃʊldɪçtə] |

| sentence | Urteil (n) | ['ʊʁ‚taɪl] |
| to sentence (vt) | verurteilen (vt) | [fɛɐ'ʔʊʁtaɪlən] |

guilty (culprit)	Schuldige (m)	['ʃʊldɪgə]
to punish (vt)	bestrafen (vt)	[bə'ʃtʀaːfən]
punishment	Strafe (f)	['ʃtʀaːfə]
fine (penalty)	Geldstrafe (f)	['gɛltʃtʀaːfə]

life imprisonment	lebenslange Haft (f)	['leːbəns,laŋə haft]
death penalty	Todesstrafe (f)	['toːdəs,ʃtʁaːfə]
electric chair	elektrischer Stuhl (m)	[e'lɛktʁɪʃə ʃtuːl]
gallows	Galgen (m)	[galgən]

| to execute (vt) | hinrichten (vt) | ['hɪn,ʁɪçtən] |
| execution | Hinrichtung (f) | ['hɪn,ʁɪçtʊŋ] |

| prison | Gefängnis (n) | [gə'fɛŋnɪs] |
| cell | Zelle (f) | ['tsɛlə] |

escort (convoy)	Eskorte (f)	[ɛs'kɔʁtə]
prison officer	Gefängniswärter (m)	[gə'fɛŋnɪs·vɛʁtə]
prisoner	Gefangene (m)	[gə'faŋənə]

| handcuffs | Handschellen (pl) | ['hantʃɛlən] |
| to handcuff (vt) | Handschellen anlegen | ['hantʃɛlən 'an,leːgən] |

prison break	Ausbruch (m)	['aʊs,bʁʊχ]
to break out (vi)	ausbrechen (vi)	['aʊs,bʁɛçən]
to disappear (vi)	verschwinden (vi)	[fɛɛ'ʃvɪndən]
to release (from prison)	aus … entlassen	['aʊs … ɛnt'lasn]
amnesty	Amnestie (f)	[amnɛs'tiː]

police	Polizei (f)	[,poli'tsaɪ]
police officer	Polizist (m)	[poli'tsɪst]
police station	Polizeiwache (f)	[poli'tsaɪ,vaχə]
truncheon	Gummiknüppel (m)	['gʊmi,knypəl]
megaphone (loudhailer)	Sprachrohr (n)	['ʃpʁaːχ,ʁoːɐ]

patrol car	Streifenwagen (m)	['ʃtʁaɪfən,vaːgən]
siren	Sirene (f)	[,zi'ʁeːnə]
to turn on the siren	die Sirene einschalten	[di ,zi'ʁeːnə 'aɪnʃaltən]
siren call	Sirenengeheul (n)	[zi'ʁeːnən·gə'hɔɪl]

crime scene	Tatort (m)	['taːt,ʔɔʁt]
witness	Zeuge (m)	['tsɔɪgə]
freedom	Freiheit (f)	['fʁaɪhaɪt]
accomplice	Komplize (m)	[kɔm'pliːtsə]
to flee (vi)	verschwinden (vi)	[fɛɛ'ʃvɪndən]
trace (to leave a ~)	Spur (f)	[ʃpuːɐ]

194. Police. Law. Part 2

search (investigation)	Fahndung (f)	['faːndʊŋ]
to look for …	suchen (vt)	['zuːχən]
suspicion	Verdacht (m)	[fɛɛ'daχt]
suspicious (e.g., ~ vehicle)	verdächtig	[fɛɛ'dɛçtɪç]
to stop (cause to halt)	anhalten (vt)	['an,haltən]
to detain (keep in custody)	verhaften (vt)	[fɛɛ'haftən]

case (lawsuit)	Fall (m), Klage (f)	[faːl], ['klaːgə]
investigation	Untersuchung (f)	[ʊntɐ'zuːχʊŋ]
detective	Detektiv (m)	[detɛk'tiːf]

investigator	**Ermittlungsrichter** (m)	[ɛɐ'mɪtlʊŋsˌʀɪçtə]
hypothesis	**Version** (f)	[vɛʁ'zjoːn]

motive	**Motiv** (n)	[mo'tiːf]
interrogation	**Verhör** (n)	[fɛɐ'høːɐ]
to interrogate (vt)	**verhören** (vt)	[fɛɐ'høːʀən]
to question	**vernehmen** (vt)	[fɛɐ'neːmən]
(~ neighbors, etc.)		
check (identity ~)	**Kontrolle, Prüfung** (f)	[kɔn'tʀɔlə], ['pʀyːfʊŋ]

round-up (raid)	**Razzia** (f)	['ʀatsɪa]
search (~ warrant)	**Durchsuchung** (f)	[dʊʁç'zuːxʊŋ]
chase (pursuit)	**Verfolgung** (f)	[fɛɐ'fɔlgʊŋ]
to pursue, to chase	**nachjagen** (vi)	['naːxˌjaːgən]
to track (a criminal)	**verfolgen** (vt)	[fɛɐ'fɔlgən]

arrest	**Verhaftung** (f)	[fɛɐ'haftʊŋ]
to arrest (sb)	**verhaften** (vt)	[fɛɐ'haftən]
to catch (thief, etc.)	**fangen** (vt)	['faŋən]
capture	**Festnahme** (f)	['fɛstˌnaːmə]

document	**Dokument** (n)	[ˌdoku'mɛnt]
proof (evidence)	**Beweis** (m)	[bə'vaɪs]
to prove (vt)	**beweisen** (vt)	[bə'vaɪzən]
footprint	**Fußspur** (f)	['fuːsˌʃpuːɐ]
fingerprints	**Fingerabdrücke** (pl)	['fɪŋəˌʔapdʀʏkə]
piece of evidence	**Beweisstück** (n)	[bə'vaɪsʃtʏk]

alibi	**Alibi** (n)	['aːlibi]
innocent (not guilty)	**unschuldig**	['ʊnʃʊldɪç]
injustice	**Ungerechtigkeit** (f)	['ʊngəˌʀɛçtɪçkaɪt]
unjust, unfair (adj)	**ungerecht**	['ʊngəˌʀɛçt]

criminal (adj)	**Kriminal-**	[kʀimi'naːl]
to confiscate (vt)	**beschlagnahmen** (vt)	[bə'ʃlaːkˌnaːmən]
drug (illegal substance)	**Droge** (f)	['dʀoːgə]
weapon, gun	**Waffe** (f)	['vafə]
to disarm (vt)	**entwaffnen** (vt)	[ɛnt'vafnən]
to order (command)	**befehlen** (vt)	[ˌbə'feːlən]
to disappear (vi)	**verschwinden** (vi)	[fɛɐ'ʃvɪndən]

law	**Gesetz** (n)	[gə'zɛts]
legal, lawful (adj)	**gesetzlich**	[gə'zɛtslɪç]
illegal, illicit (adj)	**ungesetzlich**	['ʊngəˌzɛtslɪç]

responsibility (blame)	**Verantwortlichkeit** (f)	[fɛɐ'ʔantvɔʁtlɪçkaɪt]
responsible (adj)	**verantwortlich**	[fɛɐ'ʔantvɔʁtlɪç]

NATURE

The Earth. Part 1

195. Outer space

space	**Kosmos** (m)	['kɔsmɔs]
space (as adj)	**kosmisch, Raum-**	['kɔsmɪʃ], ['ʀaʊm]
outer space	**Weltraum** (m)	['vɛltʀaʊm]
world	**All** (n)	[al]
universe	**Universum** (n)	[uni'vɛʀzʊm]
galaxy	**Galaxie** (f)	[gala'ksi:]
star	**Stern** (m)	[ʃtɛʁn]
constellation	**Gestirn** (n)	[gə'ʃtɪʁn]
planet	**Planet** (m)	[pla'ne:t]
satellite	**Satellit** (m)	[zatɛ'li:t]
meteorite	**Meteorit** (m)	[meteo'ʀi:t]
comet	**Komet** (m)	[ko'me:t]
asteroid	**Asteroid** (m)	[asteʀo'i:t]
orbit	**Umlaufbahn** (f)	['ʊmlaʊf,ba:n]
to revolve	**sich drehen**	[zɪç 'dʀe:ən]
(~ around the Earth)		
atmosphere	**Atmosphäre** (f)	[ʔatmo'sfɛ:ʀə]
the Sun	**Sonne** (f)	['zɔnə]
solar system	**Sonnensystem** (n)	['zɔnən·zʏs,te:m]
solar eclipse	**Sonnenfinsternis** (f)	['zɔnən,fɪnstɛnɪs]
the Earth	**Erde** (f)	['e:ɐdə]
the Moon	**Mond** (m)	[mo:nt]
Mars	**Mars** (m)	[maʁs]
Venus	**Venus** (f)	['ve:nʊs]
Jupiter	**Jupiter** (m)	['ju:pitɐ]
Saturn	**Saturn** (m)	[za'tʊʁn]
Mercury	**Merkur** (m)	[mɛʁ'ku:ɐ]
Uranus	**Uran** (m)	[u'ʀa:n]
Neptune	**Neptun** (m)	[nɛp'tu:n]
Pluto	**Pluto** (m)	['plu:to]
Milky Way	**Milchstraße** (f)	['mɪlç,ʃtʀa:sə]
Great Bear (Ursa Major)	**Der Große Bär**	[de:ɐ 'gʀo:sə bɛ:ɐ]
North Star	**Polarstern** (m)	[po'la:ɐ,ʃtɛʁn]
Martian	**Marsbewohner** (m)	['maʁs·bə,vo:nɐ]

extraterrestrial (n)	Außerirdischer (m)	[ˈaʊsɐˌʔɪʁdɪʃɐ]
alien	außerirdisches Wesen (n)	[ˈaʊsɐˌʔɪʁdɪʃəs ˈveːzən]
flying saucer	fliegende Untertasse (f)	[ˈfliːɡəndə ˈʊntɐˌtasə]

spaceship	Raumschiff (n)	[ˈʀaʊmʃɪf]
space station	Raumstation (f)	[ˈʀaʊmˈʃtatsjoːn]
blast-off	Raketenstart (m)	[ʀaˈkeːtənʃtaʁt]

engine	Triebwerk (n)	[ˈtʀiːpˌvɛʁk]
nozzle	Düse (f)	[ˈdyːzə]
fuel	Treibstoff (m)	[ˈtʀaɪpʃtɔf]

cockpit, flight deck	Kabine (f)	[kaˈbiːnə]
aerial	Antenne (f)	[anˈtɛnə]
porthole	Bullauge (n)	[ˈbʊlˌʔaʊɡə]
solar panel	Sonnenbatterie (f)	[ˈzɔnənˌbatəˈʀiː]
spacesuit	Raumanzug (m)	[ˈʀaʊmˌʔantsuːk]

| weightlessness | Schwerelosigkeit (f) | [ˈʃveːʀəˌloːzɪçkaɪt] |
| oxygen | Sauerstoff (m) | [ˈzaʊɐʃtɔf] |

| docking (in space) | Ankopplung (f) | [ˈaŋkɔplʊŋ] |
| to dock (vi, vt) | koppeln (vi) | [ˈkɔpəln] |

observatory	Observatorium (n)	[ɔpzɛʁvaˈtoːʀiʊm]
telescope	Teleskop (n)	[teleˈskoːp]
to observe (vt)	beobachten (vt)	[bəˈʔoːbaχtən]
to explore (vt)	erforschen (vt)	[ɛʁˈfɔʁʃən]

196. The Earth

the Earth	Erde (f)	[ˈeːɐdə]
the globe (the Earth)	Erdkugel (f)	[ˈeːɐtˈkuːɡəl]
planet	Planet (m)	[plaˈneːt]

atmosphere	Atmosphäre (f)	[ʔatmoˈsfɛːʀə]
geography	Geographie (f)	[ˌɡeoɡʀaˈfiː]
nature	Natur (f)	[naˈtuːɐ]

globe (table ~)	Globus (m)	[ˈɡloːbʊs]
map	Landkarte (f)	[ˈlantˌkaʁtə]
atlas	Atlas (m)	[ˈatlas]

Europe	Europa (n)	[ɔɪˈʀoːpa]
Asia	Asien (n)	[ˈaːziən]
Africa	Afrika (n)	[ˈaːfʀika]
Australia	Australien (n)	[aʊsˈtʀaːliən]

America	Amerika (n)	[aˈmeːʀika]
North America	Nordamerika (n)	[ˈnɔʁtʔaˌmeːʀika]
South America	Südamerika (n)	[ˈzyːtʔaˈmeːʀika]

| Antarctica | Antarktis (f) | [antˈʔaʁktɪs] |
| the Arctic | Arktis (f) | [ˈaʁktɪs] |

197. Cardinal directions

north	Norden (m)	['nɔʁdən]
to the north	nach Norden	[na:χ 'nɔʁdən]
in the north	im Norden	[ɪm 'nɔʁdən]
northern (adj)	nördlich	['nœʁtlɪç]
south	Süden (m)	['zy:dən]
to the south	nach Süden	[na:χ 'zy:dən]
in the south	im Süden	[ɪm 'zy:dən]
southern (adj)	südlich	['zy:tlɪç]
west	Westen (m)	['vɛstən]
to the west	nach Westen	[na:χ 'vɛstən]
in the west	im Westen	[ɪm 'vɛstən]
western (adj)	westlich, West-	['vɛstlɪç], [vɛst]
east	Osten (m)	['ɔstən]
to the east	nach Osten	[na:χ 'ɔstən]
in the east	im Osten	[ɪm 'ɔstən]
eastern (adj)	östlich	['œstlɪç]

198. Sea. Ocean

sea	Meer (n), See (f)	[me:ɐ], [ze:]
ocean	Ozean (m)	['o:tsea:n]
gulf (bay)	Golf (m)	[gɔlf]
straits	Meerenge (f)	['me:ɐ,ʔɛŋə]
land (solid ground)	Festland (n)	['fɛst,lant]
continent (mainland)	Kontinent (m)	['kɔntinɛnt]
island	Insel (f)	['ɪnzəl]
peninsula	Halbinsel (f)	['halp,ʔɪnzəl]
archipelago	Archipel (m)	[,aʁçi'pe:l]
bay, cove	Bucht (f)	[buχt]
harbour	Hafen (m)	['ha:fən]
lagoon	Lagune (f)	[la'gu:nə]
cape	Kap (n)	[kap]
atoll	Atoll (n)	[a'tɔl]
reef	Riff (n)	[ʀɪf]
coral	Koralle (f)	[ko'ʀalə]
coral reef	Korallenriff (n)	[ko'ʀalən,ʀɪf]
deep (adj)	tief	[ti:f]
depth (deep water)	Tiefe (f)	['ti:fə]
abyss	Abgrund (m)	['ap,gʀʊnt]
trench (e.g. Mariana ~)	Graben (m)	['gʀa:bən]
current (Ocean ~)	Strom (m)	[ʃtʀo:m]
to surround (bathe)	umspülen (vt)	['ʊmʃpy:lən]
shore	Ufer (n)	['u:fɐ]

coast	Küste (f)	['kʏstə]
flow (flood tide)	Flut (f)	[flu:t]
ebb (ebb tide)	Ebbe (f)	['ɛbə]
shoal	Sandbank (f)	['zant,baŋk]
bottom (~ of the sea)	Boden (m)	['bo:dən]

wave	Welle (f)	['vɛlə]
crest (~ of a wave)	Wellenkamm (m)	['vɛlən,kam]
spume (sea foam)	Schaum (m)	[ʃaʊm]

storm (sea storm)	Sturm (m)	[ʃtʊʁm]
hurricane	Orkan (m)	[ɔʁ'ka:n]
tsunami	Tsunami (m)	[tsʊ'na:mi]
calm (dead ~)	Windstille (f)	['vɪntʃtɪlə]
quiet, calm (adj)	ruhig	['ʁu:ɪç]

| pole | Pol (m) | [po:l] |
| polar (adj) | Polar- | [po'la:ɐ] |

latitude	Breite (f)	['bʁaɪtə]
longitude	Länge (f)	['lɛŋə]
parallel	Breitenkreis (m)	['bʁaɪtəən·kʁaɪs]
equator	Äquator (m)	[ɛ'kva:to:ɐ]

sky	Himmel (m)	['hɪməl]
horizon	Horizont (m)	[hoʁi'tsɔnt]
air	Luft (f)	[lʊft]

lighthouse	Leuchtturm (m)	['lɔɪçt,tʊʁm]
to dive (vi)	tauchen (vi)	['taʊxən]
to sink (ab. boat)	versinken (vi)	[fɛɐ'zɪŋkən]
treasure	Schätze (pl)	['ʃɛtsə]

199. Seas & Oceans names

Atlantic Ocean	Atlantischer Ozean (m)	[at,lantɪʃe 'o:tsea:n]
Indian Ocean	Indischer Ozean (m)	['ɪndɪʃe 'o:tsea:n]
Pacific Ocean	Pazifischer Ozean (m)	[pa'tsi:fɪʃe 'o:tsea:n]
Arctic Ocean	Arktischer Ozean (m)	['aʁktɪʃe 'o:tsea:n]

Black Sea	Schwarzes Meer (n)	['ʃvaʁtsəs 'me:ɐ]
Red Sea	Rotes Meer (n)	['ʁo:təs 'me:ɐ]
Yellow Sea	Gelbes Meer (n)	['gɛlbəs 'me:ɐ]
White Sea	Weißes Meer (n)	[vaɪsəs 'me:ɐ]

Caspian Sea	Kaspisches Meer (n)	['kaspɪʃəs me:ɐ]
Dead Sea	Totes Meer (n)	['to:təs me:ɐ]
Mediterranean Sea	Mittelmeer (n)	['mɪtəl,me:ɐ]

| Aegean Sea | Ägäisches Meer (n) | [ɛ'gɛ:ɪʃəs 'me:ɐ] |
| Adriatic Sea | Adriatisches Meer (n) | [adʁi'a:tɪʃəs 'me:ɐ] |

| Arabian Sea | Arabisches Meer (n) | [a'ʁa:bɪʃəs 'me:ɐ] |
| Sea of Japan | Japanisches Meer (n) | [ja'pa:nɪʃəs me:ɐ] |

| Bering Sea | Beringmeer (n) | ['be:ʀɪŋ,me:ɐ] |
| South China Sea | Südchinesisches Meer (n) | ['zy:t-çi'ne:zɪʃəs me:ɐ] |

Coral Sea	Korallenmeer (n)	[ko'ʀalən,me:ɐ]
Tasman Sea	Tasmansee (f)	[tas'ma:n-ze:]
Caribbean Sea	Karibisches Meer (n)	[ka'ʀi:bɪʃəs 'me:ɐ]

| Barents Sea | Barentssee (f) | ['ba:ʀənts-ze:] |
| Kara Sea | Karasee (f) | ['kaʀa,ze:] |

North Sea	Nordsee (f)	['nɔʁt,ze:]
Baltic Sea	Ostsee (f)	['ɔstze:]
Norwegian Sea	Nordmeer (n)	['nɔʁt,me:ɐ]

200. Mountains

mountain	Berg (m)	[bɛʁk]
mountain range	Gebirgskette (f)	[gə'bɪʁks,kɛtə]
mountain ridge	Bergrücken (m)	['bɛʁk,ʀʏkən]

summit, top	Gipfel (m)	['gɪpfəl]
peak	Spitze (f)	['ʃpɪtsə]
foot (~ of the mountain)	Bergfuß (m)	['bɛʁk,fu:s]
slope (mountainside)	Abhang (m)	['ap,haŋ]

volcano	Vulkan (m)	[vʊl'ka:n]
active volcano	tätiger Vulkan (m)	['tɛ:tɪgɐ vʊl'ka:n]
dormant volcano	schlafender Vulkan (m)	['ʃla:fəndɐ vʊl'ka:n]

eruption	Ausbruch (m)	['aʊs,bʀʊχ]
crater	Krater (m)	['kʀa:tɐ]
magma	Magma (n)	['magma]
lava	Lava (f)	['la:va]
molten (~ lava)	glühend heiß	['gly:ənt 'haɪs]

canyon	Cañon (m)	[ka'njɔn]
gorge	Schlucht (f)	[ʃlʊχt]
crevice	Spalte (f)	['ʃpaltə]
abyss (chasm)	Abgrund (m)	['ap,gʀʊnt]

pass, col	Gebirgspass (m)	[gə'bɪʁks,pas]
plateau	Plateau (n)	[pla'to:]
cliff	Fels (m)	[fɛls]
hill	Hügel (m)	['hy:gəl]

glacier	Gletscher (m)	['glɛtʃɐ]
waterfall	Wasserfall (m)	['vasɐ,fal]
geyser	Geiser (m)	['gaɪzɐ]
lake	See (m)	[ze:]

plain	Ebene (f)	['e:bənə]
landscape	Landschaft (f)	['lantʃaft]
echo	Echo (n)	['ɛço]
alpinist	Bergsteiger (m)	['bɛʁk,ʃtaɪgɐ]

rock climber	Kletterer (m)	['klɛtərɐ]
to conquer (in climbing)	bezwingen (vt)	[bə'tsvɪŋən]
climb (an easy ~)	Aufstieg (m)	['aʊfʃtiːk]

201. Mountains names

The Alps	Alpen (pl)	['alpən]
Mont Blanc	Montblanc (m)	[mon'blaŋ]
The Pyrenees	Pyrenäen (pl)	[pyʀe'nɛːən]

The Carpathians	Karpaten (pl)	[kaʁ'paːtən]
The Ural Mountains	Ural (m), Uralgebirge (n)	[u'ʀaːl], [u'ʀaːlɡə'bɪʁɡə]
The Caucasus Mountains	Kaukasus (m)	['kaʊkazʊs]
Mount Elbrus	Elbrus (m)	[ɛl'bʀʊs]

The Altai Mountains	Altai (m)	[al'taɪ]
The Tian Shan	Tian Shan (m)	['tjaːn 'ʃaːn]
The Pamirs	Pamir (m)	[pa'miːɐ]
The Himalayas	Himalaja (m)	[hima'laːja]
Mount Everest	Everest (m)	['ɛvəʀɛst]

| The Andes | Anden (pl) | ['andən] |
| Mount Kilimanjaro | Kilimandscharo (m) | [kiliman'dʒaːʀo] |

202. Rivers

river	Fluss (m)	[flʊs]
spring (natural source)	Quelle (f)	['kvɛlə]
riverbed (river channel)	Flussbett (n)	['flʊsˌbɛt]
basin (river valley)	Stromgebiet (n)	['ʃtʀoːmˌɡə'biːt]
to flow into ...	einmünden in ...	['aɪnˌmʏndən ɪn]

| tributary | Nebenfluss (m) | ['neːbənˌflʊs] |
| bank (river ~) | Ufer (n) | ['uːfɐ] |

current (stream)	Strom (m)	[ʃtʀoːm]
downstream (adv)	stromabwärts	['ʃtʀoːmˌapvɛʁts]
upstream (adv)	stromaufwärts	['ʃtʀoːmˌaʊfvɛʁts]

inundation	Überschwemmung (f)	[yːbɐ'ʃvɛmʊŋ]
flooding	Hochwasser (n)	['hoːχˌvasɐ]
to overflow (vi)	aus den Ufern treten	['aʊs den 'uːfɐn 'tʀeːtən]
to flood (vt)	überfluten (vt)	[ˌyːbɐ'fluːtən]

| shallow (shoal) | Sandbank (f) | ['zantˌbaŋk] |
| rapids | Stromschnelle (f) | ['ʃtʀoːmˌʃnɛlə] |

dam	Damm (m)	[dam]
canal	Kanal (m)	[ka'naːl]
reservoir (artificial lake)	Stausee (m)	['ʃtaʊzeː]
sluice, lock	Schleuse (f)	['ʃlɔɪzə]
water body (pond, etc.)	Gewässer (n)	[ɡə'vɛsɐ]

swamp (marshland)	Sumpf (m), Moor (n)	[zʊmpf], [moːɐ]
bog, marsh	Marsch (f)	[maʁʃ]
whirlpool	Strudel (m)	[ˈʃtʀuːdəl]

stream (brook)	Bach (m)	[baχ]
drinking (ab. water)	Trink-	[ˈtʀɪŋk]
fresh (~ water)	Süß-	[zyːs]

| ice | Eis (n) | [aɪs] |
| to freeze over (ab. river, etc.) | zufrieren (vi) | [ˈtsuːˌfʀiːʀən] |

203. Rivers names

| Seine | Seine (f) | [ˈzɛːnə] |
| Loire | Loire (f) | [luˈaːʀ] |

Thames	Themse (f)	[ˈtɛmzə]
Rhine	Rhein (m)	[ʀaɪn]
Danube	Donau (f)	[ˈdoːnaʊ]

Volga	Wolga (f)	[ˈvoːlga]
Don	Don (m)	[dɔn]
Lena	Lena (f)	[ˈleːna]

Yellow River	Gelber Fluss (m)	[ˈgɛlbɐ ˈflʊs]
Yangtze	Jangtse (m)	[ˈjangtsɛ]
Mekong	Mekong (m)	[ˈmeːkɔŋ]
Ganges	Ganges (m)	[ˈgaŋgɛs], [ˈgaŋəs]

Nile River	Nil (m)	[niːl]
Congo River	Kongo (m)	[ˈkɔŋgo]
Okavango River	Okavango (m)	[ɔkaˈvaŋgo]
Zambezi River	Sambesi (m)	[zamˈbeːzi]
Limpopo River	Limpopo (m)	[limpɔˈpo]
Mississippi River	Mississippi (m)	[mɪsɪˈsɪpi]

204. Forest

| forest, wood | Wald (m) | [valt] |
| forest (as adj) | Wald- | [ˈvalt] |

thick forest	Dickicht (n)	[ˈdɪkɪçt]
grove	Gehölz (n)	[gəˈhœlts]
forest clearing	Lichtung (f)	[ˈlɪçtʊŋ]

| thicket | Dickicht (n) | [ˈdɪkɪçt] |
| scrubland | Gebüsch (n) | [gəˈbyʃ] |

footpath (troddenpath)	Fußweg (m)	[ˈfuːsˌveːk]
gully	Erosionsrinne (f)	[eʀoˈzioːnsˈʀɪnə]
tree	Baum (m)	[baʊm]
leaf	Blatt (n)	[blat]

leaves (foliage)	**Laub** (n)	[laʊp]
fall of leaves	**Laubfall** (m)	['laʊpˌfal]
to fall (ab. leaves)	**fallen** (vi)	['falən]
top (of the tree)	**Wipfel** (m)	['vɪpfəl]
branch	**Zweig** (m)	[tsvaɪk]
bough	**Ast** (m)	[ast]
bud (on shrub, tree)	**Knospe** (f)	['knɔspə]
needle (of the pine tree)	**Nadel** (f)	['naːdəl]
fir cone	**Zapfen** (m)	['tsapfən]
tree hollow	**Höhlung** (f)	['høːˌlʊŋ]
nest	**Nest** (n)	[nɛst]
burrow (animal hole)	**Höhle** (f)	['høːlə]
trunk	**Stamm** (m)	[ʃtam]
root	**Wurzel** (f)	['vʊʁtsəl]
bark	**Rinde** (f)	['ʁɪndə]
moss	**Moos** (n)	['moːs]
to uproot (remove trees or tree stumps)	**entwurzeln** (vt)	[ɛnt'vʊʁtsəln]
to chop down	**fällen** (vt)	['fɛlən]
to deforest (vt)	**abholzen** (vt)	['apˌhɔltsən]
tree stump	**Baumstumpf** (m)	['baʊmˌʃtʊmpf]
campfire	**Lagerfeuer** (n)	['laːgɐˌfɔɪɐ]
forest fire	**Waldbrand** (m)	['valtˌbʁant]
to extinguish (vt)	**löschen** (vt)	['lœʃən]
forest ranger	**Förster** (m)	['fœʁstɐ]
protection	**Schutz** (m)	[ʃʊts]
to protect (~ nature)	**beschützen** (vt)	[bə'ʃʏtsən]
poacher	**Wilddieb** (m)	['vɪltˌdiːp]
steel trap	**Falle** (f)	['falə]
to pick (mushrooms)	**sammeln** (vt)	['zaməln]
to pick (berries)	**pflücken** (vt)	['pflʏkən]
to lose one's way	**sich verirren**	[zɪç fɛɐ'ʔɪʁən]

205. Natural resources

natural resources	**Naturressourcen** (pl)	[na'tuːɐˌʁɛ'sʊʁsən]
minerals	**Bodenschätze** (pl)	['boːdənˌʃɛtsə]
deposits	**Vorkommen** (n)	['foːɐˌkɔmən]
field (e.g. oilfield)	**Feld** (n)	[fɛlt]
to mine (extract)	**gewinnen** (vt)	[gə'vɪnən]
mining (extraction)	**Gewinnung** (f)	[gə'vɪnʊŋ]
ore	**Erz** (n)	[eːɐts]
mine (e.g. for coal)	**Bergwerk** (n)	['bɛʁkˌvɛʁk]
shaft (mine ~)	**Schacht** (m)	[ʃaxt]
miner	**Bergarbeiter** (m)	['bɛʁkʔaʁˌbaɪtɐ]
gas (natural ~)	**Erdgas** (n)	['eːɐtˌgaːs]

gas pipeline	Gasleitung (f)	['gaːsˌlaɪtʊn]
oil (petroleum)	Erdöl (n)	['eːɐtˌʔøːl]
oil pipeline	Erdölleitung (f)	['eːɐtʔøːlˌlaɪtʊn]
oil well	Ölquelle (f)	['øːlˌkvɛlə]
derrick (tower)	Bohrturm (m)	['boːɐˌtʊʁm]
tanker	Tanker (m)	['taŋkɐ]

sand	Sand (m)	[zant]
limestone	Kalkstein (m)	['kalkʃtaɪn]
gravel	Kies (m)	[kiːs]
peat	Torf (m)	[tɔʁf]
clay	Ton (m)	[toːn]
coal	Kohle (f)	['koːlə]

iron (ore)	Eisen (n)	['aɪzən]
gold	Gold (n)	[gɔlt]
silver	Silber (n)	['zɪlbə]
nickel	Nickel (n)	['nɪkəl]
copper	Kupfer (n)	['kʊpfe]

zinc	Zink (n)	[tsɪŋk]
manganese	Mangan (n)	[maŋ'gaːn]
mercury	Quecksilber (n)	['kvɛkˌzɪlbə]
lead	Blei (n)	[blaɪ]

mineral	Mineral (n)	[mɪne'ʁaːl]
crystal	Kristall (m)	[kʁɪs'tal]
marble	Marmor (m)	['maʁmoːɐ]
uranium	Uran (n)	[u'ʁaːn]

The Earth. Part 2

206. Weather

weather	Wetter (n)	['vɛtɐ]
weather forecast	Wetterbericht (m)	['vɛtɐbəˌʀɪçt]
temperature	Temperatur (f)	[tɛmpəʀa'tu:ɐ]
thermometer	Thermometer (n)	[tɛʁmo'me:tɐ]
barometer	Barometer (n)	[baʀo'me:tɐ]

humid (adj)	feucht	[fɔɪçt]
humidity	Feuchtigkeit (f)	['fɔɪçtɪçkaɪt]
heat (extreme ~)	Hitze (f)	['hɪtsə]
hot (torrid)	glutheiß	['glu:tˌhaɪs]
it's hot	ist heiß	[ist haɪs]

it's warm	ist warm	[ist vaʁm]
warm (moderately hot)	warm	[vaʁm]

it's cold	ist kalt	[ist kalt]
cold (adj)	kalt	[kalt]

sun	Sonne (f)	['zɔnə]
to shine (vi)	scheinen (vi)	['ʃaɪnən]
sunny (day)	sonnig	['zɔnɪç]
to come up (vi)	aufgehen (vi)	['aʊfˌge:ən]
to set (vi)	untergehen (vi)	['ʊntɐˌge:ən]

cloud	Wolke (f)	['vɔlkə]
cloudy (adj)	bewölkt	[bə'vœlkt]
rain cloud	Regenwolke (f)	['ʀe:gənˌvɔlkə]
somber (gloomy)	trüb	[tʀy:p]

rain	Regen (m)	['ʀe:gən]
it's raining	Es regnet	[ɛs 'ʀe:gnət]

rainy (~ day, weather)	regnerisch	['ʀe:gnəʀɪʃ]
to drizzle (vi)	nieseln (vi)	['ni:zəln]

pouring rain	strömender Regen (m)	['ʃtʀø:məntdə 'ʀe:gən]
downpour	Regenschauer (m)	['ʀe:gənˌʃaʊɐ]
heavy (e.g. ~ rain)	stark	[ʃtaʁk]

puddle	Pfütze (f)	['pfʏtsə]
to get wet (in rain)	nass werden (vi)	[nas 've:ɐdən]

fog (mist)	Nebel (m)	['ne:bəl]
foggy	neblig	['ne:blɪç]
snow	Schnee (m)	[ʃne:]
it's snowing	Es schneit	[ɛs 'ʃnaɪt]

207. Severe weather. Natural disasters

thunderstorm	Gewitter (n)	[gə'vɪtɐ]
lightning (~ strike)	Blitz (m)	[blɪts]
to flash (vi)	blitzen (vi)	['blɪtsən]
thunder	Donner (m)	['dɔnɐ]
to thunder (vi)	donnern (vi)	['dɔnɐn]
it's thundering	Es donnert	[ɛs 'dɔnɐt]
hail	Hagel (m)	['ha:gəl]
it's hailing	Es hagelt	[ɛs 'ha:gəlt]
to flood (vt)	überfluten (vt)	[ˌy:bɐ'flu:tən]
flood, inundation	Überschwemmung (f)	[y:bɐ'ʃvɛmʊŋ]
earthquake	Erdbeben (n)	['e:ɐtˌbe:bən]
tremor, shoke	Erschütterung (f)	[ɛɐ'ʃʏtəʀʊŋ]
epicentre	Epizentrum (n)	[ˌepi'tsɛntʀʊm]
eruption	Ausbruch (m)	['aʊsˌbʀʊχ]
lava	Lava (f)	['la:va]
twister	Wirbelsturm (m)	['vɪʁbəlˌʃtʊʁm]
tornado	Tornado (m)	[tɔʁ'na:do]
typhoon	Taifun (m)	[taɪ'fu:n]
hurricane	Orkan (m)	[ɔʁ'ka:n]
storm	Sturm (m)	[ʃtʊʁm]
tsunami	Tsunami (m)	[tsu'na:mi]
cyclone	Zyklon (m)	[tsy'klo:n]
bad weather	Unwetter (n)	['ʊnˌvɛtɐ]
fire (accident)	Brand (m)	[bʀant]
disaster	Katastrophe (f)	[ˌkatas'tʀo:fə]
meteorite	Meteorit (m)	[meteo'ʀi:t]
avalanche	Lawine (f)	[la'vi:nə]
snowslide	Schneelawine (f)	['ʃne:laˌvi:nə]
blizzard	Schneegestöber (n)	['ʃne:gəˌʃtø:bɐ]
snowstorm	Schneesturm (m)	['ʃne:ˌʃtʊʁm]

208. Noises. Sounds

silence (quiet)	Stille (f)	['ʃtɪlə]
sound	Laut (m)	[laʊt]
noise	Lärm (m)	[lɛʁm]
to make noise	lärmen (vi)	['lɛʁmən]
noisy (adj)	lärmend	['lɛʁmənt]
loudly (to speak, etc.)	laut	[laʊt]
loud (voice, etc.)	laut	[laʊt]
constant (e.g., ~ noise)	ständig	['ʃtɛndɪç]

cry, shout (n)	Schrei (m)	[ʃʀaɪ]
to cry, to shout (vi)	schreien (vi)	[ˈʃʀaɪən]
whisper	Flüstern (n)	[ˈflʏstən]
to whisper (vi, vt)	flüstern (vt)	[ˈflʏstən]

| barking (dog's ~) | Gebell (n) | [ɡəˈbɛl] |
| to bark (vi) | bellen (vi) | [ˈbɛlən] |

groan (of pain, etc.)	Stöhnen (n)	[ˈʃtøːnən]
to groan (vi)	stöhnen (vi)	[ˈʃtøːnən]
cough	Husten (m)	[ˈhuːstən]
to cough (vi)	husten (vi)	[ˈhuːstən]

whistle	Pfiff (m)	[pfɪf]
to whistle (vi)	pfeifen (vi)	[ˈpfaɪfən]
knock (at the door)	Klopfen (n)	[ˈklɔpfən]
to knock (on the door)	klopfen (vi)	[ˈklɔpfən]

| to crack (vi) | krachen (vi) | [ˈkʀaχən] |
| crack (cracking sound) | Krachen (n) | [ˈkʀaχən] |

siren	Sirene (f)	[ˌziˈʀeːnə]
whistle (factory ~, etc.)	Pfeife (f)	[ˈpfaɪfə]
to whistle (ab. train)	pfeifen (vi)	[ˈpfaɪfən]
honk (car horn sound)	Hupe (f)	[ˈhuːpə]
to honk (vi)	hupen (vi)	[ˈhuːpən]

209. Winter

winter (n)	Winter (m)	[ˈvɪntɐ]
winter (as adj)	Winter-	[ˈvɪntɐ]
in winter	im Winter	[ɪm ˈvɪntɐ]

snow	Schnee (m)	[ʃneː]
it's snowing	Es schneit	[ɛs ˈʃnaɪt]
snowfall	Schneefall (m)	[ˈʃneːˌfal]
snowdrift	Schneewehe (f)	[ˈʃneːˌveːə]

snowflake	Schneeflocke (f)	[ˈʃneːˌflɔkə]
snowball	Schneeball (m)	[ˈʃneːˌbal]
snowman	Schneemann (m)	[ˈʃneːˌman]
icicle	Eiszapfen (m)	[ˈaɪsˌtsapfən]

December	Dezember (m)	[deˈtsɛmbɐ]
January	Januar (m)	[ˈjanuaːɐ]
February	Februar (m)	[ˈfeːbʀuaːɐ]

| frost (severe ~, freezing cold) | Frost (m) | [fʀɔst] |
| frosty (weather, air) | frostig, Frost- | [ˈfʀɔstɪç], [fʀɔst] |

below zero (adv)	unter Null	[ˈʊntɐ ˈnʊl]
first frost	leichter Frost (m)	[ˈlaɪçtɐ fʀɔst]
hoarfrost	Reif (m)	[ʀaɪf]
cold (cold weather)	Kälte (f)	[ˈkɛltə]

it's cold	Es ist kalt	[ɛs ist kalt]
fur coat	Pelzmantel (m)	['pɛlts͵mantəl]
mittens	Fausthandschuhe (pl)	['faʊst·hant∫uːə]

to fall ill	erkranken (vi)	[ɛɐ'kʀaŋkən]
cold (illness)	Erkältung (f)	[ɛɐ'kɛltʊŋ]
to catch a cold	sich erkälten	[zɪç ɛɐ'kɛltən]

ice	Eis (n)	[aɪs]
black ice	Glatteis (n)	['glat͵ʔaɪs]
to freeze over (ab. river, etc.)	zufrieren (vi)	['tsuː͵fʀiːʀən]
ice floe	Eisscholle (f)	['aɪs∫ɔlə]

skis	Ski (pl)	[∫iː]
skier	Skiläufer (m)	['∫iː͵lɔɪfe]
to ski (vi)	Ski laufen	['∫iː 'laʊfən]
to skate (vi)	Schlittschuh laufen	['∫lɪt∫uː 'laʊfən]

Fauna

210. Mammals. Predators

predator	**Raubtier** (n)	['ʀaʊptiːɐ]
tiger	**Tiger** (m)	['tiːgɐ]
lion	**Löwe** (m)	['løːvə]
wolf	**Wolf** (m)	[vɔlf]
fox	**Fuchs** (m)	[fʊks]
jaguar	**Jaguar** (m)	['jaːguaːɐ]
leopard	**Leopard** (m)	[leo'paʁt]
cheetah	**Gepard** (m)	[ge'paʁt]
black panther	**Panther** (m)	['pantɐ]
puma	**Puma** (m)	['puːma]
snow leopard	**Schneeleopard** (m)	['ʃneːleoˌpaʁt]
lynx	**Luchs** (m)	[lʊks]
coyote	**Kojote** (m)	[kɔ'joːtə]
jackal	**Schakal** (m)	[ʃa'kaːl]
hyena	**Hyäne** (f)	['hyɛːnə]

211. Wild animals

animal	**Tier** (n)	[tiːɐ]
beast (animal)	**Bestie** (f)	['bɛstɪə]
squirrel	**Eichhörnchen** (n)	['aɪçˌhœʁnçən]
hedgehog	**Igel** (m)	['iːgəl]
hare	**Hase** (m)	['haːzə]
rabbit	**Kaninchen** (n)	[ka'niːnçən]
badger	**Dachs** (m)	[daks]
raccoon	**Waschbär** (m)	['vaʃˌbɛːɐ]
hamster	**Hamster** (m)	['hamstɐ]
marmot	**Murmeltier** (n)	['mʊʁməlˌtiːɐ]
mole	**Maulwurf** (m)	['maʊlˌvʊʁf]
mouse	**Maus** (f)	[maʊs]
rat	**Ratte** (f)	['ʀatə]
bat	**Fledermaus** (f)	['fleːdɐˌmaʊs]
ermine	**Hermelin** (n)	[hɛʁmə'liːn]
sable	**Zobel** (m)	['tsoːbəl]
marten	**Marder** (m)	['maʁdɐ]
weasel	**Wiesel** (n)	['viːzəl]
mink	**Nerz** (m)	[nɛʁts]

| beaver | Biber (m) | ['bi:bɐ] |
| otter | Fischotter (m) | ['fɪʃˌʔɔtɐ] |

horse	Pferd (n)	[pfe:ɐt]
moose	Elch (m)	[ɛlç]
deer	Hirsch (m)	[hɪʁʃ]
camel	Kamel (n)	[ka'me:l]

bison	Bison (m)	['bi:zɔn]
wisent	Wisent (m)	['vi:zɛnt]
buffalo	Büffel (m)	['bʏfəl]

zebra	Zebra (n)	['tse:bʁa]
antelope	Antilope (f)	[anti'lo:pə]
roe deer	Reh (n)	[ʁe:]
fallow deer	Damhirsch (m)	['damhɪʁʃ]
chamois	Gämse (f)	['gɛmzə]
wild boar	Wildschwein (n)	['vɪltʃvaɪn]

whale	Wal (m)	[va:l]
seal	Seehund (m)	['ze:ˌhʊnt]
walrus	Walroß (n)	['va:lˌʁɔs]
fur seal	Seebär (m)	['ze:ˌbɛ:ɐ]
dolphin	Delfin (m)	[dɛl'fi:n]

bear	Bär (m)	[bɛ:ɐ]
polar bear	Eisbär (m)	['aɪsˌbɛ:ɐ]
panda	Panda (m)	['panda]

monkey	Affe (m)	['afə]
chimpanzee	Schimpanse (m)	[ʃɪm'panzə]
orangutan	Orang-Utan (m)	['o:ʁaŋˌʔu:tan]
gorilla	Gorilla (m)	[go'ʁɪla]
macaque	Makak (m)	[ma'kak]
gibbon	Gibbon (m)	['gɪbɔn]

elephant	Elefant (m)	[ele'fant]
rhinoceros	Nashorn (n)	['na:sˌhɔʁn]
giraffe	Giraffe (f)	[ˌgi'ʁafə]
hippopotamus	Flusspferd (n)	['flʊsˌpfe:ɐt]

| kangaroo | Känguru (n) | ['kɛŋguʁu] |
| koala (bear) | Koala (m) | [ko'a:la] |

mongoose	Manguste (f)	[maŋ'gʊstə]
chinchilla	Chinchilla (n)	[tʃɪn'tʃɪla]
skunk	Stinktier (n)	['ʃtɪŋkˌti:ɐ]
porcupine	Stachelschwein (n)	['ʃtaxəlʃvaɪn]

212. Domestic animals

cat	Katze (f)	['katsə]
tomcat	Kater (m)	['ka:tɐ]
dog	Hund (m)	[hʊnt]

horse	Pferd (n)	[pfe:ɐt]
stallion (male horse)	Hengst (m)	['hɛŋst]
mare	Stute (f)	['ʃtu:tə]

cow	Kuh (f)	[ku:]
bull	Stier (m)	[ʃti:ɐ]
ox	Ochse (m)	['ɔksə]

sheep (ewe)	Schaf (n)	[ʃa:f]
ram	Widder (m)	['vɪdɐ]
goat	Ziege (f)	['tsi:gə]
billy goat, he-goat	Ziegenbock (m)	['tsi:gən‚bɔk]

| donkey | Esel (m) | ['e:zəl] |
| mule | Maultier (n) | ['maʊl‚ti:ɐ] |

pig	Schwein (n)	[ʃvaɪn]
piglet	Ferkel (n)	['fɛʁkəl]
rabbit	Kaninchen (n)	[ka'ni:nçən]

| hen (chicken) | Huhn (n) | [hu:n] |
| cock | Hahn (m) | [ha:n] |

duck	Ente (f)	['ɛntə]
drake	Enterich (m)	['ɛntəʁɪç]
goose	Gans (f)	[gans]

| tom turkey, gobbler | Puter (m) | ['pu:tɐ] |
| turkey (hen) | Pute (f) | ['pu:tə] |

domestic animals	Haustiere (pl)	['haʊs‚ti:ʁə]
tame (e.g. ~ hamster)	zahm	[tsa:m]
to tame (vt)	zähmen (vt)	['tsɛ:mən]
to breed (vt)	züchten (vt)	['tsʏçtən]

farm	Farm (f)	[faʁm]
poultry	Geflügel (n)	[gə'fly:gəl]
cattle	Vieh (n)	[fi:]
herd (cattle)	Herde (f)	['he:ɐdə]

stable	Pferdestall (m)	['pfe:ɐdə‚ʃtal]
pigsty	Schweinestall (m)	['ʃvaɪnə‚ʃtal]
cowshed	Kuhstall (m)	['ku:‚ʃtal]
rabbit hutch	Kaninchenstall (m)	[ka'ni:nçən‚ʃtal]
hen house	Hühnerstall (m)	['hy:nɐ‚ʃtal]

213. Dogs. Dog breeds

dog	Hund (m)	[hʊnt]
sheepdog	Schäferhund (m)	['ʃɛ:fɐ‚hʊnt]
German shepherd	Deutsche Schäferhund (m)	['dɔɪtʃə 'ʃɛ:fɐ‚hʊnt]
poodle	Pudel (m)	['pu:dəl]
dachshund	Dachshund (m)	['daks‚hʊnt]
bulldog	Bulldogge (f)	['bʊl‚dɔgə]

boxer	Boxer (m)	['bɔksɐ]
mastiff	Mastiff (m)	['mastɪf]
Rottweiler	Rottweiler (m)	['ʀɔtvaɪlɐ]
Doberman	Dobermann (m)	['doːbɐˌman]

basset	Basset (m)	[ba'seː]
bobtail	Bobtail (m)	['bɔpteːl]
Dalmatian	Dalmatiner (m)	[ˌdalma'tiːnɐ]
cocker spaniel	Cocker-Spaniel (m)	['kɔkɐ 'ʃpanɪəl]

| Newfoundland | Neufundländer (m) | [nɔɪ'fʊntˌlɛndɐ] |
| Saint Bernard | Bernhardiner (m) | [bɛʀnhaʀ'diːnɐ] |

husky	Eskimohund (m)	['ɛskimoˌhʊnt]
Chow Chow	Chow-Chow (m)	['tʃau'tʃau]
spitz	Spitz (m)	[ʃpɪts]
pug	Mops (m)	[mɔps]

214. Sounds made by animals

barking (n)	Gebell (n)	[gə'bɛl]
to bark (vi)	bellen (vi)	['bɛlən]
to miaow (vi)	miauen (vi)	[mi'auən]
to purr (vi)	schnurren (vi)	['ʃnʊʀən]

to moo (vi)	muhen (vi)	['muːən]
to bellow (bull)	brüllen (vi)	['bʀʏlən]
to growl (vi)	knurren (vi)	['knʊʀən]

howl (n)	Heulen (n)	['hɔɪlən]
to howl (vi)	heulen (vi)	['hɔɪlən]
to whine (vi)	winseln (vi)	['vɪnzəln]

to bleat (sheep)	meckern (vi)	['mɛkɐn]
to oink, to grunt (pig)	grunzen (vi)	['gʀʊntsən]
to squeal (vi)	kreischen (vi)	['kʀaɪʃən]

to croak (vi)	quaken (vi)	['kvaːkən]
to buzz (insect)	summen (vi)	['zʊmən]
to chirp (crickets, grasshopper)	zirpen (vi)	['tsɪʀpən]

215. Young animals

cub	Tierkind (n)	['tiːɐˌkɪnt]
kitten	Kätzchen (n)	['kɛtsçən]
baby mouse	Mausjunge (n)	['mausjʊŋə]
puppy	Hündchen (n), Welpe (m)	['hʏntçən], ['vɛlpə]

leveret	Häschen (n)	['hɛːsçən]
baby rabbit	Kaninchenjunge (n)	[ka'niːnçənjʊŋə]
wolf cub	Wolfsjunge (n)	['vɔlfsjʊŋə]

| fox cub | Fuchsjunge (n) | ['fʊksˌjʊŋə] |
| bear cub | Bärenjunge (n) | ['bɛːRənˌjʊŋə] |

lion cub	Löwenjunge (n)	['løːvənˌjʊŋə]
tiger cub	junger Tiger (m)	['jʏŋɐ 'tiːgɐ]
elephant calf	Elefantenjunge (n)	[ele'fantənˌjʊŋə]

piglet	Ferkel (n)	['fɛʁkəl]
calf (young cow, bull)	Kalb (n)	[kalp]
kid (young goat)	Ziegenkitz (n)	['tsiːgənˌkɪts]
lamb	Lamm (n)	[lam]
fawn (young deer)	Hirschkalb (n)	['hɪʁʃˌkalp]
young camel	Kamelfohlen (n)	[ka'meːlˌfoːlən]

| snakelet (baby snake) | junge Schlange (f) | ['jʊŋə 'ʃlaŋə] |
| froglet (baby frog) | Fröschlein (n) | ['fRœʃlain] |

baby bird	junger Vogel (m)	['jʏŋɐ 'foːgəl]
chick (of chicken)	Küken (n)	['kyːkən]
duckling	Entlein (n)	['ɛntlain]

216. Birds

bird	Vogel (m)	['foːgəl]
pigeon	Taube (f)	['taʊbə]
sparrow	Spatz (m)	[ʃpats]
tit (great tit)	Meise (f)	['maɪzə]
magpie	Elster (f)	['ɛlstɐ]

raven	Rabe (m)	['Raːbə]
crow	Krähe (f)	['kRɛːə]
jackdaw	Dohle (f)	['doːlə]
rook	Saatkrähe (f)	['zaːtˌkRɛːə]

duck	Ente (f)	['ɛntə]
goose	Gans (f)	[gans]
pheasant	Fasan (m)	[fa'zaːn]

eagle	Adler (m)	['aːdlɐ]
hawk	Habicht (m)	['haːbɪçt]
falcon	Falke (m)	['falkə]
vulture	Greif (m)	[gRaɪf]
condor (Andean ~)	Kondor (m)	['kɔndoːɐ]

swan	Schwan (m)	[ʃvaːn]
crane	Kranich (m)	['kRaːnɪç]
stork	Storch (m)	[ʃtɔʁç]

parrot	Papagei (m)	[papa'gaɪ]
hummingbird	Kolibri (m)	['koːlibRi]
peacock	Pfau (m)	[pfaʊ]

| ostrich | Strauß (m) | [ʃtRaʊs] |
| heron | Reiher (m) | ['Raɪɐ] |

flamingo	Flamingo (m)	[fla'mɪŋgo]
pelican	Pelikan (m)	['pe:lika:n]

nightingale	Nachtigall (f)	['naxtɪgal]
swallow	Schwalbe (f)	['ʃvalbə]

thrush	Drossel (f)	['dRɔsəl]
song thrush	Singdrossel (f)	['zɪŋˌdRɔsəl]
blackbird	Amsel (f)	['amzəl]

swift	Segler (m)	['ze:glɐ]
lark	Lerche (f)	['lɛʁçə]
quail	Wachtel (f)	['vaxtəl]

woodpecker	Specht (m)	[ʃpɛçt]
cuckoo	Kuckuck (m)	['kʊkʊk]
owl	Eule (f)	['ɔɪlə]
eagle owl	Uhu (m)	['u:hu]
wood grouse	Auerhahn (m)	['aʊɐˌha:n]
black grouse	Birkhahn (m)	['bɪʁkˌha:n]
partridge	Rebhuhn (n)	['Re:pˌhu:n]

starling	Star (m)	[ʃta:ɐ]
canary	Kanarienvogel (m)	[ka'na:Rɪənˌfo:gəl]
hazel grouse	Haselhuhn (n)	['ha:zəlˌhu:n]
chaffinch	Buchfink (m)	['bu:xfɪŋk]
bullfinch	Gimpel (m)	['gɪmpəl]

seagull	Möwe (f)	['møːvə]
albatross	Albatros (m)	['albatRɔs]
penguin	Pinguin (m)	['pɪŋguiːn]

217. Birds. Singing and sounds

to sing (vi)	singen (vt)	['zɪŋən]
to call (animal, bird)	schreien (vi)	['ʃRaɪən]
to crow (cock)	kikeriki schreien	[ˌkikəRi'ki: 'ʃRaɪən]
cock-a-doodle-doo	kikeriki	[ˌkikəRi'ki:]

to cluck (hen)	gackern (vi)	['gakɐn]
to caw (crow call)	krächzen (vi)	['kRɛçtsən]
to quack (duck call)	schnattern (vi)	['ʃnatɐn]
to cheep (vi)	piepsen (vi)	['pi:psən]
to chirp, to twitter	zwitschern (vi)	['tsvɪtʃɐn]

218. Fish. Marine animals

bream	Brachse (f)	['bRaksə]
carp	Karpfen (m)	['kaʁpfən]
perch·	Barsch (m)	[baʁʃ]
catfish	Wels (m)	[vɛls]
pike	Hecht (m)	[hɛçt]

| salmon | Lachs (m) | [laks] |
| sturgeon | Stör (m) | [ʃtø:ɐ] |

herring	Hering (m)	['he:ʀɪŋ]
Atlantic salmon	atlantische Lachs (m)	[at'lantɪʃə laks]
mackerel	Makrele (f)	[ma'kʀe:lə]
flatfish	Scholle (f)	['ʃɔlə]

zander, pike perch	Zander (m)	['tsandɐ]
cod	Dorsch (m)	[dɔʁʃ]
tuna	Tunfisch (m)	['tu:nfɪʃ]
trout	Forelle (f)	[ˌfo'ʀɛlə]

eel	Aal (m)	[a:l]
electric ray	Zitterrochen (m)	['tsɪtɐˌʀɔχən]
moray eel	Muräne (f)	[mu'ʀɛ:nə]
piranha	Piranha (m)	[pi'ʀanja]

shark	Hai (m)	[haɪ]
dolphin	Delfin (m)	[dɛl'fi:n]
whale	Wal (m)	[va:l]

crab	Krabbe (f)	['kʀabə]
jellyfish	Meduse (f)	[me'du:zə]
octopus	Krake (m)	['kʀa:kə]

starfish	Seestern (m)	['ze:ˌʃtɛʁn]
sea urchin	Seeigel (m)	['ze:ˌʔi:gəl]
seahorse	Seepferdchen (n)	['ze:ˌpfe:ɐtçən]

oyster	Auster (f)	['aʊstɐ]
prawn	Garnele (f)	[gaʁ'ne:lə]
lobster	Hummer (m)	['hʊmɐ]
spiny lobster	Languste (f)	[laŋ'gʊstə]

219. Amphibians. Reptiles

| snake | Schlange (f) | ['ʃlaŋə] |
| venomous (snake) | Gift-, giftig | [gɪft], ['gɪftɪç] |

viper	Viper (f)	['vi:pɐ]
cobra	Kobra (f)	['ko:bʀa]
python	Python (m)	['py:tɔn]
boa	Boa (f)	['bo:a]

grass snake	Ringelnatter (f)	['ʀɪŋəlˌnatɐ]
rattle snake	Klapperschlange (f)	['klapɐʃlaŋə]
anaconda	Anakonda (f)	[ana'kɔnda]

lizard	Eidechse (f)	['aɪdɛksə]
iguana	Leguan (m)	['le:gua:n]
monitor lizard	Waran (m)	[va'ʀa:n]
salamander	Salamander (m)	[zala'mandɐ]
chameleon	Chamäleon (n)	[ka'mɛ:leˌɔn]

scorpion	Skorpion (m)	[skɔʁ'pjoːn]
turtle	Schildkröte (f)	['ʃɪlt‚kʁøːtə]
frog	Frosch (m)	[fʁɔʃ]
toad	Kröte (f)	['kʁøːtə]
crocodile	Krokodil (n)	[kʁoko'diːl]

220. Insects

insect	Insekt (n)	[ɪn'zɛkt]
butterfly	Schmetterling (m)	['ʃmɛtelɪŋ]
ant	Ameise (f)	['aːmaɪzə]
fly	Fliege (f)	['fliːgə]
mosquito	Mücke (f)	['mʏkə]
beetle	Käfer (m)	['kɛːfe]

wasp	Wespe (f)	['vɛspə]
bee	Biene (f)	['biːnə]
bumblebee	Hummel (f)	['hʊməl]
gadfly (botfly)	Bremse (f)	['bʁɛmzə]

| spider | Spinne (f) | ['ʃpɪnə] |
| spider's web | Spinnennetz (n) | ['ʃpɪnən‚nɛts] |

dragonfly	Libelle (f)	[li'bɛlə]
grasshopper	Grashüpfer (m)	['gʁaːs‚hʏpfe]
moth (night butterfly)	Schmetterling (m)	['ʃmɛtelɪŋ]

cockroach	Schabe (f)	['ʃaːbə]
tick	Zecke (f)	['tsɛkə]
flea	Floh (m)	[floː]
midge	Kriebelmücke (f)	['kʁiːbəl‚mʏkə]

locust	Heuschrecke (f)	['hɔɪʃʁɛkə]
snail	Schnecke (f)	['ʃnɛkə]
cricket	Heimchen (n)	['haɪmçən]
firefly	Leuchtkäfer (m)	['lɔɪçt‚kɛːfe]
ladybird	Marienkäfer (m)	[ma'ʁiːən‚kɛːfe]
cockchafer	Maikäfer (m)	['maɪ‚kɛːfe]

leech	Blutegel (m)	['bluːt‚ʔeːgəl]
caterpillar	Raupe (f)	['ʁaʊpə]
earthworm	Wurm (m)	[vʊʁm]
larva	Larve (f)	['laʁfə]

221. Animals. Body parts

beak	Schnabel (m)	['ʃnaːbəl]
wings	Flügel (pl)	['flyːgəl]
foot (of the bird)	Fuß (m)	[fuːs]
feathers (plumage)	Gefieder (n)	[gə'fiːde]
feather	Feder (f)	['feːde]
crest	Haube (f)	['haʊbə]

gills	Kiemen (pl)	['ki:mən]
spawn	Laich (m)	[laɪç]
larva	Larve (f)	['laʁfə]
fin	Flosse (f)	['flɔsə]
scales (of fish, reptile)	Schuppe (f)	['ʃʊpə]

fang (canine)	Stoßzahn (m)	['ʃtoːsˌtsaːn]
paw (e.g. cat's ~)	Pfote (f)	['pfoːtə]
muzzle (snout)	Schnauze (f)	['ʃnaʊtsə]
mouth (cat's ~)	Rachen (m)	['ʁaxən]
tail	Schwanz (m)	[ʃvants]
whiskers	Barthaar (n)	['baːɐtˌhaːɐ]

hoof	Huf (m)	[huːf]
horn	Horn (n)	[hɔʁn]

carapace	Panzer (m)	['pantsɐ]
shell (mollusk ~)	Muschel (f)	['mʊʃl]
eggshell	Schale (f)	['ʃaːlə]

animal's hair (pelage)	Fell (n)	[fɛl]
pelt (hide)	Haut (f)	[haʊt]

222. Actions of animals

to fly (vi)	fliegen (vi)	['fliːgən]
to fly in circles	herumfliegen (vi)	[hɛ'ʁʊmˌfliːgən]
to fly away	wegfliegen (vi)	['vɛkˌfliːgən]
to flap (~ the wings)	schlagen (vi)	['ʃlaːgən]

to peck (vi)	picken (vt)	['pɪkən]
to sit on eggs	bebrüten (vt)	[bə'bʁyːtən]
to hatch out (vi)	ausschlüpfen (vi)	['aʊsˌʃlʏpfən]
to build a nest	ein Nest bauen	[aɪn nɛst 'baʊən]

to slither, to crawl	kriechen (vi)	['kʁiːçən]
to sting, to bite (insect)	stechen (vt)	['ʃtɛçən]
to bite (ab. animal)	beißen (vt)	['baɪsən]

to sniff (vt)	schnüffeln (vt)	['ʃnʏfəln]
to bark (vi)	bellen (vi)	['bɛlən]
to hiss (snake)	zischen (vi)	['tsɪʃən]

to scare (vt)	erschrecken (vt)	[ɛɐ'ʃʁɛkən]
to attack (vt)	angreifen (vt)	['anˌgʁaɪfən]

to gnaw (bone, etc.)	nagen (vi)	['naːgən]
to scratch (with claws)	kratzen (vt)	['kʁatsən]
to hide (vi)	sich verstecken	[zɪç fɛɐ'ʃtɛkən]

to play (kittens, etc.)	spielen (vi)	['ʃpiːlən]
to hunt (vi, vt)	jagen (vi)	['jagən]
to hibernate (vi)	Winterschlaf halten	['vɪntɐˌʃlaːf 'haltən]
to go extinct	aussterben (vi)	['aʊsˌʃtɛʁbən]

223. Animals. Habitats

habitat	Lebensraum (f)	['le:bəns,ʀaʊm]
migration	Wanderung (f)	['vandəʀʊŋ]
mountain	Berg (m)	[bɛʁk]
reef	Riff (n)	[ʀɪf]
cliff	Fels (m)	[fɛls]
forest	Wald (m)	[valt]
jungle	Dschungel (m, n)	['dʒʊŋəl]
savanna	Savanne (f)	[za'vanə]
tundra	Tundra (f)	['tʊndʀa]
steppe	Steppe (f)	['ʃtɛpə]
desert	Wüste (f)	['vy:stə]
oasis	Oase (f)	[o'a:zə]
sea	Meer (n), See (f)	[me:ɐ], [ze:]
lake	See (m)	[ze:]
ocean	Ozean (m)	['o:tsea:n]
swamp (marshland)	Sumpf (m)	[zʊmpf]
freshwater (adj)	Süßwasser-	['zy:s,vasɐ]
pond	Teich (m)	[taɪç]
river	Fluss (m)	[flʊs]
den (bear's ~)	Höhle (f), Bau (m)	['hø:lə], [baʊ]
nest	Nest (n)	[nɛst]
tree hollow	Höhlung (f)	['hø:,lʊŋ]
burrow (animal hole)	Loch (n)	[lɔx]
anthill	Ameisenhaufen (m)	['a:maɪzən·haʊfən]

224. Animal care

zoo	Zoo (m)	['tso:]
nature reserve	Schutzgebiet (n)	['ʃʊtsgə,bi:t]
breeder (cattery, kennel, etc.)	Zucht (f)	[tsʊχt]
open-air cage	Freigehege (n)	['fʀaɪ·gə'he:gə]
cage	Käfig (m)	['kɛ:fɪç]
kennel	Hundehütte (f)	['hʊndə'hytə]
dovecot	Taubenschlag (m)	['taʊbənʃla:k]
aquarium (fish tank)	Aquarium (n)	[a'kva:ʀiʊm]
dolphinarium	Delphinarium (n)	[dɛlfi'na:ʀɪʊm]
to breed (animals)	züchten (vt)	['tsʏçtən]
brood, litter	Wurf (m)	[vʊʁf]
to tame (vt)	zähmen (vt)	['tsɛ:mən]
to train (animals)	dressieren (vt)	[dʀɛ'si:ʀən]
feed (fodder, etc.)	Futter (n)	['fʊtɐ]
to feed (vt)	füttern (vt)	['fʏtɐn]

201

pet shop	Zoohandlung (f)	[tsoo'handlʊŋ]
muzzle (for dog)	Maulkorb (m)	['maʊl͵kɔʁp]
collar (e.g., dog ~)	Halsband (n)	['hals͵bant]
name (of an animal)	Rufname (m)	['ʁu:f͵na:mə]
pedigree (dog's ~)	Stammbaum (m)	['ʃtam͵baʊm]

225. Animals. Miscellaneous

pack (wolves)	Rudel (n)	['ʁu:dəl]
flock (birds)	Vogelschwarm (m)	['fo:gəlʃvaʁm]
shoal, school (fish)	Schwarm (m)	[ʃvaʁm]
herd (horses)	Pferdeherde (f)	['pfe:ʁdə͵he:ʁdə]

| male (n) | Männchen (n) | ['mɛnçən] |
| female (n) | Weibchen (n) | ['vaɪpçən] |

hungry (adj)	hungrig	['hʊŋʁɪç]
wild (adj)	wild	[vɪlt]
dangerous (adj)	gefährlich	[gə'fɛ:ɐlɪç]

226. Horses

| horse | Pferd (n) | [pfe:ɐt] |
| breed (race) | Rasse (f) | ['ʁasə] |

| foal | Fohlen (n) | ['fo:lən] |
| mare | Stute (f) | ['ʃtu:tə] |

mustang	Mustang (m)	['mʊstaŋ]
pony	Pony (n)	['pɔni]
draught horse	schweres Zugpferd (n)	['ʃve:ʁəs 'tsu:k͵pfe:ɐt]

| mane | Mähne (f) | ['mɛnə] |
| tail | Schwanz (m) | [ʃvants] |

hoof	Huf (m)	[hu:f]
horseshoe	Hufeisen (n)	['hu:f͵ʔaɪzən]
to shoe (vt)	beschlagen (vt)	[bə'ʃla:gən]
blacksmith	Schmied (m)	[ʃmi:t]

saddle	Sattel (m)	['zatəl]
stirrup	Steigbügel (m)	['ʃtaɪk͵by:gəl]
bridle	Zaum (m)	[tsaʊm]
reins	Zügel (pl)	['tsy:gəl]
whip (for riding)	Peitsche (f)	['paɪtʃə]

rider	Reiter (m)	['ʁaɪtɐ]
to saddle up (vt)	satteln (vt)	['zatəln]
to mount a horse	besteigen (vt)	[bə'ʃtaɪgən]

| gallop | Galopp (m) | [ga'lɔp] |
| to gallop (vi) | galoppieren (vi) | [galɔ'pi:ʁən] |

trot (n)	Trab (m)	[tʀaːp]
at a trot (adv)	im Trab	[ɪm tʀaːp]
to go at a trot	traben (vi)	['tʀaːbən]

| racehorse | Rennpferd (n) | ['ʀɛn͵pfeːɐt] |
| horse racing | Rennen (n) | ['ʀɛnən] |

stable	Pferdestall (m)	['pfeːɐdəʃtal]
to feed (vt)	füttern (vt)	['fʏtɐn]
hay	Heu (n)	[hɔɪ]
to water (animals)	tränken (vt)	['tʀɛŋkən]
to wash (horse)	striegeln (vt)	['ʃtʀiːgəln]

horse-drawn cart	Pferdewagen (m)	['pfeːɐdə͵vaːgən]
to graze (vi)	weiden (vi)	['vaɪdən]
to neigh (vi)	wiehern (vi)	['viːɐn]
to kick (to buck)	ausschlagen (vi)	['aʊsʃlaːgən]

Flora

227. Trees

tree	**Baum** (m)	[baʊm]
deciduous (adj)	**Laub-**	[laʊp]
coniferous (adj)	**Nadel-**	['naːdəl]
evergreen (adj)	**immergrün**	['ɪmɐˌgʀyːn]
apple tree	**Apfelbaum** (m)	['apfəlˌbaʊm]
pear tree	**Birnbaum** (m)	['bɪʁnˌbaʊm]
sweet cherry tree	**Süßkirschbaum** (m)	['zyːskɪʁʃˌbaʊm]
sour cherry tree	**Sauerkirschbaum** (m)	[zaʊəˈkɪʁʃˌbaʊm]
plum tree	**Pflaumenbaum** (m)	['pflaʊmənˌbaʊm]
birch	**Birke** (f)	['bɪʁkə]
oak	**Eiche** (f)	['aɪçə]
linden tree	**Linde** (f)	['lɪndə]
aspen	**Espe** (f)	['ɛspə]
maple	**Ahorn** (m)	['aːhɔʁn]
spruce	**Fichte** (f)	['fɪçtə]
pine	**Kiefer** (f)	['kiːfɐ]
larch	**Lärche** (f)	['lɛʁçə]
fir tree	**Tanne** (f)	['tanə]
cedar	**Zeder** (f)	['tseːdɐ]
poplar	**Pappel** (f)	['papəl]
rowan	**Vogelbeerbaum** (m)	['foːgəlbeːɐˌbaʊm]
willow	**Weide** (f)	['vaɪdə]
alder	**Erle** (f)	['ɛʁlə]
beech	**Buche** (f)	['buːχə]
elm	**Ulme** (f)	['ʊlmə]
ash (tree)	**Esche** (f)	['ɛʃə]
chestnut	**Kastanie** (f)	[kasˈtaːniə]
magnolia	**Magnolie** (f)	[magˈnoːlɪə]
palm tree	**Palme** (f)	['palmə]
cypress	**Zypresse** (f)	[tsyˈpʀɛsə]
mangrove	**Mangrovenbaum** (m)	[maɲˈgʀoːvənˌbaʊm]
baobab	**Baobab** (m)	['baːobap]
eucalyptus	**Eukalyptus** (m)	[ɔɪkaˈlʏptʊs]
sequoia	**Mammutbaum** (m)	['mamʊtˌbaʊm]

228. Shrubs

bush	**Strauch** (m)	[ʃtʀaʊχ]
shrub	**Gebüsch** (n)	[gəˈbʏʃ]

| grapevine | Weinstock (m) | ['vaɪnˌʃtɔk] |
| vineyard | Weinberg (m) | ['vaɪnˌbɛʁk] |

raspberry bush	Himbeerstrauch (m)	['hɪmbeːɐˌʃtʀaʊχ]
blackcurrant bush	schwarze Johannisbeere (f)	['ʃvaʁtsə joːˈhanɪsbeːʀə]
redcurrant bush	rote Johannisbeere (f)	['ʀoːtə joːˈhanɪsbeːʀə]
gooseberry bush	Stachelbeerstrauch (m)	['ʃtaχəlbeːɐˌʃtʀaʊχ]

acacia	Akazie (f)	[aˈkaːtsiə]
barberry	Berberitze (f)	[bɛʁbəˈʀɪtsə]
jasmine	Jasmin (m)	[jasˈmiːn]

juniper	Wacholder (m)	[vaˈχɔldɐ]
rosebush	Rosenstrauch (m)	['ʀoːzənˌʃtʀaʊχ]
dog rose	Heckenrose (f)	['hɛkənˌʀoːzə]

229. Mushrooms

mushroom	Pilz (m)	[pɪlts]
edible mushroom	essbarer Pilz (m)	['ɛsbaːʀɐ pɪlts]
poisonous mushroom	Giftpilz (m)	['gɪftˌpɪlts]
cap	Hut (m)	[huːt]
stipe	Stiel (m)	[ʃtiːl]

cep, penny bun	Steinpilz (m)	['ʃtaɪnˌpɪlts]
orange-cap boletus	Rotkappe (f)	['ʀoːtˌkapə]
birch bolete	Birkenpilz (m)	['bɪʁkənˌpɪlts]
chanterelle	Pfifferling (m)	['pfɪfɛlɪŋ]
russula	Täubling (m)	['tɔyplɪŋ]

morel	Morchel (f)	['mɔʁçəl]
fly agaric	Fliegenpilz (m)	['fliːgənˌpɪlts]
death cap	Grüner Knollenblätterpilz (m)	['gʀyːnɐ 'knɔlənˈblɛtəˌpɪlts]

230. Fruits. Berries

fruit	Frucht (f)	[fʀʊχt]
fruits	Früchte (pl)	['fʀʏçtə]
apple	Apfel (m)	['apfəl]
pear	Birne (f)	['bɪʁnə]
plum	Pflaume (f)	['pflaʊmə]

strawberry (garden ~)	Erdbeere (f)	['eːɐtˌbeːʀə]
sour cherry	Sauerkirsche (f)	['zaʊɐˌkɪʁʃə]
sweet cherry	Süßkirsche (f)	['zyːsˌkɪʁʃə]
grape	Weintrauben (pl)	['vaɪnˌtʀaʊbən]

raspberry	Himbeere (f)	['hɪmˌbeːʀə]
blackcurrant	schwarze Johannisbeere (f)	['ʃvaʁtsə joːˈhanɪsbeːʀə]
redcurrant	rote Johannisbeere (f)	['ʀoːtə joːˈhanɪsbeːʀə]
gooseberry	Stachelbeere (f)	['ʃtaχəlˌbeːʀə]

cranberry	Moosbeere (f)	['moːsˌbeːʀə]
orange	Apfelsine (f)	[apfəl'ziːnə]
tangerine	Mandarine (f)	[ˌmandaˈʀiːnə]
pineapple	Ananas (f)	['ananas]
banana	Banane (f)	[baˈnaːnə]
date	Dattel (f)	['datəl]

lemon	Zitrone (f)	[tsiˈtʀoːnə]
apricot	Aprikose (f)	[ˌapʀiˈkoːzə]
peach	Pfirsich (m)	['pfɪʀzɪç]
kiwi	Kiwi, Kiwifrucht (f)	['kiːvi], ['kiːviˌfʀʊχt]
grapefruit	Grapefruit (f)	['gʀɛɪpˌfʀuːt]

berry	Beere (f)	['beːʀə]
berries	Beeren (pl)	['beːʀən]
cowberry	Preiselbeere (f)	['pʀaɪzəlˌbeːʀə]
wild strawberry	Walderdbeere (f)	['valtʔeːʁətˌbeːʀə]
bilberry	Heidelbeere (f)	['haɪdəlˌbeːʀə]

231. Flowers. Plants

| flower | Blume (f) | ['bluːmə] |
| bouquet (of flowers) | Blumenstrauß (m) | ['bluːmənˌʃtʀaʊs] |

rose (flower)	Rose (f)	['ʀoːzə]
tulip	Tulpe (f)	['tʊlpə]
carnation	Nelke (f)	['nɛlkə]
gladiolus	Gladiole (f)	[ˌglaˈdɪoːlə]

cornflower	Kornblume (f)	['kɔʁnˌbluːmə]
harebell	Glockenblume (f)	['glɔkənˌbluːmə]
dandelion	Löwenzahn (m)	['løːvənˌtsaːn]
camomile	Kamille (f)	[kaˈmɪlə]

aloe	Aloe (f)	['aːloe]
cactus	Kaktus (m)	['kaktʊs]
rubber plant, ficus	Gummibaum (m)	['gʊmiˌbaʊm]

lily	Lilie (f)	['liːliə]
geranium	Geranie (f)	[geˈʀaːnɪə]
hyacinth	Hyazinthe (f)	[hyaˈtsɪntə]

mimosa	Mimose (f)	[miˈmoːzə]
narcissus	Narzisse (f)	[naʁˈtsɪsə]
nasturtium	Kapuzinerkresse (f)	[ˌkapuˈtsiːnɐˌkʀɛsə]

orchid	Orchidee (f)	[ˌɔʁçiˈdeːə]
peony	Pfingstrose (f)	['pfɪŋstˌʀoːzə]
violet	Veilchen (n)	['faɪlçən]

pansy	Stiefmütterchen (n)	['ʃtiːfˌmʏtɐçən]
forget-me-not	Vergissmeinnicht (n)	[ˌfɛɐˈgɪsˈmaɪn·nɪçt]
daisy	Gänseblümchen (n)	['gɛnzəˌblyːmçən]
poppy	Mohn (m)	[moːn]

| hemp | Hanf (m) | [hanf] |
| mint | Minze (f) | ['mɪntsə] |

| lily of the valley | Maiglöckchen (n) | ['maɪˌglœkçən] |
| snowdrop | Schneeglöckchen (n) | ['ʃneːglœkçən] |

nettle	Brennnessel (f)	['bʀɛnˌnɛsəl]
sorrel	Sauerampfer (m)	['zauɐˌʔampfɐ]
water lily	Seerose (f)	['zeːˌʀoːzə]
fern	Farn (m)	[faʀn]
lichen	Flechte (f)	['flɛçtə]

conservatory (greenhouse)	Gewächshaus (n)	[gəˈvɛksˌhaus]
lawn	Rasen (m)	['ʀaːzən]
flowerbed	Blumenbeet (n)	['bluːməənˌbeːt]

plant	Pflanze (f)	['pflantsə]
grass	Gras (n)	[gʀaːs]
blade of grass	Grashalm (m)	['gʀaːsˌhalm]

leaf	Blatt (n)	[blat]
petal	Blütenblatt (n)	['blyːtənˌblat]
stem	Stiel (m)	[ʃtiːl]
tuber	Knolle (f)	['knɔlə]

| young plant (shoot) | Jungpflanze (f) | ['juŋˌpflantsə] |
| thorn | Dorn (m) | [dɔʀn] |

to blossom (vi)	blühen (vi)	['blyːən]
to fade, to wither	welken (vi)	['vɛlkən]
smell (odour)	Geruch (m)	[gəˈʀuχ]
to cut (flowers)	abschneiden (vt)	['apˌʃnaɪdən]
to pick (a flower)	pflücken (vt)	['pflʏkən]

232. Cereals, grains

grain	Getreide (n)	[gəˈtʀaɪdə]
cereal crops	Getreidepflanzen (pl)	[gəˈtʀaɪdəˌpflantsən]
ear (of barley, etc.)	Ähre (f)	['ɛːʀə]

wheat	Weizen (m)	['vaɪtsən]
rye	Roggen (m)	['ʀɔgən]
oats	Hafer (m)	['haːfɐ]
millet	Hirse (f)	['hɪʀzə]
barley	Gerste (f)	['gɛʀstə]
maize	Mais (m)	['maɪs]
rice	Reis (m)	[ʀaɪs]
buckwheat	Buchweizen (m)	['buːχˌvaɪtsən]

pea plant	Erbse (f)	['ɛʀpsə]
kidney bean	weiße Bohne (f)	['vaɪsə 'boːnə]
soya	Sojabohne (f)	['zoːjaˌboːnə]
lentil	Linse (f)	['lɪnzə]
beans (pulse crops)	Bohnen (pl)	['boːnən]

233. Vegetables. Greens

| vegetables | Gemüse (n) | [gə'my:zə] |
| greens | grünes Gemüse (pl) | ['gʀy:nəs gə'my:zə] |

tomato	Tomate (f)	[to'ma:tə]
cucumber	Gurke (f)	['guʀkə]
carrot	Karotte (f)	[ka'ʀɔtə]
potato	Kartoffel (f)	[kaʁ'tɔfəl]
onion	Zwiebel (f)	['tsvi:bəl]
garlic	Knoblauch (m)	['kno:p‚lauχ]

cabbage	Kohl (m)	[ko:l]
cauliflower	Blumenkohl (m)	['blu:mən‚ko:l]
Brussels sprouts	Rosenkohl (m)	['ʀo:zən‚ko:l]
broccoli	Brokkoli (m)	['bʀɔkoli]

beetroot	Rote Bete (f)	[‚ʀo:tə'be:tə]
aubergine	Aubergine (f)	[‚obɛʁ'ʒi:nə]
marrow	Zucchini (f)	[tsʊ'ki:ni]
pumpkin	Kürbis (m)	['kYʁbɪs]
turnip	Rübe (f)	['ʀy:bə]

parsley	Petersilie (f)	[petɐ'zi:lɪə]
dill	Dill (m)	[dɪl]
lettuce	Kopf Salat (m)	[kɔpf za'la:t]
celery	Sellerie (m)	['zɛləʀi]
asparagus	Spargel (m)	['ʃpaʁgəl]
spinach	Spinat (m)	[ʃpi'na:t]

pea	Erbse (f)	['ɛʁpsə]
beans	Bohnen (pl)	['bo:nən]
maize	Mais (m)	['maɪs]
kidney bean	weiße Bohne (f)	['vaɪsə 'bo:nə]

pepper	Pfeffer (m)	['pfɛfɐ]
radish	Radieschen (n)	[ʀa'di:sçən]
artichoke	Artischocke (f)	[aʁti'ʃɔkə]

REGIONAL GEOGRAPHY

234. Western Europe

Europe	Europa (n)	[ɔɪˈRoːpa]
European Union	Europäische Union (f)	[ˌɔɪRoˈpɛːɪʃə ʔuˈnjoːn]
European (n)	Europäer (m)	[ˌɔɪRoˈpɛːɐ]
European (adj)	europäisch	[ˌɔɪRoˈpɛːɪʃ]
Austria	Österreich (n)	[ˈøːstəRaɪç]
Austrian (masc.)	Österreicher (m)	[ˈøːstɐRaɪçɐ]
Austrian (fem.)	Österreicherin (f)	[ˈøːstəˌRaɪçəRɪn]
Austrian (adj)	österreichisch	[ˈøːstɐRaɪçɪʃ]
Great Britain	Großbritannien (n)	[gRoːs·bRiˈtaniən]
England	England (n)	[ˈɛŋlant]
British (masc.)	Brite (m)	[ˈbRɪtə]
British (fem.)	Britin (f)	[ˈbRɪtɪn]
English, British (adj)	englisch	[ˈɛŋlɪʃ]
Belgium	Belgien (n)	[ˈbɛlgɪən]
Belgian (masc.)	Belgier (m)	[ˈbɛlgɪɐ]
Belgian (fem.)	Belgierin (f)	[ˈbɛlgɪəRɪn]
Belgian (adj)	belgisch	[ˈbɛlgɪʃ]
Germany	Deutschland (n)	[ˈdɔɪtʃlant]
German (masc.)	Deutsche (m)	[ˈdɔɪtʃə]
German (fem.)	Deutsche (f)	[ˈdɔɪtʃə]
German (adj)	deutsch	[dɔɪtʃ]
Netherlands	Niederlande (f)	[ˈniːdeˌlandə]
Holland	Holland (n)	[ˈhɔlant]
Dutch (masc.)	Holländer (m)	[ˈhɔlɛndɐ]
Dutch (fem.)	Holländerin (f)	[ˈhɔlɛndəRɪn]
Dutch (adj)	holländisch	[ˈhɔlɛndɪʃ]
Greece	Griechenland (n)	[ˈgRiːçənˌlant]
Greek (masc.)	Grieche (m)	[ˈgRiːçə]
Greek (fem.)	Griechin (f)	[ˈgRiːçɪn]
Greek (adj)	griechisch	[ˈgRiːçɪʃ]
Denmark	Dänemark (n)	[ˈdɛːnəˌmaʁk]
Dane (masc.)	Däne (m)	[ˈdɛːnə]
Dane (fem.)	Dänin (f)	[ˈdɛːnɪn]
Danish (adj)	dänisch	[ˈdɛːnɪʃ]
Ireland	Irland (n)	[ˈɪʁlant]
Irish (masc.)	Ire (m)	[ˈiːʁə]
Irish (fem.)	Irin (f)	[ˈiːRɪn]
Irish (adj)	irisch	[ˈiːRɪʃ]

Iceland	Island (n)	['i:slant]
Icelander (masc.)	Isländer (m)	['i:sˌlɛndɐ]
Icelander (fem.)	Isländerin (f)	['i:sˌlɛndəʀɪn]
Icelandic (adj)	isländisch	['i:sˌlɛndɪʃ]

Spain	Spanien (n)	['ʃpa:nɪən]
Spaniard (masc.)	Spanier (m)	['ʃpa:nɪɐ]
Spaniard (fem.)	Spanierin (f)	['ʃpa:nɪəʀɪn]
Spanish (adj)	spanisch	['ʃpa:nɪʃ]

Italy	Italien (n)	[i'ta:lɪən]
Italian (masc.)	Italiener (m)	[ˌital'ɪe:nɐ]
Italian (fem.)	Italienerin (f)	[ˌital'ɪe:nəʀɪn]
Italian (adj)	italienisch	[ˌita'lɪe:nɪʃ]

Cyprus	Zypern (n)	['tsy:pɐn]
Cypriot (masc.)	Zypriot (m)	[tsypʀi'o:t]
Cypriot (fem.)	Zypriotin (f)	[tsypʀi'o:tɪn]
Cypriot (adj)	zyprisch	['tsy:pʀɪʃ]

Malta	Malta (n)	['malta]
Maltese (masc.)	Malteser (m)	[mal'te:zɐ]
Maltese (fem.)	Malteserin (f)	[mal'te:zəʀɪn]
Maltese (adj)	maltesisch	[mal'te:zɪʃ]

Norway	Norwegen (n)	['nɔʁˌve:gən]
Norwegian (masc.)	Norweger (m)	['nɔʁˌve:gɐ]
Norwegian (fem.)	Norwegerin (f)	['nɔʁˌve:gəʀɪn]
Norwegian (adj)	norwegisch	['nɔʁve:gɪʃ]

Portugal	Portugal (n)	['pɔʁtugal]
Portuguese (masc.)	Portugiese (m)	[pɔʁtu'gi:zə]
Portuguese (fem.)	Portugiesin (f)	[pɔʁtu'gi:zɪn]
Portuguese (adj)	portugiesisch	[pɔʁtu'gi:zɪʃ]

Finland	Finnland (n)	['fɪnlant]
Finn (masc.)	Finne (m)	['fɪnə]
Finn (fem.)	Finnin (f)	['fɪnɪn]
Finnish (adj)	finnisch	['fɪnɪʃ]

France	Frankreich (n)	['fʀaŋkʀaɪç]
French (masc.)	Franzose (m)	[fʀan'tso:zə]
French (fem.)	Französin (f)	[fʀan'tsø:zɪn]
French (adj)	französisch	[fʀan'tsø:zɪʃ]

Sweden	Schweden (n)	['ʃve:dən]
Swede (masc.)	Schwede (m)	['ʃve:də]
Swede (fem.)	Schwedin (f)	['ʃve:dɪn]
Swedish (adj)	schwedisch	['ʃve:dɪʃ]

Switzerland	Schweiz (f)	[ʃvaɪts]
Swiss (masc.)	Schweizer (m)	['ʃvaɪtsɐ]
Swiss (fem.)	Schweizerin (f)	['ʃvaɪtsəʀɪn]
Swiss (adj)	schweizerisch	['ʃvaɪtsəʀɪʃ]
Scotland	Schottland (n)	['ʃɔtlant]
Scottish (masc.)	Schotte (m)	['ʃɔtə]

Scottish (fem.)	Schottin (f)	['ʃɔtɪn]
Scottish (adj)	schottisch	['ʃɔtɪʃ]

Vatican City	Vatikan (m)	[vati'ka:n]
Liechtenstein	Liechtenstein (n)	['lɪçtənˌʃtaɪn]
Luxembourg	Luxemburg (n)	['lʊksəmˌbʊʁk]
Monaco	Monaco (n)	[mo'nako]

235. Central and Eastern Europe

Albania	Albanien (n)	[al'ba:niən]
Albanian (masc.)	Albaner (m)	[al'ba:nɐ]
Albanian (fem.)	Albanerin (f)	[al'ba:nəʁɪn]
Albanian (adj)	albanisch	[al'ba:nɪʃ]

Bulgaria	Bulgarien (n)	[bʊl'ga:ʁɪən]
Bulgarian (masc.)	Bulgare (m)	[bʊl'ga:ʁə]
Bulgarian (fem.)	Bulgarin (f)	[bʊl'ga:ʁɪn]
Bulgarian (adj)	bulgarisch	[bʊl'ga:ʁɪʃ]

Hungary	Ungarn (n)	['ʊŋgaʁn]
Hungarian (masc.)	Ungar (m)	['ʊŋgaʁ]
Hungarian (fem.)	Ungarin (f)	['ʊŋgaʁɪn]
Hungarian (adj)	ungarisch	['ʊŋgaʁɪʃ]

Latvia	Lettland (n)	['lɛtlant]
Latvian (masc.)	Lette (m)	['lɛtə]
Latvian (fem.)	Lettin (f)	['lɛtɪn]
Latvian (adj)	lettisch	['lɛtɪʃ]

Lithuania	Litauen (n)	['lɪtaʊən]
Lithuanian (masc.)	Litauer (m)	['li:taʊɐ]
Lithuanian (fem.)	Litauerin (f)	['li:taʊəʁɪn]
Lithuanian (adj)	litauisch	['lɪtaʊɪʃ]

Poland	Polen (n)	['po:lən]
Pole (masc.)	Pole (m)	['po:lə]
Pole (fem.)	Polin (f)	['po:lɪn]
Polish (adj)	polnisch	['pɔlnɪʃ]

Romania	Rumänien (n)	[ʁu'mɛ:nɪən]
Romanian (masc.)	Rumäne (m)	[ʁu'mɛ:nə]
Romanian (fem.)	Rumänin (f)	[ʁu'mɛ:nɪn]
Romanian (adj)	rumänisch	[ʁu'mɛ:nɪʃ]

Serbia	Serbien (n)	['zɛʁbɪən]
Serbian (masc.)	Serbe (m)	['zɛʁbə]
Serbian (fem.)	Serbin (f)	['zɛʁbɪn]
Serbian (adj)	serbisch	['zɛʁbɪʃ]

Slovakia	Slowakei (f)	[slova'kaɪ]
Slovak (masc.)	Slowake (m)	[slo'va:kə]
Slovak (fem.)	Slowakin (f)	[slo'va:kɪn]
Slovak (adj)	slowakisch	[slo'va:kɪʃ]

Croatia	Kroatien (n)	[kʀoˈaːtsɪən]
Croatian (masc.)	Kroate (m)	[kʀoˈaːtə]
Croatian (fem.)	Kroatin (f)	[kʀoˈaːtɪn]
Croatian (adj)	kroatisch	[kʀoˈaːtɪʃ]

Czech Republic	Tschechien (n)	[ˈtʃɛçɪən]
Czech (masc.)	Tscheche (m)	[ˈtʃɛçə]
Czech (fem.)	Tschechin (f)	[ˈtʃɛçɪn]
Czech (adj)	tschechisch	[ˈtʃɛçɪʃ]

Estonia	Estland (n)	[ˈɛstlant]
Estonian (masc.)	Este (m)	[ˈɛstə]
Estonian (fem.)	Estin (f)	[ˈɛstɪn]
Estonian (adj)	estnisch	[ˈɛstnɪʃ]

Bosnia and Herzegovina	Bosnien und Herzegowina (n)	[ˈbɔsnɪən ʊnt ˌhɛʀtsəˈgɔvinaː]
North Macedonia	Makedonien (n)	[makəˈdoːnɪən]
Slovenia	Slowenien (n)	[sloˈveːnɪən]
Montenegro	Montenegro (n)	[mɔnteˈneːgʀo]

236. Former USSR countries

Azerbaijan	Aserbaidschan (n)	[ˌazɛʀbaɪˈdʒaːn]
Azerbaijani (masc.)	Aserbaidschaner (m)	[azɛʀbaɪˈdʒaːnɐ]
Azerbaijani (fem.)	Aserbaidschanerin (f)	[azɛʀbaɪˈdʒaːnəʀɪn]
Azerbaijani, Azeri (adj)	aserbaidschanisch	[ˌazɛʀbaɪˈdʒaːnɪʃ]

Armenia	Armenien (n)	[aʀˈmeːnɪən]
Armenian (masc.)	Armenier (m)	[aʀˈmeːnɪɐ]
Armenian (fem.)	Armenierin (f)	[aʀˈmeːnɪəʀɪn]
Armenian (adj)	armenisch	[aʀˈmeːnɪʃ]

Belarus	Weißrussland (n)	[ˈvaɪsˌʀʊslant]
Belarusian (masc.)	Weißrusse (m)	[ˈvaɪsˌʀʊsə]
Belarusian (fem.)	Weißrussin (f)	[ˈvaɪsˌʀʊsɪn]
Belarusian (adj)	weißrussisch	[ˈvaɪsˌʀʊsɪʃ]

Georgia	Georgien (n)	[geˈɔʀgɪən]
Georgian (masc.)	Georgier (m)	[geˈɔʀgɪɐ]
Georgian (fem.)	Georgierin (f)	[geˈɔʀgɪəʀɪn]
Georgian (adj)	georgisch	[geˈɔʀgɪʃ]

Kazakhstan	Kasachstan (n)	[ˈkaːzaχˌstaːn]
Kazakh (masc.)	Kasache (m)	[kaˈzaχə]
Kazakh (fem.)	Kasachin (f)	[kaˈzaχɪn]
Kazakh (adj)	kasachisch	[ˌkaˈzaχɪʃ]

Kirghizia	Kirgisien (n)	[ˈkɪʀgiːzɪən]
Kirghiz (masc.)	Kirgise (m)	[kɪʀˈgiːzə]
Kirghiz (fem.)	Kirgisin (f)	[kɪʀˈgiːzɪn]
Kirghiz (adj)	kirgisisch	[kɪʀˈgiːzɪʃ]
Moldova, Moldavia	Moldawien (n)	[mɔlˈdaːvɪən]
Moldavian (masc.)	Moldauer (m)	[ˈmɔldaʊɐ]

| Moldavian (fem.) | Moldauerin (f) | ['mɔldaʊə,ʀɪn] |
| Moldavian (adj) | moldauisch | ['mɔldaʊɪʃ] |

Russia	Russland (n)	['ʀʊslant]
Russian (masc.)	Russe (m)	['ʀʊsə]
Russian (fem.)	Russin (f)	['ʀʊsɪn]
Russian (adj)	russisch	['ʀʊsɪʃ]

Tajikistan	Tadschikistan (n)	[ta'dʒi:kɪsta:n]
Tajik (masc.)	Tadschike (m)	[ta'dʒi:kə]
Tajik (fem.)	Tadschikin (f)	[ta'dʒi:kɪn]
Tajik (adj)	tadschikisch	[ta'dʒi:kɪʃ]

Turkmenistan	Turkmenistan (n)	[tʊʁk'me:nɪsta:n]
Turkmen (masc.)	Turkmene (m)	[tʊʁk'me:nə]
Turkmen (fem.)	Turkmenin (f)	[tʊʁk'me:nɪn]
Turkmenian (adj)	turkmenisch	[tʊʁk'me:nɪʃ]

Uzbekistan	Usbekistan (n)	[ʊs'be:kɪsta:n]
Uzbek (masc.)	Usbeke (m)	[ʊs'be:kə]
Uzbek (fem.)	Usbekin (f)	[ʊs'be:kɪn]
Uzbek (adj)	usbekisch	[us'be:kɪʃ]

Ukraine	Ukraine (f)	[ˌukʀa'i:nə]
Ukrainian (masc.)	Ukrainer (m)	[ukʀa'i:ne]
Ukrainian (fem.)	Ukrainerin (f)	[ukʀa'i:nəʀɪn]
Ukrainian (adj)	ukrainisch	[ukʀa'i:nɪʃ]

237. Asia

| Asia | Asien (n) | ['a:ziən] |
| Asian (adj) | asiatisch | [a'zia:tɪʃ] |

Vietnam	Vietnam (n)	[vɪɛt'nam]
Vietnamese (masc.)	Vietnamese (m)	[vɪɛtna'me:zə]
Vietnamese (fem.)	Vietnamesin (f)	[vɪɛtna'me:zɪn]
Vietnamese (adj)	vietnamesisch	[ˌviɛtna'me:zɪʃ]

India	Indien (n)	['ɪndiən]
Indian (masc.)	Inder (m)	['ɪnde]
Indian (fem.)	Inderin (f)	['ɪndəʀɪn]
Indian (adj)	indisch	['ɪndɪʃ]

Israel	Israel (n)	['ɪsʀae:l]
Israeli (masc.)	Israeli (m)	[ˌɪsʀa'e:li]
Israeli (fem.)	Israeli (f)	[ˌɪsʀa'e:li]
Israeli (adj)	israelisch	[ɪsʀa'e:lɪʃ]

Jew (n)	Jude (m)	['ju:də]
Jewess (n)	Jüdin (f)	['jy:dɪn]
Jewish (adj)	jüdisch	['jy:dɪʃ]

| China | China (n) | ['çi:na] |
| Chinese (masc.) | Chinese (m) | [çi'ne:zə] |

213

| Chinese (fem.) | Chinesin (f) | [çi'ne:zɪn] |
| Chinese (adj) | chinesisch | [çi'ne:zɪʃ] |

Korean (masc.)	Koreaner (m)	[koʀe'a:nɐ]
Korean (fem.)	Koreanerin (f)	[koʀe'a:nəʀɪn]
Korean (adj)	koreanisch	[koʀe'a:nɪʃ]

Lebanon	Libanon (m, n)	['li:banɔn]
Lebanese (masc.)	Libanese (m)	[liba'ne:zə]
Lebanese (fem.)	Libanesin (f)	[liba'ne:zɪn]
Lebanese (adj)	libanesisch	[liba'ne:zɪʃ]

Mongolia	Mongolei (f)	[ˌmɔŋgo'laɪ]
Mongolian (masc.)	Mongole (m)	[mɔŋ'go:lə]
Mongolian (fem.)	Mongolin (f)	[mɔŋ'go:lɪn]
Mongolian (adj)	mongolisch	[mɔŋ'go:lɪʃ]

Malaysia	Malaysia (n)	[ma'laɪzɪa]
Malaysian (masc.)	Malaie (m)	[ma'laɪə]
Malaysian (fem.)	Malaiin (f)	[ma'lajɪn]
Malaysian (adj)	malaiisch	[ma'laɪɪʃ]

Pakistan	Pakistan (n)	['pa:kɪsta:n]
Pakistani (masc.)	Pakistaner (m)	[pakɪs'ta:nɐ]
Pakistani (fem.)	Pakistanerin (f)	[pakɪs'ta:nəʀɪn]
Pakistani (adj)	pakistanisch	[pakɪs'ta:nɪʃ]

Saudi Arabia	Saudi-Arabien (n)	[ˌzaʊdiʔa'ʀa:bɪən]
Arab (masc.)	Araber (m)	['a:ʀabɐ]
Arab (fem.)	Araberin (f)	['a:ʀabəʀɪn]
Arabic, Arabian (adj)	arabisch	[a'ʀa:bɪʃ]

Thailand	Thailand (n)	['taɪlant]
Thai (masc.)	Thailänder (m)	['taɪˌlɛndɐ]
Thai (fem.)	Thailänderin (f)	['taɪˌlɛndəʀɪn]
Thai (adj)	thailändisch	['taɪlɛndɪʃ]

Taiwan	Taiwan (n)	[taɪ'va:n]
Taiwanese (masc.)	Taiwaner (m)	[taɪ'va:nɐ]
Taiwanese (fem.)	Taiwanerin (f)	[taɪ'va:nəʀɪn]
Taiwanese (adj)	taiwanisch	[taɪ'va:nɪʃ]

Turkey	Türkei (f)	[tYʁ'kaɪ]
Turk (masc.)	Türke (m)	['tYʁkə]
Turk (fem.)	Türkin (f)	['tYʁkɪn]
Turkish (adj)	türkisch	['tYʁkɪʃ]

Japan	Japan (n)	['ja:pan]
Japanese (masc.)	Japaner (m)	[ja'pa:nɐ]
Japanese (fem.)	Japanerin (f)	[ja'pa:nəʀɪn]
Japanese (adj)	japanisch	[ja'pa:nɪʃ]

Afghanistan	Afghanistan (n)	[af'ga:nɪsta:n]
Bangladesh	Bangladesch (n)	[ˌbaŋgla'dɛʃ]
Indonesia	Indonesien (n)	[ɪndo'ne:zɪən]
Jordan	Jordanien (n)	[jɔʁ'da:nɪən]

Iraq	Irak (m, n)	[i'ʀaːk]
Iran	Iran (m, n)	[i'ʀaːn]
Cambodia	Kambodscha (n)	[kam'bɔdʒa]
Kuwait	Kuwait (n)	[ku'vaɪt]

Laos	Laos (n)	['laːɔs]
Myanmar	Myanmar (n)	['mɪanmaːɐ]
Nepal	Nepal (n)	['neːpal]
United Arab Emirates	Vereinigten Arabischen Emirate (pl)	[fɛɐ'ʔaɪnɪɡən a'ʀaːbɪʃən emi'ʀaːtə]

Syria	Syrien (n)	['zyːʀɪən]
Palestine	Palästina (n)	[palɛs'tiːna]
South Korea	Südkorea (n)	['zyːtko'ʀeːa]
North Korea	Nordkorea (n)	['nɔʁt·ko'ʀeːa]

238. North America

United States of America	Die Vereinigten Staaten	[di fɛɐ'ʔaɪnɪçtən 'ʃtaːtən]
American (masc.)	Amerikaner (m)	[ameʀi'kaːnɐ]
American (fem.)	Amerikanerin (f)	[ameʀi'kaːnəʀɪn]
American (adj)	amerikanisch	[ameʀi'kaːnɪʃ]

Canada	Kanada (n)	['kanada]
Canadian (masc.)	Kanadier (m)	[ka'naːdɪɐ]
Canadian (fem.)	Kanadierin (f)	[ka'naːdiəʀɪn]
Canadian (adj)	kanadisch	[ka'naːdɪʃ]

Mexico	Mexiko (n)	['mɛksikoː]
Mexican (masc.)	Mexikaner (m)	[mɛksi'kaːnɐ]
Mexican (fem.)	Mexikanerin (f)	[mɛksi'kaːnəʀɪn]
Mexican (adj)	mexikanisch	[mɛksi'kaːnɪʃ]

239. Central and South America

Argentina	Argentinien (n)	[ˌaʁgɛn'tiːnɪən]
Argentinian (masc.)	Argentinier (m)	[aʁgɛn'tiːnɪɐ]
Argentinian (fem.)	Argentinierin (f)	[aʁgɛn'tiːniəʀɪn]
Argentinian (adj)	argentinisch	[aʁgɛn'tiːnɪʃ]

Brazil	Brasilien (n)	[bʀa'ziːlɪən]
Brazilian (masc.)	Brasilianer (m)	[bʀazi'lɪaːnɐ]
Brazilian (fem.)	Brasilianerin (f)	[bʀazi'lɪaːnəʀɪn]
Brazilian (adj)	brasilianisch	[bʀazi'lɪanɪʃ]

Colombia	Kolumbien (n)	[ko'lʊmbɪən]
Colombian (masc.)	Kolumbianer (m)	[kolʊm'bɪaːnɐ]
Colombian (fem.)	Kolumbianerin (f)	[kolʊm'bɪaːnəʀɪn]
Colombian (adj)	kolumbianisch	[kolʊm'bɪaːnɪʃ]

| Cuba | Kuba (n) | ['kuːba] |
| Cuban (masc.) | Kubaner (m) | [ku'baːnɐ] |

| Cuban (fem.) | Kubanerin (f) | [ku'ba:nəʀɪn] |
| Cuban (adj) | kubanisch | [ku'ba:nɪʃ] |

Chile	Chile (n)	['tʃi:lə]
Chilean (masc.)	Chilene (m)	[tʃi'le:nə]
Chilean (fem.)	Chilenin (f)	[tʃi'le:nɪn]
Chilean (adj)	chilenisch	[tʃi'le:nɪʃ]

Bolivia	Bolivien (n)	[bo'li:vɪən]
Venezuela	Venezuela (n)	[ˌvene'tsue:la]
Paraguay	Paraguay (n)	['pa:ʀagvaɪ]
Peru	Peru (n)	[pe'ʀu:]

Suriname	Suriname (n)	[syʀi'na:mə]
Uruguay	Uruguay (n)	['u:ʀugvaɪ]
Ecuador	Ecuador (n)	[ˌekua'do:ɐ]

The Bahamas	Die Bahamas	[di ba'ha:ma:s]
Haiti	Haiti (n)	[ha'i:ti]
Dominican Republic	Dominikanische Republik (f)	[dominiˌka:nɪʃə ʀepu'blik]
Panama	Panama (n)	['panama:]
Jamaica	Jamaika (n)	[ja'maɪka]

240. Africa

Egypt	Ägypten (n)	[ɛ'gyptən]
Egyptian (masc.)	Ägypter (m)	[ɛ'gyptɐ]
Egyptian (fem.)	Ägypterin (f)	[ɛ'gyptəʀɪn]
Egyptian (adj)	ägyptisch	[ɛ'gyptɪʃ]

Morocco	Marokko (n)	[ˌma'ʀɔko]
Moroccan (masc.)	Marokkaner (m)	[maʀɔ'ka:nɐ]
Moroccan (fem.)	Marokkanerin (f)	[maʀɔ'ka:nəʀɪn]
Moroccan (adj)	marokkanisch	[maʀɔ'ka:nɪʃ]

Tunisia	Tunesien (n)	[tu'ne:zɪən]
Tunisian (masc.)	Tunesier (m)	[tu'ne:zɪɐ]
Tunisian (fem.)	Tunesierin (f)	[tu'ne:zɪəʀɪn]
Tunisian (adj)	tunesisch	[tu'ne:zɪʃ]

Ghana	Ghana (n)	['ga:na]
Zanzibar	Sansibar (n)	['zanziba:ɐ]
Kenya	Kenia (n)	['ke:nia]
Libya	Libyen (n)	['li:byən]
Madagascar	Madagaskar (n)	[ˌmada'gaskaɐ]

Namibia	Namibia (n)	[na'mi:bia]
Senegal	Senegal (m)	['ze:negal]
Tanzania	Tansania (n)	[tan'za:nɪa]
South Africa	Republik Südafrika (f)	[ʀepu'bli:k zy:tˌʔa:fʀika]

African (masc.)	Afrikaner (m)	[afʀi'ka:nɐ]
African (fem.)	Afrikanerin (f)	[afʀi'ka:nəʀɪn]
African (adj)	afrikanisch	[afʀi'ka:nɪʃ]

241. Australia. Oceania

Australia	Australien (n)	[aʊsˈtʀaːlɪən]
Australian (masc.)	Australier (m)	[aʊsˈtʀaːlɪɐ]
Australian (fem.)	Australierin (f)	[aʊsˈtʀaːlɪəʀɪn]
Australian (adj)	australisch	[aʊsˈtʀaːlɪʃ]

New Zealand	Neuseeland (n)	[nɔɪˈzeːlant]
New Zealander (masc.)	Neuseeländer (m)	[nɔɪˈzeːˌlɛndɐ]
New Zealander (fem.)	Neuseeländerin (f)	[nɔɪˈzeːˌlɛndəʀɪn]
New Zealand (as adj)	neuseeländisch	[nɔɪˈzeːˌlɛndɪʃ]

| Tasmania | Tasmanien (n) | [tasˈmaːnɪən] |
| French Polynesia | Französisch-Polynesien (n) | [fʀanˈtsøːzɪʃ polyˈneːzɪən] |

242. Cities

Amsterdam	Amsterdam (n)	[ˌamstɐˈdam]
Ankara	Ankara (n)	[ˈaŋkaʀa]
Athens	Athen (n)	[aˈteːn]
Baghdad	Bagdad (n)	[ˈbakdat]
Bangkok	Bangkok (n)	[ˈbaŋkɔk]
Barcelona	Barcelona (n)	[ˌbaʀsəˈloːnaː]

Beijing	Peking (n)	[ˈpeːkɪŋ]
Beirut	Beirut (n)	[baɪˈʀuːt]
Berlin	Berlin (n)	[bɛʀˈliːn]
Mumbai (Bombay)	Bombay (n)	[ˈbɔmbeɪ]
Bonn	Bonn (n)	[bɔn]

Bordeaux	Bordeaux (n)	[bɔʀˈdoː]
Bratislava	Bratislava (n)	[bʀatɪsˈlaːva]
Brussels	Brüssel (n)	[ˈbʀʏsəl]
Bucharest	Bukarest (n)	[ˈbukaʀɛst]
Budapest	Budapest (n)	[ˈbuːdaˌpɛst]

Cairo	Kairo (n)	[ˈkaɪʀo]
Kolkata (Calcutta)	Kalkutta (n)	[kalˈkʊta]
Chicago	Chicago (n)	[ʃɪˈkaːgo]
Copenhagen	Kopenhagen (n)	[ˌkopənˈhaːgən]

Dar-es-Salaam	Daressalam (n)	[daʀɛsaˈlaːm]
Delhi	Delhi (n)	[ˈdɛli]
Dubai	Dubai (n)	[ˈduːbaɪ]
Dublin	Dublin (n)	[ˈdablɪn]
Düsseldorf	Düsseldorf (n)	[ˈdʏsəlˌdɔʀf]

Florence	Florenz (n)	[floˈʀɛnts]
Frankfurt	Frankfurt (n)	[ˈfʀaŋkfʊʀt]
Geneva	Genf (n)	[gɛnf]

| The Hague | Den Haag (n) | [den ˈhaːk] |
| Hamburg | Hamburg (n) | [ˈhambʊʀk] |

Hanoi	Hanoi (n)	[ha'nɔɪ]
Havana	Havanna (n)	[ha'vana]
Helsinki	Helsinki (n)	['helsiŋki]
Hiroshima	Hiroshima (n)	[hiʀo'ʃiːma]
Hong Kong	Hongkong (n)	['hɔŋkɔŋ]

Istanbul	Istanbul (n)	['ɪstambuːl]
Jerusalem	Jerusalem (n)	[je'ʀuːzalɛm]
Kyiv	Kiew (n)	['kiːɛf]
Kuala Lumpur	Kuala Lumpur (n)	[ku'ala 'lʊmpʊʀ]
Lisbon	Lissabon (n)	['lɪsabɔn]
London	London (n)	['lɔndɔn]
Los Angeles	Los Angeles (n)	[lɔs'ændʒəlɪs]
Lyons	Lyon (n)	[li'ɔŋ]

Madrid	Madrid (n)	[ma'dʀɪt]
Marseille	Marseille (n)	[maʀ'sɛːj]
Mexico City	Mexiko-Stadt (n)	['mɛksiko 'ʃtat]
Miami	Miami (n)	[maj'ɛmɪ]
Montreal	Montreal (n)	[mɔntʀe'al]
Moscow	Moskau (n)	['mɔskaʊ]
Munich	München (n)	['mʏnçən]

Nairobi	Nairobi (n)	[naɪ'ʀoːbi]
Naples	Neapel (n)	[ne'apəl]
New York	New York (n)	[nju: 'jɔːk]
Nice	Nizza (n)	['nɪtsaː]
Oslo	Oslo (n)	['ɔsloː]
Ottawa	Ottawa (n)	[ɔ'tava]

Paris	Paris (n)	[pa'ʀiːs]
Prague	Prag (n)	[pʀaːk]
Rio de Janeiro	Rio de Janeiro (n)	['ʀiːo deː ʒa'neːʀo]
Rome	Rom (n)	[ʀoːm]

Saint Petersburg	Sankt Petersburg (n)	['sankt 'peːtɐsbʊʀk]
Seoul	Seoul (n)	[ze'uːl]
Shanghai	Schanghai (n)	[ʃaŋ'haɪ]
Singapore	Singapur (n)	['zɪŋgapuːɐ]
Stockholm	Stockholm (n)	['ʃtɔkhɔlm]
Sydney	Sydney (n)	['sɪdnɪ]

Taipei	Taipeh (n)	[taɪ'peː]
Tokyo	Tokio (n)	['toːkɪoː]
Toronto	Toronto (n)	[to'ʀɔnto]
Venice	Venedig (n)	[ve'neːdɪç]
Vienna	Wien (n)	[viːn]
Warsaw	Warschau (n)	['vaʀʃaʊ]
Washington	Washington (n)	['vɔʃɪŋtən]

243. Politics. Government. Part 1

| politics | Politik (f) | [poli'tɪk] |
| political (adj) | politisch | [po'liːtɪʃ] |

politician	Politiker (m)	[po'li:tikɐ]
state (country)	Staat (m)	[ʃtaːt]
citizen	Bürger (m)	['bʏʁgɐ]
citizenship	Staatsbürgerschaft (f)	['ʃtaːtsbʏʁgɐˌʃaft]

| national emblem | Staatswappen (n) | ['ʃtaːtsˌvapən] |
| national anthem | Nationalhymne (f) | [natsjo'naːlˌhʏmnə] |

government	Regierung (f)	[ʀeˈgiːʀʊŋ]
head of state	Staatschef (m)	['ʃtaːtsʃɛf]
parliament	Parlament (n)	[paʁlaˈmɛnt]
party	Partei (f)	[paʁˈtaɪ]

| capitalism | Kapitalismus (m) | [kapitaˈlɪsmʊs] |
| capitalist (adj) | kapitalistisch | [kapitaˈlɪstɪʃ] |

| socialism | Sozialismus (m) | [zotsɪaˈlɪsmʊs] |
| socialist (adj) | sozialistisch | [zotsɪaˈlɪstɪʃ] |

communism	Kommunismus (m)	[ˌkɔmuˈnɪsmʊs]
communist (adj)	kommunistisch	[kɔmuˈnɪstɪʃ]
communist (n)	Kommunist (m)	[kɔmuˈnɪst]

democracy	Demokratie (f)	[demokʀaˈtiː]
democrat	Demokrat (m)	[demoˈkʀaːt]
democratic (adj)	demokratisch	[demoˈkʀaːtɪʃ]
Democratic party	demokratische Partei (f)	[demoˈkʀaːtɪʃə paʁˈtaɪ]

| liberal (n) | Liberale (m) | [libeˈʀaːlɐ] |
| Liberal (adj) | liberal | [libeˈʀaːl] |

| conservative (n) | Konservative (m) | [ˌkɔnzɛʁvaˈtiːvə] |
| conservative (adj) | konservativ | [ˌkɔnzɛʁvaˈtiːf] |

republic (n)	Republik (f)	[ʀepuˈbliːk]
republican (n)	Republikaner (m)	[ʀepubliˈkaːnɐ]
Republican party	Republikanische Partei (f)	[ʀepubliˈkaːnɪʃə paʁˈtaɪ]

elections	Wahlen (pl)	['vaːlən]
to elect (vt)	wählen (vt)	['vɛːlən]
elector, voter	Wähler (m)	['vɛːlɐ]
election campaign	Wahlkampagne (f)	['vaːlˌkamˌpanjə]

voting (n)	Abstimmung (f)	['apˌʃtɪmʊŋ]
to vote (vi)	abstimmen (vi)	['apˌʃtɪmən]
suffrage, right to vote	Abstimmungsrecht (n)	['apʃtɪmʊŋsˌʀɛçt]

candidate	Kandidat (m)	[kandiˈdaːt]
to run for (~ President)	kandidieren (vi)	[kandiˈdiːʀən]
campaign	Kampagne (f)	[kamˈpanjə]

| opposition (as adj) | Oppositions- | [ɔpoziˈtsjoːns] |
| opposition (n) | Opposition (f) | [ɔpoziˈtsjoːn] |

| visit | Besuch (m) | [bəˈzuːx] |
| official visit | Staatsbesuch (m) | ['ʃtaːtsbəˌzuːx] |

219

international (adj)	international	[ˌɪntɛnatsjɔ'naːl]
negotiations	Verhandlungen (pl)	[fɛɐ'handlʊŋən]
to negotiate (vi)	verhandeln (vi)	[fɛɐ'handəln]

244. Politics. Government. Part 2

society	Gesellschaft (f)	[gə'zɛlʃaft]
constitution	Verfassung (f)	[fɛɐ'fasʊŋ]
power (political control)	Macht (f)	[maχt]
corruption	Korruption (f)	[kɔrʊp'tsjoːn]

| law (justice) | Gesetz (n) | [gə'zɛts] |
| legal (legitimate) | gesetzlich | [gə'zɛtslɪç] |

| justice (fairness) | Gerechtigkeit (f) | [gə'ʀɛçtɪç·kaɪt] |
| just (fair) | gerecht | [gə'ʀɛçt] |

committee	Komitee (n)	[komi'teː]
bill (draft law)	Gesetzentwurf (m)	[gə'zɛtsʔɛntˌvʊʁf]
budget	Budget (n)	[by'dʒeː]
policy	Politik (f)	[poli'tɪk]
reform	Reform (f)	[ʀe'fɔʁm]
radical (adj)	radikal	[ʀadi'kaːl]

power (strength, force)	Macht (f)	[maχt]
powerful (adj)	mächtig	['mɛçtɪç]
supporter	Anhänger (m)	['anˌhɛŋɐ]
influence	Einfluss (m)	['aɪnˌflʊs]

regime (e.g. military ~)	Regime (n)	[ʀe'ʒiːm]
conflict	Konflikt (m)	[kɔn'flɪkt]
conspiracy (plot)	Verschwörung (f)	[fɛɐ'ʃvøːʀʊŋ]
provocation	Provokation (f)	[pʀovoka'tsjoːn]

to overthrow (regime, etc.)	stürzen (vt)	['ʃtʏʁtsən]
overthrow (of a government)	Sturz (m)	[ʃtʊʁts]
revolution	Revolution (f)	[ʀevolu'tsjoːn]

| coup d'état | Staatsstreich (m) | ['ʃtaːtsˌʃtʀaɪç] |
| military coup | Militärputsch (m) | [mili'tɛːɐˌpʊtʃ] |

crisis	Krise (f)	['kʀiːzə]
economic recession	Rezession (f)	[ʀetsɛ'sjoːn]
demonstrator (protester)	Demonstrant (m)	[demɔn'stʀant]
demonstration	Demonstration (f)	[demɔnstʀa'tsjoːn]
martial law	Ausnahmezustand (m)	['aʊsnaːməˌtsuːʃtant]
military base	Militärbasis (f)	[mili'tɛːɐˌbaːzɪs]

| stability | Stabilität (f) | [ʃtabili'tɛːt] |
| stable (adj) | stabil | [ʃta'biːl] |

exploitation	Ausbeutung (f)	['aʊsˌbɔɪtʊŋ]
to exploit (workers)	ausbeuten (vt)	['aʊsˌbɔɪtən]
racism	Rassismus (m)	[ʀa'sɪsmʊs]

racist	Rassist (m)	[ʀa'sɪst]
fascism	Faschismus (m)	[fa'ʃɪsmʊs]
fascist	Faschist (m)	[fa'ʃɪst]

245. Countries. Miscellaneous

foreigner	Ausländer (m)	['aʊs͵lɛndɐ]
foreign (adj)	ausländisch	['aʊs͵lɛndɪʃ]
abroad (in a foreign country)	im Ausland	[ɪm 'aʊslant]

emigrant	Auswanderer (m)	['aʊs͵vandɐʀɐ]
emigration	Auswanderung (f)	['aʊs͵vandɐʀʊŋ]
to emigrate (vi)	auswandern (vi)	['aʊs͵vandɐn]

the West	Westen (m)	['vɛstən]
the East	Osten (m)	['ɔstən]
the Far East	Ferner Osten (m)	['fɛʀnɐ 'ɔstən]
civilization	Zivilisation (f)	[tsiviliza'tsjoːn]
humanity (mankind)	Menschheit (f)	['mɛnʃhaɪt]
the world (earth)	Welt (f)	[vɛlt]
peace	Frieden (m)	['fʀiːdən]
worldwide (adj)	Welt-	[vɛlt]

homeland	Heimat (f)	['haɪmaːt]
people (population)	Volk (n)	[fɔlk]
population	Bevölkerung (f)	[bə'fœlkəʀʊŋ]
people (a lot of ~)	Leute (pl)	['lɔɪtə]
nation (people)	Nation (f)	[na'tsjoːn]
generation	Generation (f)	[genɛʀa'tsjoːn]
territory (area)	Territorium (n)	[tɛʀi'toːʀiʊm]
region	Region (f)	[ʀe'gjoːn]
state (part of a country)	Staat (m)	[ʃtaːt]

tradition	Tradition (f)	[tʀadi'tsjoːn]
custom (tradition)	Brauch (m)	[bʀaʊx]
ecology	Ökologie (f)	[͵økolo'giː]

Indian (Native American)	Indianer (m)	[ɪn'dɪaːnɐ]
Gypsy (masc.)	Zigeuner (m)	[tsi'gɔɪnɐ]
Gypsy (fem.)	Zigeunerin (f)	[tsi'gɔɪnɐʀɪn]
Gypsy (adj)	Zigeuner-	[tsi'gɔɪnɐ]

empire	Reich (n)	['ʀaɪç]
colony	Kolonie (f)	[kolo'niː]
slavery	Sklaverei (f)	[sklavə'ʀaɪ]
invasion	Einfall (m)	['aɪn͵fal]
famine	Hunger (m)	['hʊŋɐ]

246. Major religious groups. Confessions

| religion | Religion (f) | [ʀeli'gjoːn] |
| religious (adj) | religiös | [ʀeli'gɪøːs] |

faith, belief	Glaube (m)	['glaʊbə]
to believe (in God)	glauben (vt)	['glaʊbən]
believer	Gläubige (m)	['glɔɪbɪgə]

| atheism | Atheismus (m) | [ate'ʔɪsmʊs] |
| atheist | Atheist (m) | [ate'ɪst] |

Christianity	Christentum (n)	['kʀɪstəntu:m]
Christian (n)	Christ (m)	[kʀɪst]
Christian (adj)	christlich	['kʀɪstlɪç]

Catholicism	Katholizismus (m)	['katolizɪsmus]
Catholic (n)	Katholik (m)	[kato'li:k]
Catholic (adj)	katholisch	[ka'to:lɪʃ]

Protestantism	Protestantismus (m)	[pʀotɛs'tantɪsmʊs]
Protestant Church	Protestantische Kirche (f)	[pʀotɛs'tantɪʃə 'kɪʀçə]
Protestant (n)	Protestant (m)	[pʀotɛs'tant]

Orthodoxy	Orthodoxes Christentum (n)	[ɔʀto'dɔksəs 'kʀɪstəntu:m]
Orthodox Church	Orthodoxe Kirche (f)	[ɔʀto'dɔksə 'kɪʀçə]
Orthodox (n)	orthodoxer Christ (m)	[ɔʀto'dɔks]

Presbyterianism	Presbyterianismus (m)	[pʀɛsbyte'ʀɪa:nɪsmʊs]
Presbyterian Church	Presbyterianische Kirche (f)	[pʀɛsbyte'ʀɪa:nɪʃə 'kɪʀçə]
Presbyterian (n)	Presbyterianer (m)	[pʀɛsbyte'ʀɪa:nɐ]

| Lutheranism | Lutherische Kirche (f) | ['lʊtəʀɪʃə 'kɪʀçə] |
| Lutheran (n) | Lutheraner (m) | [lʊtə'ʀa:nɐ] |

| Baptist Church | Baptismus (m) | [bap'tɪsmʊs] |
| Baptist (n) | Baptist (m) | [bap'tɪst] |

| Anglican Church | Anglikanische Kirche (f) | [aŋgli'ka:nɪʃə 'kɪʀçə] |
| Anglican (n) | Anglikaner (m) | [aŋgli'kanɐ] |

| Mormonism | Mormonismus (m) | [mɔʀmo:'nɪsmʊs] |
| Mormon (n) | Mormone (m) | [mɔʀ'mo:nə] |

| Judaism | Judentum (n) | ['ju:dəntu:m] |
| Jew (n) | Jude (m) | ['ju:də] |

| Buddhism | Buddhismus (m) | [bʊ'dɪsmʊs] |
| Buddhist (n) | Buddhist (m) | [bʊ'dɪst] |

| Hinduism | Hinduismus (m) | [hɪndu'ʔɪsmʊs] |
| Hindu (n) | Hindu (m) | ['hɪndu] |

Islam	Islam (m)	[ɪs'la:m]
Muslim (n)	Moslem (m)	['mɔslɛm]
Muslim (adj)	moslemisch	[mɔs'le:mɪʃ]

Shiah Islam	Schiismus (m)	[ʃi'ɪsmʊs]
Shiite (n)	Schiit (m)	[ʃi'i:t]
Sunni Islam	Sunnismus (m)	[zʊ'nɪsmʊs]
Sunnite (n)	Sunnit (m)	[zʊ'ni:t]

247. Religions. Priests

priest	Priester (m)	['pʀiːstɐ]
the Pope	Papst (m)	[papst]
monk, friar	Mönch (m)	[mœnç]
nun	Nonne (f)	['nɔnə]
pastor	Pfarrer (m)	['pfaʀɐ]
abbot	Abt (m)	[apt]
vicar (parish priest)	Vikar (m)	[vi'kaːɐ]
bishop	Bischof (m)	['bɪʃɔf]
cardinal	Kardinal (m)	[ˌkaʁdi'naːl]
preacher	Prediger (m)	['pʀeːdɪgɐ]
preaching	Predigt (f)	['pʀeːdɪçt]
parishioners	Gemeinde (f)	[gə'maɪndə]
believer	Gläubige (m)	['glɔɪbɪgə]
atheist	Atheist (m)	[ate'ɪst]

248. Faith. Christianity. Islam

Adam	Adam	['aːdam]
Eve	Eva	['eːva]
God	Gott (m)	[gɔt]
the Lord	Herr (m)	[hɛʁ]
the Almighty	Der Allmächtige	[deːɐ al'mɛçtɪgə]
sin	Sünde (f)	['zʏndə]
to sin (vi)	sündigen (vi)	['zʏndɪgən]
sinner (masc.)	Sünder (m)	['zʏndɐ]
sinner (fem.)	Sünderin (f)	['zʏndəʀɪn]
hell	Hölle (f)	['hœlə]
paradise	Paradies (n)	[paʀa'diːs]
Jesus	Jesus (m)	['jeːzʊs]
Jesus Christ	Jesus Christus (m)	['jeːzʊs 'kʀɪstʊs]
the Holy Spirit	der Heiliger Geist	[deːɐ 'haɪlɪgɐ 'gaɪst]
the Saviour	der Erlöser	[deːɐ ɛɐ'løːzɐ]
the Virgin Mary	die Jungfrau Maria	[di 'jʊŋfʀaʊ ma'ʀiːa]
the Devil	Teufel (m)	['tɔɪfl]
devil's (adj)	teuflisch	['tɔɪflɪʃ]
Satan	Satan (m)	['zaːtan]
satanic (adj)	satanisch	[za'taːnɪʃ]
angel	Engel (m)	['ɛŋəl]
guardian angel	Schutzengel (m)	['ʃʊts,ʔɛŋəl]
angelic (adj)	Engel(s)-	['ɛŋəls]

apostle	Apostel (m)	[a'pɔstəl]
archangel	Erzengel (m)	['e:ɐts͜ˌʔɛŋəl]
the Antichrist	Antichrist (m)	['antiˌkrɪst]

Church	Kirche (f)	['kɪʁçə]
Bible	Bibel (f)	['bi:bl]
biblical (adj)	biblisch	['bi:blɪʃ]

Old Testament	Altes Testament (n)	['altəs tɛsta'mɛnt]
New Testament	Neues Testament (n)	['nɔɪəs tɛsta'mɛnt]
Gospel	Evangelium (n)	[evaŋ'ge:lɪʊm]
Holy Scripture	Heilige Schrift (f)	['haɪlɪgə ʃʁɪft]
Heaven	Himmelreich (n)	['hɪməlˌʁaɪç]

Commandment	Gebot (n)	[gə'bo:t]
prophet	Prophet (m)	[pʁo'fe:t]
prophecy	Prophezeiung (f)	[pʁofe'tsaɪʊŋ]

Allah	Allah	['ala]
Mohammed	Mohammed (m)	['mo:hamɛt]
the Koran	Koran (m)	[ko'ʁa:n]

mosque	Moschee (f)	[mɔ'ʃe:]
mullah	Mullah (m)	['mʊla]
prayer	Gebet (n)	[gə'be:t]
to pray (vi, vt)	beten (vi)	['be:tən]

pilgrimage	Wallfahrt (f)	['valˌfa:ɐt]
pilgrim	Pilger (m)	['pɪlgɐ]
Mecca	Mekka (n)	['mɛka]

church	Kirche (f)	['kɪʁçə]
temple	Tempel (m)	['tɛmpəl]
cathedral	Kathedrale (f)	[kate'dʁa:lə]
Gothic (adj)	gotisch	['go:tɪʃ]
synagogue	Synagoge (f)	[zyna'go:gə]
mosque	Moschee (f)	[mɔ'ʃe:]

chapel	Kapelle (f)	[ka'pɛlə]
abbey	Abtei (f)	[ap'taɪ]
convent	Nonnenkloster (n)	['nɔnənˌklo:stɐ]
monastery	Frauenkloster (n)	['fʁaʊənˌklo:stɐ]
monastery	Kloster (n), Konvent (m)	['klo:stɐ], [kɔn'vɛnt]

bell (church ~s)	Glocke (f)	['glɔkə]
bell tower	Glockenturm (m)	['glɔkənˌtʊʁm]
to ring (ab. bells)	läuten (vi)	['lɔɪtən]

cross	Kreuz (n)	[kʁɔɪts]
cupola (roof)	Kuppel (f)	['kʊpl]
icon	Ikone (f)	[i'ko:nə]

soul	Seele (f)	['ze:lə]
fate (destiny)	Schicksal (n)	['ʃɪkˌza:l]
evil (n)	das Böse	['bø:zə]
good (n)	Gute (n)	['gu:tə]

vampire	Vampir (m)	[vam'pi:ɐ]
witch (evil ~)	Hexe (f)	['hɛksə]
demon	Dämon (m)	['dɛ:mɔn]
spirit	Geist (m)	[gaɪst]

| redemption (giving us ~) | Sühne (f) | ['zy:nə] |
| to redeem (vt) | sühnen (vt) | ['zy:nən] |

church service	Gottesdienst (m)	['gɔtəsˌdi:nst]
to say mass	die Messe lesen	[di 'mɛsə 'le:zən]
confession	Beichte (f)	['baɪçtə]
to confess (vi)	beichten (vi)	['baɪçtən]

saint (n)	Heilige (m)	['haɪlɪgə]
sacred (holy)	heilig	['haɪlɪç]
holy water	Weihwasser (n)	['vaɪˌvasɐ]

ritual (n)	Ritual (n)	[ʁi'tua:l]
ritual (adj)	rituell	[ʁi'tuɛl]
sacrifice	Opfer (n)	['ɔpfɐ]

superstition	Aberglaube (m)	['a:bɐˌglaʊbə]
superstitious (adj)	abergläubisch	['a:bɐˌglɔɪbɪʃ]
afterlife	Nachleben (n)	['na:xˌle:bən]
eternal life	ewiges Leben (n)	['e:vɪgəs 'le:bn]

MISCELLANEOUS

249. Various useful words

background (green ~)	**Hintergrund** (m)	[ˈhɪntɐˌɡʀʊnt]
balance (of the situation)	**Bilanz** (f)	[biˈlants]
barrier (obstacle)	**Barriere** (f)	[baˈʀiɛːʀə]
base (basis)	**Basis** (f)	[ˈbaːzɪs]
beginning	**Anfang** (m)	[ˈanfaŋ]
category	**Kategorie** (f)	[ˌkateɡoˈʀiː]
cause (reason)	**Ursache** (f)	[ˈuːɐˌzaχə]
choice	**Auswahl** (f)	[ˈaʊsvaːl]
coincidence	**Zufall** (m)	[ˈtsuːˌfal]
comfortable (~ chair)	**bequem**	[bəˈkveːm]
comparison	**Vergleich** (m)	[fɛɐˈɡlaɪç]
compensation	**Kompensation** (f)	[kɔmpɛnzaˈtsjoːn]
degree (extent, amount)	**Grad** (m)	[ɡʀaːt]
development	**Entwicklung** (f)	[ɛntˈvɪklʊŋ]
difference	**Unterschied** (m)	[ˈʊntɐˌʃiːt]
effect (e.g. of drugs)	**Effekt** (m)	[ɛˈfɛkt]
effort (exertion)	**Anstrengung** (f)	[ˈanˌʃtʀɛŋʊŋ]
element	**Element** (n)	[eleˈmɛnt]
end (finish)	**Ende** (n)	[ˈɛndə]
example (illustration)	**Beispiel** (n)	[ˈbaɪˌʃpiːl]
fact	**Tatsache** (f)	[ˈtaːtˌzaχə]
frequent (adj)	**häufig**	[ˈhɔɪfɪç]
growth (development)	**Wachstum** (n)	[ˈvakstuːm]
help	**Hilfe** (f)	[ˈhɪlfə]
ideal	**Ideal** (n)	[ideˈaːl]
kind (sort, type)	**Art** (f)	[aːɐt]
labyrinth	**Labyrinth** (n)	[labyˈʀɪnt]
mistake, error	**Fehler** (m)	[ˈfeːlɐ]
moment	**Moment** (m)	[moˈmɛnt]
object (thing)	**Gegenstand** (m)	[ˈɡeːɡənˌʃtant]
obstacle	**Hindernis** (n)	[ˈhɪndɐnɪs]
original (original copy)	**Original** (n)	[oʀigiˈnaːl]
part (~ of sth)	**Anteil** (m)	[ˈanˌtaɪl]
particle, small part	**Teilchen** (n)	[ˈtaɪlçən]
pause (break)	**Pause** (f)	[ˈpaʊzə]
position	**Position** (f)	[poziˈtsjoːn]
principle	**Prinzip** (n)	[pʀɪnˈtsiːp]
problem	**Problem** (n)	[pʀoˈbleːm]
process	**Prozess** (m)	[pʀoˈtsɛs]

progress	Fortschritt (m)	['fɔʁtʃʁɪt]
property (quality)	Eigenschaft (f)	['aɪɡənʃaft]
reaction	Reaktion (f)	[ˌʁeak'tsjoːn]
risk	Risiko (n)	['ʁiːziko]

secret	Geheimnis (n)	[ɡə'haɪmnɪs]
series	Serie (f)	['zeːʁiə]
shape (outer form)	Form (f)	[fɔʁm]
situation	Situation (f)	[zitua'tsjoːn]
solution	Lösung (f)	['løːzʊŋ]

standard (adj)	Standard-	['standaʁt]
standard (level of quality)	Standard (m)	['standaʁt]
stop (pause)	Halt (m)	[halt]
style	Stil (m)	[ʃtiːl]

system	System (n)	[zʏs'teːm]
table (chart)	Tabelle (f)	[ta'bɛlə]
tempo, rate	Tempo (n)	['tɛmpo]
term (word, expression)	Fachwort (n)	['faχˌvɔʁt]
thing (object, item)	Ding (n)	[dɪŋ]

truth (e.g. moment of ~)	Wahrheit (f)	['vaːʁhaɪt]
turn (please wait your ~)	Reihe (f)	['ʁaɪə]
type (sort, kind)	Typ (m)	[tyːp]
urgent (adj)	dringend	['dʁɪŋənt]
urgently	dringend	['dʁɪŋənt]

utility (usefulness)	Nutzen (m)	['nʊtsən]
variant (alternative)	Variante (f)	[va'ʁɪantə]
way (means, method)	Weise (f)	['vaɪzə]
zone	Zone (f)	['tsoːnə]

250. Modifiers. Adjectives. Part 1

additional (adj)	ergänzend	[ɛɛ'ɡɛntsənt]
ancient (~ civilization)	alt	[alt]
artificial (adj)	künstlich	['kʏnstlɪç]
back, rear (adj)	Hinter-	['hɪntə]
bad (adj)	schlecht	[ʃlɛçt]

beautiful (~ palace)	schön	[ʃøːn]
beautiful (person)	schön	[ʃøːn]
big (in size)	groß	[ɡʁoːs]
bitter (taste)	bitter	['bɪtə]
blind (sightless)	blind	[blɪnt]

calm, quiet (adj)	ruhig	['ʁuːɪç]
careless (negligent)	nachlässig	['naːχˌlɛsɪç]
caring (~ father)	sorgsam	['zɔʁkzaːm]
central (adj)	zentral	[tsɛn'tʁaːl]

| cheap (low-priced) | billig | ['bɪlɪç] |
| cheerful (adj) | froh | [fʁoː] |

children's (adj)	Kinder-	['kɪndɐ]
civil (~ law)	bürgerlich	['bʏɐɡelɪç]
clandestine (secret)	Untergrund-	['ʊntɐ͵ɡʀʊnt]

clean (free from dirt)	sauber	['zaʊbɐ]
clear (explanation, etc.)	klar	[klaːɐ]
clever (intelligent)	klug	[kluːk]
close (near in space)	nah	[naː]
closed (adj)	geschlossen	[ɡə'ʃlɔsən]

cloudless (sky)	wolkenlos	['vɔlkən͵loːs]
cold (drink, weather)	kalt	[kalt]
compatible (adj)	kompatibel	[kɔmpa'tiːbəl]
contented (satisfied)	zufrieden	[tsu'fʀiːdən]
continuous (uninterrupted)	ununterbrochen	['ʊnʔʊntɐ͵bʀɔχən]

cool (weather)	kühl	[kyːl]
dangerous (adj)	gefährlich	[ɡə'fɛːɐlɪç]
dark (room)	dunkel	['dʊŋkəl]
dead (not alive)	tot	[toːt]
dense (fog, smoke)	dicht	[dɪçt]

destitute (extremely poor)	in Armut lebend	[ɪn 'aɐmuːt 'leːbənt]
different (not the same)	unterschiedlich	['ʊntɐ͵ʃiːtlɪç]
difficult (decision)	schwierig	['ʃviːʀɪç]
difficult (problem, task)	schwierig	['ʃviːʀɪç]
dim, faint (light)	gedämpft	[ɡə'dɛmpft]

dirty (not clean)	schmutzig	['ʃmʊtsɪç]
distant (in space)	fern	[fɛɐn]
dry (clothes, etc.)	trocken	['tʀɔkən]
easy (not difficult)	einfach	['aɪnfaχ]

empty (glass, room)	leer	[leːɐ]
even (e.g. ~ surface)	glatt	[ɡlat]
exact (amount)	genau	[ɡə'naʊ]
excellent (adj)	ausgezeichnet	['aʊsɡə͵tsaɪçnət]
excessive (adj)	übermäßig	['yːbɐ͵mɛːsɪç]

expensive (adj)	teuer	['tɔɪɐ]
exterior (adj)	Außen-, äußer	['aʊsən], ['ɔɪsɐ]
far (the ~ East)	fern	[fɛɐn]
fast (quick)	schnell	[ʃnɛl]
fatty (food)	fett	[fɛt]

fertile (land, soil)	fruchtbar	['fʀʊχtbaːɐ]
flat (~ panel display)	platt	[plat]
foreign (adj)	ausländisch, Fremd-	['aʊslɛndɪʃ], [fʀɛmt]
fragile (china, glass)	zerbrechlich	[tsɛɐ'bʀɛçlɪç]

free (at no cost)	kostenlos, gratis	['kɔstənloːs], ['ɡʀaːtɪs]
free (unrestricted)	frei	[fʀaɪ]
fresh (~ water)	Süß-	[zyːs]
fresh (e.g. ~ bread)	frisch	[fʀɪʃ]
frozen (food)	tiefgekühlt	['tiːfɡə͵kyːlt]
full (completely filled)	voll	[fɔl]

gloomy (house, forecast)	düster	['dy:stɐ]
good (book, etc.)	gut	[gu:t]
good, kind (kindhearted)	gut	[gu:t]
grateful (adj)	dankbar	['daŋkba:ɐ]

happy (adj)	glücklich	['glʏklɪç]
hard (not soft)	hart	[haʁt]
heavy (in weight)	schwer	[ʃve:ɐ]
hostile (adj)	feindlich	['faɪntlɪç]
hot (adj)	heiß	[haɪs]

huge (adj)	riesig	['ʁi:zɪç]
humid (adj)	feucht	[fɔɪçt]
hungry (adj)	hungrig	['hʊŋʁɪç]
ill (sick, unwell)	krank	[kʁaŋk]
immobile (adj)	unbeweglich	['ʊnbəˌve:klɪç]

important (adj)	wichtig	['vɪçtɪç]
impossible (adj)	unmöglich	['ʊnmøːklɪç]
incomprehensible	unverständlich	['ʊnfɛɐˌʃtɛntlɪç]
indispensable (adj)	notwendig	['no:tvɛndɪç]
inexperienced (adj)	unerfahren	['ʊnʔɛɐˌfaːʁən]

insignificant (adj)	unbedeutend	['ʊnbəˌdɔɪtənt]
interior (adj)	innen-	['ɪnən]
joint (~ decision)	gemeinsam	[gə'maɪnzaːm]
last (e.g. ~ week)	vorig	['foːʁɪç]

last (final)	der letzte	[de:ɐ 'lɛtstə]
left (e.g. ~ side)	link	[lɪŋk]
legal (legitimate)	gesetzlich	[gə'zɛtslɪç]
light (in weight)	leicht	[laɪçt]
light (pale color)	licht	[lɪçt]

limited (adj)	begrenzt	[bə'gʁɛntst]
liquid (fluid)	flüssig	['flʏsɪç]
long (e.g. ~ hair)	lang	[laŋ]
loud (voice, etc.)	laut	[laʊt]
low (voice)	leise	['laɪzə]

251. Modifiers. Adjectives. Part 2

main (principal)	Haupt-	[haʊpt]
matt, matte	matt	[mat]
meticulous (job)	sorgfältig	['zɔʁkfɛltɪç]
mysterious (adj)	rätselhaft	['ʁɛːtsəlˌhaft]
narrow (street, etc.)	eng, schmal	[ɛŋ], [ʃmaːl]

native (~ country)	Heimat-	['haɪmaːt]
nearby (adj)	nah	[naː]
needed (necessary)	nötig	['nøːtɪç]
negative (~ response)	negativ	['neːgatiːf]
neighbouring (adj)	Nachbar-	['naxˌbaːɐ]
nervous (adj)	nervös	[nɛʁ'vøːs]

229

new (adj)	neu	[nɔɪ]
next (e.g. ~ week)	nächst	[nɛ:çst]
nice (agreeable)	nett	[nɛt]

pleasant (voice)	angenehm	[ˈangəˌne:m]
normal (adj)	normal	[nɔʁˈma:l]
not big (adj)	nicht groß	[nɪçt gʁo:s]
not difficult (adj)	nicht schwierig	[nɪçt ˈʃviːʁɪç]

obligatory (adj)	obligatorisch, Pflicht-	[ɔbligaˈtoːʁɪʃ], [pflɪçt]
old (house)	alt	[alt]
open (adj)	offen	[ˈɔfən]
opposite (adj)	gegensätzlich	[ˈgeːgənˌzɛtslɪç]
ordinary (usual)	gewöhnlich	[gəˈvøːnlɪç]

original (unusual)	original	[oʁigiˈna:l]
past (recent)	vergangen	[fɛʁˈgaŋən]
permanent (adj)	beständig	[bəˈʃtɛndɪç]
personal (adj)	persönlich	[pɛʁˈzøːnlɪç]
polite (adj)	höflich	[ˈhøːflɪç]

poor (not rich)	arm	[aʁm]
possible (adj)	möglich	[ˈmøːklɪç]
present (current)	gegenwärtig	[ˈgeːgənˌvɛʁtɪç]
previous (adj)	früher	[ˈfʁyːɐ]
principal (main)	hauptsächlich	[ˈhaʊptˌzɛçlɪç]

private (~ jet)	privat	[pʁiˈva:t]
probable (adj)	wahrscheinlich	[vaːˈɐ̯ˈʃaɪnlɪç]
prolonged (e.g. ~ applause)	andauernd	[ˈanˌdaʊənt]
public (open to all)	öffentlich	[ˈœfəntlɪç]

punctual (person)	pünktlich	[ˈpʏŋktlɪç]
quiet (tranquil)	still	[ʃtɪl]
rare (adj)	selten	[ˈzɛltən]
raw (uncooked)	roh	[ʁoː]

right (not left)	recht	[ʁɛçt]
right, correct (adj)	richtig	[ˈʁɪçtɪç]
ripe (fruit)	reif	[ʁaɪf]
risky (adj)	riskant	[ʁɪsˈkant]
sad (~ look)	traurig, unglücklich	[ˈtʁaʊʁɪç], [ˈʊnˌglʏklɪç]

sad (depressing)	traurig	[ˈtʁaʊʁɪç]
safe (not dangerous)	sicher	[ˈzɪçɐ]
salty (food)	salzig	[ˈzaltsɪç]
satisfied (customer)	zufrieden	[tsuˈfʁiːdən]

second hand (adj)	gebraucht	[gəˈbʁaʊxt]
shallow (water)	seicht	[zaɪçt]
sharp (blade, etc.)	scharf	[ʃaʁf]
short (in length)	kurz	[kʊʁts]

short, short-lived (adj)	kurz	[kʊʁts]
short-sighted (adj)	kurzsichtig	[ˈkʊʁtsˌzɪçtɪç]
significant (notable)	bedeutend	[bəˈdɔɪtənt]

| similar (adj) | ähnlich | ['ɛ:nlɪç] |
| simple (easy) | einfach | ['aɪnfaχ] |

skinny	abgemagert	['apgəˌmaːget]
small (in size)	klein	[klaɪn]
smooth (surface)	glatt	[glat]
soft (~ toys)	weich	[vaɪç]
solid (~ wall)	fest, stark	[fɛst], [ʃtaʁk]

sour (flavour, taste)	sauer	['zaʊɐ]
spacious (house, etc.)	geräumig	[gə'ʀɔɪmɪç]
special (adj)	speziell, Spezial-	[ʃpe'tsɪɛl], [ʃpe'tsɪaːl]
straight (line, road)	gerade	[gə'ʀaːdə]
strong (person)	stark	[ʃtaʁk]

stupid (foolish)	dumm	[dʊm]
suitable (e.g. ~ for drinking)	brauchbar	['bʀaʊχbaːɐ]
sunny (day)	sonnig	['zɔnɪç]
superb, perfect (adj)	ausgezeichnet	['aʊsgəˌtsaɪçnət]
swarthy (dark-skinned)	dunkelhäutig	['dʊŋkəlˌhɔɪtɪç]

sweet (sugary)	süß	[zy:s]
tanned (adj)	gebräunt	[gə'bʀɔɪnt]
tasty (delicious)	lecker	['lɛkɐ]
tender (affectionate)	zärtlich	['tsɛ:ɐtlɪç]

the highest (adj)	höchst	[hø:çst]
the most important	das wichtigste	[das 'vɪçtɪçstə]
the nearest	nächst	[nɛ:çst]
the same, equal (adj)	gleich	[glaɪç]

thick (e.g. ~ fog)	dick	[dɪk]
thick (wall, slice)	dick	[dɪk]
thin (person)	dünn	[dʏn]
tight (~ shoes)	knapp	[knap]
tired (exhausted)	müde	['my:də]

tiring (adj)	ermüdend	[ɛɐ'my:dənt]
transparent (adj)	durchsichtig	['dʊʁçˌzɪçtɪç]
unclear (adj)	undeutlich	['ʊnˌdɔɪtlɪç]
unique (exceptional)	einzigartig	['aɪntsɪçˌʔaːɐtɪç]
various (adj)	verschieden	[fɛɐ'ʃiːdən]

warm (moderately hot)	warm	[vaʁm]
wet (e.g. ~ clothes)	nass	[nas]
whole (entire, complete)	ganz	[gants]
wide (e.g. ~ road)	breit	[bʀaɪt]
young (adj)	jung	[jʊŋ]

231

MAIN 500 VERBS

to accompany (vt)	begleiten (vt)	[bə'glaɪtən]
to accuse (vt)	anklagen (vt)	['anˌklaːgən]
to acknowledge (admit)	zugeben (vt)	['tsuːˌgeːbən]
to act (take action)	handeln (vi)	['handəln]
to add (supplement)	hinzufügen (vt)	[hɪn'tsuːˌfyːgən]
to address (speak to)	adressieren an ...	[adʀɛ'siːʀən an]
to admire (vi)	bewundern (vt)	[bə'vʊndɛn]
to advertise (vt)	werben (vt)	['vɛʀbən]
to advise (vt)	raten (vt)	['ʀaːtən]
to affirm (assert)	behaupten (vt)	[bə'haʊptən]
to agree (say yes)	zustimmen (vi)	['tsuːˌʃtɪmən]
to aim (to point a weapon)	zielen auf ...	['tsiːlən aʊf]
to allow (sb to do sth)	erlauben (vt)	[ɛɐ'laʊbən]
to amputate (vt)	amputieren (vt)	[ampu'tiːʀən]
to answer (vi, vt)	antworten (vi)	['antˌvoʀtən]
to apologize (vi)	sich entschuldigen	[zɪç ɛnt'ʃʊldɪgən]
to appear (come into view)	erscheinen (vi)	[ɛɐ'ʃaɪnən]
to applaud (vi, vt)	applaudieren (vi)	[aplaʊ'diːʀən]
to appoint (assign)	ernennen (vt)	[ɛɐ'nɛnən]
to approach (come closer)	sich nähern	[zɪç 'nɛːɐn]
to arrive (ab. train)	ankommen (vi)	['anˌkɔmən]
to ask (~ sb to do sth)	bitten (vt)	['bɪtən]
to aspire to ...	anstreben (vt)	['anˌʃtʀeːbən]
to assist (help)	assistieren (vi)	[asɪs'tiːʀən]
to attack (mil.)	attackieren (vt)	[ata'kiːʀən]
to attain (objectives)	erzielen (vt)	[ɛɐ'tsiːlən]
to avenge (get revenge)	sich rächen	[zɪç 'ʀɛçən]
to avoid (danger, task)	vermeiden (vt)	[fɛɐ'maɪdən]
to award (give a medal to)	auszeichnen (vt)	['aʊsˌtsaɪçnən]
to battle (vi)	kämpfen (vi)	['kɛmpfən]
to be (vi)	sein (vi)	[zaɪn]
to be a cause of ...	verursachen (vt)	[fɛɐ'ʔuːɐˌzaxən]
to be afraid	Angst haben	['aŋst 'haːbən]
to be angry (with ...)	verärgert sein	[fɛɐ'ɛʀgɐt zaɪn]
to be at war	Krieg führen	[kʀiːk 'fyːʀən]
to be based (on ...)	beruhen auf ...	[bə'ʀuːən 'aʊf]
to be bored	sich langweilen	[zɪç 'laŋˌvaɪlən]

232

to be convinced	sich überzeugen	[zɪç yːbɐ'tsɔɪɡən]
to be enough	ausreichen (vi)	['aʊsˌʀaɪçən]
to be envious	beneiden (vt)	[bə'naɪdən]
to be indignant	sich empören	[zɪç ɛm'pøːʀən]
to be interested in ...	sich interessieren	[zɪç ɪntəʀɛ'siːʀən]
to be lost in thought	in Gedanken versinken	[ɪn ɡə'daŋkən fɛɐ'zɪŋkən]
to be lying (~ on the table)	gelegen sein	[ɡə'leːɡən zaɪn]
to be needed	nötig sein	['nøːtɪç zaɪn]
to be perplexed (puzzled)	verblüfft sein	[fɛɐ'blʏft zaɪn]
to be preserved	sich erhalten	[zɪç ɛɐ'haltən]
to be required	notwendig sein	['noːtvɛndɪç zaɪn]
to be surprised	überrascht sein	[yːbɐ'ʀaʃt zaɪn]
to be worried	sich Sorgen machen	[zɪç 'zɔɐɡən 'maxən]
to beat (to hit)	schlagen (vt)	['ʃlaːɡən]
to become (e.g. ~ old)	werden (vi)	['veːɐdən]
to behave (vi)	sich benehmen	[zɪç bə'neːmən]
to believe (think)	meinen (vt)	['maɪnən]
to belong to ...	gehören (vi)	[ɡə'høːʀən]
to berth (moor)	anlegen (vi)	['anˌleːɡən]
to blind (other drivers)	blenden (vt)	['blɛndən]
to blow (wind)	wehen (vi)	['veːən]
to blush (vi)	erröten (vi)	[ɛɐ'ʀøːtən]
to boast (vi)	prahlen (vi)	['pʀaːlən]
to borrow (money)	leihen (vt)	['laɪən]
to break (branch, toy, etc.)	brechen (vt)	['bʀɛçən]
to breathe (vi)	atmen (vi)	['aːtmən]
to bring (sth)	mitbringen (vt)	['mɪtˌbʀɪŋən]
to burn (paper, logs)	verbrennen (vt)	[fɛɐ'bʀɛnən]
to buy (purchase)	kaufen (vt)	['kaufən]
to call (~ for help)	rufen (vi)	['ʀuːfən]
to call (yell for sb)	rufen (vt)	['ʀuːfən]
to calm down (vt)	beruhigen (vt)	[bə'ʀuːɪɡən]
can (v aux)	können (v mod)	['kœnən]
to cancel (call off)	zurückziehen (vt)	[tsu'ʀʏkˌtsiːən]
to cast off (of a boat or ship)	ablegen (vi)	['apˌleːɡən]
to catch (e.g. ~ a ball)	fangen (vt)	['faŋən]
to change (~ one's opinion)	ändern (vt)	['ɛndən]
to change (exchange)	tauschen (vt)	['taʊʃən]
to charm (vt)	entzücken (vt)	[ɛnt'tsʏkən]
to choose (select)	wählen (vt)	['vɛːlən]
to chop off (with an axe)	abhacken (vt)	['aphakən]
to clean (e.g. kettle from scale)	reinigen (vt)	['ʀaɪnɪɡən]
to clean (shoes, etc.)	putzen (vt)	['pʊtsən]
to clean up (tidy)	aufräumen (vt)	['aʊfˌʀɔɪmən]
to close (vt)	schließen (vt)	['ʃliːsən]

to comb one's hair	sich kämmen	[zɪç 'kɛmən]
to come down (the stairs)	herabsteigen (vi)	[hɛ'rapˌʃtaɪgən]
to come out (book)	erscheinen (vi)	[ɛɐ'ʃaɪnən]
to compare (vt)	vergleichen (vt)	[fɛɐ'glaɪçən]
to compensate (vt)	kompensieren (vt)	[kɔmpɛn'ziːɾən]

to compete (vi)	konkurrieren (vi)	[kɔŋkʊ'ʁiːʁən]
to compile (~ a list)	erstellen (vt)	[ɛɐ'ʃtɛlən]
to complain (vi, vt)	klagen (vi)	['klaːgən]
to complicate (vt)	erschweren (vt)	[ɛɐ'ʃveːʁən]

to compose (music, etc.)	komponieren (vt)	[kɔmpo'niːʁən]
to compromise (reputation)	kompromittieren (vt)	[kɔmpʁomɪ'tiːʁən]
to concentrate (vi)	sich konzentrieren	[zɪç kɔntsɛn'tʁiːʁən]
to confess (criminal)	gestehen (vi)	[gə'ʃteːən]

to confuse (mix up)	verwechseln (vt)	[fɛɐ'vɛksəln]
to congratulate (vt)	gratulieren (vi)	[gʁatu'liːʁən]
to consult (doctor, expert)	sich konsultieren mit ...	[zɪç kɔnzʊl'tiːʁən mɪt]
to continue (~ to do sth)	fortsetzen (vt)	['fɔʁtˌzɛtsən]

to control (vt)	kontrollieren (vt)	[kɔntʁo'liːʁən]
to convince (vt)	überzeugen (vt)	[y:bə'tsɔɪgən]
to cooperate (vi)	zusammenarbeiten (vi)	[tsu'zamənˌʔaʁbaɪtən]
to coordinate (vt)	koordinieren (vt)	[koʔɔʁdi'niːʁən]

to correct (an error)	korrigieren (vt)	[kɔʁi'giːʁən]
to cost (vt)	kosten (vt)	['kɔstən]
to count (money, etc.)	rechnen (vt)	['ʁɛçnən]
to count on ...	auf ... zählen	[aʊf ... 'tsɛːlən]

to crack (ceiling, wall)	bersten (vi)	['bɛʁstən]
to create (vt)	schaffen (vt)	['ʃafən]
to crush, to squash (~ a bug)	zertreten (vt)	[tsɛɐ'tʁeːtən]
to cry (weep)	weinen (vi)	['vaɪnən]
to cut off (with a knife)	abschneiden (vt)	['apˌʃnaɪdən]

253. Verbs D-G

to dare (~ to do sth)	wagen (vt)	['vaːgən]
to date from ...	sich datieren	[zɪç da'tiːʁən]
to deceive (vi, vt)	täuschen (vt)	['tɔɪʃən]
to decide (~ to do sth)	entscheiden (vt)	[ɛnt'ʃaɪdən]

to decorate (tree, street)	schmücken (vt)	['ʃmʏkən]
to dedicate (book, etc.)	widmen (vt)	['vɪtmən]
to defend (a country, etc.)	verteidigen (vt)	[fɛɐ'taɪdɪgən]
to defend oneself	sich verteidigen	[zɪç fɛɐ'taɪdɪgən]

to demand (request firmly)	verlangen (vt)	[fɛɐ'laŋən]
to denounce (vt)	denunzieren (vt)	[denʊn'tsiːʁən]
to deny (vt)	verneinen (vt)	[fɛɐ'naɪnən]
to depend on ...	abhängen von ...	['apˌhɛŋən fɔn]
to deprive (vt)	nehmen (vt)	['neːmən]

to deserve (vt)	verdienen (vt)	[fɛɐ'diːnən]
to design (machine, etc.)	projektieren (vt)	[pʀojɛk'tiːʀən]
to desire (want, wish)	wünschen (vt)	['vʏnʃən]
to despise (vt)	verachten (vt)	[fɛɐ'ʔaxtən]

to destroy (documents, etc.)	vernichten (vt)	[fɛɐ'nɪçtən]
to differ (from sth)	sich unterscheiden	[zɪç ˌʊntɐ'ʃaɪdən]
to dig (tunnel, etc.)	graben (vt)	['gʀaːbən]
to direct (point the way)	richten (vt)	['ʀɪçtən]

to disappear (vi)	verschwinden (vi)	[fɛɐ'ʃvɪndən]
to discover (new land, etc.)	entdecken (vt)	[ɛnt'dɛkən]
to discuss (vt)	besprechen (vt)	[bə'ʃpʀɛçən]
to distribute (leaflets, etc.)	verbreiten (vt)	[fɛɐ'bʀaɪtən]

to disturb (vt)	stören (vt)	['ʃtøːʀən]
to dive (vi)	tauchen (vi)	['tauxən]
to divide (math)	dividieren (vt)	[divi'diːʀən]
to do (vt)	machen (vt)	['maxən]

to do the laundry	waschen (vt)	['vaʃən]
to double (increase)	verdoppeln (vt)	[fɛɐ'dɔpəln]
to doubt (have doubts)	zweifeln (vi)	['tsvaɪfəln]
to draw a conclusion	einen Schluss ziehen	['aɪnən ʃlʊs 'tsiːən]

to dream (daydream)	träumen (vi, vt)	['tʀɔɪmən]
to dream (in sleep)	träumen (vi, vt)	['tʀɔɪmən]
to drink (vi, vt)	trinken (vt)	['tʀɪŋkən]
to drive a car	lenken (vt)	['lɛŋkən]
to drive away (scare away)	verjagen (vt)	[fɛɐ'jaːgən]

to drop (let fall)	fallen lassen	['falən 'lasən]
to drown (ab. person)	ertrinken (vi)	[ɛɐ'tʀɪŋkən]
to dry (clothes, hair)	trocknen (vt)	['tʀɔknən]
to eat (vi, vt)	essen (vi, vt)	['ɛsən]

to eavesdrop (vi)	belauschen (vt)	[bə'lauʃən]
to emit (diffuse - odor, etc.)	verbreiten (vt)	[fɛɐ'bʀaɪtən]
to enjoy oneself	sich amüsieren	[zɪç amy'ziːʀən]
to enter (on the list)	einschreiben (vt)	['aɪnˌʃʀaɪbən]

to enter (room, house, etc.)	hereinkommen (vi)	[hɛ'ʀaɪnˌkɔmən]
to entertain (amuse)	amüsieren (vt)	[amy'ziːʀən]
to equip (fit out)	einrichten (vt)	['aɪnˌʀɪçtən]
to examine (proposal)	erörtern (vt)	[ɛɐ'ʔœʀtən]

to exchange (sth)	wechseln (vt)	['vɛksəln]
to excuse (forgive)	entschuldigen (vt)	[ɛnt'ʃʊldɪgən]
to exist (vi)	existieren (vi)	[ˌɛksɪs'tiːʀən]
to expect (anticipate)	erwarten (vt)	[ɛɐ'vaʀtən]

to expect (foresee)	voraussehen (vt)	[fo'ʀausˌzeːən]
to expel (from school, etc.)	ausschließen (vt)	['ausˌʃliːsən]
to explain (vt)	erklären (vt)	[ɛɐ'klɛːʀən]
to express (vt)	ausdrücken (vt)	['ausˌdʀʏkən]
to extinguish (a fire)	löschen (vt)	['lœʃən]

to fall in love (with ...)	sich verlieben	[zɪç fɛɛ'li:bən]
to fancy (vt)	gefallen (vi)	[gə'falən]
to feed (provide food)	füttern (vt)	['fʏtən]

to fight (against the enemy)	kämpfen (vi)	['kɛmpfən]
to fight (vi)	schlagen (mit ...)	['ʃla:gən mɪt]
to fill (glass, bottle)	füllen (vt)	['fʏlən]
to find (~ lost items)	finden (vt)	['fɪndən]

to finish (vt)	beenden (vt)	[bə'ʔɛndən]
to fish (angle)	fischen (vt)	['fɪʃən]
to fit (ab. dress, etc.)	passen (vi)	['pasən]
to flatter (vt)	schmeicheln (vi)	['ʃmaɪçəln]

to fly (bird, plane)	fliegen (vi)	['fli:gən]
to follow ... (come after)	folgen (vi)	['fɔlgən]
to forbid (vt)	verbieten (vt)	[fɛɛ'bi:tən]
to force (compel)	zwingen (vt)	['tsvɪŋən]

to forget (vi, vt)	vergessen (vt)	[fɛɛ'gɛsən]
to forgive (pardon)	verzeihen (vt)	[fɛɛ'tsaɪən]
to form (constitute)	bilden (vt)	['bɪldən]
to get dirty (vi)	sich beschmutzen	[zɪç bə'ʃmʊtsən]

to get infected (with ...)	sich anstecken	[zɪç 'anʃtɛkən]
to get irritated	gereizt sein	[gə'ʀaɪtst zaɪn]
to get married	heiraten (vi)	['haɪʀa:tən]
to get rid of ...	loswerden (vt)	['lo:s,ve:ɐdən]

to get tired	müde werden	['my:də 've:ɐdən]
to get up (arise from bed)	aufstehen (vi)	['aʊfʃte:ən]
to give (vt)	geben (vt)	['ge:bən]
to give a bath (to bath)	baden (vt)	['ba:dən]

to give a hug, to hug (vt)	umarmen (vt)	[ʊm'ʔaʁmən]
to give in (yield to)	nachgeben (vi)	['na:x,ge:bən]
to glimpse (vt)	erblicken (vt)	[ɛɛ'blɪkən]
to go (by car, etc.)	fahren (vi)	['fa:ʀən]

to go (on foot)	gehen (vi)	['ge:ən]
to go for a swim	schwimmen gehen	['ʃvɪmən 'ge:ən]
to go out (for dinner, etc.)	ausgehen (vi)	['aʊs,ge:ən]
to go to bed (go to sleep)	schlafen gehen	['ʃla:fən 'ge:ən]

to greet (vt)	begrüßen (vt)	[bə'gʀy:sən]
to grow (plants)	züchten (vt)	['tsʏçtən]
to guarantee (vt)	garantieren (vt)	[gaʀan'ti:ʀən]
to guess (the answer)	erraten (vt)	[ɛɛ'ʀa:tən]

254. Verbs H-M

to hand out (distribute)	austeilen (vt)	['aʊs,taɪlən]
to hang (curtains, etc.)	hängen (vt)	['hɛŋən]
to have (vt)	haben (vt)	[ha:bən]

to have a bath	sich waschen	[zɪç 'vaʃən]
to have a try	versuchen (vt)	[fɛɛ'zu:χən]

to have breakfast	frühstücken (vi)	['fʀy:ʃtʏkən]
to have dinner	zu Abend essen	[tsu 'a:bənt 'ɛsən]
to have lunch	zu Mittag essen	[tsu 'mɪta:k 'ɛsən]
to head (group, etc.)	führen (vt)	['fy:ʀən]
to hear (vt)	hören (vt)	['hø:ʀən]

to heat (vt)	wärmen (vt)	['vɛʀmən]
to help (vt)	helfen (vi)	['hɛlfən]
to hide (vt)	verstecken (vt)	[fɛɛ'ʃtɛkən]
to hire (e.g. ~ a boat)	mieten (vt)	['mi:tən]
to hire (staff)	einstellen (vt)	['aɪnʃtɛlən]

to hope (vi, vt)	hoffen (vi)	['hɔfən]
to hunt (for food, sport)	jagen (vi)	['jagən]
to hurry (vi)	sich beeilen	[zɪç bə'ʔaɪlən]
to imagine (to picture)	sich vorstellen	[zɪç 'fo:ɐʃtɛlən]
to imitate (vt)	imitieren (vt)	[imi'ti:ʀən]

to implore (vt)	anflehen (vt)	['anfle:ən]
to import (vt)	importieren (vt)	[ɪmpɔʀ'ti:ʀən]
to increase (vi)	sich vergrößern	[zɪç fɛɛ'gʀø:sen]
to increase (vt)	vergrößern (vt)	[fɛɛ'gʀø:sen]
to infect (vt)	anstecken (vt)	['anʃtɛkən]

to influence (vt)	beeinflussen (vt)	[bə'ʔaɪnflʊsən]
to inform	mitteilen (vt)	['mɪttaɪlən]
(e.g. ~ the police about ...)		
to inform (vt)	informieren (vt)	[ɪnfɔʀ'mi:ʀən]
to inherit (vt)	erben (vt)	['ɛʀbən]
to inquire (about ...)	sich nach ... erkundigen	[zɪç na:χ ... ɛɛ'kʊndɪgən]

to insert (put in)	einsetzen (vt)	['aɪnzɛtsən]
to insinuate (imply)	andeuten (vt)	['andɔɪtən]
to insist (vi, vt)	bestehen auf	[bə'ʃte:ən aʊf]
to inspire (vt)	ermutigen (vt)	[ɛɛ'mu:tɪgən]
to instruct (teach)	instruieren (vt)	[ɪnstʀu'i:ʀən]

to insult (offend)	kränken (vt)	['kʀɛŋkən]
to interest (vt)	interessieren (vt)	[ɪntəʀɛ'si:ʀən]
to intervene (vi)	sich einmischen	[zɪç 'aɪnmɪʃən]
to introduce (sb to sb)	bekannt machen	[bə'kant 'maχən]

to invent (machine, etc.)	erfinden (vt)	[ɛɛ'fɪndən]
to invite (vt)	einladen (vt)	['aɪnla:dən]
to iron (clothes)	bügeln (vt)	['by:gəln]
to irritate (annoy)	ärgern (vt)	['ɛʀgen]
to isolate (vt)	isolieren (vt)	[izo'li:ʀən]

to join (political party, etc.)	sich anschließen	[zɪç 'anʃli:sən]
to joke (be kidding)	Witz machen	[vɪts 'maχən]
to keep (old letters, etc.)	behalten (vt)	[bə'haltən]
to keep silent, to hush	schweigen (vi)	['ʃvaɪgən]
to kill (vt)	ermorden (vt)	[ɛɛ'mɔʀdən]

to knock (on the door)	anklopfen (vi)	['an͵klɔpfən]
to know (sb)	kennen (vt)	['kɛnən]
to know (sth)	wissen (vt)	['vɪsən]
to laugh (vi)	lachen (vi)	['laxən]
to launch (start up)	lancieren (vt)	[lan'si:ʀən]

to leave (~ for Mexico)	wegfahren (vi)	['vɛk͵fa:ʀən]
to leave (forget sth)	verlassen (vt)	[fɛɐ'lasən]
to leave (spouse)	verlassen (vt)	[fɛɐ'lasən]
to liberate (city, etc.)	befreien (vt)	[bə'fʀaɪən]
to lie (~ on the floor)	liegen (vi)	['li:gən]

to lie (tell untruth)	lügen (vi)	['ly:gən]
to light (campfire, etc.)	anzünden (vt)	['an͵tsʏndən]
to light up (illuminate)	beleuchten (vt)	[bə'lɔɪçtən]
to limit (vt)	begrenzen (vt)	[bə'gʀɛntsən]

to listen (vi)	hören (vt)	['hø:ʀən]
to live (~ in France)	wohnen (vi)	['vo:nən]
to live (exist)	leben (vi)	['le:bən]
to load (gun)	laden (vt)	['la:dən]
to load (vehicle, etc.)	laden (vt)	['la:dən]

to look (I'm just ~ing)	sehen (vt)	['ze:ən]
to look for ... (search)	suchen (vt)	['zu:xən]
to look like (resemble)	ähnlich sein	['ɛ:nlɪç zaɪn]

| to lose (umbrella, etc.) | verlieren (vt) | [fɛɐ'li:ʀən] |
| to love (e.g. ~ dancing) | gernhaben (vt) | ['gɛʀn͵ha:bən] |

to love (sb)	lieben (vt)	['li:bən]
to lower (blind, head)	herunterlassen (vt)	[hɛ'ʀʊnte͵lasən]
to make (~ dinner)	zubereiten (vt)	['tsu:bə͵ʀaɪtən]

| to make a mistake | einen Fehler machen | ['aɪnən 'fe:lɐ 'maxən] |
| to make angry | ärgern (vt) | ['ɛʀgən] |

to make easier	erleichtern (vt)	[ɛɐ'laɪçten]
to make multiple copies	vervielfältigen (vt)	[fɛɐ'fi:l͵fɛltɪgən]
to make the acquaintance	kennenlernen (vt)	['kɛnən͵lɛʀnən]

| to make use (of ...) | benutzen (vt) | [bə'nʊtsən] |
| to manage, to run | managen (vt) | ['mɛnɪdʒən] |

to mark (make a mark)	markieren (vt)	[maʀ'ki:ʀən]
to mean (signify)	bedeuten (vt)	[bə'dɔɪtən]
to memorize (vt)	memorieren (vt)	[memo'ʀi:ʀən]

| to mention (talk about) | erwähnen (vt) | [ɛɐ'vɛ:nən] |
| to miss (school, etc.) | versäumen (vt) | [fɛɐ'zɔɪmən] |

to mix (combine, blend)	mischen (vt)	['mɪʃən]
to mock (make fun of)	spotten (vi)	['ʃpɔtən]
to move (to shift)	verschieben (vt)	[fɛɐ'ʃi:bən]
to multiply (math)	multiplizieren (vt)	[mʊltipli'tsi:ʀən]
must (v aux)	müssen (v mod)	['mʏsən]

255. Verbs N-R

to name, to call (vt)	benennen (vt)	[bə'nɛnən]
to negotiate (vi)	verhandeln (vi)	[fɛɐ'handəln]
to note (write down)	notieren (vt)	[no'ti:ʀən]
to notice (see)	bemerken (vt)	[bə'mɛʀkən]

to obey (vi, vt)	gehorchen (vi)	[gə'hɔʀçən]
to object (vi, vt)	einwenden (vt)	['aɪnˌvɛndən]
to observe (see)	beobachten (vt)	[bə'ʔo:baxtən]
to offend (vt)	beleidigen (vt)	[bə'laɪdɪgən]

to omit (word, phrase)	weglassen (vt)	['vɛkˌlasən]
to open (vt)	öffnen (vt)	['œfnən]
to order (in restaurant)	bestellen (vt)	[bə'ʃtɛlən]
to order (mil.)	befehlen (vt)	[ˌbə'fe:lən]
to organize (concert, party)	veranstalten (vt)	[fɛɐ'ʔanʃtaltən]

to overestimate (vt)	überschätzen (vt)	[y:bɐ'ʃɛtsən]
to own (possess)	besitzen (vt)	[bə'zɪtsən]
to participate (vi)	teilnehmen (vi)	['taɪlˌne:mən]
to pass through (by car, etc.)	vorbeifahren (vi)	[fo:ɐ'baɪˌfa:ʀən]
to pay (vi, vt)	zahlen (vt)	['tsa:lən]

to peep, to spy on	gucken (vi)	[gʊkən]
to penetrate (vt)	eindringen (vi)	['aɪnˌdʀɪŋən]
to permit (vt)	erlauben (vt)	[ɛɐ'laʊbən]
to pick (flowers)	pflücken (vt)	['pflʏkən]
to place (put, set)	stellen (vt)	['ʃtɛlən]

to plan (~ to do sth)	planen (vt)	['pla:nən]
to play (actor)	spielen (vi, vt)	['ʃpi:lən]
to play (children)	spielen (vi, vt)	['ʃpi:lən]
to point (~ the way)	zeigen (vt)	['tsaɪgən]

to pour (liquid)	gießen (vt)	['gi:sən]
to pray (vi, vt)	beten (vi)	['be:tən]
to prefer (vt)	vorziehen (vt)	['foɐˌtsi:ən]
to prepare (~ a plan)	vorbereiten (vt)	['fo:ɐbəˌʀaɪtən]

to present (sb to sb)	vorstellen (vt)	['fo:ɐʃtɛlən]
to preserve (peace, life)	bewahren (vt)	[bə'va:ʀən]
to prevail (vt)	überwiegen (vi)	[ˌy:bɐ'vi:gən]
to progress (move forward)	vorankommen	[fo:'ʀanˌkɔmən]

to promise (vt)	versprechen (vt)	[fɛɐ'ʃpʀɛçən]
to pronounce (vt)	aussprechen (vt)	['aʊsˌʃpʀɛçən]
to propose (vt)	vorschlagen (vt)	['fo:ɐʃla:gən]
to protect (e.g. ~ nature)	bewachen (vt)	[bə'vaxən]

to protest (vi)	protestieren (vi)	[pʀotɛs'ti:ʀən]
to prove (vt)	beweisen (vt)	[bə'vaɪzən]
to provoke (vt)	provozieren (vt)	[pʀovo'tsi:ʀən]
to pull (~ the rope)	ziehen (vt)	['tsi:ən]
to punish (vt)	bestrafen (vt)	[bə'ʃtʀa:fən]

to push (~ the door)	schieben (vt)	['ʃiːbən]
to put away (vt)	weglegen (vt)	['vɛkˌleːgən]
to put in order	in Ordnung bringen	[ɪn 'ɔʁdnʊŋ 'bʁɪŋən]
to put, to place	stellen (vt)	['ʃtɛlən]

to quote (cite)	zitieren (vt)	[ˌtsiˈtiːʁən]
to reach (arrive at)	erreichen (vt)	[ɛʁˈʁaɪçən]
to read (vi, vt)	lesen (vi, vt)	['leːzən]
to realize (a dream)	verwirklichen (vt)	[fɛʁˈvɪʁklɪçən]
to recognize (identify sb)	anerkennen (vt)	['anɛʁˌkɛnən]

to recommend (vt)	empfehlen (vt)	[ɛmˈpfeːlən]
to recover (~ from flu)	genesen (vi)	[gəˈneːzən]
to redo (do again)	nochmals tun (vt)	['nɔχmaːls tuːn]
to reduce (speed, etc.)	verringern (vt)	[fɛʁˈʁɪŋɛn]

to refuse (~ sb)	absagen (vt)	['apˌzaːgən]
to regret (be sorry)	bedauern (vt)	[bəˈdaʊɐn]
to reinforce (vt)	befestigen (vt)	[bəˈfɛstɪgən]
to remember (Do you ~ me?)	sich erinnern	[zɪç ɛʁˈʔɪnɐn]

to remember (I can't ~ her name)	zurückdenken (vi)	[tsuˈʁʏkˌdɛŋkən]
to remind of ...	erinnern (vt)	[ɛʁˈʔɪnɐn]
to remove (~ a stain)	entfernen (vt)	[ɛntˈfɛʁnən]
to remove (~ an obstacle)	beseitigen (vt)	[bəˈzaɪtɪgən]

to rent (sth from sb)	mieten (vt)	['miːtən]
to repair (mend)	reparieren (vt)	[ʁepaˈʁiːʁən]
to repeat (say again)	noch einmal sagen	[nɔχ 'aɪnmaːl 'zaːgən]
to report (make a report)	berichten (vt)	[bəˈʁɪçtən]

to reproach (vt)	vorwerfen (vt)	['foːɐˌvɛʁfən]
to reserve, to book	reservieren (vt)	[ʁezɛʁˈviːʁən]
to restrain (hold back)	zurückhalten (vt)	[tsuˈʁʏkˌhaltən]
to return (come back)	zurückkehren (vi)	[tsuˈʁʏkˌkeːʁən]

to risk, to take a risk	riskieren (vt)	[ʁɪsˈkiːʁən]
to rub out (erase)	ausradieren (vt)	['aʊsˌʁaˈdiːʁən]
to run (move fast)	laufen (vi)	['laʊfən]
to rush (hurry sb)	zur Eile antreiben	[tsuːɐ 'aɪlə 'anˌtʁaɪbən]

256. Verbs S-W

to satisfy (please)	befriedigen (vt)	[bəˈfʁiːdɪgən]
to save (rescue)	retten (vt)	['ʁɛtən]
to say (~ thank you)	sagen (vt)	['zaːgən]
to scold (vt)	schelten (vt)	['ʃɛltən]

to scratch (with claws)	kratzen (vt)	['kʁatsən]
to select (to pick)	auswählen (vt)	['aʊsˌvɛːlən]
to sell (goods)	verkaufen (vt)	[fɛʁˈkaʊfən]
to send (a letter)	abschicken (vt)	['apˌʃɪkən]
to send back (vt)	zurückschicken (vt)	[tsuˈʁʏkˌʃɪkən]

to sense (~ danger)	**fühlen** (vt)	['fy:lən]
to sentence (vt)	**verurteilen** (vt)	[fɛɐ'ʔʊɐtaɪlən]
to serve (in restaurant)	**bedienen** (vt)	[bə'di:nən]

to settle (a conflict)	**regeln** (vt)	['ʀe:gəln]
to shake (vt)	**schütteln** (vt)	['ʃʏtəln]
to shave (vi)	**sich rasieren**	[zɪç ʀa'zi:ʀən]
to shine (gleam)	**glänzen** (vi)	['glɛntsən]

to shiver (with cold)	**zittern** (vi)	['tsɪtən]
to shoot (vi)	**schießen** (vi)	['ʃi:sən]
to shout (vi)	**schreien** (vi)	['ʃʀaɪən]
to show (to display)	**zeigen** (vt)	['tsaɪgən]

to shudder (vi)	**zusammenzucken** (vi)	[tsu'zamən͵tsʊkən]
to sigh (vi)	**aufseufzen** (vi)	['aʊf͵zɔɪftsən]
to sign (document)	**unterschreiben** (vt)	[͵ʊntɐ'ʃʀaɪbən]
to signify (mean)	**bezeichnen** (vt)	[bə'tsaɪçnən]

to simplify (vt)	**vereinfachen** (vt)	[fɛɐ'ʔaɪnfaxən]
to sin (vi)	**sündigen** (vi)	['zʏndɪgən]
to sit (be sitting)	**sitzen** (vi)	['zɪtsən]
to sit down (vi)	**sich setzen**	[zɪç 'zɛtsən]

to smell (emit an odor)	**riechen** (vi)	['ʀi:çən]
to smell (inhale the odor)	**riechen** (vt)	['ʀi:çən]
to smile (vi)	**lächeln** (vi)	['lɛçəln]
to snap (vi, ab. rope)	**zerreißen** (vi)	[tsɛɐ'ʀaɪsən]

to solve (problem)	**lösen** (vt)	['lø:zən]
to sow (seed, crop)	**säen** (vt)	['zɛ:ən]
to spill (liquid)	**vergießen** (vt)	[fɛɐ'gi:sən]
to spill out, scatter (flour, etc.)	**verschütten** (vt)	[fɛɐ'ʃʏtən]

to spit (vi)	**spucken** (vi)	['ʃpʊkən]
to stand (toothache, cold)	**aushalten** (vt)	['aʊs͵haltən]
to start (begin)	**beginnen** (vt)	[bə'gɪnən]
to steal (money, etc.)	**stehlen** (vt)	['ʃte:lən]

to stop (for pause, etc.)	**stoppen** (vt)	['ʃtɔpən]
to stop (please ~ calling me)	**einstellen** (vt)	['aɪnʃtɛlən]
to stop talking	**verstummen** (vi)	[fɛɐ'ʃtʊmən]
to stroke (caress)	**streicheln** (vt)	['ʃtʀaɪçəln]

to study (vt)	**lernen** (vt)	['lɛʁnən]
to suffer (feel pain)	**leiden** (vi)	['laɪdən]
to support (cause, idea)	**unterstützen** (vt)	[͵ʊntɐ'ʃtʏtsən]
to suppose (assume)	**vermuten** (vt)	[fɛɐ'mu:tən]

to surface (ab. submarine)	**auftauchen** (vi)	['aʊf͵taʊxən]
to surprise (amaze)	**erstaunen** (vt)	[ɛɐ'ʃtaʊnən]
to suspect (vt)	**verdächtigen** (vt)	[fɛɐ'dɛçtɪgən]
to swim (vi)	**schwimmen** (vi)	['ʃvɪmən]

to take (get hold of)	**nehmen** (vt)	['ne:mən]
to take a rest	**sich ausruhen**	[zɪç 'aʊs͵ʀu:ən]

to take away	fortbringen (vt)	[ˈfɔʁtˌbʁɪŋən]
(e.g. about waiter)		
to take off (aeroplane)	starten (vi)	[ˈʃtaʁtən]
to take off	abnehmen (vt)	[ˈapˌneːmən]
(painting, curtains, etc.)		
to take pictures	fotografieren (vt)	[fotoɡʁaˈfiːʁən]
to talk to ...	sprechen mit ...	[ˈʃpʁɛçən mɪt]
to teach (give lessons)	lehren (vt)	[ˈleːʁən]
to tear off, to rip off (vt)	abreißen (vt)	[ˈapˌʁaɪsən]
to tell (story, joke)	erzählen (vt)	[ɛɐˈtsɛːlən]
to thank (vt)	danken (vi)	[ˈdaŋkən]
to think (believe)	glauben (vi)	[ˈɡlaʊbən]
to think (vi, vt)	denken (vi, vt)	[ˈdɛŋkən]
to threaten (vt)	drohen (vi)	[ˈdʁoːən]
to throw (stone, etc.)	werfen (vt)	[ˈvɛʁfən]
to tie to ...	anbinden (vt)	[ˈanˌbɪndən]
to tie up (prisoner)	binden (vt)	[ˈbɪndən]
to tire (make tired)	ermüden (vt)	[ɛɐˈmyːdən]
to touch (one's arm, etc.)	berühren (vt)	[bəˈʁyːʁən]
to tower (over ...)	überragen	[ˌyːbɐˈʁaːɡən]
to train (animals)	dressieren (vt)	[dʁɛˈsiːʁən]
to train (sb)	trainieren (vt)	[tʁɛˈniːʁən]
to train (vi)	trainieren (vi)	[tʁɛˈniːʁən]
to transform (vt)	transformieren (vt)	[ˌtʁansfoʁˈmiːʁən]
to translate (vt)	übersetzen (vt)	[ˌyːbeˈzɛtsən]
to treat (illness)	behandeln (vt)	[bəˈhandəln]
to trust (vt)	vertrauen (vt)	[fɛɐˈtʁaʊən]
to try (attempt)	versuchen (vt)	[fɛɐˈzuːχən]
to turn (e.g., ~ left)	abbiegen (vi)	[ˈapˌbiːɡən]
to turn away (vi)	sich abwenden	[zɪç ˈapˌvɛndən]
to turn off (the light)	ausschalten (vt)	[ˈaʊsˌʃaltən]
to turn on (computer, etc.)	einschalten (vt)	[ˈaɪnˌʃaltən]
to turn over (stone, etc.)	umdrehen (vt)	[ˈʊmˌdʁeːən]
to underestimate (vt)	unterschätzen (vt)	[ˌʊnteˈʃɛtsən]
to underline (vt)	unterstreichen (vt)	[ˌʊnteˈʃtʁaɪçən]
to understand (vt)	verstehen (vt)	[fɛɐˈʃteːən]
to undertake (vt)	unternehmen (vt)	[ˌʊnteˈneːmən]
to unite (vt)	vereinigen (vt)	[fɛɐˈʔaɪnɪɡən]
to untie (vt)	losbinden (vt)	[ˈloːsˌbɪndən]
to use (phrase, word)	gebrauchen (vt)	[ɡəˈbʁaʊχən]
to vaccinate (vt)	impfen (vt)	[ˈɪmpfən]
to vote (vi)	stimmen (vi)	[ˈʃtɪmən]
to wait (vt)	warten (vi)	[ˈvaʁtən]
to wake (sb)	wecken (vt)	[ˈvɛkən]
to want (wish, desire)	wollen (vt)	[ˈvɔlən]
to warn (of a danger)	warnen (vt)	[ˈvaʁnən]

to wash (clean)	waschen (vt)	['vaʃən]
to water (plants)	begießen (vt)	[bə'giːsən]
to wave (the hand)	winken (vi)	['vɪŋkən]

to weigh (have weight)	wiegen (vi)	['viːgən]
to work (vi)	arbeiten (vi)	['aʁbaɪtən]
to worry (make anxious)	beunruhigen (vt)	[bə'ʔʊnˌʁuːɪgən]
to worry (vi)	sich aufregen	[zɪç 'aʊfˌʁeːgən]

to wrap (parcel, etc.)	einpacken (vt)	['aɪnˌpakən]
to wrestle (sport)	ringen (vi)	['ʁɪŋən]
to write (vt)	schreiben (vi, vt)	['ʃʁaɪbən]
to write down	aufschreiben (vt)	['aʊfˌʃʁaɪbən]